FOREIGN BUSINESS IN JAPAN BEFORE WORLD WAR II

FOREIGN

The International Conference on Business History 16

BUSINESS

Proceedings of the Fuji Conference

IN JAPAN

edited by TAKESHI YUZAWA MASARU UDAGAWA

BEFORE

WORLD WAR II

UNIVERSITY OF TOKYO PRESS

This volume is the proceedings of the First Session of the Fourth Series of the Conference, which took place from January 4 to 7, 1989. We would like to express our deepest gratitude to the Taniguchi Foundation for its continuing sponsorship of the Conference.

Published by University of Tokyo Press
Printed in Japan

ISBN 4–13–047036–1
ISBN 0–86008–455–8

Contents

Introduction

Takeshi Yuzawa

Since 1974 the Japanese Business History Society has been running a series of conferences sponsored by the Taniguchi Foundation and has published 15 volumes of the proceedings of the conferences. These international business history conferences held in Japan are now known as the Fuji Conferences, because all of the conferences, except one, were held at the foot of Mt. Fuji. One of the main topics we have taken up is the comparison between Japan and other foreign countries. In the preface to the first volume of this series, Keiichirō Nakagawa stressed that "it seemed it would be most effective to have joint meetings of foreign and Japanese business historians to discuss problems relating to the different characteristics of business among the nations. We believe that through such joint meetings we will be able to gain clues to understanding what should be accepted as internationally common features and what should be regarded as the peculiarities of each country." We might say that we could contribute to breaking through "the end of insularity" (if we follow the usage of R. Davenport-Hines and Geoffrey Jones) in the study of business history and could clarify the differences and similarities of the business climates and practices among the various countries, although it might be difficult to say that we are totally satisfied with reasoning those backgrounds from business history viewpoints.

The fourth series of the Fuji Conferences has been organized under a new committee, and the main themes to be addressed concern themselves with international business relations. There are two major reasons for proposing these themes. First, we have to deepen comparative studies by considering the conflicts that have been occurring at the front lines of international business and investment. In fact, to analyze various forms of contacts among the different cultures and ways of business may provide the essential keys for understanding the true reasons behind them. Secondly, in the course of these fifteen years, the situation of the Japanese economy in the world has drastically changed, and not only Japanese but also foreign scholars want to know the secrets of Japanese success which might produce new ideas on economic and business development and serve as good examples for the developing countries. The traditional method of considering the Japanese economy has involved a tendency to stress the peculiar aspects of Japan, and could not solve the problem of the adaptability of Japan's experience to other countries. To consider the Japanese case from the international perspective would better elucidate the objective situation of the Japanese economy in coping with different cultures and business climates than just by understanding the peculiarities of Japan.

The topic of the sixteenth Fuji Conference is "Foreign Business in Japan Before World War II." Historically speaking, modernization of the Japanese economy began under the strong influence of foreign business. Major manufacturing industries were transplanted from western countries and the traditional merchant houses introduced western-style trade methods. However, Japanese industrialization was not realized only by the newly introduced western method: traditional business methods were also preserved, and it is important to see the mixtures of these two methods in Japanese business. This harmonization of western and oriental traditions brought on rapid economic growth. Therefore it is important to analyze the business activities of such foreign companies, their successes as well as their failures, and to investigate the relationship between their experience and Japan's industrial and business development, the evolution of "Japanese-style management," and Japanese industrial policy. Although this conference dealt mainly with the prewar experience, many of the issues explored have a direct bearing on contemporary problems of foreign companies attempting to do business in Japan.

Masaru Udagawa read an introductory paper presenting the framework of the conference and pointed out the main points which we should discuss. After that, he reviewed foreign direct investment in Japan, looking back to the Meiji period, when foreign businesses played an important role in Japanese industrialization while indigenous firms were forming their foundations to cope with their foreign counterparts.

Nobuhisa Fujita's paper mainly concentrated on the Mitsubishi zaibatsu, one of the biggest concerns, in which the case of Mitsubishi Electric and Mitsubishi Oil were important for tie-ups with foreign companies. The former was established as a joint venture with Westinghouse Electric, the latter with Associated Oil. Fujita analyzed the motivation and attitude of Mitsubishi in forming tie-up policies with foreign firms.

Toshiaki Chokki's paper concentrated on the development of the Japanese electrical industry with special attention to foreign interests.

As Mark Mason and Fujita also said in regard to joint ventures of electrical firms, the electrical industry was one of the most important to considering the role of foreign capital and technology in Japan. Chokki compared the foreign tie-up companies with the indigenous firms and discussed the competitive relations between them which resulted in the rapid growth of the Japanese electrical industry as a whole.

Mira Wilkins presented a paper on American multinationals in Japan with special attention to the oil and car industries. Her main contribution to this conference was her discussion of the uniqueness of Japan in terms of accepting foreign business, the result of her wide range of studies on American multinational enterprises.

Mark Mason also discussed subsidiaries of American multinationals, particularly the case of NEC, which was launched by Western Electric and is now one of the biggest telecommunications companies in the world independent of its parent company. He especially analyzed the characteristics of Japanese government dealings with the foreign enterprises.

Stephen Nicholas gave an overview of the British firms in Japan, modeled on the theory of transaction cost. He took the case of ICI, which confronted severe competition with Japanese firms but could not make a direct investment. He also detailed the cases of Babcock and Morgan Crucible, which had production facilities in Japan, and contrasted both companies' policies dealing with changing business circumstances.

Clive Trebilcock analyzed British armament businesses in Japan, especially Vickers and Armstrong. Modern Japan was eager to buy foreign armaments and to establish the industry itself within its borders. He described the British armament trade in Japan and detailed the case of Nihon Seikō Sho, a joint venture that was the largest foreign investment by Vickers in 1914. The firm was also strategically important for the Japanese armament industry but was not successful in its management, which leads to a new explanation of British business in Japan.

Erich Pauer presented the case of German companies in Japan, which were quite active in entering the Japanese market—all the more because they were comparative latecomers to Japan. After World War I the favorable business circumstances for German firms in Japan paved the way for the joint venture of Siemens and Furukawa and the vigorous strategy of I.G. Farben in the Japanese market, especially for dyestuffs. However, Pauer pointed out several difficulties German firms encountered in Japan.

Jin-Mieung Li presented a paper on a French case of a multinational breaking into the Japanese market at the end of the Meiji era, and the case of L'Air Liquide may also be a good example of French business in Japan in terms of changing patterns of control by the parent company. The manufacturing subsidiaries enjoyed a prosperous business in the 1920s, while they experienced hardship after business circumstances were reversed.

François Jequier read a paper on the origins and development of Swiss commercial activities in Japan, which began before the Meiji Restoration. Jequier focused on the watch industry, which is a good example of the transfer of technology from Switzerland to Japan. He also explained the case of Nestlé, which became a successful Swiss multinational in Japan after surmounting various difficulties.

Ten papers were read, and we reserved three hours exclusively for the concluding discussion, which the readers can refer to in the last chapter. The whole conference lasted only four days, but the organizing committee and speakers frequently exchanged ideas throughout, and we allowed the speakers to refine their papers as a result of these discussions. In this sense, this book represents more than the official proceedings of the conference; rather, we would like to say that this book is the result of extended cooperation between our committee and the participants.

Business Management and Foreign-Affiliated Companies in Japan Before World War II

Masaru Udagawa

I. Introduction

Recently there has been a movement among Japanese business historians to review Japan's rapid industrialization and business development after the late 19th century from the viewpoint of international relations. In the midst of this movement the Business History Society of Japan organized its 1986 conference with a central theme of "Modern Business Development and Its International Relations." Professor Keiichirō Nakagawa, the organizer of the conference under this theme, pointed out, "There is no business history of any nation that can be understood without considering its international relations. It is particularly true for the countries that lagged behind others in industrialization, where international relations were woven fast into their business histories from the very beginning." He emphasized that historical study of industrialization and business activities in Japan inevitably requires an approach with an international point of view because the country had to start after the West had already executed and, to some extent, achieved the industrial revolution, and yet had to compete with the West.[1]

As the project leader of the Fuji Conference of January 1989, I have chosen the theme "Foreign Business in Japan Before World War II" because it is important to understand what role business played in international relations in the course of Japan's business history. Another reason for choosing this theme is that it forms a domain that combines the business history of foreign countries with that of Japan, and thus serves as the most appropriate theme for the Fuji Conference—a forum of collaboration and enlightenment for scholars from abroad as well as from Japan.

In order to make the conference fruitful, I would like to suggest that the following topics of discussion be examined thoroughly.

The first one considers Japan as a host country of foreign capital operations, specifically: (1) how foreign governments and companies regarded the Japanese market, (2) what influences the Japanese government's policies on tariffs, industries, and foreign capital had on foreign companies' business expansion into Japan and the companies' business operations, and (3) how Japanese business managers reacted to the business expansion of the foreign companies.

The second topic focuses on the business activities of foreign companies in Japan, such as (1) what motives they had in entering the Japanese market and with what strategies and operations, (2) what difficulties they encountered in the Japanese market and how they coped with them, and (3) what business results they achieved and how these results affected their business activities at home and in other countries.

The third topic concerns the impact of the foreign companies on Japanese companies, such as (1) what roles their business activities played in Japan's industrialization and the development of business management, (2) how their production facilities, technology, business management methods, and know-how were transferred to Japanese companies, and (3) what efforts Japanese companies made to introduce and anchor the said hardware and software in their own business management and how the foreign counterparts helped in such an attempt.

It is well known that, before the outbreak of World War II, many foreign companies had achieved access to the Japanese market by means of commodity exports, direct investment, and technical or capital affiliation with Japanese companies, and for this reason had been developing active business operations. Due to space considerations, my paper deals mainly with foreign manufacturing companies which extended investment in the Japanese market by themselves and the foreign manufacturers which took a form of capital affiliation with the Japanese companies in order to enter this market. In my paper, both are called foreign-affiliated companies. It is my hope that such an examination of their business activities will serve as material to develop discussions of the above-mentioned topics.

II. The Expansion Process of Foreign Affiliates

1. Outline of Japan's Policy Toward Foreign Capital

After winning the Sino-Japanese War of 1895, which enabled Japan to free itself from the threat of colonial domination by the western powers, Japan changed the course of its foreign capital policies from exclusion to acceptance of foreign investment.[2] The basis for foreigners and foreign-affiliated companies to conduct business in Japan was gradually prepared after the war through the establishment of the gold-standard system in 1897; the full enforcement of the Commercial Law of 1899, which secured free business activities by foreigners and allowed the application of Japanese standards for foreign affiliates as they established business organizations in Japan; and, in 1899, the complete abolishment of the principle of extraterritoriality. In 1905, Japan defeated Russia in the Russo-Japanese War and thereby gained international prestige. This led to the achievement of long-desired tariff autonomy in 1911. With the outbreak of World War I, the importation of manufactured goods from overseas was stopped. It served as an opportunity, as industrial activities were further promoted in Japan, for the foreign-affiliated manufacturers to establish their branches and factories, or to make a solid start of capital affiliation and joint venture with Japanese companies.

However, after the worldwide depression that followed the 1929 crash of the American stock market, Japan's policy toward foreign capital again turned to exclusive measures: the Ministry of Commerce and Industry took the initiative in the "Buy Japanese" campaign; the international environment was aggravated following the occurrence of the Manchurian Incident in 1931; and military intervention in politics and economy became more active. Japan left the gold standard in 1931 and adopted the Foreign Exchange Control Law in 1933. Consequently, business activities of foreign affiliates were strictly restricted, and various types of suppressive measures were taken.

2. *The State of Foreign-Affiliated Manufacturers*

Table 1 shows the state of the foreign-affiliated manufacturing companies operating in Japan surveyed by the Ministry of Commerce and Industry in 1931. According to this survey, there were 88 companies, including 29 foreign corporations—i.e., sales offices with overseas headquarters—and 59 companies that had been established under Japanese laws. As for ownership and management of the latter, 13 of them were exclusively financed and managed by foreigners, and 10 were mainly financed by foreigners, with management in their hands. The remaining 36 companies were owned by both foreigners and Japanese, and the latter had the right of management. As for the nationalities of the 88 companies, 36 were from the United States, 21 from Britain, 17 from Germany, and 14 from other countries, including 6 that were unidentified. By type of industry, 24 were classified as machinery and equipment companies, 13 as electrical machinery, followed by 7 cotton yarn and knitting companies and 6 record companies.

It is also interesting to consider what manufacturing companies overseas expanded their business into the Japanese market before World War II. As Table 2 indicates, most of them were leading multinational

Table 1 Foreign-Affiliated Corporations in Japan (Manufacturing) by Product and by Type of Ownership (as of January 1931)

I. Foreign Corporations (Sales Offices): 29 Companies			
By Nationality		By Product	
U.S.A.	15	Machinery	18
U.K.	5	Electric apparatus	3
Germany	5	Food	3
Switzerland	2	Movies	2
Czechoslovakia	1	Art	1
Luxembourg	1	Petroleum	1
		Silk yarn	1
II. Corporations Under Japanese Law			
A. Fully Owned and Operated by Foreigners: 13 Companies			
By Nationality		By Product	
U.S.A.	6	Electric apparatus, machinery, automobiles, and food—2 in each	
U.K.	5	Records, rubber products, petroleum, machinery, and photographic paper—1 in each	
Germany	2		
B. Mostly Owned and Operated by Foreigners: 10 Companies			
By Nationality		By Product	
U.S.A.	6	Records	5
U.K.	2	Machinery	3
Germany	2	Automobiles and rubber products —1 in each	
C. Jointly Owned by Foreigners and Japanese and Operated by the Latter: 36 Companies			
By Nationality		By Product	
U.S.A.	9	Electric apparatus	8
U.K.	9	Cotton yarn	6
Germany	8	Rayon	3
China	2	Steel	3
Switzerland	1	Wool products	2
France	1	Machinery, gas, glass, ice, celluloid, matches—1 in each	
Unidentified	6	Unidentified	6

Source: Gaimushō, Tokubetsu Shiryōbu (Special Resource Center, Ministry of Foreign Affairs), ed., *Nippon ni Okeru Gaikoku Shihon* (Foreign Capital in Japan), (Kasumigasekikai, Tokyo), 1948.

enterprises that had been, at the time, actively operating in the world market by establishing their production and sales bases abroad.[3] It is further shown that many of them came to Japan after World War I, which means that the Japanese market after the war constituted a part of a worldwide strategy for the multinational enterprises. It should also be noted that when such multinationals undertook capital affiliation or joint ventures with Japanese companies, most of the Japanese partners were major zaibatsu group companies which held a dominant position in the Japanese industry at that time.

III. Business Activities of Major Foreign-Affiliated Manufacturing Companies

Unfortunately, it is impossible to determine the amount of the invested capital by the foreign affiliates which made their advance into the Japanese market before World War II. But it is easy to assume that it was not so large. Parenthetically, "Investment to Japanese Banks and Companies by Foreigners (Estimate)," by the Ministry of Finance, disclosed that their outstanding investment exceeded ¥100 million in 1928—however, only by ¥13,830,000, and this amount was the largest for some time after 1928.[4]

Although their investment was small, it did not mean that the role that the foreign affiliates played in the Japanese market was commensurately small. Most of them were giant enterprises which developed worldwide business operations with excellent technology, sales organizations, and massive information resources. Therefore, their impact on business management in Japan was not limited to their relative industrial sector; instead it spread into Japanese business in general. This chapter deals with four of the then newly rising industrial sectors where their operations were most active—namely, petroleum, tires, heavy electric apparatuses, and automobiles—and discusses part of their activities.

1. The Petroleum Industry

The first sales base established in Japan directly by a foreign-affiliated oil company was the Yokohama Branch of Standard Company of New York in 1893. It was followed by the establishment of the Rising Sun Petroleum Company (Shell group) in 1900, a divested petroleum sales division of Britain's Samuel Samuel & Co. (a subsidiary of Marcus Samuel & Co.), which had been active in trade with Japan since 1880.[5]

Standard Co. and Rising Sun dominated the then rapidly growing lamp-oil market in a short period of time. Their status as the big two was not shaken even when domestic crude-oil production and refining were promoted in the 1900s, and together they secured more than 65% of the market share in the first sales agreement reached with two domestic companies, Nippon Sekiyu (Nippon Oil Company) and Hōden Sekiyu (Hōden Oil Company).[6]

In the meantime Standard expanded its business into crude-oil pro-

TABLE 2 Major Foreign-Affiliated Manufacturing Companies in Prewar

Company Name	Year	Capital	Foreign Corporation (Capital Ratio)
New York Standard (Japan Branch)	1893	—	Standard Oil of New York (U.S.A.) (100)
Nippon Denki	1899	200	Western Electric (U.S.A.) (54)
Murai Kyōdai Shōkai	1899	10,000	American Tobacco (U.S.A.) (60)
Rising Sun	1900	250	Samuel Samuel & Co. (U.K.) (100)
Singer Sewing Machine (Japan Branch)	1901	—	Singer Sewing Machine (U.S.A.) (100)
Osaka Gas	1902	4,000	Anthony N. Brady (U.S.A.) (55)
Tokyo Denki	1905	400	General Electric (U.S.A.) (55)
Nippon Bakuhatsubutsu Seizōsho	1905	£1 mil.	Armstrong Whitworth, Chilworth Gunpowder, Nobel's Explosives (U.K.) (100)
Siemens-Schuckertwerke (Japan Branch)	1905	250	Siemens-Schuckertwerke (Ger.) (100)
Nihon Seikō Sho	1907	10,000	Armstrong, Vickers (U.K.) (50)
Teikoku Seishi	1907	1,500	J. & P. Coats (U.K.) (60)

Japan (Unit: ¥1000, %)

Japanese Investor	Rate of Foreign Capital 1930	1941	Note
	100	100	Before Japan Branch, Standard sold oil through China & Japan Trading, and Anglo-American Oil Co. It founded International Oil Co. in 1900 with capital ¥10 million and sold the total assets to Nippon Sekiyu in 1907.
Iwadare Kunihiko Maeda Takeshirō	59	33	Before affiliation, WE sold through Takata Shōkai. ND became an affiliate of Sumitomo in 1932.
Murai Kichibei	—	—	MKS became government-owned in 1904 by the Government Monopoly in Tobacco Act.
	100	100	
	100	100	
Asano Sōichirō	—	—	Brady withdrew capital in 1925.
Tamura Eiji	57	27	GE appointed Mitsui Bussan as its agent in 1906.
Fujioka Ichirō			TD merged with Shibaura Seisakusho in 1939 to form Tokyo Shibaura Denki.
	—	—	HQ was located in London, an office and plant in Japan. Became the navy's powder mill in 1919.
	100	100	
Hokkaido Tankō Kisen	25	6	
Murai Kyōdai Shōkai	60	60	

Table 2 (Continued)

Company Name	Year	Capital	Foreign Corporation (Capital Ratio)
Dunlop Far East (Japan Branch)	1909	——	Dunlop of Far East (U.K.) (100)
Shibaura Seisakusho	1909	2,000	General Electric (U.S.A.) (25)
Nihon Oxygen & Acetylene	1910	FF 400 thou.	L'Air Liquide (France) (100)
Lever Brothers (Amagasaki Plant)	1913	——	Lever Brothers (U.K.) (100)
Yokohama Gomu Seizō	1917	2,500	B.F. Goodrich (U.S.A.) (50)
Nichibei Ita garasu	1918	3,000	Libbey-Owens Sheet Glass (U.S.A.) (35)
Nihon Kenchiku Zairyō	1919	1,000	American Trading, Truscon Steel (U.S.A.) (100)
Gotō Fuundō	1919	750	Siemens & Halske (Ger.) (10)
Asahi Kenshoku	1922	2,000	Vereinigte Glanzstoff Fabriken (Ger.) (20)

Japanese Investor	Rate of Foreign Capital 1930	1941	Note
	100	100	Before Japan Branch, Dunlop sold through Guria Shōkai. Became Nippon Dunlop, a Japanese corporation, in 1917 with capital ¥1.18 million.
Mitsui Gōmei	32	27	Merged with Tokyo Denki in 1939 to form Tokyo Shibaura Denki.
	88	88	Became Teikoku Sanso, a Japanese corporation in 1930 and accepted capital of Sumitomo zaibatsu.
	—	—	Kobe Gas took over management in 1925; became Velvet Sekken the following year. Became a subsidiary of Nissan Combine in 1936; incorporated in to Nippon Yushi.
Yokohama Densen Seizō	59	9	Goodrich started direct sales in Japan in 1912.
Sumitomo Kichizaemon	30	17	Became an affiliate of Sumitomo zaibatsu in 1922.
Asahi Garasu			Changed name to Nippon Itagarasu in 1931.
	100	23	Immediately after establishment, changed name to Nihon Truscon Kōzai, then to Nihon Kōzai in 1930, Tōyō Kōzai in 1934. Became a subsidiary of Mitsui Bussan in 1933; merged with Sanki Kōgyō in 1943.
Gotō Setsuzō	10	9	
Kita Matazō Noguchi Shitagau (Jun)	30	5	Became a company of Nitchitsu Combine in 1929. Merged with other subsidiaries, Nippon Bemberg Kenshi and Nobeoka Anmonia Kenshi in 1933 to form Asahi Bemberg Kenshi.

Table 2 (Continued)

Company Name	Year	Capital	Foreign Corporation (Capital Ratio)
Fuji Denki Seizō	1923	10,000	Siemens-Schuckert-werke, Siemens & Halske (Ger.) (30)
Mitsubishi Denki	1923	15,000	Westinghouse Electric (U.S.A.) (10)
Ford Japan	1925	4,000	Ford Motor (U.S.A.) (100)
General Motors Japan	1927	8,000	General Motors (U.S.A.) (100)
Nihon Chikuonki Shōkai	1927	2,100	Columbia (U.K.) (67)
Nippon Victor	1927	2,000	Victor Talking Machine (U.S.A.) (100)
Tōyō Kamibukuro	1927	250	Bates International Bag (U.S.A.) (99)
Daidō Match	1927	6,000	Sweden Match (Sweden) (50)
Tōyō Babcock Seizō	1928	1,750	Babcock & Wilcox (U.K.) (71)
Nihon Bemberg Kenshi	1929	10,000	J.P. Bemberg (Ger.) (20)
Tōyō Carrier Kōgyō	1930	300	Carrier Corp. (U.S.A.) (50)
Mitsubishi Sekiyu	1931	5,000	Associated Oil (U.S.A.) (50)
Sumitomo Aluminum	1931	3,500	Aluminum Ltd. (Can.) (50)

Japanese Investor	Rate of Foreign Capital 1930	1941	Note
Furukawa Denki Kōgyō	30	30	
Mitsubishi Zōsen	10	5	Westinghouse appointed Takata Shōkai as an agent in 1899. Sales operation was assigned to Hishimi Denki Shōkai in 1929.
	100	100	Before FJ, FM sold through Sale & Frazar.
	100	100	Before GMJ, GM sold through Mitsui Bussan and Yanase Jidōsha.
	67	3	Became an affiliate of Nissan Combine in 1935 and of Tokyo Denki in 1938.
	68	0	Accepted capital of Mitsubishi and Sumitomo in 1929, became an affiliate of Nissan Combine in 1935 and of Tokyo Denki in 1938.
	99	65	Accepted capital of Asano Cement in 1935.
Takikawa Gisaku	50	0	SM contributed capital to Nippon Match in 1923. DM became an affiliate of Nissan Combine in 1932.
Mitsui Bussan	71	67	Babcock started direct sales in Japan in 1906.
Nippon Chisso Hiryō	30	5	Merged with Asahi Kenshoku and Nobeoka Anmonia Kenshi in 1933 to form Asahi Bemberg Kenshi.
Sanki Kōgyō	50	46	
Mitsubishi Gōshi, Shōji, Kōgyō	—	25	Mitsubishi Shōji was awarded the sales rights to products of AO in Japan in 1923.
Sumitomo Shindōkōkan	—	38	

TABLE 2 (Continued)

Company Name	Year	Capital	Foreign Corporation (Capital Ratio)
Sakuma Kōgyō	1931	1,000	Paraffin Co. (U.S.A.) (60)
Tōyō Otis Elevator	1932	10,000	Otis Elevator (U.S.A.) (60)
Sumitomo Densen Seizōsho	1932	15,000	International Standard Electric (U.S.A.) (12)
Nippon Kinsen Tōrokuki	1933	750	National Cash Register (U.S.A.) (100)
Titan Kōgyō	1936	1,500	Titan Gesellschaft (Ger.) (50)
Nippon Watson Tōkei Kaikeikikai	1937	500	International Business Machine (U.S.A.) (100)
Shibaura Kyōdō Kōgyō	1939	16,000	United Engineering & Foundary (U.S.A.) (49)

Note: Foreign-affiliated companies in this table are defined as those with 10% or more of the foreign capital ratio at the time of affiliation.
Sources: Nippon Kōgyō Ginkō Gaijibu (Foreign Affairs Div., Industrial Bank of Japan, Ltd.), ed., *Gaikoku Kaisha no Honpō Tōshi* (Foreign Capital Investment in Japan), (Nippon Kōgyō Ginkō, Tokyo), 1948;

duction and refining in Japan and established International Sekiyu (International Oil Company) in 1900 with capital of ¥10 million. Rising Sun planned a project to refine Bornean crude oil in Japan and completed a large refinery in Saitozaki, Fukuoka Prefecture. But International Oil was not successful in developing oil wells and sold the total asset to Nippon Oil Co. in 1907. On the other hand, the project of Rising Sun was severely hurt by raised tariffs on crude oil in 1908. Moreover, with the outbreak of World War I, transportation costs rose dramatically. As a result, Rising Sun stopped operation of the Saitozaki refinery in 1915.[7]

Japanese Investor	Rate of Foreign Capital 1930	1941	Note
Sakuma Eikichi	—	60	
Mitsui Bussan	—	60	OE Japan Branch was founded in 1927, affiliated with Mitsui Bussan.
Sumitomo Gōshi	—	12	SDS started technical affiliation with Western Electric through Nippon Denki, changed name to Sumitomo Denki Kōgyō in 1939.
	—	70	Merged with Nippon Kinsen Tōrokuki, a company of Fujiyama group in 1935, to form Nippon National Kinsen Tōrokuki.
Kokusan Kōgyō	—	50	KK was an affiliate of Nissan Combine.
	—	100	Before NWTK, IBM sold first through Morimura Shōji and then Kurosawa Shōten.
Shibaura Seisakusho	—	49	

Gaimushō, Tokubetsu Shiryōbu (Special Resource Center, Ministry of Foreign Affairs), ed., *Nippon ni Okeru Gaikoku Shihon* (Situation of the Foreign Capital in Japan), (Kasumigasekikai, Tokyo), 1948; and histories of each company.

After this, both Standard and Rising Sun concentrated their business operations on the importation and sale of oil products, and this change in their management policies turned out to be a good choice. Hitting its highest in 1915, crude-oil production in Japan kept decreasing. Diversification in oil products continued after World War I, and demand for various types of products increased. On top of these considerations, there was a worldwide surplus of crude oil, and thus its price fell. With all these factors as a background, Japanese companies made a solid start in refining imported crude petroleum. Therefore, after World War I, Standard and Rising Sun put more emphasis on their importation and sales activities of various oil products and at the same time supplied crude to the imported oil refineries, thereby establishing themselves firmly in the Japanese oil market.[8]

Vigorous sales activities of the two foreign affiliates gave way to the establishment of Mitsubishi Sekiyu (Mitsubishi Oil Company), a result of a Japan-U.S. affiliation.[9] In 1924, Mitsubishi Shōji (Mitsubishi Trading Company) was awarded the exclusive sales right on behalf of Associated Oil Co. However, although Mitsubishi Trading had the powerful support of the Mitsubishi zaibatsu, it was still a difficult task to expand its sales channels to compete with the strong sales organizations of Standard and Rising Sun. Mitsubishi then decided to move into crude-oil refining rather than the importation oil products, and in 1931 it established Mitsubishi Oil Co., a joint investment by Mitsubishi Gōshi (Mitsubishi Limited Partnership), Mitsubishi Trading, Mitsubishi Kōgyō (Mitsubishi Mining Company), and Associated Oil Co., which then supplied crude oil and provided facilities and techniques. Mitsubishi Oil Co. made its first shipment by the end of the year through Mitsubishi Trading.

2. *The Tire Industry*

Rubber-related industries in Japan were developed primarily through the business activities of the Japan branch of Kyokutō Dunlop (Dunlop Far East).[10] This was a subsidiary of Britain's Dunlop Rubber, established in Kobe in 1909, and became a Japanese corporation in 1917. Dunlop was exporting rubber-related products to Japan from 1903 through an agent, but it was determined to establish its own branch after the Russo-Japanese War, expecting that Japan would recover its tariff autonomy.[11]

As Dunlop expected, when Japan regained its tariff autonomy in 1911, it immediately lowered the tariff on raw rubber and raised it drastically on rubber products. The rubber-related industry in Japan, since then, prospered under a protective tariff, which at that time meant a progressive domination of the Japanese rubber market by Nippon Dunlop (Dunlop Japan), which had, as a parent company, one of the world's largest rubber companies standing behind it. Dunlop Japan was especially powerful in the automobile tire market. It had an outstanding market share until the early 1930s, when Yokohama Gomu Seizō (Yokohama Rubber Manufacturing Company) and Burijisuton Taiya (Bridgestone Tire Company) began producing tires.[12]

Of the two newcomers in the tire industry, Yokohama Rubber was established in 1917 as a joint-venture company of B.F. Goodrich of the United States, which had a plan to establish a manufacturing plant in

Asia, and Yokohama Densen Seizō (Yokohama Electric Wire Manufacturing Company), a subsidiary of the Furukawa zaibatsu.[13] The company started out producing automobile tires in 1921, but before it went into full production the Great Kantō Earthquake of 1923 destroyed its plant facilities. In 1928, Yokohama Rubber again reached an agreement with Goodrich concerning automobile tire production, and started operation of its new factory in 1930. Also, Bridgestone, a domestic corporation, started production of automobile tires in 1931.

In this way the monopoly of Dunlop Japan in the tire market ended. Since then a keen competition has unfolded among Dunlop Japan, a foreign affiliate, Yokohama Rubber, a Japan–U.S. joint venture, and Bridgestone, a Japanese corporation. The market share of each of them in 1935, including Manchukuo as a part of the Japanese market, was 40%, 28%, and 32%, respectively.[14]

3. *The Heavy Electric Machinery Industry*

Most of the major electric machinery manufacturers in Japan before World War II were financially supported by zaibatsu, and were strengthening and establishing their business basis through affiliation with their overseas counterparts by introducing their major equipment and facilities, technology, business management systems, and know-how. Actually, in the heavy electric industry, four companies which established themselves as dominating market powers by the latter half of the 1920s—namely, Shibaura Seisakusho (Shibaura Engineering Works), Hitachi Seisakusho (Hitachi Engineering Works), Mitsubishi Denki (Mitsubishi Electric Manufacturing Company), and Fuji Denki Seizō (Fuji Electric Manufacturing Company)—were all zaibatsu affiliates and, except for Hitachi, were affiliated with foreign heavy electric machinery manufacturers. Specifically, Shibaura Engineering, an affiliate of Mitsui zaibatsu, formed an affiliation with General Electric (GE) in 1909 and transferred one-fourth of its stock to GE in 1910. Mitsubishi Electric, an affiliate of the Mitsubishi zaibatsu, formed an affiliation with Westinghouse Electric in 1923 and offered 10% of its stocks. Fuji Electric Co. was established in 1923 as a joint venture company of Furukawa Denki Kōgyō (Furukawa Electric Industry, a company of the Furukawa zaibatsu) and Siemens.

Japanese companies ventured into affiliation or partnership with major foreign heavy electric enterprises in order to introduce and learn about their advanced production facilities and technologies, modern business management systems, and know-how. The foreign heavy electric manufacturers, on the other hand, regarded Japan as a prospective market and had been active in exporting their products through their agents and sales offices even before they launched their affiliations and joint ventures with Japanese companies. However, the situation turned out to be more advantageous for the Japanese companies as tariffs on the foreign products were raised and the domestic manufacturers gained power, and competition among the foreign affiliates grew more intense, and therefore unstable, in the long run.

In general, overseas activities of the major foreign heavy electric manufacturers saw a change in direction in the 20th century, particularly in the 1920s, from a strategy of exporting products to a more stable means of maintaining and increasing their market shares by signing agreements with the major manufacturers in target markets such as capital consolidation, patent exchange, and market separation.[15] They sought a similar strategy in the Japanese market and, at the request of a powerful zaibatsu and its subsidiaries or at their own initiative, planned affiliations or joint ventures with Japanese companies. This allowed them to secure the execution of their patent rights and to expand their business possibilities in the East Asian market, including Japan, through "complementary" exports to their Japanese partners.

4. *The Automobile Industry*

The great earthquake of September 1923, which destroyed south Kantō (including Tokyo and Yokohama), was one of the key factors which influenced the popularization of automobiles in Japan. In the reconstruction following the earthquake, automobiles played an especially important role in transporting goods and people, and thereby their usefulness was widely recognized.[16] However, those who enjoyed opportunities in the rapidly growing automobile market after the earthquake were not Japanese but, instead, American automobile manufacturers. Ford was the first to seize the opportunity. It had had a plan to advance to East Asia with Shanghai as its base when it received an urgent order for 800 units of buses and trucks from the municipal authorities of Tokyo, which suffered a crushing blow to its streetcar network. Taking this opportunity, Ford decided to change its target from Shanghai to Japan. In 1925, it established Nippon Ford (Ford Japan) in Yokohama and commenced production using the "knockdown" assembly method. The company canceled its sales contract with an American trading company, Sale & Frazar Ltd., and launched a direct sales system based on the franchise method. This movement of Ford stimulated General Motors (GM), which established Nippon GM (GM Japan) in Osaka in 1927 and developed assembly production and direct sales activities. Chrysler followed them and, in 1928, founded Kyōritsu Jidōsha Seisakusho (Kyōritsu Automobile Works) in Yokohama with the joint capital contribution of its import agent. Its assembly production started in 1928.

Because the "big three" American automobile manufacturers successively made inroads into the Japanese market, domestic manufacturers, as yet lacking mass production and marketing techniques, could not compete, and consequently most of them had to withdraw from the automobile market. Importation of automobiles from Europe gradually ceased as well. As a result, by the end of 1930s, the Japanese automobile market was almost completely dominated by the American big three, particularly Ford and GM.

IV. The Impact of Foreign Affiliates

The effect of the inroads made by foreign-affiliated companies and their activities in Japan was great in many spheres of Japanese business management. This section discusses, among many, three aspects of their impact, i.e., technology transfer, industrial structure, and managerial ideology.

1. Technology Transfer

The Japanese companies which went into capital affiliation with the foreign companies or the new companies established as joint ventures between the foreigners and Japanese were provided by their foreign partners with production facilities, technology, and methodology and business management know-how such as plant management, sales organizations, and accounting systems. Both parties were eager to start personnel interchanges, and for this reason the Japanese side was able to introduce advanced production technology and modern management systems comprehensively and, by learning and assimilating them, could establish a leading position in the industry in the early stages of its development.

To illustrate this point, the following statement is quoted from a history of Mitsubishi Electric Mfg. Co., which entered the heavy electric machinery industry after World War I.

> As soon as the company was founded, we started, in high spirits, to diversify our production lines, and began receiving orders for various types of products. However, we were definitely lacking technology and experience in terms of the production quality, especially for voltage equipment with large capacity. The number of failures and defects which were found in the transformer equipment ordered by the

Ministry of Railways for its electrification project, large-scale induction motors for milling, electrical equipment for submarines, etc., caused substantial trouble for our customers.

The causes of these failures were found in various stages of production, such as inappropriate judgment about material suitability, insufficient machine design, unskilled machining, and defective plant management. In short, we were far behind the modern production management and business management.[17]

In order to make a breakthrough, Mitsubishi Electric ventured into an affiliation with Westinghouse in 1923, two years after its foundation. Mitsubishi obtained from Westinghouse patent rights as well as "drawings, technical data, machine work specifications, etc." in order to learn design principles and machine work methods and to introduce "its [Westinghouse's] management techniques."[18] In the meantime, in order to accelerate the learning and assimilation process of such engineering, Mitsubishi not only invited engineers from Westinghouse but sent 35 of its own personnel there in the period from 1923 to 1931.[19]

As a result of this cooperation with Westinghouse, production technology and product quality at Mitsubishi were enhanced dramatically, and the company, thus, was able to establish itself as a major manufacturer of heavy electric apparatus by the late 1920s.

What is more important is that a substantial part of such advanced production technology and modern management systems which Japanese companies had introduced from its affiliated partners was disseminated widely throughout the industry through the modeling of one company after another in the same trade, activities within the business circle, and workers who changed companies. For example, Hitachi Works started producing large-scale generators in 1924 by imitating and modifying insulation technology which Shibaura Engineering had introduced from GE.[20] Also, scientific management techniques such as time study and wage management that Mitsubishi Electric had learned from Westinghouse were transferred to Kure Kaigun Kōshō (Kure Naval Dockyard) and the Kokura factory of the Ministry of Railways through external activities of the company's engineers, and further gave much influence on the scientific management campaign carried out with the leadership of the Interim Bureau of Industrial Rationalization of the Ministry of Commerce and Industry in the early 1930s.[21]

The production technology and business management systems and know-how of the "pure" foreign companies in Japan were transferred through their Japanese employees, who "spun out" from the company and set out on business of their own or changed their occupations. As an illustration of this, many of the production techniques in the rubber-related industry were derived from Dunlop Japan so that "almost all the rubber companies have personnel who have been at Dunlop."[22] Bridgestone, the first domestic rubber company to go into the automobile tire business, was no exception. In its early stages, the company depended totally upon the engineers and skilled workers who left Dunlop Japan for its production technology.[23] It is also well known that those who formulated the sales organization of Toyota Jidōsha (Toyota Motor Company) were personnel who had learned American marketing methods and know-how while working for GM Japan.

It is worth pointing out that, when introducing production technology and business management systems and know-how, the Japanese companies did not adopt methodologies practiced in the foreign companies as they were but, in many cases, modified them, taking into account such factors as labor-management relations, social customs, and business practices unique to Japan. As Mitsubishi Electric introduced scientific management methods from Westinghouse in 1925, instead of accepting the F. W. Taylor method employed at Westinghouse, the management explained to the workers before carrying out the time study that "standard time study is not meant to set severe labor as the standard, but to standardize the amount of labor that an average worker can perform continuously." Moreover, when setting the wage rate based on this time study, it assured its employees that it would "guarantee the present income."[24]

Toyota Motor's earlier sales organizations and marketing methods were transplanted from GM Japan, but not exactly in their original forms. GM Japan imported from the United States the method of high-pressure marketing activities and was mechanically exercising an exclusive franchise system on dealers. But Toyota made a significant modification as it applied them to its own system. It made much of ordinary business practices in Japan and tried to build up its marketing activities and sales organizations on the foundation of mutual understanding and cooperation of the manufacturer and dealers.[25]

These examples illustrate that the foreign-affiliated companies served as an entrance for advanced technology, both hard- and software, from abroad, and at the same time as an exit for such technology to spread out in the country. The Japanese companies, on the other hand, absorbed and assimilated the foreign technology and strove for the blending of the Japanese way of doing business and western systems.

2. Industrial Structure

With a background of ample funds, technical superiority, stable raw-material supply sources, and large sales organizations, the foreign-affiliated companies in Japan operated their business strategies to seek so-called economics of scale, and thereby secured themselves the leading positions in their industries. Consequently, although circumstances differed in each industry, it became a general tendency among the sectors with foreign affiliates that an oligopolistic structure would emerge at a relatively early stage. In order for the domestic companies to survive in competition with their foreign counterparts, they had to expand and strengthen their business through mergers with other companies. Or when a Japanese company tried to enter the industrial sector where a foreign company was already dominating the market, it had to construct a business organization comparable in size to that of the foreign company.

In the oil industry, as mentioned, Standard founded International Oil Company with a capital of ¥10 million while Nippon Oil had a capital of ¥1.2 million and Hōden Oil ¥600,000, although they were the largest in Japan at that time. Therefore the emergence of giant International was quite shocking to the industry, and thus drove many of the smaller oil companies to form trusts with Nippon Oil and Hōden Oil. As a result, the two companies were able to expand their business in the industry. Moreover, after World War I, the aggressive marketing activities of Standard and Rising Sun became the major cause of the consolidation of Nippon Oil and Hōden Oil.[26]

As for the automotive industry, the emergence of Ford Japan and GM Japan put an end to the stage of so-called trial and error for Japanese enterprises. Since then, mass production and mass sales systems practiced by these two foreign affiliates became the criteria to enter this industry. The only Japanese manufacturers that could satisfy these criteria were Toyota Motor and Nissan Jidōsha (Nissan Motor Company).

The activities of the foreign-affiliated companies served to develop the related fields of their business and promote the technical level. An example is found in the rubber-processing industry of Japan, which grew rapidly in Hyōgo and Osaka prefectures after 1915. This was a result of the establishment of a Dunlop plant in Kobe, which caused the formation of related businesses located around it like so many satellites.[27] Another example is to be found in the auto industry. Ford Japan and GM Japan adopted a policy of using some assembly parts of Japanese manufacture. This contributed to a great extent to the development of vehicle parts engineering in Japan and its technological improvement, because the two companies imposed strict quality inspections at their headquarters in the

United States as they employed important parts from Japanese companies. The tires made by Bridgestone passed the quality inspections of Ford and GM in 1932, and this became the major force for the company to compete with the two foreign affiliates, Dunlop Japan and Yokohama Rubber, and to expand its sales channels.[28]

The emergence of car dealers, a new distribution industry in Japan, is also attributable to Ford Japan and GM Japan, which took great interest in perfecting their sales networks. What is important is that the vehicle parts and material manufacturers and the car dealers raised by Ford Japan and GM Japan were later handed down to Toyota Motor and Nissan Motor together with their employees when the two foreign affiliates had to withdraw from Japan according to the Jidōsha Seizō Jigyō Hō (Automobile Manufacturing Industry Law) of 1936, which will be discussed later.

3. *Managerial Ideology*

Construction of branch offices and factories of the foreign corporations or the emergence of the foreign-affiliated companies in Japan saw its full development in the 20th century. It was a favorable phenomenon for Japan, a less-developed country that had to seek industrialization and modernization by adopting capital, production systems, and business management systems from the advanced western nations. This phenomenon, on the other hand, shows that industrial leaders and business managers in Japan at that time were quite internationally minded. This tendency was particularly obvious in the zaibatsu group companies, where participation of salaried managers in the top management was realized at an early stage, and in such enterprises whose founders had experience studying abroad, since they did not hesitate to form affiliations with the foreign corporations as they entered the new sector of heavy industry.

However, at the same time, such activities of the foreign affiliates and their progressive market domination triggered "All-Japanese" principles and "nationalism" advocated by the local corporations that were operating their business activities in severe competition with the foreign affiliates.[29] This was especially evident among companies characterized by their "engineers' groups" in the newly established industry, which were formulated on the basis of an increasing number of engineers being educated at domestic universities and colleges after the 1910s. Such companies supported, as the spiritual strut of their business foundation, the "Principle of All-Japanese Technology" and actively operated their business according to that ideology.[30]

Odaira Namihei, for example, founded Hitachi Works in order to begin home production of electric machinery in Japan. He tried to indoctrinate his ideology of "All-Japanese Technology" into young engineers with college training, and succeeded in his attempt to form a typical "engineers' group."[31] Due to the company's business performance and support from the engineers, Odaira successfully persuaded the owner, Kuhara Fusanosuke, who had been considering affiliation with Siemens, and gained independence from Kuhara Kōgyō (Kuhara Mining) in 1920. He made Hitachi Engineering Works one of the major heavy electricapparatus manufacturers by the late 1920s.

Generally speaking, such "nationalism" or the "Principle of All-Japanese Technology" advocated by a number of Japanese corporations was an effective managerial ideology both in-house and outside the companies when facing competition with the foreign affiliates.[32] And the intensive competition between the foreign corporations and their Japanese counterparts, which had a completely different business basis and managerial ideology, resulted in self-reliance for the Japanese industry. As a result, home production in the industry was achieved at an early stage. Emergence and growth of such Japanese enterprises based on domestic technology encouraged the Japanese engineers working for the foreign affiliates to develop their own technology instead of relying upon foreign technology for copy production. As a result, after World War I, many of the Japanese partners of the foreign affiliates established their own technical laboratories in spite of the opposition raised by the latter.[33]

V. Japan's Industrial Policy in 1930s and Foreign Affiliates

In the early 1930s, the government's policy toward foreign capital turned back to the exclusive one mentioned above, and business activities of the foreign corporations were strictly restricted accordingly. With such changes in the business environment, many of the foreign affiliates adopted a policy of "Japanizing" themselves in order to ensure continuation of their business activities or reservation of their assets. That is, as Table 2 indicates, the foreign-affiliated companies increased the proportion of capital contribution by the Japanese partners, and many of the pure foreign corporations in Japan established joint capital with Japanese companies. Also, they increased the number of Japanese in their top management and the ratio of locally manufactured parts.

However, there were some companies which could not continue their Japanization policies or which persisted in their conventional managerial policies. Among them, Standard and Rising Sun in the oil industry and Ford and GM in the automotive industry are worth mentioning. These four companies firmly established their business foundations in their respective sectors and were leading their domestic competitors. Moreover, these two sectors were the focus of the attention of the military authorities at that time because of their growing influence upon politics and economy.

This section, therefore, discusses the Japanese government's policies toward the two industries, and the response from the foreign corporations or their governments.

1. Governmental Policies on Oil and Standard and Rising Sun

After the Manchurian Incident, the international environment for Japan deteriorated, and so did the performance of the domestic petroleum companies and stability in the oil market, because Standard and Rising Sun started a dumping contest against a backdrop of a worldwide oil surplus. Now the formulation of a strong oil policy was inevitable both for the sake of the industry and for military purposes. In particular, the military authorities were anxious to secure a fuel supply in time of war, and demanded that the government take measures to control the oil industry. The government set up the Rinji Nenryō Chōsakai (Interim Fuel Research Committee) in 1932 to study oil policies, and came out with "Sekiyu Kokusaku Jisshi Yōkō" (Outline of National Oil Policies), which had two primary objectives: one was to impose on oil companies the obligation to store petroleum for emergency use, and the other was to establish a licensing system for the oil industry. In accordance with this outline, in July 1933 the government enacted the Sekiyu Gyō Hō (Petroleum Industry Law), which authorized the government to allocate oil production and sales amounts to licensed companies and placed these companies under the obligation to store imported crude oil and various petroleum products equivalent to half of their business result of the previous year. The law also aimed to protect the domestic companies and to control the business of the foreign corporations.[34]

Enforcement of the law placed the foreign oil companies at a disadvantage. For example, Standard and Rising Sun, which had held more than 50% of the gasoline market share before the law, were awarded only 45% of the share at the first allotment in 1934, and this ratio was reduced further to 38% by 1937. The situation was the same for crude oil and other oil products.[35] Moreover, the obligation to hold in storage the equivalent of six months' worth of business became a significant financial burden for the two companies, which originally were oil importers. In order to fulfill their duty, both of them would have had to expend ¥70 to ¥80 million.[36]

Standard and Rising Sun filed a stiff protest with the Ministry of Commerce and Industry, which had jurisdiction over the industry, against the allotment of the sales share, and submitted that they could not accept the storage requirement of six months' worth of oil but could store three months' worth. The governments of the United States and Britain, at the request of the two companies, advanced a claim to the Japanese government to respect the companies' vested rights and to give them equal rights with the Japanese companies.

The Japanese government, however, ignored these requests. In September 1934, Standard and Rising Sun filed requests to their own governments to temporarily stop crude oil exports to Japan and to Manchukuo. But the two governments decided that they could not take such retaliatory measures because they could jeopardize their relations with Japan.[37]

After this, Standard and Rising Sun continued their business activities in Japan until August 1941, when the two governments exercised an embargo on petroleum against Japan, without either company having in storage six months' worth of oil in spite of the pressure from the Japanese government. But their sales share gradually decreased, and so did their influence over the industry.

2. Government Policies on Automobiles and Ford/GM

At the outbreak of the Manchurian Incident, the Japanese army requisitioned many civilian automobiles to service military transport. Discovering that the domestic vehicles performed poorly compared with Fords and Chevrolets, the army started negotiations with other authorities to consider "Kokusan Jidōsha Kōgyō Juritsu Saku" (Measures to Establish Domestic Automotive Industry) with a primary purpose of taking steps to produce trucks comparable to the Fords and Chevrolets for the mass market and to boycott Ford Japan and GM Japan, two obstacles to that purpose.[38] Although the related ministries opposed the radical position of the army, the latter exercised its growing power to demand that the cabinet approve its position. As a result, in August 1935, the cabinet accepted the demand from the army and started preparing the draft of the Automobile Manufacturing Industry Law.

The automotive policies fostered by the army forced Ford and GM, which had been virtually monopolizing the Japanese market, to take measures to protect their continued operation and assets. GM sought ways to remain in Japan by becoming affiliated with a Japanese manufacturer, and finally chose the Nissan combine, which was planning to take a decisive step into the automobile business. In October 1934, GM announced the following agreements with Nissan: (1) Nissan would own 51% of GM Japan's stock; (2) GM Japan would own 100% of stocks of Nissan Motor Co., a subsidiary of the Nissan combine.

Although this Nissan-GM cooperation plan was approved by the Ministry of Commerce and Industry as well as the Ministry of Finance, the army voiced strong opposition, and thereby the first attempt ended in failure. In October 1935, Nissan and GM plotted the second cooperation plan to merge GM Japan and Nissan Motor to establish a new company and to obtain a license under the impending Automobile Manufacturing Industry Law, but again it was not successful.[39]

Ford, on the other hand, sought a strategy to retain Ford Japan by way of establishing local manufacturing facilities. In August 1934, Ford started negotiations to purchase a parcel of reclaimed land owned by the city of Yokohama to build a plant under this strategy. But when this plan became known to the army, it demanded that the Yokohama city government call off the sale. Nevertheless, Ford did not abandon the plan and, in May 1935, succeeded in purchasing 90 acres of land owned by Tokyo Wan Umetate Kaisha (Tokyo Bay Reclamation Company), a company of the Asano zaibatsu. The sale was carried out despite the army's opposition because Tokyo Bay Reclamation acted on its own judgment that "Ford will build factories and provide technology. Even if a war breaks out, they cannot take the factories back to America."[40] Having purchased land, Ford began implementing the plan to build new facilities before the Automobile Manufacturing Industry Law was announced.

Against this action of Ford, the Japanese government hurried to legislate the Automobile Manufacturing Industry Law. In the meantime the U.S. government offered an objection to the proposed law stating that the law conflicted with the U.S.–Japan Treaty of Commerce and Navigation. Even in Japan, there was a strong voice against the law. However, citing Article 1 of the law, "The purpose of this law is to foster the automobile manufacturing industry in the Empire in order to complete national defense and develop industry," the advocates overruled all objections and opposition. That is, they took a view that the law should be enacted for the sake of national defense.[41]

The Automobile Manufacturing Industry Law passed the Diet in May 1936 and was put into effect in July. As a result, the application for the plant construction permit that Ford Japan submitted to the Kanagawa prefectural government was rejected. The Japanese government immediately granted licenses to Toyoda Jidōshokki Seisakusho (Toyoda

Automatic Loom Works)[42] and Nissan Motor. In contrast, Ford Japan and GM Japan were ordered to keep assembly production under 12,360 and 9,470 vehicles respectively.

Ford, as its plan for a new factory failed and production was restricted, changed its strategy and sought cooperation with a Japanese company. It approached the Mitsubishi zaibatsu, the Furukawa zaibatsu, Toyota Motor, and Nissan Motor, but was not successful in any attempts. Also GM, after abandoning the cooperation plan with the Nissan combine, began negotiations for affiliation with the Sumitomo zaibatsu and Toyota Motor, but in vain.[43]

In the meantime the business environment of both Ford Japan and GM Japan continued to deteriorate, and in January 1941 they terminated their operations in Japan.

VI. Conclusion

Before the outbreak of World War II, many foreign corporations were making inroads in the Japanese market either by themselves or by way of joint ventures or capital affiliations with Japanese companies. Most of them were the leading multinationals which were conducting worldwide manufacturing and sales activities at that time. The fact that they made notable advances into Japan after World War I indicates that this market was incorporated in their global strategies and that they regarded Japan as a basis for their further advance into East Asia.

However, it should also be noticed that the amount of their investment was not very large. It proves that, in the global strategy of the multinationals, the East Asian market including Japan was not a major concern.

Nevertheless, the foreign-affiliated companies in Japan deserved much attention. Their newest technology, managerial organization, and business activities based on abundant information, in the long run, promoted the transfer of production facilities and technology, and business management systems and know-how, to Japanese companies; oligopolized their participating sector in the early stage; brought up personnel for management and engineering; and caused the "Principles of All-Japanese Technology" to arise, thereby contributing greatly to independence of the Japanese industry and to the modernization of Japanese business activities.

Japan's policies on foreign capital after winning the Sino-Japanese War of 1895 showed a turnabout with the outbreak of the Manchurian Incident of 1931 from the former receptive-to-foreign-investment principle to restrictive and exclusive measures. The most illustrative of the oppressive measures against foreign capital after the incident were the Petroleum Industry Law and the Automobile Manufacturing Industry Law, both legislated with an aim to regulate and exclude foreign corporations.

The Petroleum Industry Law was modeled after a similar law enacted in France in 1928. But the French law was different from that of Japan in that the former gave sufficient consideration to foreign companies' business performance in the past and in that, in case they built new refineries, it would assure safety of their investment for the next 20 years.[44] Ford and GM, on the other hand, possessed assembly plants in Germany. In 1929, the government of Germany approved the purchase of Adam Opel, a domestic corporation, by GM and in 1931 gave permission to Ford's local production plan. As these examples show, Japan's effort to exclude foreign capital in the 1930s was the most decisive of any nation's to pursue obstructing and protective policies for the sake of its own domestic industries.

In other words, the enactment of the Petroleum Industry Law and the Automobile Manufacturing Industry Law was epoch-making in the sense that they became a prototype of various wartime regulations which would later be established in other industrial sectors. Simultaneously, however, it was the beginning of international isolation for Japan's industrial and business activities.

Notes

This study was supported by the 1988 special research subsidy fund of Hōsei University.

1. Nakagawa Keiichirō, "Kokusai Kankei Keieishi e no Mondai Teiki (Topics of Discussion in International Business History)," in *Keieishi Gakkai Dai 22-Kai Taikai Hōkoku Shū* (Report of the 22nd Conference of Business History), 1986, p. 83.
2. Horie Yasuzo, *Gaishi Yunyū no Kaiko to Tenbō* (The Importation of Foreign Capital: Retrospect and Prospect) (Yūhikaku, Tokyo), 1950, pp. 35–36.
3. On this point, see the following references: Wilkins, Mira, *The Emergence of Multinational Enterprise: American Business Abroad from the Colonial Era to 1914* (Harvard University Press, Cambridge, MA), 1970; Wilkins, Mira, *The Maturing of Multinational Enterprise: American Business Abroad from 1914 to 1970* (Harvard University Press, Cambridge, MA), 1974; Franko, Lawrence G., "The Origins of Multinational Manufacturing by Continental European Firms," *Business History Review*, vol. XLVIII, no. 3, Autumn 1974; and Stopford, John M., "The Origins of British-Based Multinational Manufacturing Enterprise," *Business History Review*, vol. XLVIII, no. 3, Autumn 1974.
4. Ōkurashō (Ministry of Finance), ed., *Dai 2-Ji Taisen ni Okeru Rengōkoku*

Zaisan Shori (1) (Confiscated Assets of the Allied Powers During World War II, Vol. I) (Ōkurashō, Tokyo), 1966, pp. 145–46.

5. Iguchi Tosuke, *Gendai Nippon Sangyō Hattatsu Shi (II): Sekiyu* (History of Industrial Development in Modern Japan, II: Petroleum Industry) (Kojun-sha, Tokyo), 1963, pp. 91–92.

6. Nippon Sekiyu KK (Nippon Oil Co., Ltd.), ed., *Nippon Sekiyu Shi* (History of the Oil Industry in Japan) (Nippon Sekiyu KK, Tokyo), 1958, p. 77.

7. Mobil Sekiyu KK (Mobil Oil Co. Ltd.), ed., *Sekiyu Monogatari: Mobil Sekiyu Shōshi* (Oil Story: A Brief History of Mobil Sekiyu) (Mobil Sekiyu KK, Tokyo), 1984, pp. 78–84; Shell Sekiyu KK (Shell Oil Co. Ltd.) ed., *Shell Sekiyu 60-Nen no Ayumi* (60-Year History of Shell Sekiyu) (Shell Sekiyu KK, Tokyo), 1960, p. 6.

8. Iguchi, *op. cit.*, p. 246. After this, Standard underwent the following changes: Standard Oil of New York merged with Vacuum Oil Company in 1931 and became Socony Vacuum Corporation; the latter established Standard Vacuum Oil Company in 1933 with a 50-50 capital contribution with Standard Oil Company of New Jersey.

9. Refer to the following sources for the description of Mitsubishi Oil Company: Mitsubishi Sekiyu KK (Mitsubishi Oil Co. Ltd.), *Mitsubishi Sekiyu 50 Nen Shi* (50-Year History of Mitsubishi Oil) (Mitsubishi Sekiyu KK, Tokyo), 1981; and Kawabe Nobuo, *Sōgō Shōsha no Kenkyū* (Study of General Trading Companies) (Jikkyō Shuppan, Tokyo), 1982, Chapter 1.

10. Nippon Gomu Kōgyō Kai (Rubber Industry Association of Japan), ed., *Nippon Gomu Kōgyō Shi (1)* (History of Rubber Industry in Japan, Vol. 1) (Tōyō Keizai Shinpōsha, Tokyo), 1969, pp. 203–5.

11. Jones, Geoffrey, "The Growth and Performance of British Multinational Firms Before 1939: The Case of Dunlop," in *Economic History Review*, vol. XXXVII, no. 1, February 1984, p. 39.

12. Nippon Gomu Kōgyō Kai, ed., *op. cit.*, p. 311.

13. Yokohama Gomu Seizō KK (Yokohama Rubber Mfg. Co., Ltd.), ed., *40 Nen Shi* (40-Year History) (Yokohama Gomu KK, Tokyo), 1959, pp. 5–14.

14. Burijisuton Taiya KK (Bridgestone Tire Co., Ltd.), ed., *Bridgestone 50 Nen Shi* (50-Year History of Bridgestone) (Burijisuton Taiya KK, Tokyo), 1982, p. 64.

15. On this point, refer to: Itagaki Hiroshi, "1920 Nendai America Denki Sangyō no Kaigai Shinshutsu (Overseas Business Expansion of the American Electric Machinery Industry in the 1920s)," in *Kokumin Keizai* (National Economics), no. 136, March 1977; and Wilkins, *The Emergence of Multinational Enterprise*, pp. 93–96.

16. Nippon Jidōsha Kōgyōkai (Automobile Industry Association of Japan), ed., *Nippon Jidōsha Kōgyō Shiko (2)* (Outline of the History of the Japanese Automobile Industry, Vol. 2) (Nippon Jidōsha Kōgyōkai, Tokyo), 1967, p. 8. The description that follows is based on: Udagawa, Masaru, "The Prewar Japanese Automobile Industry and American Manufacturers," in Nakagawa Keiichirō and Morikawa Hidemasa, eds., *Japanese Yearbook on Business History*, no. 2, 1985.

17. Mitsubishi Denki KK (Mitsubishi Electric Mfg. Co. Ltd.), ed., *Mitsubishi Denki Shashi* (History of Mitsubishi Electric Mfg. Co. Ltd.) (Mitsubishi Denki KK, Tokyo), 1982, p. 30.

18. *Ibid.*, p. 33.

19. Mitsubishi Denki KK (Mitsubishi Electric Mfg. Co. Ltd.), ed., *Kengyō*

Kaiko (Retrospective of the Company's Foundation) (Mitsubishi Denki KK, Tokyo), pp. 69–70. Out of the 35 delegates, 13 were later promoted to the top management above directors.

20. Hasegawa Shin, "Electrical Equipment Industry in the 1920s (English title)," *Rekishigaku Kenkyū* (Journal of Historical Studies), no. 486, November 1980, p. 30.

21. Sasaki Satoshi, "The Introduction of Time Study Method into Mitsubishi Electric Co. at Kobe Works (English title)," *Keiei Shigaku* (Japan Business History Review), vol. 21, no. 4, January 1987, pp. 51–54.

22. Nippon Gomu Kōgyō Kai, *op. cit.* p. 205.

23. Burijisuton Taiya KK, *op. cit.*, p. 35, p. 46.

24. Sasaki, *op. cit.*, p. 38.

25. Toyota Jidōsha Hanbai KK (Toyota Motor Sales Co., Ltd.), ed., *Motorization to Tomo ni* (Along with Motorization) (Toyota Jidōsha Hanbai KK, Nagoya), 1970, pp. 38–47.

26. Iguchi, *op. cit.*, pp. 108–18.

27. Nippon Gomu Kōgyō Kai, *op. cit.*, p. 204.

28. Burijisuton Taiya KK, *op. cit.*, pp. 47–54.

29. Chokki, Toshiaki, "Foreign Joint Ventures and Modernization of Business Management in Japan (English title)," *Keiei Shirin* (The Hōsei Journal of Business), vol. 17, no. 4, January 1981, p. 314.

30. The number of the engineers with a college education was 1,921 in 1910, but this number increased to 5,025 in 1920. Sixty-five % of them were working for private corporations, according to Hoshimi Uchida, "Distribution of University Graduate Engineers in Japan, 1920 (English title)" in *Tokyo Keizai Daigaku Kaishi* (The Journal of Tokyo Keizai University), no. 152, September 1987, p. 105.

31. Hitachi Seisakusho KK (Hitachi Works Co., Ltd.), ed., *Hitachi Kōjō 50 Nen Shi* (50-Year History of Hitachi Factory) (Hitachi Seisakusho KK, Tokyo), 1961, p. 2. Parenthetically, all of the 11 executives (above managing director) of Hitachi Works before World War II started their careers as engineers.

32. Chokki, *op. cit.*, p. 315.

33. Uchida Hoshimi, "Gijutsu Kaihatsu (Development of Technology)," in Nakagawa Keiichirō, ed., *Nihon Teki Keiei* (Japanese Business Management) (Nippon Keizai Shinbun Sha, Tokyo), 1977, p. 145.

34. This description is based on Takeda Haruhito, *Nenryō Kyoku Sekiyu Gyōsei Zenshi* (History of the Preceding Age of Oil Administration by the Fuel Bureau), Sangyō Seisaku Shi Kenkyūjo (Research Center of Industrial Policies, Tokyo), 1979.

35. *Ibid.*, pp. 233–34.

36. Anderson, Irvine H., Jr., *The Standard Vacuum Oil Company and United States East Asian Policy, 1933–1941* (Princeton University Press, Princeton), 1975, p. 160; and Shell Sekiyu, *op. cit.*, p. 9.

37. Wilkins, *The Maturing of Multinational Enterprise*, pp. 230–33.

38. Udagawa, Masaru, "Historical Development of the Japanese Automobile Industry, 1917–1971," in *Keiei Shirin* (The Hōsei Journal of Business), vol. 19, no. 4, January 1983, p. 35.

39. Udagawa, "The Prewar Japanese Automobile Industry and American Manufacturers," pp. 86–91.

40. Nippon Jidōsha Kōgyōkai (Automobile Industry Association of Japan),

ed., *Nippon Jidōsha Kōgyō Shiko* (*3*) (Outline of the History of the Japanese Automobile Industry, Vol. 3) (Nippon Jidōsha Kōgyōkai, Tokyo), 1969, p. 38.

41. *Ibid.*, pp. 43–45.

42. In August 1937, the Toyoda Automatic Loom Works separated its automobile division and created an independent company, Toyota Motor. Note that the original company name, Toyoda, was modified to Toyota for the independent automobile company.

43. Udagawa, "The Prewar Japanese Automobile Industry and American Manufacturers," pp. 94–95.

44. Iguchi, *op. cit.*, pp. 245–55.

Comment

Hiroaki Yamazaki

Professor Udagawa presents a bird's-eye view of the activities of foreign-affiliated companies in Japan before World War II. He explains what kind of foreign-affiliated companies existed in prewar Japan, how they acted and affected Japanese business activities, and how Japan's policy on foreign capital changed, then summarizes his conclusion. I evaluate his paper highly as an introduction to a history of foreign-affiliated companies in Japan and basically agree with his conclusion. But in order to stimulate discussions in this conference, I would like to raise three points in regard to his paper.

My first point concerns the effect of the activities of foreign-affiliated companies on the development of Japanese businesses before 1931. Udagawa says that Japanese government policy with regard to foreign capital changed around 1931 from a receptive one to a restrictive one. However, he also emphasizes that the foreign-affiliated companies, in the long run, promoted the transfer of production facilities, technology, business management systems, and know-how to Japanese companies and contributed greatly to the independence of the Japanese industry and to the modernization of Japanese business activities. If this is so, when we divide the period in consideration in two—before and after 1931—and firstly take up the earlier period when foreign-affiliated companies acted freely, we should be able to see differences in their effects on the development of Japanese businesses. For example, in the case of the automobile industry, GM and Ford almost monopolized the Japanese market and it seems to me that they checked the development of Japanese businesses, while on the other hand, in the case of the heavy electric machinery industry, Japanese managers could take the leadership in the top management of foreign-affiliated companies and these companies as such could develop by absorbing foreign technologies and know-how. The questions are then (1) Is my judgment about the two industries mentioned above correct? (2) If so, how should we arrange the cases of other main industries taken up in this paper in relation to the two contrasting cases cited above?

And (3) What factors were responsible for the industry differences in their effects on the development of Japanese businesses.

My second comment concerns the evaluation of the position of foreign investment in the Japanese economy. According to Udagawa, foreign investment was rather small. I agree with this statement. But at the same time we should not overlook the fact that in several growing heavy and chemical industries which occupied important positions in the Japanese industrial structure, foreign affiliates oligopolized the market. As shown in Table 1, among heavy and chemical industries which developed during the 1920s and occupied important positions in the Japanese industrial structure in 1929, automobile manufacturing, petroleum importing and refining, and electrical machinery manufacturing were industries which foreign affiliates entered and in which they occupied the dominant position. In this sense, foreign-affiliated companies had a significant influence on the development of the Japanese heavy and chemical industries, although the actual amount of foreign investment in the Japanese economy as a whole was not so large.

My third comment concerns the necessity of taking into account technical affiliation if we are to consider the whole effect of foreign affiliates in Japan on Japan's industrial development. Let me illustrate this point with the case of the rayon industry. At the end of the 1920s, the six largest rayon manufacturers in Japan were Teikoku Jinzō Kenshi (Teijin), Asahi Kenshoku, Tōyō Rayon, Nippon Rayon, Kurashiki Kenshoku, and Tōyō Bōseki. Teijin was established in 1918 and tried to affiliate itself with renowned foreign manufacturers, such as Courtaulds and Société de la Viscose, but all such efforts failed. As a result, it was forced to develop its own technology through trial and error.

Response

Masaru Udagawa

In response to the first comment: The outbreak of the Manchurian Incident in 1931 triggered changes in the Japanese government's policies toward foreign capital. It is also true that the business activities of foreign-affiliated companies rapidly became more difficult after 1931. However, from a long-term point of view, there was no major difference in the foreign-affiliated companies' contribution to the development of Japanese industries and businesses before and after the Manchurian Incident. Professor Yamazaki is right in suggesting that business activities by Ford and GM, which entered Japan in the 1920s, heavily damaged the domestic manufacturers. But the two companies' activities did not disturb the development of Japan's automotive industry itself; instead they led to the formation of an "infrastructure" vital for the industry's development. In the 1930s, Toyota and Nissan emerged in the automotive industry and took full advantage of the infrastructure created by foreign companies. In the electric machinery industry, Japan-foreign joint-venture partners maintained good relations, and the foreign companies lent full support to these joint ventures even after the Manchurian Incident. Basically such a situation applies to joint ventures in other industrial sectors as well.

It is difficult to quantify the importance of the role played by foreign businesses in each industry. However, the impact of the foreign businesses in the automotive industry was significantly large. On the other hand, such impact was moderate in the electric-machinery industry. The foreign businesses in the petroleum industry had an impact similar to the one in the automotive industry, and such an impact in the rubber industry was comparable to that in the electric machinery industry.

In response to the second comment: I agree with Yamazaki on this issue. Although the exact figure is not available for the amount of money invested by foreign-affiliated companies in each industrial sector, we can assume that the largest portion was invested in the sector of new heavy and chemical industries which led the Second Industrial Revolution. Therefore, I believe that the foreign-affiliated companies played a significant role in the development process of the Japanese heavy and chemical industries, which progressed largely in the period between the two world wars.

In response to the third comment: My treatise covered only the direct investment to Japan made by the foreign manufacturing companies. But as Yamazaki suggested, discussions of the contribution of the foreign affiliates to the development of industry and businesses in Japan should inevitably incorporate consideration of technical affiliations formed by foreign and Japanese companies. It is true that, in such affiliations, general trading companies such as Mitsui Bussan played an important role. In this matter I also agree with Yamazaki. I personally think that the number of such technical affiliations concluded between Japanese and foreign companies was larger than the number of cases of direct investment by foreign companies. However, I still assume that the direct investment made a larger contribution and had a larger impact on the development of Japanese industry and businesses than affiliations. The specific industrial sectors in which many technical affiliations were formed were the chemical industry, the steel industry, and the shipbuilding industry.

The Contributions of Foreign Enterprises to Japanese Economic Development

Mira Wilkins

There now exists a body of literature that deals with host countries and multinational enterprises—a literature that is both historical and contemporaneous.[1] In considering the contributions of foreign companies, there are many economic and political questions that we must ask. The economic ones are both macro and micro in nature. The macro questions include the magnitude of the investment impact. What were the employment consequences? What were the net tax revenue results (net of any governmental spending required)? What was the effect on the balance of payments? What was the influence on economic development? Did the foreign direct investment cause "immiserizing growth" as the country continued to import capital-intensive goods and as the terms of trade turned adverse (export prices fell relative to import ones)? Did the burden of paying dividends to the foreign owner exceed the benefits of the investment?[2]

The micro questions relate to the specifics of the economic impact of individual companies. Did the foreign company introduce new technology? Did it teach new skills? Were there alternative ways—aside from the foreign enterprise—of obtaining the technology more cheaply? Here we want not only to define technology in traditional terms of new processes but also to consider "social technology," that is, new management methods. Was the technology provided appropriate? What were the linkage effects on suppliers, on dealers, on competitors? Did the foreign company "crowd out" other firms? Did the foreign firm, by borrowing in the host country or through involvement in joint ventures, divert domestic savings from more productive alternatives? Were remitted profits "excessive"? Did the foreign enterprise introduce new products? Were these appropriate ones? What, from a sectoral standpoint, was the impact on industrial development?

Some economists view foreign business as encouraging a wide range of new domestic enterprises—as *complementary*. By contrast, others, in the counterpart to the macroeconomic arguments on "immiserizing growth," see firms from abroad as *substituting* for host nation enterprises by creating insuperable obstacles to their expansion; foreign companies, these economists believe, preempt the most profitable projects, intimidating and discouraging savers from investing in their own countries and prompting those savers to send their capital abroad (flight capital). The very existence of strong foreign business, it is sometimes maintained, deters and defeats domestic capital and domestic entrepreneurship. Since foreign companies have "preferred access to funds," the argument proceeds, they can effectively overwhelm and suppress the disadvantaged domestic firm.

An added set of economic considerations deals with the success of the foreign company and how such success or failure is to be evaluated in terms of host nation benefits. A foreign firm can be "successful" yet create a burden on a host nation in the form of huge profit remittances. It can be a "failure"—that is, unprofitable—but can leave in its wake productive resources. Ultimately, if we are evaluating the contributions of foreign business, we must judge success and failure in terms of national interests, since from a host country view this is the only legitimate criterion.

The political issues deal with the interactions between the host government and the foreign company. On the one hand, there has been discussion of the extent to which the host government encouraged, regulated, or restricted foreign business—and the degree to which the host government was responsive to popular opinion prevailing in the host nation. On the other hand, students of international business frequently seek to identify the degree to which such companies from abroad (whether or not aided by their home governments) influenced host government policies: Was the sovereignty of the capital-recipient country at bay?

All of these general topics can be, and have been, looked at in relation to particular host countries in particular time periods. In this paper I want to consider foreign companies in Japan in the decades before World War II.[3] What were the relevant economic contributions? Did foreign firms add to or subtract from Japanese industrial business development more or less than the foreign companies present in other host nations? Did foreign companies encounter in Japan a special "Japanese style of management" that was nowhere else present, and did this mean that their path in Japan had to be unique? Did the Japanese government play an economic role totally unlike that of any other sovereign state? To what extent were Japanese conditions sui generis?

I. Foreign Business in Japan in an Overall Context

In the early 20th century, many countries (including Japan) were *homes* to companies that operated over borders.[4] Yet, were we to rank by importance such home countries, Great Britain would be first, followed by the United States and Germany.[5]

Many more countries were hosts to foreign multinationals. The most important host was the United States.[6] According to John Dunning, in 1914 Japan received only 0.2% of worldwide foreign direct investment.[7] This figure is an approximation, but it does suggest that Japan was far down on the list of candidates for multinational enterprise expansion.

In the pre–World War I years, however, Japan did attract Great Britain's leading multinational business, J. & P. Coats.[8] According to Geoffrey Jones, Dunlop built its first factory in Kobe in 1909.[9] Even earlier, the British firms Vickers and Armstrong (in 1907) had entered into a joint venture in Japan.[10] Likewise, from the United States, Western Electric and General Electric had established manufacturing facilities in Japan well before 1914.[11] In 1900 the world's largest oil company, Standard Oil, launched a short-lived but fully integrated producing, refining, and marketing enterprise in Japan.[12] Clearly, Japan was part of the broad international expansion of all these British and American companies.

So, too, German banks—in connection with their general overseas growth—made direct investments in Japan. The Deutsche Bank had for a very brief interlude a branch in Yokohama from 1872 to 1874. By the end of 1908, the Deutsch-Asiatische Bank had 12 branches, including two in Japan (in Yokohama and Kobe).[13] Siemens & Halske had a Japanese subsidiary in 1901.[14]

The years of World War I (1914–18) marked a sharp change in the world economy. The United States—a debtor country in world accounts in 1914—became a key creditor nation. While U.S. multinationals were already important before World War I,[15] after the war their business activities expanded dramatically.[16] However, Dunning believes that British multinationals were still more in evidence than American ones in 1938.[17] The First World War had devastating effects on the German economy. Nonetheless, German business revived and resumed international expansion.

As for the host countries, I do not know the sequence of nations that were the most attractive to foreign multinationals in the interwar years. For 1938, Dunning has placed Canada first in rank, drawing 9.4% of the total inward direct investment from abroad. Japan, he estimated, obtained a mere 0.4% of worldwide foreign direct investment, albeit this was double his estimate of 0.2% in 1914.[18]

The size of U.S. direct investment in Japan was small. The book value of U.S. direct investment in Japan in 1929 was put by the U.S. Department of Commerce at a mere $60.7 million, or 0.8% of total U.S. direct investment abroad.[19] Among countries in Asia, Japan ranked fourth as a host to U.S. multinationals.[20] While the number of new entries into Japan from the United States, the United Kingdom, and Germany rose in the 1920s, Japan still was a secondary or even tertiary locale for international business.

II. The Economic and Political Impacts

All this said, were the economic and political impacts on Japan equally minor? Were the impacts substantially less than on other countries that pulled in larger sums from abroad?

From a macroeconomic standpoint, the size of the investment by foreign companies in Japan must have been a tiny fraction of the total. Japan's labor force was about 30.5 million in the years 1928–37;[21] Mark Mason has provided some 1932 figures from official Japanese sources that indicate 24,000 Japanese were employed in firms in which there was substantial foreign direct investment.[22] That is less than .08% of the labor force. The 10,000 people employed in 1932 in U.S. branch factories, again identified by Mason,[23] represented a mere .03% of the Japanese labor force. In terms of tax revenues, I have no idea of the impact of the multinationals. According to William Lockwood, as late as 1933, all Japanese national taxes on personal income, business profits, and interest still yielded little more than the liquor tax[24]—and, of course, foreign investors had no role in the production and distribution of liquor (and the impact of foreign managers on liquor consumption, and thus on the liquor tax—while possibly considerable—certainly had no macroeconomic significance). Yet, in net, the contribution of the foreign direct investors to tax revenues was undoubtedly positive (there was no Japanese subsidizing of foreign business).

Once more, we have little concrete evidence of the effects on the balance of payments of the multinationals in Japan. In that most were importers of goods, that effect was negative. Most companies from overseas appear to have produced principally for Japanese domestic consumption rather than for export, although some did export to far eastern markets. The positive items on the balance of payments would be the capital flow to Japan to establish the new enterprise, along with any product exports. The negative flows would be for imports of machinery and imports of parts for assembly and products for distribution, plus the remittances home of earnings. There is little to suggest that foreign companies had a favorable effect on the Japanese balance of payments, *unless* one establishes a counterfactual development model and assumes that Japan would import all the goods that were produced by the foreign enterprises in Japan and that, by virtue of the import substitution, the outflow for imports was sufficiently reduced to offset the new imports and the profit remittances.

But it is just as easy to set up an alternative counterfactual model, arguing (more plausibly) that Japan's contacts with the West—through multinational enterprises—created a "demonstration effect," a desire for new products, many of which had to be imported; in this scenario the presence of the multinationals created the demand for added products from overseas, which, in turn, encouraged imports and had adverse effects on the balance of payments.

How do these macroeconomic considerations compare with those in other host countries? In very few host nations worldwide have foreign direct investors accounted for a sizable proportion of the *total* labor force, albeit there appear to be many countries where the percentages exceeded those of Japan. In terms of tax revenues, in a number of nations foreign companies' activities have in times past generated the bulk of government tax revenues (this was the case, for example, in the principal oil-exporting countries, when foreign multinationals dominated production). When companies from abroad produced in nations *for export*, the general pattern was a sizable positive impact on the balance of payments. There are many countries in which the balance-of-payment impacts—positive or negative—have clearly been material.

Did foreign direct investment in Japan before World War II cause "immiserizing growth"? Here the answer seems to be a resounding no. In many instances, output of foreign companies was in producer goods. While the terms of trade do appear to have deteriorated in the pre–World War II years,[25] the reason does not seem to lie in the presence of foreign direct investors.[26] When there was concern by the Japanese on profit remittances, controls were imposed. The burden of dividends paid never seems to have been excessive. Indeed, foreign direct investors seem to have contributed to real economic growth.

This brings us to the microeconomic influences. If from a macroeconomic viewpoint the role of foreign companies in Japan appears to be far from overwhelming, when we discuss particular sectors and particular impacts, then the consequences seem of much more significance.[27] At the request of the conveners of this conference, I will concentrate on the specific impacts of American oil and automobile companies. The impacts in these two sectors were different, but in each case the impacts were substantial. Whereas in the oil industry American and the British-Dutch companies shared in the foreign influence, in the automobile industry it was primarily American enterprises that had an impact.[28] First, I will discuss the American role in the oil industry and then turn to the U.S. automobile makers.

In 1900 the marketing manager of Standard Oil of New York proposed that Standard Oil start an oil-producing and -refining business in Japan. Japanese mining law had been amended in 1900 to make this possible. There was then a prevailing belief that Japan had substantial oil resources. Accordingly the International Oil Company, Ltd. was established in November 1900 with an authorized capital of ¥10 million—almost half of which was supplied by Standard Oil. The other half was authorized but not subscribed, albeit there does seem to have been participation by certain Japanese interests and possibly by Shell interests as well.[29]

American drillers went to work in Hokkaido and other promising producing areas. In Naoetsu, on the Japan Sea coast, some 150 kilometers southwest of Niigata and less than 300 kilometers from Tokyo, the new company built the "best equipped and most modern refinery in Japan." In the early 1900s, refineries were typically near crude-oil production sites. The assumption was that Japan would produce adequate raw materials to supply this facility. The prediction did not come to pass. The International Oil Company, Ltd.'s crude-oil output came to barely one-third of the new refinery's capacity. After seven years, in 1907, Standard Oil withdrew from production and refining in Japan; it sold out to a Japanese company, Nippon Sekiyu, leaving the Japanese with its modern refinery.[30] Nippon Sekiyu became Japan's largest non-foreign-owned oil company.[31]

The principal U.S. oil company in the Far East was Standard Oil of New York (Socony). It had large Asiatic interests in distribution and continued as a marketer of products in Japan after the sale of the International Oil Company, Ltd.[32] Also important was Vacuum Oil (mainly in lubricating oil). By the 1920s, Tide Water Oil Company had agents in Japan.[33] Texaco once sold in Japan, but in the wake of the 1923 earthquake it retreated from Japanese business. Mitsubishi Trading Company, which was the agent for the American firm Associated Oil Company and for Tide Water Oil Company, took over Texaco's former distributors.[34]

In 1931, Socony and Vacuum Oil merged in the United States to form

Socony-Vacuum (later Mobil Oil), and in 1933, Socony-Vacuum combined its Asiatic distribution network with Standard Oil of New Jersey's producing and refining operations in the Netherland East Indies. The result was Standard-Vacuum Oil Company, which never refined in Japan. It sold imported refined-oil products throughout the Far East, including Japan.[35] Meanwhile, and by contrast, in 1931, Associated Oil Company (a subsidiary of Tidewater Associated Oil Company) joined with Mitsubishi interests in a 50-50 refining venture called Mitsubishi Oil Company.[36] Its refinery in 1939 had a daily average capacity of 5,500 barrels of crude oil (the American 50% share was 2,750).[37] Unlike International Oil Company, from the start it was intended to operate using imported crude oil. By 1939, Japan (and Manchukuo) had refineries with a capacity of 85,470 barrels daily; thus the U.S. share was a trivial 3.2%. (By contrast, in 1939, American-owned refineries represented 62.1% of capacity in Canada, 37.2% in Germany, 26.7% in France, and 13.1% in the United Kingdom.) Japan in 1939 had a larger refinery capacity than Germany (54,285 barrels) and almost as large a capacity as the United Kingdom (91,500 barrels).[38] Only 15 years earlier, in 1924, Japan's daily refinery capacity had been a mere 3,000 barrels; at that time Germany's was 10,000 and the British Isles had 45,000.[39]

Although Mitsubishi Oil Company was a 50-50 joint venture, it was Japanese-managed. Americans gave technical assistance, trained Japanese personnel to run the refinery, and provided the imported crude-oil inputs.[40] Mitsubishi Oil Company seems to have learned from the technical advice provided by the Americans. Thus, even though it was relatively small, it did offer an example to be followed by other Japanese enterprises.

By 1933–34 the Japanese desire for domestic oil refineries had become very apparent to the much larger Standard-Vacuum Oil Company (known as Stanvac).[41] It appears that Stanvac tried to *thwart* Japanese moves in this direction, hoping to continue its export of refined-oil products to Japan; however, its efforts to prevent Japanese refinery expansion proved futile.[42] Instead, the Japanese were able to manipulate the American oil company. To maintain its newly threatened position in Japan, in December 1935, Stanvac (and Shell) agreed to provide the Japanese with research results on the hydrogenation process for obtaining oil from coal.[43] This was a major concession.

In the 1930s, Stanvac was caught in the vise of Japan's foreign exchange difficulties. It sold some land it owned in Japan in 1937, but was not given permission to remit the proceeds.[44] It marketed all its refined-oil products "on consignment" and thus had no profits in Japan—and none to remit.[45] As noted, it never built refineries in Japan before World War II.

In sum, Japan's modern economy depended on oil from abroad, which came from foreign companies. What Japan did in the 1930s was develop a refining industry (crude-oil imports were less costly than refined ones) and develop reserve stockpiling. The relatively small Mitsubishi Oil Company excepted, Japan's sizable refining industry emerged as wholly domestic. As for its reserve needs, under the Petroleum Industry Law of 1934, the Japanese government set the standards.

In microeconomic terms, Associated Oil—in connection with its joint venture in Mitsubishi Oil Company—introduced new technology and skills to Japan. Stanvac was prepared to do so when it agreed to share hydrogenation research results. Stanvac's distribution system was important in Japan. There were no questions on "appropriate" technology; the Japanese made their own choices. The linkage effects were substantial: Oil is vital. Stanvac's opposition notwithstanding, Japanese refinery capacity expanded greatly in the 1930s. There was no "crowding-out" effect. The Mitsubishi Oil Company joint venture was desired by the Japanese. There was no diversion of domestic resources in a way adverse to Japanese wishes. Stanvac booked its profits abroad. As for Tidewater Associated Oil, its profits on Japanese business seem modest.[46]

The products introduced by Stanvac were obviously appropriate and in demand. The availability of oil was crucial to Japan's industrial development. Stanvac survived in the highly nationalistic Japan of the 1930s, only because it filled Japanese needs. It survived after 1934 under the growing restrictions. Its strong bargaining power was tempered by a Japanese government that had a clear vision of national requirements. Stanvac turned to the U.S. government for aid,[47] but never was Japanese sovereignty at bay.

Like the oil industry, motor vehicles are identified with modern economic development. The Japanese automobile industry emerged under the aegis of American influence. In the 1920s both Ford and General Motors were expanding internationally.[48] The companies were establishing assembly plants in many countries, principally to save on shipping expenses. It was far cheaper to ship "knocked-down" units than "built-up" ones.

Ford had long exported to Japan using an export-import house, Sale & Frazar, as its exclusive distributor.[49] In 1924, Robert Roberge, head of Ford's export department, visited Japan and decided that the company was not well served by its agent. "Dealers as we know them," he wrote the home office, "do not exist. We must start from the very beginning to develop a real organization."[50]

With approval from Dearborn, early in 1925, Roberge formed a Japanese Ford company, which would have an assembly facility as well as manage sales and service. Ford-Dearborn agreed to furnish its Japanese subsidiary with "engineering and technical advice and assistance" and to send to Japan engineers, technical experts, and managers, as required. To run the Japanese company, Roberge selected Benjamin Kopf, who had been born in Argentina and was an Argentine citizen of German background. Kopf had been hired by Ford Motor Company in Buenos Aires in January 1917 not long after its assembly plant had been started there. He had served Ford in Argentina, Brazil, Uruguay, and Chile. He knew nothing about the Orient, but more important, he had been a Ford employee for some nine years. By 1925, Ford had assembly facilities in all four of those Latin American countries.

Kopf discovered that business prospects in Japan were excellent. In 1925 and 1926 a total of 16,909 American and Canadian vehicles were exported to Japan, and of these 16,689 were Fords! In Ford-Japan's first two years, Kopf reported a profit of $1.9 million. Ford's initial assembly operations took place in some sheds that Roberge had rented from the Yokohama Dock Company. At once Kopf began creating a dealer network.[51]

General Motors must have been impressed, although it could not know about the profits. In 1926, GM resolved to follow the leader and to assemble vehicles in Japan. The spectacular Ford performance had been in a market that the U.S. Department of Commerce had predicted could absorb a maximum of 3,500 units annually![52]

In the late 1920s both Ford and General Motors prospered in the Japanese market. After General Motors had built its large plant in Osaka (it opened in 1927), Ford decided its leased Japanese sheds were totally inadequate; it bought about nine acres and constructed an "earthquake proof" factory in Yokohama in order to assemble 100 cars a day. Ford's new facility assembled its first units in 1929, coincident with Ford's introduction of the Model A. The plant, it was said, would employ as many as 600 Japanese workers. With the exception of the period of the changeover from the Model T to the Model A, Ford was always ahead of GM in Japan.[53]

As Ford and General Motors inaugurated assembly operations, according to their worldwide practice, they began to buy certain parts locally. There was considerable cost savings in so doing. Table 1 shows Ford Motor Company's domestic purchases in Japan and the rising savings per car. Japanese parts makers started up to fill the needs for both original equipment and also for repair parts. One of Ford Motor Company's early suppliers was Nissan.[54] Ford produced far more trucks than cars. Ford typically sold truck chassis and Japanese body builders made the bodies.[55] To sell cars and trucks, the American companies required dealers, and each developed Japanese dealer organizations. By about 1930, Ford and General Motors each had between 70 and 80 franchised dealers. Likewise, to run the plants, managers and workers were required; both Ford and GM hired in Japan. In the case of Ford, the early staff was made up largely of "foreigners"; Kopf, over time, learned the Japanese language and hired more Japanese staff members. As of September 30, 1941, Ford in Japan had 19 salaried employees. Kopf was, of course, an Argentine; there were two Americans, one Dane, one Greek, one Swede, and thirteen Japanese.[56] In both companies all the workers were Japanese.[57] The linkage effects in this industry were formidable, as was the role of the American firms.

As early as 1918 a U.S. Department of Commerce official had written, "Japan is ambitious to build motor vehicles." He noted that the Japanese government was encouraging motor truck production.[58] Despite this, in 1930 only 458 motor vehicles were manufactured in Japan (all by Japanese producers). Imports totaled 18,663; these were, in the main, assembled by Ford and General Motors, with Ford in the lead.[59] In 1931, Japan moved into Manchuria—the first step in its military expansion. That year Japan went off the gold standard, which in effect devalued the yen. Imports became more expensive. That same year the Japanese Ministry of Commerce and Industry set up a Committee for the Establishment of a Japanese Automobile Industry.[60] The three events were interrelated. Japanese military moves, foreign exchange shortages, and the need for more trucks went together.

Increasingly, in Japan added parts were made locally, and Ford and General Motors trained Japanese parts producers. Soon the output of Japanese cars and trucks began to rise. In December 1933, Toyoda Automatic Loom Works made the decision to develop and to manufacture motor vehicles.[61] Ayukawa Yoshisuke at Nissan Motor Company was also making similar plans.[62] By 1934, Japanese car and truck production was 2,701 vehicles; by 1935 it was 5,355 units.[63]

The mounting Japanese output made both Ford and General Motors aware that their monopoly position in vehicle sales was gone, and unless they responded, their sales would deteriorate. Meanwhile, in 1933–34, General Motors was in negotiations for a joint venture with Nissan; this came to naught.[64] Later, Kopf would write that the GM-Nissan deal had fallen through because of army opposition.[65] In February 1935 three Ford men inspected the Nissan facility. They found a plant that was 25% larger than Ford's at Yokohama and described it as well equipped. It was then producing one or two cars a day with plans for 20 a day by year end. Kopf did not think Nissan would provide "serious competition" in the Japanese market.[66]

By the spring of 1935, Kopf was, however, pressing Dearborn to establish a *manufacturing* facility in Japan with a capacity of 200 units a day, of which 60% would be trucks.[67] Kopf believed Ford could not survive merely as an assembler of imported units. The Ford men were aware that numerous small- and medium-size parts manufacturers had sprung up increased in size and number by Ford's local purchases. These would be future suppliers of Ford's new manufacturing operation. Also there were the big companies that would serve as suppliers: Shibaura Engineering (a GE subsidiary); Dunlop Rubber (a subsidiary of Dunlop of England); Yokohama Rubber (an affiliate of Goodrich); and Nippon Denki (an affiliate of International Telephone and Telegraph Corporation, for storage batteries). In addition, there was the large, 100% Japanese group: Bridgestone Tire (tires); Yuasa Battery (storage batteries); Teikoku Hatsujo (railway-car springs); Izumi Seisakujo (railway and bus upholstery); and Kyosan Seisakujo (railway signaling systems). Nissan, which was making its own cars, would not be a Ford supplier.[68] Indeed, the Ford men found that in 1935, many potential suppliers had lots of government work "and are not interested in working for Ford Motor Company."[69]

Nonetheless, Kopf was convinced that "the urge to industrialize" in Japan was so great that it would not be stopped; that Japanese-made products would be exported throughout the Far East; and that, since Japan's move into Manchuria, the army was committed to motor vehicles and would play an important role in the future of the industry. Ford would have to manufacture "before we are shut out of the market."[70]

With this in mind, in 1935, Kopf, assisted by men from Ford headquarters in Michigan, found a 91.5-acre site on the Yokohama waterfront, purchased the land, and in June 1936 applied for permits to erect manufacturing and assembly facilities and to operate them.[71] Japan, which was mobilizing for war, had immense needs for motor vehicles, particularly trucks, but the Japanese government preferred to buy from domestic firms. Kopf's applications to manufacture in Japan were not approved. On July 30, 1936, Kopf wrote home that, under the new Japanese motor car manufacturing act, the Japanese government intended to license as manufacturers only Toyoda and Nissan.[72]

Meanwhile, Toyoda (Toyota as of October 1936) had begun to take advantage of what Ford and General Motors had created. Suppliers, which had been trained by and had served Ford, were urged to defect and to sell to Toyoda.[73] Toyoda hired Kamiya Shōtarō from General Motors.[74] He became Toyota's legendary sales manager.

Kamiya had joined the General Motors organization in Osaka in January 1928. His first position was in GM's sales and publicity department, which had "charge of dealer outlets, sales planning, advertising and publicity." By 1930, Kamiya was a department manager, the highest position of any Japanese in the American subsidiary. Kamiya was impressed with his rapid rise, which was based on merit (rather than seniority, school, or family). In 1931, Kamiya had become General Motors' liaison with the Japanese government. By 1934, however, as a "loyal" Japanese, knowing that the government was openly promoting domestic industry, he began to think about leaving General Motors. As he later would describe it, he felt the Americans at GM were "much colder than simple economic rationalism might dictate," that their policy toward dealers "was especially merciless," and that they disregarded "the local situation." Kamiya had told GM that the company should be more sensitive to dealer needs, but his complaints went unheeded.[75]

Thus, Kamiya decided in 1935 to join Toyoda. In doing so, he brought with him Hinode Motors, a leading GM dealer. He also recruited from GM two of his principal subordinates in GM's sales and publicity department. At GM, Kamiya had learned the importance of a good after-sales service system. Toyoda adopted this. Kamiya knew the value of a dealer network and immediately sought to convince Ford and GM dealers to join the Toyoda organization.[76] On July 30, 1936, Kopf of Ford Motor Company wrote Dearborn that the Toyoda people had made rapid progress in producing a truck "of the Ford and Chevrolet type." Toyoda had just announced a car that looked like a De Soto (a Chrysler model), which would be sold at a lower price than the Ford and Chevrolet. Kopf felt Toyoda would provide competition in Japan "from unexpected quarters."[77] Toyoda Kiichirō openly stated that he wanted to combine the best of Ford and Chevrolet features, together with Japanese requirements, and compete with foreign models in price and performance. He set out to develop a method of production based on the American system of mass production, but adapted to Japanese conditions.[78] In short, Toyota was building on the experiences of the foreign automobile companies.

As noted earlier, Nissan had started in the motor vehicle industry as a Ford parts supplier. When it began its own manufacturing, it stopped supplying Ford with parts.[79] Nonetheless its 1933–34 negotiations with GM for a joint venture reveal its desire to continue an alliance with American companies—and we will see that this wish persisted in the 1930s.

The Japanese government assigned Ford and General Motors import quotas, while Toyota and Nissan moved forward with their manufacturing plans. Ford, forbidden to expand in Yokohama, now sought a Japanese partner. Kopf explored the possibility of a merger with Furukawa Electric and Mitsubishi interests; Nissan at this point said it wanted to buy Ford's Japanese company. All of these 1936 ideas came to naught.[80]

In 1937, Nissan's Ayukawa suggested a joint venture between Ford and Nissan in Manchuria, another plan that was not realized.[81] What was evident in Nissan's discussions, first with GM and then with Ford, was that Nissan felt that there was much to be learned from the American companies. In 1937, Nissan brought to Japan a number of "foreign experts" to help get its production going, but Kopf did not believe Nissan would be an important factor in the market for some time.[82] By 1937, Nissan seemed to be most popular with the army, which certainly gave it an advantage.[83]

Increasingly, Japanese suppliers emerged to assist the *Japanese* enterprises, and talents grew within the Toyota and Nissan companies. In 1937, Kopf thought the Toyota truck was doing well, while "their passenger car has been a miserable failure."[84] Toyota sources explained that in order to comply with government policy, the firm had stopped car production and concentrated on building trucks.[85] Military orders for the war in China (which Japan had invaded in 1937) helped provide a large market.[86]

In September 1938 a director of Toyota called on Kopf, telling him that government officials wanted a Toyota-Ford merger. Kopf was agreeable, if a satisfactory agreement could be reached.[87] In November 1938, Kopf was negotiating with Nissan as well.[88] When it looked as though nothing would work out with Ford, in November 1938, the Toyota people went "to sound out" General Motors.[89]

As late as December 1939, Toyota and Nissan were still interested in a merger with Ford; recently Ford officials have located an agreement of December 19, 1939, signed by Benjamin Kopf of Ford, Toyoda Risaburō of Toyota, and Ayukawa Yoshisuke of Nissan, to create a joint venture in Japan (Ford would provide 40% of the capital, Toyota 30%, and Nissan 30%). This plan, like so many prior ones, never came to pass.[90] It is of interest, however, that Toyota and Nissan continued to see value in such an arrangement. For Ford the advantages were obvious: It was being replaced. After 1938 the Japanese government had reduced import quotas. Ford wanted to continue in Japan, but its future was obviously bleak. By 1940–41, Ford and General Motors' sales were sharply reduced.[91]

This, then, in brief is a chronicle of the American car companies in Japan. Their presence seems to have had major consequences, both direct and indirect. Both Ford and GM introduced new assembly technology. They trained Japanese men in assembly, purchasing, and sales who later staffed Japanese companies. Parts suppliers developed in many cases because of the American presence and then became the basis for much of the new Japanese industry. The American companies' products were the models for Japanese production. Professor Udagawa has pointed out that before Ford and GM began operations in Japan, there were "no sales agents dealing in durable consumer goods such as automobiles."[92] This was an American contribution. Japanese nationalism, however, was most fundamental to the creation of the pre–World War II Japanese motor industry. American companies were held back by the Japanese government, allowing Japanese industry to emerge.

Was there a clash of cultures? Was GM's "merciless" dealer policy inappropriate in Japan? GM's dealers were expected to perform; those who did not were as unhappy in the United States as in Japan. In the case of Ford, one sees little evidence of a clash of cultures. Benjamin Kopf was very much admired by all accounts. While there was involvement from Dearborn in auditing and in major decisions, on a day-by-day basis Kopf seems to have encountered few cases of "culture shock" or cultural clashes. Clearly the presence of the foreign companies provided a stimulant to the expansion of Japanese enterprise.

The story of the Japanese automobile industry offers an effective antidote to those who have insisted on the insuperable bargaining advantage of foreign enterprises in host nations. What is apparent is that such critics know no Japanese economic history. Those who argue that foreign companies with their technology, skills, access to capital, and origins in a country economically in advance of the recipient nation will by their very nature overwhelm domestic enterprise ignore the important case of Japan. In Japan there was no "crowding-out" effect *as traditionally defined*; indeed, it was the newly emerging domestic (Japanese) automobile industry that "crowded out" the foreign investors, not vice versa. Foreign enterprise in the automobile industry, kept under controls, created the infrastructure needed for domestic endeavors.

According to Ford Motor Company records, Ford's business in Japan was profitable. From the inception of the Japanese Ford company to the time that it was taken over by the Japanese government in December 1941 (after Pearl Harbor), the company had annual dollar sales ranging from $2,700,000 to $18,400,000; its annual profits after taxes ranged from $450,000 to $4,100,000; and, most important, dividends received by Ford-U.S. during the entire period totaled $17.6 million. Ford's investment in Japan as of December 1941 was $3,873,000.[93] I do not have comparable figures for General Motors, but data on its profits from 1927 to 1934 indicate that it, too, was highly profitable, although GM may have been less wise than Ford on the matter of remittances.[94]

The success of Ford and General Motors was not at the expense of Japan, which, as we have seen, borrowed from, learned from, replicated, and incorporated into its own industry the offerings from America. Ford and General Motors were not shy about letting the Japanese know about their technology. Because of their strength internationally, they had no fears about a future Japanese automobile industry. Japanese companies never copied blindly: They always adapted what they learned. Ford and General Motors' profits *encouraged* domestic firms to enter the industry.[95]

From a political standpoint, Ford and General Motors each negotiated with the Japanese government, presenting the company viewpoint. Yet, the Japanese government always had the advantage. The Japanese government experimented with encouraging and discouraging joint-venture arrangements, all the while creating an environment that prompted the development of domestic industry. Its handling of the American companies was critical to the rise of the Japanese industry.

III. Conclusions

Within every host country, there is ambivalence toward foreign investment. There are those who applaud it and those who deplore it. The predominant views along the spectrum not only vary in intensity (i.e., in degree of passion) by country but also by period and industry in each country. Government policies lead or reflect, depending on the nation, the ambivalence, differing not only in intensity (number and seriousness of such policies) by country but also, once again, by period and industry in each country.

The ambivalence stems from an inherent clash between "us" and "them," nationals and foreigners, "our sort" and "aliens." It is a clash between nationalism and internationalism. Patriotism, nationalism, and militarism each leads to a turning inward. There is also a deep-seated feeling—evident in many contexts—that the more distant the involvement is from a locale, the less appropriate.[96] By contrast, it has long been recognized that foreign investors offer needed capital, and foreign direct investors, in particular, provide business experience, technology, product designs, and jobs (often most important in the public perception and in government policy to encourage inward foreign direct investment).

The Japanese experience with inward foreign direct investment is *not* unique in the ambivalence, nor, in general, in the fact that government policies came to be designed to tailor foreign direct investment to national requirements. Nor is the identification of extremes of nationalism and more restrictive measures confined to Japan. "National security" is always linked with fear of foreigners' intrusions.[97] Only in specifics (the particulars of how industries were promoted, the details of governmental actions, and, of course, the exact timing)—not in the general principles—was the Japanese experience sui generis.

In the 1920s, Japan was quite open to foreign investment. In the 1930s, as the government and the army shaped Japan's path, the nation became increasingly committed to using foreign companies to its own ends. The shift was not peculiar. Many countries have changed policies toward foreign direct investment even more radically.[98] The particular measures Japan adopted vis-à-vis foreign investors were often distinctive to Japan. The way in which Japan proceeded in developing, for example, its own oil refining and automobile industries while using foreign companies was special. Yet, Japan's desire for national production and its ambivalent views toward foreign enterprises were far from out-of-the-ordinary. Likewise, the major contribution of foreign companies to shaping the modern industrial sector in Japan was not totally unlike what took place elsewhere. In short, the Japanese experience was unique in detail, but only that.[99]

Notes

1. The literature is vast. For a sample of the variety, see Neil Hood and Stephen Young, *The Economics of Multinational Enterprise* (London: Longman, 1979), ch. 5; Geoffrey Jones, "The British Government and Foreign Multinationals," forthcoming; and Mira Wilkins, *The History of Foreign Investment in the United States to 1914* (Cambridge, Mass.: Harvard University Press, 1989).

2. For the specific literature on "immiserizing growth," see Wilkins, *ibid.*, p. 939n.38.

3. The history of U.S. enterprises, in particular, in Japan is far from virgin territory. See, for example, Mira Wilkins, "The Role of U.S. Business," in Dorothy Borg and Shumpei Okamoto, eds., *Pearl Harbor as History: Japanese-American Relations 1931–1941* (New York: Columbia University Press, 1973), pp. 341–76;

idem., "American-Japanese Direct Foreign Investment Relationships, 1930–1952," *Business History Review*, LVI (Winter 1982), 497–518. In addition, see Mira Wilkins and Frank Ernest Hill, *American Business Abroad: Ford on Six Continents* (Detroit: Wayne State University Press, 1964); Mira Wilkins, *The Emergence of Multinational Enterprise: American Business Abroad from the Colonial Era to 1914* (Cambridge, Mass.: Harvard University Press, 1970); and *idem.*, *The Maturing of Multinational Enterprise: American Business Abroad from 1914 to 1970* (Cambridge, Mass.: Harvard University Press, 1974), all of which deal with U.S. business in Japan in the broad context of American business abroad. More recent work includes Mark Mason, "Foreign Direct Investment and Japanese Economic Development, 1899–1931," in *Business and Economic History*, 2nd ser., XVI (1987), 93–107, and *idem.*, "The Development of United States Enterprise in Japan: Studies in Government Policy and Corporate Strategy," Ph.D. thesis, Harvard University, 1988. Also, there have been specific studies of particular U.S. enterprises in Japan, e.g., Irvine H. Anderson, *The Standard-Vacuum Oil Company and United States East Asian Policy, 1933–1941* (Princeton: Princeton University Press, 1975). R.P.T. Davenport-Hines and Geoffrey Jones have a chapter on British business in Japan in their edited volume, *British Business in Asia* (Cambridge: Cambridge University Press, 1989), pp. 217–44, 288–94.

4. On early Japanese multinational enterprise, see Mira Wilkins, "Japanese Multinational Enterprise before 1914," *Business History Review*, LX (Summer 1986), 199–231.

5. Mira Wilkins, "European and North American Multinationals, 1870–1914: Comparisons and Contrasts," *Business History*, XXX (January 1988), pp. 13–14.

6. Wilkins, *The History of Foreign Investment in the United States*, passim.

7. John Dunning, "Changes in the Level and Structure of International Production," in Mark Casson, ed., *The Growth of International Business* (London: Allen & Unwin, 1983), p. 88.

8. Information from Kuwahara Tetsuya. See also Masaru Udagawa, "Business Management and Foreign-Affiliated Companies in Japan Before World War II," Table 2 (pp. 6–13), in this volume. On the far larger, and earlier, J. & P. Coats investments in the United States, see Wilkins, *The History of Foreign Investment in the United States*, pp. 72, 130, 361–68.

9. Geoffrey Jones, "The Multinational Expansion of Dunlop 1890–1939," in *idem.*, ed., *British Multinationals* (Aldershot: Gower, 1986), pp. 25–27. Jones writes that this was for rickshaw tires. According to Eisuke Daitō in "From Natural Rubber to Synthetic Resin" (paper presented to Anglo-Japanese Business History Conference, September 1988), Dunlop's Kobe factory, which started production in the spring of 1910, made bicycle tires. In 1911, Dunlop bought out another British investor in Japan that manufactured tires for rickshaws (Ingram Rubber Co.).

10. R.P.T. Davenport-Hines, "Vickers as a Multinational before 1945," in Jones, ed., *British Multinationals*, pp. 46, 52.

11. Wilkins, *The Emergence*, pp. 94, 103.

12. Ralph Hidy and Muriel Hidy, *Pioneering in Big Business 1882–1911* (New York: Harper & Bros., 1955), p. 498.

13. J. Riesser, *The German Great Banks and Their Concentration* (1911, Rpt. New York: Arno Press, 1977), pp. 422–24, 455.

14. See data in SAA 68/LS 913, Siemens-Museum, Munich.
15. Wilkins, *The Emergence.*
16. Wilkins, *The Maturing.*
17. Dunning, "Changes in the Level," p. 87.
18. *Ibid.*, p. 88.
19. Wilkins, *The Maturing*, pp. 55 (for total) and 58 (for Japan).
20. Wilkins, "The Role of U.S. Business," p. 374, for fourth rank in U.S. foreign direct investment in 1930, 1936, and 1940.
21. William W. Lockwood, *The Economic Development of Japan* (Princeton: Princeton University Press, 1954), p. 169.
22. Mason, "Foreign Direct Investment," p. 104.
23. *Ibid.*, pp. 104–5.
24. Lockwood, *Economic Development*, p. 525.
25. *Ibid.*, p. 317.
26. It might be interesting to do a study on foreign investors' proportion of Japanese imports. Such calculations would seem possible but are beyond the scope of the present paper.
27. In a sense, the distinction between macro and micro impacts may explain why William Lockwood felt the contribution of foreign business to Japanese economic development was meager, while George Allen and Audrey Donnithorne saw it as important. Mason, in "Foreign Direct Investment," pp. 93 and 96, notes the variation in viewpoints. Lockwood was interested in the macroeconomic consequences, while Allen and Donnithorne were more interested in the specifics of western firms.
28. The Royal Dutch-Shell Group's subsidiary was a major participant in selling oil products in Japan. There were several British companies that had arrangements with Japanese vehicle producers: Isuzu, which built army trucks, had a royalty agreement with British Leyland, while another Japanese firm had an arrangement with the British Wolseley, related to the latter's trucks. Mira Wilkins interview with Benjamin Kopf, Mexico City, Dec. 11, 1961 (henceforth cited as Kopf interv.).
29. See Hidy and Hidy, *Pioneering*, pp. 498, 779n.5. One Kumamoto Eiichirō was a participant from Japan.
30. *Ibid.*, p. 498. On the sale to Nippon Sekiyu, see Udagawa, "Business Management," Table 2.
31. In early 1934, Nippon Sekiyu's gasoline sales in Japan represented 22% of the market, compared with 29% held by Royal Dutch-Shell's subsidiary, Rising Sun, and 19% by Stanvac. Anderson, *Standard-Vacuum*, p. 77. See also Table 1 (p. 141) in Morikawa Hidemasa's, "Comment" to Nobuhisa Fujita's paper in this volume.
32. Wilkins, *The Emergence*, pp. 210–11.
33. U.S. Senate, Special Committee Investigating Petroleum Resources, *American Petroleum Interests in Foreign Countries*, 79th Cong., 1st Sess., 1945, 404. Henceforth cited as *Petroleum Hearings.*
34. Wilkins, "The Role of U.S. Business," p. 362. Texaco did remain in Manchuria—as an oil distributor. See Nobuhisa Fujita, "Ties Between Foreign Makers and Zaibatsu Enterprises in Prewar Japan: Case Studies of Mitsubishi Oil Co. and Mitsubishi Electric Manufacturing Co.," p. 126, in this volume, on Mitsubishi Trading Company's acquisition of the Texaco distributorships.

35. Anderson, *Standard-Vacuum*, pp. 26, 32, and passim.
36. Wilkins, *The Maturing*, pp. 211–12. In 1936, Tidewater Associated Oil Company took over the interests of its subsidiary, Associated Oil Company. *Ibid.*, p. 212.
37. *Petroleum Hearings*, p. 207.
38. *Ibid.*, p. 208.
39. *Ibid.*, p. 387.
40. Wilkins, *The Maturing*, p. 213.
41. Wilkins, "The Role of U.S. Business," p. 362.
42. *Ibid.*, pp. 363–66. For more detail, see Anderson, *Standard-Vacuum*, ch. 3.
43. Wilkins, "The Role of U.S. Business," p. 365.
44. Kopf to J. Crawford, June 22, 1937, Acc. 390, Box 85, Ford Archives, Dearborn.
45. Kopf to Ford Motor Co., Jan. 7, 1938, in *ibid.*
46. Anderson, *Standard-Vacuum*, pp. 78–79n., estimates Tidewater Associated's annual return on its refinery investment in 1932–40 was 5%; he says nothing about what was remitted home. The firm also made profits on its crude oil exports, so this 5% may be a meaningless figure.
47. See details in Anderson, *Standard-Vacuum.*
48. Wilkins and Hill, *American Business Abroad.* See also Abo Tetsuo, "American Automobile Enterprises Abroad in the Interwar Period," in *The Annals of the Institute of Social Science*, 22 (1981), pp. 183–224. Chrysler, formed in 1925, was also developing foreign business on a much more modest scale.
49. Apparently, Sale & Frazar had acquired the exclusive agency for Ford cars in Japan in 1909 or 1910. *Ford Times*, IV (March 1911), back page, and *Fortune*, XXXIII (Nov. 1945), p. 135. The *Fortune* article is particularly good on Sale & Frazar, which introduced a number of American products into Japan.
50. Wilkins and Hill, *American Business Abroad*, p. 150.
51. Agreement between Ford Motor Company of Japan, Ltd. and Ford Motor Company, March 7, 1925, Acc. 363, Box 1, Ford Archives; Wilkins and Hill, *American Business Abroad*, pp. 150–51, 434–35; and Kopf interv.
52. U.S. Department of Commerce, Bureau of Foreign and Domestic Commerce, *Japan as an Automotive Market* (Washington, 1922), p. 48.
53. Wilkins and Hill, *American Business Abroad*, p. 159; *Japan Advertiser*, Tokyo, April 15, 1928 (projected employment). I have not included data on Chrysler, since it was never an important factor in the Japanese market. In Japan, according to Udagawa Masaru, Chrysler, with its import agent, in 1928 founded the Kyōritsu Automobile Works to assemble Chryslers. Udagawa, "Business Management," pp. 16–17. Output was very small. See Udagawa Masaru, "The Prewar Japanese Automobile Industry and American Manufacturers," *Japanese Yearbook on Business History* (1985), p. 82.
54. H. R. Hesser to Sorensen, April 10, 1935, Acc. 390, Box 85, Ford Archives, says Nissan Jidōsha K.K. started as makers of parts for Ford of Japan. See also Kopf interv.
55. Kopf interv.
56. Udagawa Masaru, "Japan's Automobile Marketing," in Akio Okochi and Koichi Shimokawa, *Development of Mass Marketing* (Tokyo: University of Tokyo Press, 1981), p. 166 (number of dealers). Mason, "Foreign Direct Investment," p. 105, found that in 1932 Ford had 41 non-Japanese employees com-

pared with only 12 at GM. On the transition to more Japanese employees, see Kopf interv. W. W. Townsend, Memo, Dec. 15, 1941, Acc. 6, Box 369, Ford Archives, gives the 1941 Ford staff.

57. Mason, "Foreign Direct Investment," p. 105, reports that in 1932, GM had 719 Japanese employees compared with Ford's 381. The difference is remarkable, considering that Ford's production in 1932 in Japan exceeded GM's. Could it be that GM, with its larger Japanese staff, had more difficulty in cutting back Japanese labor in the poor production year of 1932, while Ford had no qualms on that score? See Table 1 for Ford's lower output in 1932.

58. U.S. Department of Commerce, Bureau of Foreign and Domestic Commerce, *Motor Vehicles in Japan, China, and Hawaii*, by Tom O. Jones, Spec. Agents Ser. No. 170 (Washington, 1918), pp. 28–30. This report commented on the existence of a body-building industry in Japan—"the only branch of motor vehicle construction that has been developed . . . " *Ibid.*, p. 30.

59. Wilkins, "American-Japanese Direct Foreign Investment," p. 499.

60. Kamiya Shōtarō, *My Life with Toyota* (n.p.: Toyota Motor Sales Company, 1976), p. 29. Even earlier, in 1929, the Ministry of Commerce and Industry had set up a consultative body to develop a policy for promoting domestic industry.

61. Toyoda Eiji, *Toyota: Fifty Years in Motion* (Tokyo: Kodansha International, 1985), p. 40.

62. According to Kamiya, *My Life*, p. 30, the Nissan Motor Company was established in December 1933. On Ayukawa Yoshisuke, see Johannes Hirschmeier and Tsunehiko Yui, *The Development of Japanese Business 1600–1973* (Cambridge, Mass.: Harvard University Press, 1975), p. 168.

63. Wilkins and Hill, *American Business Abroad*, p. 254.

64. Kamiya, *My Life*, p. 30. Kamiya took part in the negotiations. See also Udagawa, "The Prewar Japanese Automobile Industry," p. 87, which shows that as early as 1932, R. M. May, executive director of GM of Japan, unofficially informed the Ministry of Commerce and Industry that it was "prepared to participate" in a joint venture with Japanese automobile manufacturers.

65. Kopf to J. Crawford, Oct. 12, 1937, Acc. 38, Box 38, Ford Archives. See also Udagawa, "The Prewar Japanese Automobile Industry," p. 88, for full confirmation of this.

66. H. R. Hesser to Charles E. Sorensen, Feb. 25, 1935, Acc. 390, Box 85, Ford Archives.

67. Kopf to F. Riecks and Hesser, March 28, 1935, in *ibid.*

68. Hesser to Sorensen, April 10, 1935, in *ibid.*

69. Hesser to A. M. Wibel, March 12, 1935, in *ibid.*

70. Kopf to Riecks, March 28, 1935, in *ibid.*

71. Wilkins and Hill, *American Business Abroad*, p. 254.

72. Kopf to J. Crawford, July 30, 1936, Acc. 390, Box 85. The "outline" for the Automobile Manufacturing Industry Law had been approved by the Japanese Cabinet on August 9, 1935; the Imperial Diet passed the act (without revision) on May 23, 1936; on July 11, 1936 the regulations to implement the act were issued. See Udagawa, "The Prewar Japanese Automobile Industry," pp. 85, 92–93. This sequence is *very* important. Until the regulations to implement the act were passed, Kopf had believed that Ford could manufacture and qualify under the act.

73. Toyoda, *Toyota*, p. 48.

74. *Ibid.*
75. Kamiya, *My Life*, pp. 26–31.
76. *Ibid.*, pp. 34–41.
77. Kopf to J. Crawford, July 30, 1936, Acc. 390, Box 85, Ford Archives.
78. Kamiya, *My Life*, p. 107.
79. Kopf interv. and Hesser to Sorenson, April 10, 1935, Acc. 390, Box 85, Ford Archives.
80. Wilkins, "American-Japanese Direct Foreign Investment," p. 501.
81. *Ibid.*
82. Kopf to Crawford, March 24, 1937, Acc. 390, Box 85, Ford Archives.
83. Kopf to Crawford, Oct. 12, 1937, Acc. 38, Box 38, Ford Archives.
84. Kopf to Crawford, March 24, 1937, Acc. 390, Box 85, Ford Archives.
85. Kamiya, *My Life*, p. 107, but see *ibid.*, p. 111, which shows that very limited car production did continue as Toyota built mainly trucks.
86. At the same time, after the Japanese invasion of China, the yen fell on world markets, raising the price of imports. This gave added protection to Japanese manufacturers and made life more difficult for Ford and GM. Kamiya, *My Life*, p. 108.
87. Kopf to Crawford, Sept. 1, 1938, Acc. 390, Box 85, Ford Archives.
88. Kopf to Crawford, Nov. 4, 1938, Acc. 38, Box 38, and Jan. 27, 1939, Acc. 390, Box 85, Ford Archives.
89. Kopf to Crawford, Nov. 4, 1938 (2nd letter), Acc. 38, Box 38, Ford Archives.
90. Toyoda, *Toyota*, p. 61.
91. Wilkins, "American-Japanese Direct Foreign Investment," p. 501.
92. Udagawa, "Japan's Automobile Marketing," p. 167.
93. Data Book on Foreign Operations, July 15, 1958, Ford Motor Company, Dearborn. Ford seems to have remitted its profits as fast as it could. Kopf interv. In December 1937, despite strict exchange controls, Ford received permission to remit ¥1 million in dividends. At that time General Motors left its profits in Japan and did not remit. Kopf to Ford Motor Company, Jan. 7, 1938, Acc. 390, Box 85, Ford Archives.
94. On GM profits in yen, 1927–34, see Udagawa, "The Prewar Japanese Automobile Industry," p. 86. See note 93 above on remittances. Mark Mason has uncovered in State Department records a report from Consul Richard F. Boyce in Yokohama to the U.S. Embassy in Tokyo, March 24, 1938, which indicates that Kopf told Boyce that the Japanese Ford Company in August 1937 had some ¥15 to 20 million blocked in Japan. The Japanese Finance Ministry made the "informal suggestion" that the Ford Company buy ¥1 million of the government "China Incident" bonds; Ford-Japan complied. Boyce reported that subsequently the Ford Company received "permission to transfer to Detroit all of its surplus funds"; Kopf had attributed (in conversations with Boyce) the Japanese "generosity" in allowing the remittances to (1) his buying of the Japanese bonds and (2) the wish of the Japanese to obtain credit in the United States. The consul also noted that Singer Sewing Machine Company had obtained permission to send home ¥3 million. I am indebted to Mason for photocopies of material he located in RG 59, National Archives. In 1937–38, American companies worried that yen left in Japan would depreciate in value with yen devaluations.
95. Toyoda, *Toyota*, p. 53.

96. In the United States, welfare programs are financed nationally but administered locally, *because* it is assumed people in the locale know more than those in Washington about local problems. Similarly, over and over again in the reaction to foreign direct investment, we hear that what the foreigner is offering is inappropriate in the host country, because the foreigner cannot understand the needs of the host country. This is the "benign" approach. The malign approach says the foreigner *ignores*—could not care less about—the needs of the host country, being concerned only with profits.

97. See, for example, Wilkins, *The History of Foreign Investment in the United States*, ch. 16.

98. Take, for instance, the shift that occurred with the Russian Revolution.

99. Regrettably, there is not space here to spell out the parallels, but from this author's own research it is very clear that U.S. oil companies and Ford and General Motors in other nations made economic contributions very similar to those made in Japan. In the particular industries covered in this paper, oil and automobiles, other governments have, for example, encouraged domestic refining (to save on foreign exchange) and have created the basis for a domestic automobile industry. Brazil, for instance, which had foreign-owned car assembly plants *before* Japan, now has an automobile manufacturing industry. How it was promoted, the government policies pursued, and the timing were all unlike what occurred in Japan. While the outcome also differed, both Japan and Brazil now have automobile manufacturing. To take developed countries for purposes of comparison, I could elaborate on comparable contributions of the U.S. oil and automobile companies to British and German industrial development.

TABLE 1 Summary of Savings Effected by Ford Motor Company Limited of Japan Through Local Purchase of Production Materials, 1930–36 (Inclusive)

Year	Value Mat'l Purchased	Laid-down Cost of This Material	Amount of Saving	Percent of Saving	Exchange Rate 1 Yen—$	Production for Year	Saving per Car
1930	$560339.22	$654161.39	$93822.17	14.3	.4950	10633	$ 8.82
1931	669995.71	762408.41	92412.70	12.1	.4940	11432	8.08
1932	298131.43	450371.34	152239.91	33.8	.3000	7480	20.35
1933	496282.29	692007.47	195725.18	28.8	.2500	8056	24.30
1934	1202637.51	1713910.06	511272.53	29.8	.3000	17185	29.75
1935	1365967.65	2115759.61	749791.96	35.4	.2900	14865	50.44
1936	1605597.31	2334653.80	729056.49	31.2	.2850	13822	52.75
Totals & Averages	6198951.12	8723272.08	2524520.96	28.94		83473	30.24

Note: The figures shown above represent the value of production parts which were approved for local purchase. Supplies and equipment purchased locally are not included.

Source: The table was prepared by William R. Loughran, Purchasing Department, Ford Motor Company, April 15, 1937. It was circulated to seven key executives in the company, including Edsel Ford and C. E. Sorensen. The original is in Acc. 38, Box 38, Ford Archives, Dearborn, Michigan.

Comment

Kensuke Hiroyama

Professor Mira Wilkins's paper deals with American multinationals in Japan before World War II. These companies had a significant impact on the creation of modern Japanese industry, especially the technologically advanced sectors. In general, multinational investment expansion is based on advantage, and in these cases the American advantage was in manufacturing.

In automobiles, oil refining, and machinery, western influence was substantial through demonstration by example and/or direct participation. Later the American multinationals were crowded out by the Japanese. In short, as Wilkins has mentioned in her 1982 paper, "U.S. business in Japan had been copied, absorbed, manipulated, and molded to Japanese requirements—by the rules of the Japanese state and by the initiative of Japanese business leaders."[1]

Wilkins has also said, "Nor is the identification of extremes of nationalism and more restrictive measures confined to Japan. . . . The major contribution of foreign companies to shaping the modern industrial sector in Japan was not totally unlike what took place elsewhere. In short, the Japanese experience was *unique in detail, but only that* [italics mine]." From the viewpoint of an economist, I agree, but from that of a historian, I wish to know what Wilkins thinks the characteristics of Japanese uniqueness were in detail? This is the first question.

The second question is from a business historian's standpoint. Wilkins mentions the importance of technology transfer. I agree with her microeconomic discussion. But business is based on organization, and each organization has its own policy. So, in any case of technology transfer, there are at least two policies—that of the giving side and that of the receiving side. My question concerns what the policies of American companies in Japan were before World War II, especially those of Ford and General Motors. The answer to this question will show us the characteristics of American business expansion before the war, because in the 1920s there was remarkable growth in American automobile output, and mass production techniques were exported from the United States.

In the oil refining industry a Japanese zaibatsu interest, Mitsubishi, joined Associated Oil Company in 1931 and established a joint venture, Mitsubishi Oil Company. This case shows us that Americans contributed technical assistance, training of workers, and so on. As Japan produces little crude oil, in this industry Japan could not be a competitor then. On the other hand, in the automobile industry Japan was to become an American competitor in the future. But Americans followed the same path in many industries—automobile, electric, chemical, etc.

The last question concerns the rank an American multinational in Japan held in regard to its company's worldwide network. If it played a very small role in multinational corporate strategy, I think it was free to take actions without considering its headquarters' strategy. If so, Japanese companies easily accepted advanced technology, both in manufacturing and in management.

Note

1. Mira Wilkins, "American-Japanese Direct Foreign Investment Relationship, 1930–1952," *Business History Review*, Vol. LVI, No. 4 (Winter, 1982).

Response

Mira Wilkins

The first question is on Japanese uniqueness. Each country's history is unique, and the historian's function is to chart the distinguishing features; in no way do I disagree with this. However, my paper was looking at the contributions of foreign enterprises, the responses in Japan to such businesses, and how the reactions from the private and public sectors shaped the impacts. In this regard, the uniqueness of the Japanese experience (based on Japan's history) is, I would repeat, *only one of detail.* Japan, like other countries, was special in the timing of its measures, the ways in which its national industries developed, and in the specifics of government legislation and policies. Japan was extraordinary in its abilities to imitate and innovate. But the very same multinationals, in the same industries, went to other countries around the world. In many countries they made similar contributions; in other nations private-sector enterprises sprung up to complement their activities and to compete; in other nations governments acted to develop domestic manufacturing facilities. Accordingly, the Japanese experience was far from sui generis.

The second question is on technology transfer. Ford and General Motors were investing in Japan to sell cars and to make profits in the process. Because automobile *manufacturing* at low cost involved large-scale operations and substantial investment, the barriers to entry into car manufacturing by the 1920s were very high. Ford Motor Company, for example, was never secretive about its technology. Anyone could visit the Rouge. The assumption was that because the economies of scale, the size, and the complexities of the business were so great, no outsider could easily copy the basic technology. As for the technology of individual parts manufacturing, that was another matter. Ford was eager to transfer that technology. It wanted low-cost production of parts in Japan. In Germany, in a very similar fashion, when Ford recognized the wisdom of buying parts there, it sent men from the United States to train parts manufacturers.

Question three is on the creation of competition. In the automobile industry in the 1930s, American companies never envisaged that Japanese firms would become competitors in the world industry. True, protected by their government, they might compete in Japan or perhaps even in far eastern markets, but no one imagined that they would do so on a worldwide basis. Since the Japanese were determined to have an automobile industry, both Ford and General Motors were prepared to manufacture in Japan. By contrast, the Mitsubishi Oil Company played a small part in the Japanese refining industry, as my paper shows. In this case, the far more important American company, Standard-Vacuum Oil Company, desired to impede the development of Japanese refining, since it wished to continue to sell *refined oil* in Japan.

Question four: If Japan was only a minor locale in American multinationals' overseas business, did this mean that the management of the affiliates had more independence? Probably, but in the Ford case, for instance, on all major strategic decisions, top management in Dearborn participated.

British Business Interests in Japan Before 1941: Origins, Evolution, and Operations

Stephen Nicholas

I. Introduction

Japan was not a major market for British business. The pre-1914 value of direct U.K.–Japan trade was small, and during the interwar period Britain exported about £4 million worth of goods per year to Japan while importing roughly twice that amount. Newly industrializing and separated from Britain by space and culture, Japan attracted a small proportion of total British manufacturing foreign direct investment (FDI). Table 1 displays the geographical spread of British pre- and post-1914 FDI, with Japan accounting for between 1 and 2% of total British investment in sales or production facilities. Yet, with the mid-19th-century opening of Japan, British firms, led by those mercantile houses with far eastern connections, quickly established commercial interests in Japan's major trading centers, particularly Kobe, Nagoya, Osaka, Tokyo, and Yokohama. In addition, British solicitors, advertisers, and agents clustered in these same cities, creating the externalities which attracted, in turn, British manufacturing firms. By the late 1930s, Britain was a major foreign investor in Japan with the amount and value of British property roughly equivalent to that of the United States and overshadowing that of the third largest investor, the Netherlands (see Table 2). While the total value of British and American assets in Japan were comparable, they were of a somewhat different nature. In 1941, property owned by commercial firms was much higher for Britain than for the United States, with ¥3.2 million invested by British firms in warehouses and offices.[1] American firms had a larger investment in Japanese manufacturing enterprises than British multinationals, but these investments usually accounted for less than 50% of the total assets needed to give effective control.[2] British multinationals tended to keep control in British hands, allowing only minority Japanese involvement.

While Britain was a major foreign investor in Japan, total foreign investment accounted for only a very small share of total Japanese

TABLE 1 Distribution of British Manufacturing Foreign Direct Investment, 1870–1939 (percent)

	Pre-1914		Post-1914	
	Sales	Production	Sales	Production
Developed Empire	39	29	42	46
U.S.A.	8	12	10	9
Developed Europe	25	22	17	17
Japan	1	2	1	1
Underdeveloped Empire	7	8	12	11
Underdeveloped	9	9	13	9
Other Underdeveloped	12	18	6	8

Source: Private Database on Pre-1939 British Multinationals.

TABLE 2 British, American, and Dutch Property in Japan, 1941 (¥ million)

Country	U.K.	U.S.A.	Netherlands	Total
Number of Establishments	600	614	71	1285
Value (lands, buildings, movables)	29.4	38.6	3.1	71.1

Reference: *Property in Japan*, PRO, FO371/54191.

capital formation. In 1930 the total value of British, American, and Dutch property (including land, building, and movables) was about .0013% of total Japanese land, buildings, and movables. Of course, this small overall foreign holding should not disguise the dominance foreign firms exercised in select industries and sectors. The six main British manufacturing multinationals operating in Japan in 1941 were market leaders, able to command a measure of market power; the same was true of American multinationals in Japan, such as Ford, GM, and Western Electric. Moreover, British investments had important technological and managerial spin-offs, of which both the Japanese and the British were equally aware. This paper is concerned with the evolution of British commercial interests in Japan and the problems British multinationals experienced in operating in the domestic Japanese market, particularly in the 1930s. Section II describes the extent of British trade, service, and manufacturing investment in Japan. Section III briefly derives a theoretical and empirical model of British FDI, while Section IV applies the model to the growth of merchant houses and specialist agents in Japan. Section V analyzes the activities and strategies of ICI, and Section VI assesses Babcock's and Morgan Crucible's investments in production facilities. Section VII concludes the paper with a short summary.

II. Extent of British Investment in Japan

British commercial interests in Japan can be categorized into merchant houses (both the large investment, or managing agency, houses and the specialist houses), banks, insurance companies, stevedoring and shipping firms, specialist agents, petroleum distribution companies, and manufacturing firms.[3] A number of far eastern mercantile houses operated in Japan, including Butterfield and Swire (in Yokohama from 1867; in Kobe from 1887), Wallace Brothers (1915–1937), Dodwell (from the late 1870s in Yokohama and Kobe), Mackinnon, Mackenzie (until 1939), and Cooper Findlay. While most of these houses specialized in particular products in the early years, by the interwar period they were general merchants carrying on a varied export and import trade, acting as shipping agents, holding London insurance agencies, and acting as agents for British, American, and European manufacturers. There is some evidence that these firms tended to spin off their specialist trade to subsidiary firms; Cooper Findlay, for example, founded the Anglo-American Direct Tea Trading Company, and Ralli Brothers established Shōwa Menka to trade in raw cotton and jute.

Besides these investment houses, British trade was served by specialist mercantile houses, either arranged around one particular product or mainly concerned with Japanese (including Formosan, Korean, and Manchurian) trade. Table 3 categorizes these specialized traders according to the export and import of primary products (tea, soybean oil, beancakes, and coal), textiles (piece goods, raw silk, and jute), and specific goods, such as paper and medicines. The specialist Japan-based general trading firms handled a range of products, including straw, tobacco, porcelain, and wine, as well as acted as agents for British firms. Generally, these specialist merchant houses had only one location, although a few operated branches in three or more Japanese cities.

Two British banks were represented in Japan, the Charter Bank of India, Australia and China, and the Hong Kong and Shanghai; Thomas Cook had an office for banking and travel, and, besides 29 insurance companies with representatives in Japan, the Commercial Union, Liverpool and London and Globe, Norwich Union and Fire, Sun and York-

TABLE 3 Specialist Merchant Houses, 1941

Primary Products	Piece Goods Clothing	General Merchants	Wines, Spirits	Paper	Stevedoring	Medicine
Anglo-Chinese Eastern Trading	Berrick & Co.	Abraham L&D	Curnow	Lendrum	Owston & Co.	Sim
Holmes, Ringer	Graham & Co.	Cornes & Co.	Caudrelu	Gordon & Gotch	Nickel & Lyons	
Dawes, S.H.	Jarman Davis	Marcus, Harris				
Japan & Eastern Trading Co.	Lane, Crawford	Gibbs & Lewis				
Anglo-American Direct Tea Trading Co.		Nelson, C.H.				
		Macnaughton				
		Patten Mackenzie				
		Pearce & Co.				
		Priest, Marians				
		Stracham, W.M.				
		Walker & Co.				
		Witkowski				
		Cameron & Co.				
		Curnow & Co.				
		Strong & Co.				
		Blundell & Co.				
		Sale & Co.				
		Crockford, Heath				
		Hammond, F.W.				
		Horseley & Co.				
		James, Co.				
		Gillon & Co.				
		Mayer, K.				
		Ollivant, G.B.				
		Duff, William				

Sources: *British-owned Property in Japan*, PRO, BT60/96/5; *U.K. Liaison Mission Tokyo*, PRO, BT11 3581; H. A. Macrae, *Survey of U.K. Pre-War Economic and Commercial Interest Japan, Manchuria, Formosa and Korea* (Board of Trade, Oct. 1945); company archives.

shire Insurance had branch offices with British managers. Lloyd's Register of Shipping had branches in Kobe, Yokohama, and Dairen, and two firms of charter accountants, with British parents, operated in Japan.

British stevedoring and transportation was controlled by F. Owston & Co., Yokohama, which owned Shibusawa Sōkō, and Nickel & Lyons, Osaka. Both firms were shipping agents, but undertook lighterage, warehousing, and custom and insurance brokerage. These firms, and Mackinnon, Mackenzie; Dodwell; and Butterfield and Swire, performed agency functions for the regular British steamship services, which included Ben Line, British India Steam Navigation, P&O, Glen Line, Eastern & Australian Steamship, Ocean Steamship (Blue Funnel), and India-China Steam Navigation. Besides being represented through merchant houses and British manufacturers' representatives, like Muller, Phipps & Sellers in Osaka, British firms established their own branch offices in Japan. Brunner, Mond established a branch office in 1920; Alfred Herbert, the Coventry machine-tool maker, had a large establishment in Osaka, with branches in Tokyo and Nagoya; Arthur Balfour established a Tokyo office in 1911; W.H. Allen Sons established a Tokyo branch to sell steam turbines, pumps, and diesel engines; Beldam Packing and Rubber had a Kobe office, Armstrong Withworth an office in Tokyo, and the Huddersfield valve maker, Hopkinson, a representative in Yokohama. Other British firms had connections with Japanese firms. G & W Weir had close links with the Japanese Admiralty from before 1900 and a special arrangement with Mitsubishi and Kawasaki, as did the other armament makers, such as Vickers.[4] The Asiatic Petroleum Company, through its subsidiary, Rising Sun Petroleum, had bulk storage and distribution installations valued at £2.2 million and stocks of £2 million in Japan in November 1914.

A number of British manufacturers established production facilities as well as marketing and distribution branches in Japan. The growth of British FDI in Japan, especially after World War I, was reversed in the 1930s. Several companies left the market before 1941, including Lever Brothers, Vickers, and the Far Eastern Card Clothing Co. (Tōyō Shimpu), which sold out to Japanese interests for £72,500 in 1940. This company was established by the English Card Clothing Company, Cleckheaton, in 1932, with a 20% holding by Mitsui, and employed 75 workers with sales of £35,000 per year. The Board of Trade reported that the company found that before the war it was "getting almost impossible to carry on their Company in Japan, owing to the difficulties and restrictive instructions which the Japanese Government were enforcing" and that

TABLE 4 British Multinationals in Japan, 1941

Name	Location	Year Founded	Employment (number)	Value (¥ million)	Shareholding (%)	Other Branches
Babcock & Wilcox (Tōyō Babcock)	Yokohama	1906	850–900	Assets 13	66.6 Babcock 33.3 Mitsui	France, Germany, Italy, Canada, Australia, Spain, Brazil, China, Poland
J. & P. Coats (Teikoku Seishi) Teikoku Katan-Ito Hanbai wholly owned selling subsidiary	Osaka	1907	650	8	60.0 Coats 40.0 Murai family	Austria, Germany, U.S.A., Russia, Czechoslovakia, Hungary, Yugoslavia, Poland, Mexico, Italy, Canada, Portugal, France, Argentina, Brazil

Dunlop (Nippon Dunlop Gomu)	Kobe	1909	1400	14	99.7 Dunlop	Canada, Australia, U.S.A., India, South Africa, France, Germany, Brazil, Ireland
International Paint & Composition (Bankoku Toryō Seizō Sho Gōshi)	Kobe	1911	15	.25	85.0 Int'l Paint 15.0 Japanese	Canada
Mather & Platt (Nippon Grinned Sprinkler)	Hyōgo Prefecture	1936	—	—	—	France, Germany, Italy, India, Egypt
Morgan Crucible (Morganite Carbon)	Osaka	1930	23	.012	99.0 Morgan	Russia, France, U.S.A., South Africa, Canada, Australia, Italy

Sources: *British-owned Property in Japan*, PRO, BT60 96/5; *U.K. Liaison Mission Tokyo*, PRO BT11 3581; H. A. Macrae, *Survey of U.K. Pre-War Economic and Commercial Interest Japan, Manchuria, Formosa and Korea* (Board of Trade, Oct. 1945); company archives.

the company was "more or less forced to sell."[5] However, a strong British manufacturing presence remained, with Babcock, J. & P. Coats, Dunlop, Mather & Platt, Morgan Crucible, and International Paint and Composition Co. the largest British manufacturing multinationals operating in the period immediately before the outbreak of war in 1941. As shown in Table 4, these firms fall into two groups: Babcock, Coats, and Dunlop had large subsidiaries in Japan, with substantial assets and employment, while the branches of International Paint, Mather & Platt, and Morgan were much smaller. However, all the parent firms were large multinationals with numerous branches, as can be seen from Table 4. Below, I briefly sketch a model of British international involvement, which is then used to explain the evolution of merchant houses, sales branches, and production facilities of British firms in Japan.

III. The Theory and Empirical Estimation of Multinational Investment

Firms transact internationally to transfer goods and services across national boundaries and to earn quasi-rents on firm-specific assets, including technology, marketing know-how, product differentiation advantages, and management skills.[6] If markets worked costlessly, there would be no international firms. But there are costs of operating the market system, such as the costs of gaining information, bargaining, and negotiating contracts, and the costs of monitoring and enforcing those contracts in arm's-length markets. These costs of using markets are labeled transaction costs, and firms economize on markets by replacing markets with managers organized in hierarchies. Of course, hierarchy is not the only governance structure which attenuates transaction costs. Long-term contracts, agencies, franchises, and joint ventures are intermediate governance structures falling between arm's-length markets and hierarchical firms which economize on the cost of transacting. Transaction-cost economizing is an alternative institutional undertaking which explicitly recognizes that different transactions have to be matched to the appropriate governance structure.

The choice of the appropriate governance structure depends on the nature of transactions and on the comparative costs of the alternative governance structures. Non-market governance structures, intermediate, modes and hierarchy, have costs due to agency.[7] Agency problems arise whenever there is asymmetric information and uncertainty. Imperfect information and uncertainty means that the relationship between principals and agents (franchiser-franchisee, licenser-licensee, higher-level managers–lower-level managers) is subject to hidden action (moral hazard) and hidden information (adverse selection). Hidden action is typically related to the effort the agent puts into task completion, especially the energy the agent devotes to supervision or sales promotion. Hidden information relates to the observations available to the agent but not the principal. This means that principals cannot assess whether agents employ information in the principal's or their own self-interest. Hidden action and hidden information mean that agents can behave opportunistically, taking actions which harm the principal. Therefore, principals must monitor agents. Opportunism, and the costly mechanisms employed by both intermediate modes and hierarchical firms for assessing the performance and behavior of agents, are the costs attached to non-market arrangements. The best mode is that which economizes most on the costs of operating market and non-market institutions, subject to the nature of the transactions.

Transactions affect the choice of governance structure, depending on the volume, frequency, and need for idiosyncratic investments. When transactions require no transaction-specific capital and the frequency of transacting is occasional, then market modes are efficient governance structures; when there is a need for highly specific capital investments, like a physical plant and skilled manpower tailored to a particular firm or product, and transacting is recurrent, then hierarchy is the optimal mode. Intermediate governance structures fall between these two extremes. Whether markets or non-market institutions are selected as the governance institution, the choice depends on the costs of each mode relative to the nature of the transaction.

Transaction-cost theory is consistent with the historical evidence that multinationals first export to foreign markets, sometimes using merchant houses, then develop an agency system as the volume and frequency of transacting increases and the goods and services require idiosyncratic investments, such as advertising, repair shops, and credit facilities.[8] When transactions become recurrent, the agents are replaced by sales branches. The shift from sales branches to production plants can also be understood in transaction-cost terms. Two types of transactions costs are internalized in production branches: the rents from production-based knowledge, which is not easily codified, and scope economies related to managing at a distance. Scope economies arise when the costs of joint production, particularly related to management knowledge, are less within a single international firm located in two or more different countries than the costs of producing in separately owned firms in each country. Recent empirical work, reported in the Appendix, shows that the number of branches is a good proxy for scope economies and that the number of branches is a highly significant variable in explaining the decision to invest in production facilities.[9] Theory predicts that British multinationals in Japan have many overseas branches; Table 4 confirms this prediction.

Firms determine the choice of location at the same time that they choose a governance structure. Generally the location decision depends on host-country variables, costs related to distance, and production costs. While a locational Empire–non-Empire model is outlined in the Appendix, the results are briefly reported here because they have implications for British multinational investment in Japan.[10] Firstly, the most important factor which discouraged non-Empire investment was psychic distance—dissimilarities in the level of development between home and host country, including education, language, culture, customs, and legal and commercial systems. Psychic distance was particularly great between Japan and Britain. Secondly, the lack of host-government incentives to British firms was the next most important factor in discouraging non-Empire investment. Finally, the older the firm and the more complex its internal structure, proxied by the number of different product groups in which the firm produced, the more likely the firm was to invest in non-Empire locations. Using transaction-cost theory and the evidence from the empirical studies, I explain the origins and evolution of merchant houses, agents, sales, branches, and production facilities by British firms in Japan.

IV. Merchant Houses and Agents

Already well established in India, the Far East, and Africa, the investment houses which entered the Japanese market were multiproduct trading companies purchasing goods both on "their own account" and on commission. The geographical span of the investment houses, and the partnership connections which bound "branches" of the trading companies together, created a powerful economic institution for economizing on the market in the trade for standardized goods.[11] With the opening of the Japanese market, British trading houses, particularly those based in China or India, entered the Japanese market to trade in tea, sugar, camphor, raw silk, and jute. The successful entry of British trading companies can be understood largely in terms of scope economies. While Japan was a new market, the firm-specific advantages related to knowledge of the supply and demand for primary products, the financing of raw-material purchases, the grading and loading of cargoes, and the marketing and distribution of primary products learned in the Indian and Chinese markets could be easily applied to Japan. These advantages flowed from the investment houses' organizational structure, whose specialized departments for tea, jute, sugar, and coal generated large information flows which allowed the merchant houses to invest profitably in primary products for future demand. In addition, the firms had developed an extensive experience related to penetrating new markets, which was utilized in their expansion into Japan. The multiproduct and multimarket investment houses also had risk-diversifying advantages, which were exploited through the expansion into the growing Japanese market. These firm-specific skills could not be easily or costlessly traded on the market and gave rise to scope economies which allowed multi-branch British investment houses to operate more cheaply than separate individual firms.

As the investment houses matured, especially after 1900, the branch offices in Japan began to handle both a wider range of products and more sophisticated goods requiring transaction-specific investments. For example, Dodwell imported textile yarns, piece goods, metalware, ships, munitions, pharmaceuticals, and chemicals, and exported coal, tea, raw silk, straw braid, and rice. During the Russo-Japanese War, Dodwell acted as the government's exclusive agent for chartering ships and greatly increased its contracts for the supply of coal for the Japanese navy.[12] The firm also secured the agency rights for more sophisticated goods, such as Underwood typewriters, which required investments in skilled sales staff, stock, repair shops, and promotional, advertising, and distributional facilites. In the period before 1914, Dodwell's greatest profit in Japan came from its shipping-agency services, where local knowledge of commodities and merchants guaranteed high returns on the organization of whole shiploads of bulky, seasonal goods.[13] As Japanese firms began to deal directly with overseas customers in the 1920s, the decline in Dodwell's export-import business resulted in big losses. As a result, from 1925, Dodwell acted only as an agent, and no longer as a principal. This seems to have been typical of British investment houses generally, with some large British investment houses, such as Wallace Brothers in 1937 and Mackinnon, Mackenzie in 1939, exiting the Japanese market.[14]

Transaction-cost theory is also useful in describing the rise of the specialist merchant houses, which concentrated on one product line or traded just with Japan. As the volume and frequency of transactions rose, and specialized knowledge of one product created an important firm-specific asset, specialized traders were formed. Sometimes those specialist Japan-based general traders took on agency work when their knowledge of the market could be easily applied to different products. For example, Witkowski & Co. represented John Haig, Yardley, and J. J. Coleman, and Cameron & Co. fronted for Nobel, Sanderson Bros., and Renold Chain. Without investing in sales facilities themselves, many British manufacturing firms found strong representatives in the investment and specialist trading houses.

Of course, many British firms did invest in sales branches. The agency agreements required expensive monitoring to measure the effort agents put into product selling and promotion which could be reduced by establishing a branch. Further, as the product became more complex, requiring specialist knowledge of repair, credit, and demonstration needed to market the product, and the volume of trade demanded large stocks, many British firms opened their own sales branches. The firms which established their own offices in Japan—Herbert in machine tools, Balfour in specialist steel, Allen in engines, and Hopkinson in valves—all fit this model. So, too, did the manufacturing firms who formed sales offices as the first step in their multinational expansion in Japan. The next section provides a case study of ICI's strategy of using a sales branch rather than a production plant to penetrate the Japanese market.

V. ICI's Sales Branch and the Japanese Market for Soda Ash

Brunner, Mond, ICI's predecessor, established a small Japanese office in 1902 under the control of Edward Little.[15] In 1920, following a visit to Japan by J. G. Nicholson, one of Brunner, Mond's Winnington directors, a selling company was established.[16] Japan was an important and profitable market for Brunner, Mond, with the company supplying 110,000 tons of the total Japanese demand of 120,000 tons in 1924. Brunner, Mond's dominance in the market fell, but as late as 1929, Brunner, Mond still accounted for about 40,000 tons of soda ash, which was equivalent to Japanese domestic production.[17] Brunner, Mond was the market leader, and its place in the Japanese market had been hard won during 1921 and 1922 when the company fought a price war with the Magadi Soda Co., which sold very low-priced natural soda from Lake Magadi in Kenya. Accepting losses on every ton of soda sold in Japan, Brunner, Mond successfully bankrupted Magadi in 1925 and entrenched its own position in the Japanese market.[18]

During and just after the war, two Japanese firms began to produce soda ash: the Asahi Glass Co., a subsidiary of Mitsubishi, which was founded in 1917, and the Nippon Soda Co. (which hovered on the brink of bankruptcy), founded in 1919.[19] Both firms were handicapped by the failure to secure the Solvay patents in 1909 and by shortages of cheap salt supplies. Even with knowledge of the Solvay process gained through the advice of a former Solvay engineer, the local industry came to depend on government subsidies and government support from "unfair competition."[20] As early as 1898, Brunner, Mond had estimated the costs of manufacturing in Japan—a process repeated many times up to 1930—and judged, correctly, that soda ash production was not feasible because of the lack and high cost of salt and the scarcity and high cost of coal.[21] The problems revealed by Brunner, Mond's cost calculations explain the high cost and intermittent production of the Japanese soda firms. The Nippon plant frequently lay idle, and the Asahi Glass Co. only kept the soda ash plant going to keep and gain technical knowledge.[22] Yet, the commitment of the Japanese firms to soda production was not in doubt: when ICI took over Brunner, Mond in 1926, Edward Little, the director in Japan, warned that the creation of a Japanese alkali industry was a national issue, although local production would require government protection and subsidies.

ICI understood that the "national feeling which encourages home production" was only partially driving the policy of local production. Equally important was the Magadi price war and rise of soda prices after 1924, which laid bare ICI's price leadership in the market.[23] The Japanese market for ICI's soda was substantial, with a turnover in 1924 valued at £2.5 million, which returned substantial profits.[24] ICI's Japanese market was worth protecting.[25]

ICI's strategy in the soda market was based on three premises: that direct foreign investment was neither feasible nor profitable; that Winnington's costs and ICI's prices in Japan were cheaper than local prices by Asahi; and that the Magadi price war showed that ICI had a powerful weapon to use in any struggle for market shares. The Japanese producers reached a similar conclusion: in October 1930, ICI, the Japanese Alkali Manufacturers (represented by the general sales manager of Asahi), and the Japanese commercial counselor in London (because any agreement would require government enforcement) met to discuss a market-sharing arrangement. The minor parts of the original Japanese proposal, such as the takeover of Nippon by Asahi and the restriction of Japanese producers, gained ICI's favor; the market split, 70% to the Japanese makers and 30% to ICI, was rejected. ICI demanded 40,000 tons of the 120,000-ton market and an equal share with the Japanese producers of any increase in sales.[26] The Japanese government was expected to guarantee the agreement, giving ICI exclusive rights to import (thus eliminating 20,000 tons of American and Chinese soda ash) and prohibiting Japanese firms from exporting. ICI believed that constraints on salt supplies would limit the expansion of the Japanese producers as the market expanded and the firm remained supremely confident of its ability to undercut the Japanese makers. During 1931 and 1932, ICI reduced its prices (which sharply cut its profits) to force the Japanese to negotiate.[27] The policy succeeded. Late in 1932, negotiations were reopened and a favorable settlement was agreed on. However, a new government committed to a strong Japanese alkali industry enabled the agreement to slip from ICI's hands. Unable to enter the market because local production was uneconomical, ICI had used its cost advantage to force an outcome. Unfortunately, ICI was unable to control for government, whose commitment to a local alkali industry meant that local producers were subsidized. After 1932, ICI was left with that share of the Japanese market which local firms could not supply.

VI. Babcock and Morgan Crucible in Japan in the 1930s

Six British multinationals, not including the Card Clothing Company, which sold out in 1940, had production facilities in Japan in the 1930s. In each case, the company had firm-specific technologies, providing a competitive advantage and market leadership. For example, Babcock's competitive advantage was based on the economics of high pressure and temperature steam, and Morgan Crucible was a market leader in carbon, graphite, and metallic blocks.[28] While technology licensing and joint ventures were alternative transfer mechanisms to multinational investment, these modes frequently failed to protect fully the firm's property rights in new methods and techniques of production. This weighed heavily in Morgan Crucible's decision to reject subcontracting with a Japanese firm, since the company feared that a Japanese partner would "take advantage to their own ends of everything we taught them."[29]

FDI was also the preferred vehicle for entering foreign markets by British firms when the volume and frequency of transactions rose above some minimum. Both Babcock and Morgan Crucible were typical of the general tendency of British sales and production branches to evolve out of agency arrangements as the size of the market expanded.[30] While describing their agency with L. J. Healing of London, Tokyo, and Osaka as a "pleasant arrangement," Morgan Crucible wrote to Arthur Balfour in early 1929 asking for information on starting and running a Japanese branch for the sale and distribution of carbon products and the manufacture of brushes.[31] Balfour's experience and method of business in Japan encouraged Morgan Crucible, but the success of the company's FDI in Japan depended heavily on Healing; the manager of the new Japanese branch, A. W. Drane, had previously been employed by Healing (with Morgan Crucible contributing half his salary), as had two salesmen and an office assistant. Babcock's dependence on their agent was even more dramatic. When B. A. Muster decided to retire due to age after acting as an agent for 30 years, he suggested that the company establish its own sales office. Agreeing to help Babcock establish its office, Muster advised H. E. Metcalf, who was sent from London to manage the new office.[32] The branch sales office was an effective device for increasing the frequency of Babcock's transactions, which increased ten times between 1906 and 1928.[33] Both of these examples highlight the importance of gaining market-specific information during the establishment of sales subsidiaries, particularly in an economy where psychic distance posed an acute problem.

While Morgan Crucible established a sales and production plant simultaneously, Babcock first formed a sales subsidiary in 1906, then diversified into production in 1911. The decision to produce owed something to forthcoming duties, the chance to save on freight costs, and the opportunity to purchase the Zemma Engineering Works, with a predicted 9% yield. The *Minute Book* also reported that the investment was a "step towards the appearance of nationalizing the business."[34] In addition, Babcock (and Morgan Crucible) fit the profile of all the British firms operating production plants in Japan: They were large multinationals with sales and production facilities in several countries. As shown in the econometric tests reported in the Appendix, the number of different locations performed well as a proxy for scope economies related to a firm's ability to manage at a distance. Such advantages meant that a multinational with production branches in several markets was more efficient than separate national firms in each market. The scope economies related to managing at a distance were particularly important in overcoming psychic distance.

Morgan Crucible and Babcock were both successful. The monthly reports on Babcock's Japanese branch indicated that the factory was fully and regularly employed, earning profits, and returning a healthy dividend. After a shaky start in 1932, Morgan Crucible's profits rose rapidly, placing the firm in the super-tax bracket by 1935. Both firms exercised close control over their overseas branches from the head office.[35] Neither firm evidenced slack administrative control or managerial failure, which allegedly plagued other British multinationals.[36]

While both firms were "economic" successes in profit and rate of return terms, each "failed" in the mid-1930s due to political factors. Babcock's purchase of the Zemma Works in 1911 was seen as "a step towards the appearance of nationalizing our business," a concern which continued with Babcock's commitment in early 1918 to "meet more of our requirements through local manufacture."[37] By early 1919, Mitsui was pressuring Babcock to "form our business into a Japanese company and take them in."[38] Although Mitsui was "an important—almost dominant—factor in our trade," Babcock resisted Mitsui's advances while at the same time expanding their factory to mark a continuing commitment to the Japanese market. The policy paid off, whether measured in profits (which were declared "most satisfactory"), full capacity working, or yields (which outperformed Babcock's other branches by averaging 10% during the 1920s).

By early 1927, political events and Mitsui's role as Babcock's largest customer saw Mitsui gaining a one-third holding in the Zemma Works with the floating of Tōyō Babcock. The company admitted that the float, which also involved a £20,000 expansion of the capital base, was a response to "nationalistic feelings."[39] Further attempts by Mitsui to increase their stake in 1930 met with the reply that Babcock was "committed to a majority shareholding in all its subsidiaries."[40] Local production grew, and in 1938 Babcock reported that trade was "satisfactory" and in that year sales were £433,000, with net profits of £58,870.[41]

However, in early 1939 the *Minute Book* revealed serious problems concerning the Japanese branch: "Prospects of Japan Babcock and Wilcox obtaining a proper share of the Japanese trade [are] negligible if under British ownership."[42] Mitsui proposed that they become the owners of Babcock Japan by buying out half of Babcock's holdings. Left with only a 33.3% holding, Babcock would become "only a shareholder with royalties from technology" with work on pressure parts coming to an end in Babcock's Scottish plant. Worse still, Japanese control would mean that Babcock would give up technical information as well as open the prospect of the new company competing with Scotland on world markets.[43] Finally, even if the offer from Mitsui were fair (and Babcock thought Mitsui's offer insufficient to cover existing assets), the firm would have difficulty repatriating the payment. While the existing arrangements held few prospects for Babcock, the firm rejected Mitsui's offer but considered outright sale to Mitsui. The Mitsui's terms involved an offer of ¥4.37 million with a government guarantee of a Sterling payment, a territorial limit on Japanese boiler exports, and Babcock supplying drawings and technical aid. Negotiations were eclipsed by the war, with Babcock bargaining for a ¥5.5 million settlement and payment of £350,000 Sterling.

After signs of increasing profitability in late 1932, Morganite Carbon found that it took time to get permission from the Ministry of Finance to take money out of Japan, but there was "no hold-up."[44] This sanguine attitude was disturbed in 1933 when a meeting at Battersea reported "concern over the internal political situation in Japan and the fear of a trend towards an aggressive Fascism with the possible nationalisation of industry."[45] Concern was expressed again in early 1935 when the director-manager in Japan, A. Kenward, wrote that the "Japanese authorities are increasingly suspicious of everything 'foreign' (by which I mean not Japanese)."[46] During 1938, permits for foreign exchange were even more difficult to get passed, with approvals of only £420 between January and September as against the need for £3,500.[47]

After rejecting an offer by Tōkai Denkyoku Seizō to subcontract the Morganite factory, Battersea turned its attention to the options available to the Japanese company. Four options were canvassed, none of which commanded a clear solution to the firm's difficulties.[48] First, the firm could cease production and appoint agents. However, the Japanese branch allowed Morgan Crucible to keep an eye on their Japanese competitors and their export activity, besides which good agents were difficult to find and "cannot be expected to take the same trouble as a Branch." Second, the firm could expand the present organization and plant, but "English colour was a disadvantage" and this alternative "did not make sense." The third option called for the input of Japanese capital in some form of joint venture. While this alternative solved the problem of nationalistic criticism, it did mean Japanese control. Such a partnership offered the prospect of opening a much larger market to Morganite Carbon, especially if the Japanese partner could guarantee sales to their brush-using subsidiaries. In order to attract Japanese capital, Morganite would have to begin the production of carbon blocks in Japan. This last requirement was the basis of the fourth option: their own factory producing carbon products "from the ground up." This would answer the criticism that the product should be locally made and would put the branch on an equal footing with the Japanese makers, if Morganite received permits to import carbon powder. This was a very big *if*, which ran the danger of leaving the firm with a large plant standing idle or working short time. Further, the import of carbon to make blocks meant that the Japanese could analyze the imported powder, thereby gaining secret information and eroding Morgan Crucible's technical lead.

By late 1939, Morgan Crucible declared a Japanese policy: to prevent the extension of Japanese competition; to watch developments in the Japanese brush industry; to make a profit; and to consolidate their position.[49] This "wait-and-see" policy was not surprising, considering that none of the four options offered a clear solution to Morganite's problems. But the policy held out one hope: that Morganite Carbon's technical excellence and continued existence would lead to future cooperation with a Japanese brush maker. In the remaining years before the war, an approach by a Japanese maker never eventuated, leaving the firm to fill the orders of "old friends," to produce on short time, and to badger the Japanese authorities to allow more import permits.

VII. Conclusion

From the opening of Japan in the mid-19th century, British firms were major foreign direct investors, with business interests spread widely across banking, insurance, shipping, trading, and manufacturing. While accounting for only a small proportion of total British FDI, Japan was a profitable, but sometimes difficult, market for British firms before 1930. After 1930 the difficulty of operating in Japan increased markedly, with a concomitant decline in profitability. Psychic distance, government policy, and the tyranny of physical distance meant that British firms required a competitive advantage, both technological and managerial, to operate in Japan. The major British manufacturing multinationals in 1941 were all large technically advanced firms, able to utilize their experience of operating numerous branches in diverse foreign markets. These advantages were not sufficient to overcome the xenophobia, the cost of psychic distance, and the political restrictions experienced by ICI, Babcock, and Morgan Crucible after 1930. These firms were not unique: Davenport-Hines found that Vickers's holdings in Japan suffered most of all from the "difficulties confronting overworked businessmen in penetrating and mastering the opposing business cultures of the two island empires."[50] While Dunlop had an "expanding turnover and profit position in Japan," Jones found that "the political environment was so hostile that the only rational course was to retrieve as much money as possible from the Japanese investment."[51] The market messages encouraging local production and local color were read correctly, and acted on quickly, as British firms became more "Japanese." All British manufacturing multinationals either took on local partners or tried to sell out to Japanese interests, although Morgan Crucible and Dunlop were not able to complete their arrangements before 1941. But there were no options which could rescue British multinationals in this xenophobic market from the increasingly restrictive set of government policies. By 1941 most forms of British business investment in Japan faced economic ruin, not because of economic failure but because of political policy.

Statistical Appendix

Two econometric models of British FDI were estimated: one for the location of FDI and the other for the form of FDI. Generally the location decision depends on host-country variables, costs related to distance, and production costs. Since observations on many of the variables were not available for the full range of 58 countries receiving British FDI between 1870 and 1939, a number of proxy variables were constructed. Host-market locational factors were represented by PSYCHIC, GOVT, RAW, and TARIFF. PSYCHIC was psychic distance, which discouraged the flow of goods; GOVT measured host-government disincentives; RAW measured backward vertical integration; and TARIFF measured tariff barriers. The hypothesized signs are positive for RAW and negative for PSYCHIC, GOVT, and TARIFF. Production costs were proxied by industry dummy variables for CHEMICAL, ENGINEER, and FOOD. Finally, the impact of distance was measured by AGE and the span of the enterprise, DIVER. The older the firm, the better it was expected to be at managing at a distance, hence its hypothesized sign was positive; the more diversified the firm, measured by the number of two-digit SIC product groups in which the firm produced, the more complex its internal structure and, thus, the more able it was expected to be at managing at a distance.

In the model on the form of FDI, DIVER was again used to proxy the complexity of internal structure and, as a result, the likelihood that the firm had scope economies. NUMBER, the number of overseas branches, was also used to proxy scope economies, since NUMBER captures directly the idea that managerial knowedge yields economies related to operating a number of branches at a distance.

The two logit models were estimated by maximum likelihood methods: Model 1 on the choice of location used Empire–non-Empire as the binary dependent variable, while Model 2 on the choice of form used the binary sales branch–production plant as the dependent variable. The parameter estimates in Table 5 are the log of the probabilities and, therefore, provide a measure of the *relative* importance of the various variables in the location and form of investment decision. Only by the statistical estimation of such models can we discriminate between competing hypotheses and competing variables in the decision to invest abroad, where the size of the coefficient measures the importance of the variable.

The results are not reviewed at length here, but PSYCHIC and GOVT disincentives in Model 1 have a large negative impact on the probability of investing in a host country. The Japanese market, particularly in the 1930s, was characterized by psychic distance and a government policy which discouraged investment. NUMBER and DIVER were significant variables in Model 2, both providing a positive impact on the decision to invest. Insofar as these proxies reflect scope economies,

TABLE 5 Location and Form of FDI Models

	Model 1 Empire–non-Empire[t]	Model 2 Sales Branch-Production Plant[t]
Age	0.014	—
	(2.570)	
Diver	0.743	0.30
	(1.128)	(1.19)
Raw	0.789	2.63
	(1.150)	(2.51)
Food/Drink	−1.027	1.44
	(−1.735)	(2.53)
Chemical	0.262	0.90
	(0.514)	(2.48)
Engineer	0.185	—
	(0.366)	
Tariff	−0.948	—
	(−2.009)	
Psychic	−3.306	−0.85
	(−5.380)	(−3.28)
Govt	−2.096	—
	(−3.513)	
Number	—	0.17
		(2.39)
Constant	0.055	−0.45
	(0.121)	(−1.80)
X^2	67.348	54.34
d.f.	9	6
No. of cases	176	380

[t] Asymptotic t ratios in parentheses.

British multinationals which have a large number of locations and are diversified across several product groups have a high probability of investing abroad. From the discussion in the text, it is clear that British multinationals in Japan fulfilled both these characteristics. The empirical results are consistent with the qualitative evidence on British multinationals in Japan, providing clear evidence of the relative importance of these factors in the FDI decision.

NOTES

1. *British Property in Japan*, Public Record Office (PRO), Foreign Office (FO) 371/637123.

2. *Allied Property in Japan*, PRO, FO371/54191; FO371/54192.
3. This section depends on H. A. Macrae, *Survey of UK Pre-War Economic and Commercial Interests in Japan, Manchuria, Formosa and Korea* (Board of Trade, Oct. 1945); *Firms with Pre-1941 Investment in Japan*, PRO, Board of Trade (BT)11/3346; *UK Liaison Mission Tokyo* PRO, BT 11/3581; *Plants and Installations in Japan Owned by the UK*; PRO, BT60/95/5; *British Property in Japan*, PRO, FO371 63723; FO371/54301; *Return of British Property in Japan*, PRO, BT11/3581.
4. W. J. Reader, *The Weir Group* (London, 1971), pp. 40–1.
5. *British-Owned Property in Japan*, PRO, BT60 96/5.
6. For transaction cost approaches to multinationals, see M. Casson, *Alternatives to the Multinational Enterprise* (London, 1979); D. Teece, "Economies of Scope and the Scope of the Enterprise," *Journal of Economic Behaviour and Organisation*, 1 (1980); O. Williamson, *The Economic Institutions of Capitalism* (N.Y., 1985); S. Nicholas, "Agency Contracts, Institutional Modes and the Transition to Foreign Direct Investments by British Manufacturing Multinationals Before 1939," *Journal of Economic History* 43 (1983).
7. For the agency literature, see K. J. Arrow, "The Economies of Agency," in J. Pratt and R. Zeckhauses (eds.), *Principals and Agents: The Structure of Business* (Boston, 1984); M. Jensen and W. Meckling, "Theory of the Firm: Managerial Behaviour, Agency Costs and Ownership Structure," *Journal of Financial Economies* 3 (1978).
8. Nicholas, *op. cit.*, pp. 675–77.
9. S. Nicholas, "Empirical Tests of the Transaction Cost Model: The Evolution of the Pre-1939 British Manufacturing Multinational," *Business and Economic History* 16 (1987), pp. 140–42.
10. S. Nicholas, "Locational Choice, Performance and the Growth of British Multinational Firms," *Business History* 31 (1989).
11. S. Nicholas, "Overseas Marketing Performance of British Industry, 1870–1914," *Economic History Review* 37 (1984), pp. 497–502.
12. S. Jones, *Two Centuries of Overseas Trading: The Origins and Growth of the Inchcape Group* (London, 1986), pp. 177–80.
13. *Ibid.*, p. 80.
14. A. C. Pointon, *Wallace Brothers* (Oxford, 1974), pp. 58–68.
15. ICI Archives, Mond House, uncataloged.
16. ICI Archives, Mond House, uncataloged.
17. ICI Archives, Mond House, W377/19/2, Oct. 1930; W45/6/88, no date.
18. W. Reader, *Imperial Chemical Industries: A History: Volume 1, The Forerunners 1870–1926* (London, 1970), pp. 342–45.
19. E. Daito, "The Development of the Ammonia-Soda Process in Japan, 1917–1932," in A. Okochi and H. Uchida (eds.), *Development and Diffusion of Technology: Electrical and Chemical Industries* (Tokyo, 1980), pp. 185–95.
20. ICI Archives, Mond House, W45/6/228, March 1930; W377/19/1, Sept. 1931; Daito, *op. cit.*, pp. 188–89.
21. *Ibid.*, W45/6/10, March 1916; W55/6/15, March 1916; W45/6/80, May 1925; W45/3/73, March 1929; W377/19/3, Aug. 1931.
22. *Ibid.*, W56/6/104, April 1926.
23. *Ibid.*, W377/19/5, Jan. 1929.
24. Reader, *op. cit.*, p. 341.
25. ICI Archives, Mond House, W377/19/1, Nov. 1931.

26. *Ibid.*, W377/19/1, Sept. 1931.
27. *Ibid.*, W45/3/74, Feb. 1933.
28. Babcock Archives, *Historical Notes 1958*, n. p.
29. Morgan Crucible Archives, *Memorandum on China and Japan*, 3-10-1938.
30. See S. Nicholas, " British Multinational Investment Before 1939," *Journal of European Economic History* 11 (1982), pp. 621–22; Nicholas, "Agency Contracts," pp. 675–87.
31. Morgan Crucible Archives, SU589, *Correspondence*, 26-12-1929.
32. H. E. Metcalf, *On Britain's Business* (N.Y., 1943), pp. 30–32.
33. Babcock Archives, *Typescript History* (no date), pp. 21–22.
34. Babcock Archives, *Minute Book*, 6 April 1911; Metcalf, *Britain's Business*, p. 34.
35. Babcock Archives, *Minute Book*, 13 Feb. 1930.
36. See G. Jones (ed.), *British Multinationals: Origins, Management and Performance* (London, 1986).
37. Babcock Archives, *Minute Book*, 9 May 1918.
38. *Ibid.*, 25 Feb. 1919.
39. Babcock Archives, *Historical Notes 1958*, no pages.
40. Babcock Archives, *Minute Book*, 31 March 1927.
41. *Ibid.*, 12 April 1936; 6 Oct. 1938.
42. *Ibid.*, 17 May 1939.
43. *Ibid.*, 17 May 1939.
44. Morgan Crucible Archives, SU590, *Correspondence*, 22-7-1932.
45. *Ibid.*, SU591, 3-10-1933.
46. *Ibid.*, 23-5-1935.
47. Morgan Crucible Archives, SU593, *Private File*, 1-11-1938.
48. This section is based on Morgan Crucible Archives, SU593, *Private File*, 4-10-1939.
49. *Ibid.*, 9-11-1939.
50. R. Davenport-Hines, "Vickers as a Multinational Before 1945," in Jones, *British Multinationals*, pp. 53–54.
51. G. Jones, "The Multinational Expansion of Dunlop, 1890–1939," in Jones, *British Multinationals*, p. 37.

Comment

Nobuo Kawabe

Professor Nicholas applies the transaction-cost theory to the explanation of evolution of merchant houses, agents, sales branches, and production facilities of British companies before the war. The main idea of the transaction-cost theory is the choice of governance structures: market, organizational hierarchy and intermediate, and choice of location based upon variables of host countries, costs related to distance, and production cost. The choice depends upon the nature of transactions and the comparative cost of alternative governance structure.

Nicholas's approach, the application of a theory by processing statistical data to the historical evidence, is quite new to Japanese business historians, and his paper gives us a very insightful methodology as well as results.

Nicholas's discussion is very clear, and I do not need to add many things. But I would like to raise some questions considering the experience of Japanese companies.

First, British companies had a whole spectrum of business activities from trading to manufacturing in Japan before World War II. Although Japanese companies developed their activities in foreign countries, we can find direct investment by manufacturing companies not in such advanced countries as the United States but in developing countries such as China. For example, foreign direct investment by Japanese companies in the United States before the war were mainly trade-related businesses such as trading, banking, insurance, and shipping. The role and behavior of multinationals in advanced countries are different from those in less developed countries.

In the Japanese market, as Nicholas mentioned, we can find differences in the types of industries between British and U.S. companies, although both had firm-specific advantage. There were many British commercial firms, and the British companies wanted to keep tight control over them, compared with their American counterparts. I would like to know what brought about these difference.

Second, Nicholas referred to the spin-offs by merchant houses. He mentioned that as volume and frequency of transactions increased, some companies like Cooper Findlay and Ralli Brothers had spin-offs. I think these spin-offs reduced economies of scope. For example, such Japanese *sōgō shosha* as Mitsui Bussan and Mitsubishi Shōji increased their transactions, adding product lines, branches, and functions, enjoying scope economies. When Mitsui Bussan's raw cotton department spun off to establish Tōyō Menka in 1920, it did so considering the nature of the transaction of raw cotton and negative financial influence over Mitsui Bussan. Why did British merchant houses have spin-offs and how did they trade off cost-benefit between specialization and diversification?

Third, it is interesting that both Babcock and Morgan Crucible evolved their sales and production branches out of agency arrangement. Nicholas mentioned that British firms developed manufacturing when the volume and frequency of transacting rose above some minimum. How did they decide these minimum points? In addition, when manufacturing companies canceled the agency agreement, did the agency not oppose them? Moreover, what caused differences in ICI's policy to establish only sales branches, not manufacturing branches, from the policy of Babcock and Morgan Crucible to manufacture in Japan in spite of the fact that all three had technological and managerial advantages.

Finally, Nicholas insists that British investment in Japan faced economic ruin not because of economic failure but because of political policy. When I studied the operations of business activities of Mitsubishi Shōji in the United States, they often complained about the restrictive economic policies developed by the U.S. government even before the war. I think that one of the characteristics of business activities in foreign countries is influence of the government policies of host countries.

Therefore, I think that in addition to the transaction cost, stages of economic development and the needs of host countries exert a strong influence over the activities of multinationals, particularly in the less developed countries more than home countries.

In addition, Japanese government influence went to an extreme to cause a war, which completely stopped all activities of British companies. However, we can see the increase in competition from the domestic companies. *Sōgō shosha*, which were deeply involved in the domestic market as organizers of industries, controlled the flow of products. I think even in the manufacturing sectors, many Japanese companies gained strong competitive positions, although they enjoyed support from the government. Therefore, I would like to know how transaction-cost theory explains the changing competitive positions between foreign companies and domestic firms.

Response

Stephen Nicholas

The tendency of British firms to retain more control and to resist Japanese participation relative to American firms can be explained, in large part, by the different industry characteristics. American firms entered joint ventures in industries, such as electrical engineering, where there were already large Japanese concerns. British firms tended to enter industries without strong local firms, and where British firms had a technological lead. It should be remembered that British multinationals in Japan were large multilocational firms operating in several foreign countries and with considerable experience in international operations. This experience meant that British multinationals had developed mechanisms for tight control over their Japanese subsidiaries and had broken through the barrier of psychic distance. Of course, there was a major exception to British dominance: The nature of the defense industry dictated that British defense firms enter into joint arrangements with Japanese firms.

Professor Kawabe correctly identifies the need to more fully develop the specialization-diversification trade-off needed to explain the spin-offs of specialized houses by British trading companies. This must remain, to a large extent, an area of future research. Briefly, the theory needed to develop a trade-off matrix would be Adam Smith's proposition that the division of labor is limited by the extent of the market. Besides scope interdependencies, merchant houses also experienced congestion, and the cost functions of different activities were not always complementary. A downward-sloping cost function for one or two activities implies that this activity should be hived off when the extent of the market allows a specialist firm to handle a particular product line. This is what happened in the case of Cooper Findlay and Ralli Brothers.

Finally, Kawabe asks how firms decided the switch point from sales to production branches based on the volume and frequency of transacting. This is an excellent question. The full answer awaits the empirical definition of the transaction-cost functions facing each firm. While in theory it is comparatively easy to specify transaction-cost factors, the complete specification of the empirical function is some way off. From the archives, British managers were aware of the importance of the volume and frequency of transacting in the decision to shift from sales to production branches. Of course, the sales/production-branch choice did not depend on transaction-cost factors alone. ICI did not invest in production because of production cost factors: the lack of cheap salt and coal supplies meant that alkali production was not economical in Japan, although the frequency and volume of transacting worked in favor of a shift to a production plant. The failure to specify transaction-cost functions empirically is a serious constraint on the transaction-cost model. Perhaps one of the most important contributions to transaction-cost economics by business historians will be empirical evidence on the trade-off between the volume and frequency of transacting. I agree with Kawabe that transaction-cost factors were simply one important element in understanding the development of multinationals, and that locational factors and government, as my paper argues, were equally important in explaining British multinationals in Japan.

British Multinationals in Japan, 1900–41: Vickers, Armstrong, Nobel, and the Defense Sector

Clive Trebilcock

I. Introduction

Before 1914, the major defense industries of the world were the British, German, French, American, Italian, and Austro-Hungarian. This list descends in rough order of sophistication and success. Certainly, in naval armament, the British industry was the world leader in export performance and, in many ways, in product development. The technological malaise and falling away of overseas sales which afflicted many British industries in the period 1870–1914 were not features of the defense sector. Within this global leading sector, Vickers became, in the period 1905–14, the strongest competitor, able to offer a complete range of weaponry from a single machine gun to a complete battleship. To achieve this position, it overtook the previous market leader, Armstrong, and easily outpaced a number of generalist metal and shipbuilding firms with an interest in defense work, such as Firth, John Brown, Cammell Laird, and Beardmore.

The tendency for British defense producers to create foreign subsidiaries became marked during the 1900s. Vickers' involvement in Japan was by no means its only operation in the multinational role; in fact, by 1914 it had established similar projects in Spain, Italy, Canada, Turkey, and Russia. And it was by no means the only British defense producer to employ this tactic: again by 1914, overseas production connections had been formed by Armstrong in Italy, Spain, and Turkey; by Brown in Spain and Russia; by Beardmore and Firth in Russia; and by the explosives group, Nobel, almost everywhere. Perhaps the most complete multinational in the sector, the Nobel conglomerate also created a Japanese production base during the 1900s. Together, Vickers and Nobel Explosives, excepting their mutual links with Armstrong, were the only major U.K. defense producers of the pre-1914 era able to supply the Japanese government from factories located in Japan.

There were special reasons for such levels of activity in the 1900s.

Supply-side incentives certainly existed. In a time of advancing protectionism, defense multinationals saw advantages in locating production facilities behind tariff walls. And in a time of rampant competition for the international armorers, there was an advantage in locating as close as possible to client governments. Before 1890, most big defense suppliers had relied upon simple exportation for their overseas trade. But around the turn of the century, they perceived a point in a change of strategy. However, the major influences lay on the demand side. The contentious international relations of the period 1870–1914 convinced many smaller powers that they could not rely on the vagaries of international trade for vital defense goods and that they needed effective means of supply within their own frontiers. Moreover, the years 1896–1914 saw a world manufacturing upswing which included the industrial "takeoff" of a new generation of economies, among them Italy, Sweden, very nearly Russia, and certainly Japan. Many of these states exhibited high levels of industrial growth alongside high levels of political nationalism. These countries had a manufacturing competence, a political will, and a sense of insecurity sufficient to create an appetite for advanced defense industries. Yet, they lacked crucial elements of expertise.

Clearly, there were influences on both sides of the military-industrial complex before 1914 which pointed toward the growth of multinationals within the defense sector of developing economies. Radical critics of the arms trade have frequently cited these cases as examples of monopoly capitalism or economic imperialism. However, in operation—certainly in Vickers' operation—the companies actually created did not much resemble this model. Rarely were they full-owned subsidiaries of the British mother company. We are not talking of multinationals in the sense, for example, that Vauxhall or Opel are overseas departments of General Motors of America. The characteristic method for the pre-1914 arms firms was a partnership with domestic manufacturing and capital interests. The foreigners would usually take up between 5% and 40% of equity in the new venture, rarely more. Their major obligation, under their agreement with the domestic interests—often supervised by the home government—was to provide technical guidance on plant construction and equipment and, most important, design advice and the designs themselves for the finished products. Sometimes a requirement to provide management services, and even skilled labor, might be written into the agreement. However, substantial managerial control and, usually, overall financial control remained with the indigenous interests. The return for the foreign operator was a guaranteed share of the domestic market underwritten by the home government, a monetary fee for its "consultancy" role, the royalty fee for the use of its designs, and, of course, any dividend on its shareholding. This cannot be described as the "penetration" associated with "monopolistic" or "imperialistic" capitalistic interests: too much initiative remained with domestic economic and political forces.

Nevertheless, few of the multinational diversifications of the British armaments industry before 1914 proved profitable in the longer term. This was not because the schemes were misconceived by the standards of the 1900s, nor because the objective of raising indigenous technological standards in such a demanding industry was unattainable. It was rather because after 1918, market conditions changed in a way that could not have been foreseen at any time before World War I. The multinational arms operations of the pre-1914 era could exist only within a strategic structure which functioned upon the assumptions of deterrence and limited warfare. High-technology armaments were meant to deter aggression or fight swift forensic campaigns to defeat aggression. Those assumptions failed amid the drawn-out attrition of World War I.

In the postwar world, after the deterrent had failed, a different set of values and assumptions predominated. Disillusion, disarmament, and retrenchment were the order of the decade. The dangerous mélange of nationalistic enthusiasm and economic expansion which had characterized the antebellum phase was replaced by national isolationism and economic contraction. If the interwar years were bad for international capitalism, they were particularly bad for the international armaments industry. The fortunes of this industry are affected not only by the rhythm of the international business cycle but also by the separate pulse rate of international tension. This conjunction was particularly potent in the period 1919–39.

II. The British Arms Industry and the Japanese Market, 1890–1914

Japan was a locus classicus for many of these effects. Political modernization dated from 1868; the industrial "takeoff" is conventionally dated from the mid-1880s. From the beginning, industrial modernization contained a political purpose: the creation of a national system strong enough to resist western penetration. By the 1900s the Japanese defense industries were themselves highly competent. It was becoming possible, for instance, to purchase the lead ship of a new warship class from the West and to copy it, building the rest of the class in Japan's own yards. Nevertheless, most of the ships which trounced the Russians in the central battle of the Russo-Japanese War at Tsushima in 1905 had been built in Europe, and by far the largest number—no less than ten—in Britain. After Tsushima, the next stage was to improve the Japanese capacity for independent design and production of ships, turrets, and guns. At this stage it is worth remembering that probably the most complex manufactured product of the pre-1914 years was the hydraulically and electrically driven turret system of a major warship. Building these machines was the contemporary equivalent of producing a ballistic missile or a communications satellite and, around 1907, had been managed by about as many countries as have managed the latter tasks in the late 1980s.

For some years before 1907, the Imperial Japanese Navy had been disturbed by the lack of big-gun technology and turret-engineering capacity in Japan. It was for this reason that the government decided "to induce a foreign firm of repute to join with Japanese capitalists in founding an Ordnance Factory on a large scale."[1] Invitations to tender were sent out to Vickers and Armstrong and to a selection of other British, American, and European producers. But whom to choose?

Armstrong had been the greatest naval exporter in the world in the period 1885–1900, but by the 1900s its management was aging and in some disarray.[2] The younger armory of Vickers, which had achieved the status of a major defense supplier only in 1897,[3] was determined to replace Armstrong. But determination alone would not dispel the competition which was already stiff in the Asian markets of the 1900s and would worsen in the 1910s. The Americans had already taken Japanese orders. Krupp was a nuisance but could not break into the Japanese market (although it penetrated the Chinese one), despite offering vessels "exactly like the best English designs." It was a market—one of the relatively few—where "English designs" still enjoyed a clear edge over American or German types.

In 1903 the IJN announced a major competition for a new lead battleship, the *Katori*, and named a short list of acceptable contractors. Vickers' representation in Japan was strong: they had their own full-time agent in Tokyo, Basil Winder, and they retained Mitsui Bussan Kaisha——"probably the most powerful business institution in Japan"[4]—as their general agent until 1913, when Mitsubishi took over. Mitsui pressed hard for Vickers in 1903, and the British embassy in Tokyo also let it be known that the Foreign Office would prefer the order to go to Vickers. The clinching factor was a visit of a Japanese naval commission to Barrow in 1903. They came away much impressed by the technology on view. The combination of forces was sufficient to procure the *Katori* for Barrow. The fact that the orders for both the Japanese flagship at Tsushima, the

Mikasa, and for the *Katori*—the most important ships in the IJN—fell to Vickers marked a turning point. When the IJN wished to order another state-of-the-art warship in 1910, the enormous battle cruiser *Kongō*, and to use it as the model for copies built in Japan, they again went to Vickers.

The *Kongō* contract, signed on 17 November 1910, was worth £2.4 million. The rationale for placing the order abroad was, firstly, capacity—Japanese yards were already bursting with warship orders—and, secondly, technology—naval designs were changing so fast that the IJN needed to go to an innovational leader for a convincing design.[5]

But, of course, from the mid-1900s the IJN wanted more than western ships of imposing strength. The special needs posed by national security explain why large foreign defense firms serving the Japanese market experienced the pressure to shift from exporting products to exporting technology somewhat earlier—characteristically, some two decades earlier—than was the case for the bulk of civilian high-technology producers with interests in Japan.

III. An Armament Multinational in Japan: The Creation of the Nihon Seikō Sho, 1907

The plan to create an advanced gun-making and turret-engineering plant in Japan formed amid these rapidly changing markets. The Japanese decision to select British firms as partners clearly reflects both superior British competitiveness in the armament industry and the recent successes of U.K. suppliers in meeting Japanese demand for warships. But if several British firms could supply warships, only Armstrong, Vickers, and Coventry Ordnance Works could supply as well the largest guns. The Japanese government selected one traditional supplier, Armstrong, and the up-and-coming firm of Vickers.

The agreement to create Nihon Seikō Sho was signed on 30 July 1907. The business was to be a large steel foundry, gun works, and engineering factory located in Muroran on Hokkaido. It was to be headed by Baron Yamanouchi, previously "the most powerful man in our Navy Department"[6] prior to taking up the presidency of Nihon Seikō Sho. The Japanese partner which was to collaborate with Vickers and Armstrong was Hokkaido Tankō Kisen Kaisha (Hokkaido Colliery and Steamship Co., familiarly Hokutan), a venture both entrepreneurial and semi-official. Its dynamic chairman, Inoue Kakugorō—a friend of Andrew Noble of Armstrong—was flush with compensation funds from the nationalization of company-owned railway undertakings and anxious to diversify into metal products. On the other hand, his largest shareholder was the

Imperial Household Agency.[7] The British firms could scarcely have wished for a more impressive combination of investment power and public status.

The arrangement was, of course, most unusual. Given the nature of Japanese industrialization as a device to secure and conserve national independence, it was not surprising that a certain suspicion of foreign capital had been evident throughout the "takeoff" phase. Japanese businesses had eagerly borrowed foreign technology but had resisted prudently the incursions of both foreign capital and foreign capitalists. Even though this constraint weakened during the 1900s, it by no means fell away. Special explanation is needed as to why it proved ineffective in the defense sector. Such explanation is fairly readily forthcoming. Firstly, the technology was so difficult of access that direct instruction was necessary if it was to be absorbed successfully. Secondly, military need produced a special urgency. Thirdly, years of purchasing highly refined defense products from a few British suppliers had built up a relationship of trust between Japanese naval officials and British armorers.

How, then, was this direct guidance to be administered? The conditions were not dissimilar from those agreed for similar schemes in Spain, Italy, and Russia. The British firms promised to provide Nihon Seikō Sho with all the information, advice, and designs needed for constructing the new plant. Not only the production process was covered; the western armorers also agreed to supply their best patterns for the advanced weaponry which was the government's ultimate objective. Supervision was guaranteed by an undertaking to send to Japan "skilled officials to assist in production for a long period," which in practice came to mean workers as well as managers.[8] In return, the multinationals received a good deal more than the dividends on their shares (which was just as well). They were given the preferential right to manufacture all the equipment for Seikō Sho which the new plant could not make for itself or otherwise acquire in Japan. Above all, any orders for warships or armaments which could not be met in Japan were to be transferred solely to Vickers and Armstrong. On such transfers, Seikō Sho was to earn a 2.5% commission. The intention was that Seikō Sho "should have the first share of the ordnance orders the Japanese Government have to place."[9] But in practice, the effect was to convert Seikō Sho not only into a manufactory but into an enormously valuable additional agency remitting surplus orders to Britain. Not least, it gave Vickers and Armstrong a duopoly of the foreign contracts of the IJN for heavy weaponry. Certainly, they did not depend for their earnings merely on the profits of Seikō Sho.

The distribution of the shares which were to make these profits was highly significant. Seikō Sho's initial capital was ¥10 million, increased to ¥15 million in 1909. Vickers and Armstrong were allotted equal shares at 25% of the equity, so in 1909 they each controlled ¥3.75 million worth of shares for which they had each paid ¥383,306. The two British concerns maintained this 50% combined interest only during the period 1907–17. They were bound not to sell or transfer shares without the consent of the Japanese interests. Hokutan, with ¥7.5 million in 1909, controlled the balance of the equity until 1917.

For delicate if obvious reasons, defense multinationals rarely pressed for large proportions of equity in their foreign outstations (see Table 1, note b). Governments were naturally sensitive on this score: joint ventures,

TABLE 1 Vickers' Holdings in Major Foreign Subsidiaries as Proportions of Vickers' Total Foreign Investment, 1914

Country	Company	Date commenced	Holding	% total FI
Spain	1. Placencia de las Armas	1897	£31,877	1.9
	2. La Naval	1908/9		
U.S.A.	Electric Boat	1902	£128,678	7.6
Italy	1. Vickers-Terni	1905	£166,991	9.9
	2. It. Whitehead Torpedo	1913	£5,000	0.3
Austria-Hungary	Whitehead, Fiume	1906	£200,456	11.9
Japan	Nihon Seikō Sho	1907	£383,306	22.7
Russia	1. Chantiers de Nicolaiev	1910	£189,960	11.2
	2. Tsaritsyn Gun Foundry	1913	£300,000	17.7
	3. Russian Whitehead	1914	£50,000	2.9
Canada	Vickers, Canada	1910	£102,881	6.1
Turkey	Turkish Docks Co.	1913	£125,000	7.4
France	Torpilles Whitehead	1914	£7,197	0.4
Total			£1,691,346	100.0

Notes (a) All holdings are in 1914 values.
(b) With the exception of Vickers, Canada, all are minority holdings, e.g., about 13% in La Naval, about 8% in Nicolaiev, about 20% in Turkey and at Tsaritsyn, and about 28% in Terni. Whitehead holdings were usually 25%. The Electric Boat holding may have risen close to 50%, but this is speculation.

Source: Vickers Archive, Cambridge University Library.

TABLE 2 Vickers' Receipts on Work Completed at Barrow, 1906–16

Origin of payment	Amount
Spain	£40,454
Japan	£2,432,119
Brazil	£1,646,161
Chile	£405,850
China	£292,762
Italy	£140,791
Russia	£1,129,972
Argentina	£31,733
Peru	£518,394

Source: Vickers Archive, Cambridge University Library.

TABLE 3 Work Listed to Account of Japanese Government at Vickers' Barrow Shipyard, 1903–14

Year	Item	Value/profit	% of total annual shipyard profit or work in progress
Hulls, etc.			
1906	*Katori*	£125,423	22.6 (profit)
1908	submarines	£36,733	13.0 (profit)
1909	sub. engines	£15,832	2.3 (w.i.p)
1910	sub. engines	£25,898	4.7 (profit)
1910	*Kongō*	£28,752	2.6 (w.i.p)
1911	*Kongō*	£553,048	81.4 (w.i.p)
1912	*Kongō*	£1,547,530	72.7 (w.i.p)
Gun mountings			
1909	12″ mountings	£12,220	3.7 (w.i.p)
1910	″ ″	£97,966	20.8 (w.i.p)
1911	14″ ″	£51,714	10.8 (w.i.p)
1911	″ ″	£31,084	11.0 (profit)
1912	″ ″	£275,833	50.3 (w.i.p)
1913	″ ″	£69,218	31.1 (profit)

Notes: (a) Work in progress is the total value being worked in the yard on 31 December each year.
(b) The percentages represent the share in total w.i.p or total annual profit within each category (hulls or mountings) provided by work for Japan.
(c) Barrow was Vickers' shipbuilding base in the U.K. The steel-making base was in Sheffield. It would certainly have received Japanese orders. But no equivalent set of accounts exists for the Sheffield plant.

Source: Vickers Archive, Returns of Profit and Work in Progress, Barrow Shipyard, 1903–16.

with restrained foreign participation, were more appropriate for both political and technological reasons.

Indeed, it is somewhat surprising that the British share in Seikō Sho was so high, at least in the limited period to 1917. As Table 1 shows, Vickers' stake in the Muroran arsenal claimed the largest share of the company's total overseas investment embodied in a single plant before 1914. The explanation for this is the high ranking in its worldwide markets attributed by Vickers to Japan. In terms of product exports alone, tables 2 and 3 reveal just how valuable Japanese trade was to the British firm: between 1900 and 1914, Japan was the most important foreign customer for the most powerful British arms firm. So an investment commitment to Japan was also worth special attention.

At the aggregate level, it may be true that trade with Japan was not a dominant interest for the western economies before 1914 and that investment in Japan was not a major feature of global investment by multinationals before 1940. But at the sector level the perspective can look very different. Certainly it looked different within the defense sector by the late 1900s. Japanese naval demand was a vital trade for the British defense multinationals. And in the ranking of the various satellite factories within the worldwide production network of the most active British arms producer, the Seikō Sho works clearly take pride of place.

IV. The Working of the Nihon Seikō Sho Agreement, 1907–14

By June 1908, the foundations of machine shops A and B at Muroran were complete. The Japanese government had supplied the Nihon Seikō Sho in secret with estimates of orders likely to be placed with them over the next seven years: 144 large guns as well as drive shafts for battleships and heavy cruisers, castings for ships' stems, and steam turbines for propulsion units. All armor plate contracts, on the other hand, were to be reserved for the state arsenal at Kure.[10] Nevertheless, the British interests were well pleased with this report, believing that it heralded full order books in the near future.

This was the honeymoon period. As so often happens when dealing with state customers, the British multinationals found that promises of orders were not the same as busy factories. By early 1910, Albert Vickers, chairman of Vickers, was complaining to Andrew Noble, chairman of Armstrong, that the Japanese government had reneged on its undertakings. The expected large orders had been postponed. Albert Vickers commented indignantly, "Orders for Admiralty requirements of steel should be given to our two firms on the grounds that we were building these works for Japan . . . they have certainly broken all their promises as to the large orders they were going to give us."[11]

However, all was not lost: there was still the agency role of Nihon Seikō Sho to exploit for current profit, and there was still the technology level at Muroran to promote as an investment in the future. By late 1909, Vickers was well pleased with the profitability of the submarine work they had won through the Seikō Sho connection. Albert Vickers reported to the American patent holders that "we are now manufacturing [at Barrow] three sets of machinery for Japan for which the prices are so good that you may count the order equal to three [complete] boats."[12] By 1910 the artillery work being carried out in England on orders transferred from Japan was worth £300,000. In 1911, Vickers was making components for large (12-inch) guns to be finished at Muroran. More importantly, at about the same time, they were providing weaponry for the Japan-built copies of the *Kongō* and supplying turbines "in accordance with the latest [British] Admiralty practice" for the *Kongō*-clone being built by Mitsui Shipbuilding.[13] Later in the same year, Armstrong was providing forgings both for the Vickers-built *Kongō* and for the Japanese copy being built at Yokosuka. Simultaneously, Vickers itself was quoting for £50,000 worth of turbine rotor forgings required for the Japanese versions.[14] Whatever happened at Muroran, therefore, the agency aspect of the Seikō Sho agreement gave Vickers and Armstrong enviable control of the Japanese market for many types of armaments, at least down to 1914.

But what happened at Muroran should not be discounted. The promise to send "skilled officials to assist in production" was made good. A senior engineer from Vickers, L.D. Renwick, spent many months at Muroran in 1910 and 1911 advising on management practices.[15] Moreover, in order to provide guidance at the shop-floor level, Vickers dispatched skilled workers from Sheffield and Barrow to Muroran. Letter Book 14 records on 28 May 1912 that "British foremen, smelters and workmen have been sent out to Japan."[16] And, of course, Japanese officials and managers came the other way, in order to study how matters were managed in Vickers' shipyards and steel mills. Mr. Hosoya from Muroran visited the U.K. to inspect leading British steel works in 1910.[17] There is evidence also that Vickers' guidance extended outside strict organizational and technical advice into the realms of financial management and cost accounting. Thus, in 1911, Seikō Sho sent a deputation of Japanese accountants from Muroran to study the bookkeeping methods employed by Vickers at its major plants.[18] Indeed, 1911 was the year of visits. In August, Captain Ansaka and Commander Yoshida of the IJN visited Sheffield and Newcastle to study gun-making from the scientific perspective. One month previously, no less a figure than Admiral Tōgō, the victor of Tsushima, had come with the entire Second Japanese Cruiser

Squadron to see the new Royal Navy battleships building at Barrow.[19] And a month into the new year, 1912, Professor Kamo, professor of Marine Engineering at Tokyo University, came to Barrow for a period of research into turbine manufacturing, one of the most difficult areas of current big-ship technology.

This was a particularly active period for Japanese visitors to the senior British armament firms, but it was only a more intense phase of a practice that had become almost routine. Throughout the period 1905–14 there was a constant stream of Japanese technical, naval, and industrial missions through these works. And, of course, while Japanese ships were building in British yards, naval officers, inspectors of the IJN construction department, were billeted permanently with the firms. They provided important channels for technical information back to Japan and invaluable commercial contacts with the Japanese Admiralty for the British builders. The cumulative effect of these various fact-finding devices upon the level of Japanese practice, both at Muroran and elsewhere, must have been considerable. Testimony to one set of effects elsewhere is provided by a letter of January 1912 from Admiral Matsumoto, chief controller of the IJN, thanking Vickers for their help "concerning the manufacture of certain mechanisms in Japanese Government Arsenals."[20]

However, not every stroke of the British multinational strategy in the Japanese armament market worked so well. There were basically two problems affecting the Seikō Sho venture: one was the postponed IJN orders for Muroran itself; the other was increasing competition in Japan from both indigenous and foreign producers. The first inevitably led to the British multinationals placing a certain discount on the importance of their direct operation in Japan, and rather more emphasis on its agency role. The second created strains even within the agency relationship.

By 1911, competition was pressing from all sides. In order to meet competition from Mitsubishi Shipbuilding at the end of the year, Vickers was having to provide a 5% discount on all forging work executed for Japan.[21] In the same month of October, Vickers noted with some trepidation the arrival in the Far East of the formidable Charles M. Schwab of the United States Steel Trust and the Bethlehem Steel Company. He went first to China and then to Japan. Vickers commented, "He is after the same object here, not only warships but bridges, docks and railway material . . . a great reception will be given him in commercial circles."[22] With somewhat more irritation, Vickers had recorded in August 1911 that the Kawasaki Dockyard had been appointed agents for the turbine and machinery designs of their British rivals, the Coventry Ordnance Works and John Brown of Clydebank.[23]

By 1912, Vickers was sufficiently worried by the level of competition to ask Seikō Sho to waive its commission on work remitted to England and Mitsui to reduce theirs from 5 to 3%. Their aim, of course, was to be able to quote a keener price to the final consumer. In February 1912, they were considering, as a device for averting attacks from a powerful Japanese source, an alliance with Mitsubishi. During the next month both Vickers and Armstrong, each on its own account, pursued an agreement with this great Japanese concern, but, for the time being, without success.[24] This episode possessed a twin significance: first, if the two British firms were seeking independently to come to terms with Mitsubishi, conditions must have been severe (rivalry between these two close associates was a sure sign of trouble); and secondly, if this agreement had succeeded, Vickers and Armstrong would have been connected, through Mitsubishi as well as through Nihon Seikō Sho and Mitsui Bussan, with a massive concentration of zaibatsu power, the very highest echelons of the Japanese corporate structure and the two most powerful business enterprises in Japan.

Relations between the British multinationals and Seikō Sho undoubtedly suffered as a result of these pressures. In particular, the British multinationals came to suspect that Seikō Sho regarded them as a gravy train. The basis of this belief was Seikō Sho's habit of charging commissions not only on the orders passed on by themselves to their British associates but on *all* orders which were placed by the Japanese authorities with the British armorers.

Understandably enough, Vickers was upset by this but professed to see no way of escaping the imposition. Douglas Vickers lamented, "If we do not do so, the whole influence of the Seikō Sho may be used against our types and systems so as to turn orders towards Armstrong."[25] Vickers were also concerned that any unfriendly action by Seikō Sho would let other British competitors, especially John Brown and the Coventry Ordnance Works, into the market. But in fact they had already developed an answer to the problem: it was to bypass Seikō Sho, and even their own agent in Japan, and seek Japanese orders directly from Barrow and Sheffield. What allowed them to do so was the connection built up through the Japanese delegations to England and the Japanese naval inspectors stationed at their British works. Douglas Vickers explained to Winder in April 1912 that "our relations with the Japanese staff here [Barrow] have been so good that we look upon them as the best channel for approach to the Japanese Government."[26]

Speaking of engines, armor, and turrets for cruisers being built in Japan, Vickers told their agent in Tokyo, "We are quite aware of the very large orders that are pending and some of them are even absolutely promised to us already . . . We are so directly in touch with the authorities who have the sole power of giving out contracts . . . We have negotiations in hand of which you are ignorant." He was then given his instructions: "Let us know all you hear and say nothing."[27] It was remarkable that Vickers should have developed such close relations with the Japanese Admiralty that they could afford to dispense with the services of their own highly competent agent in Japan. Of course, it was true that these relations were built up within a process of which the Seikō Sho arrangement was itself a stage. Nevertheless, in the final years before World War I, the more successful of the two British armament multinationals was employing those relations to dominate the Japanese weaponry market not only through but also *around* its associated company.

In one sense, however, Vickers was too successful at this. The extreme of friction between Seikō Sho and Vickers was reached at the end of 1910. Both the Japanese interests and the British shipyard tendered independently for the massive battle cruiser *Kongō*. Mitsui Bussan won the contract for Vickers Barrow. And it was clearly enabled to do so by the famously cordial contacts between the procurement officials of the IJN—many of whom would have served a term or so at Barrow—and the shipyard officials back in Britain. Vickers was very anxious to secure this exceptionally valuable order and to cut through the complications in their Japanese representation in order to get it. It proved in the Japanese courts in 1914 that they had been over anxious, for Sir James McKechnie, Vickers' managing director of shipbuilding, was shown to have passed large sums of money to high officials of the Japanese Admiralty, most notably Admiral Fujii, in order to put the *Kongō* contract beyond doubt. The irony is that Vickers would probably have taken it anyway. But clearly, concern over competitive conditions in the Japanese market, including competition with Seikō Sho, seduced McKechnie into an ill-considered act. It was the most celebrated, or infamous, and best-documented, of the prewar armament scandals.[28]

However, the main effect of the Fujii affair, apart from causing some embarassment to Vickers and some discomfort to a number of high Japanese officials, was to change the manner of Vickers' representation in Japan. Mitsui Bussan, which was deeply implicated in the case, felt it wiser to resign as agent. Also, it seems that maneuvering among the shareholders of Hokutan—the British partners having no monopoly on fraternal disputation—may have permitted the Mitsui interests to exercise an influence upon Seikō Sho by alternative methods, that is, through equity leverage upon its Japanese parent.[29] In any event, the outcome for Vickers was primarily to move its direct connection with the highest levels of Japanese business from one part of the zaibatsu structure to another. For the desired relationship with Mitsubishi was now accomplished: this second major Japanese conglomerate became Vickers's agent in Japan in 1913.

V. Nihon Seikō Sho: The Medium-Term Outcome

Despite the frictions between the British and Japanese parts of the international consortium, Nihon Seikō Sho began to come right as an investment in 1914. In that year it paid its first dividend, a very restrained 1%. But it followed this with 2.5% in 1915, 6.5% in 1916, and a very creditable 12.5% in 1917. Many Japanese engineering and defense suppliers profited from European demand during World War I, and Seikō Sho was no exception. By 1928, Vickers and Armstrong had received jointly £723,067 in dividends from the Muroran venture. This represented 94% of the cost of the original investment. So, viewed purely as a financial transaction, the Japanese diversification of the British armament empire had at least virtually paid for itself in its first two decades of existence. But, of course, Nihon Seikō Sho could not be viewed simply as an investment. It was part of a British armament industry presence in Japan which brought Vickers' U.K. factories contracts worth around £10 million between 1907 and 1914. The profit on the *Kongō* alone would have exceeded comfortably Vickers' entire earnings on its Seikō Sho shares over twenty-odd years. The judgment of J. D. Scott, the official historian of Vickers, on the Muroran venture—that by 1914 it "had hardly emerged from tutelage"— is neither especially true nor especially relevant.[30]

The profitable year 1917 saw some important rearrangements in the Vickers–Armstrong–Seikō Sho agreement. The Mitsui Bank, the largest creditors of Hokutan, extended the interest created in 1913 and bought out the debtor company entirely at this time. Thus the array of forces behind Seikō Sho became more explicitly: Vickers–Armstrong–Mitsui–Mitsubishi. Mitsubishi had been Vickers' agent since 1913, but in September 1917 the nature of its relationship with the British firm was expanded. The most important of the alterations was a license to make and sell submarines to Vickers' designs. The new accord realized the British ambition of the prewar years to associate *both* Mitsui and Mitsubishi directly with their ventures in Japan. It was consolidated by a new agreement between the British multinationals and Seikō Sho which largely superseded the compact of 1907. Under its terms, Seikō Sho became the sole agents in Japan for both the armaments and commercial products of Vickers and Armstrong.

VI. The Dénouement

At the time of the new agreement, Vickers was pinning a substantial measure of hope on their Japanese links. Their large-scale Turkish dockyard had been confiscated in 1914 and their interests in the Tsaritsyn armory and the Nicolaiev shipyard had gone the same way in the Russian Revolution of 1917. Only their works in Spain and Japan had shown any success in recent years.

To begin with, they were not disappointed. Seikō Sho, under the guidance of Mitsui, entered an expansive phase in 1918 and 1919, absorbing a string of subsidiaries, including two iron foundries, one of them the important Wanishi works. However, in the process, Seikō Sho became a much more distinctively Japanese concern. In order to finance the acquisitions, Mitsui raised the total equity of Seikō Sho to ¥30 million, while the joint British share remained at ¥7.5 million. Within two years, therefore, Mitsui had raised the share of Japanese capital in the venture from 50% to 75%. For the first time, but not for the last, the British interests felt themselves being moved to the margin. And they were entering a period in world economic history, and especially in Japanese economic history, when the margin was not a comfortable place to be.

This was not the only ominous development. Relations between Vickers and Armstrong within the Seikō Sho scheme, as within many of their joint prewar ventures, had often been stormy, sometimes acrimonious. In 1920, Vickers found the going particularly rough. At this point they discovered that three years previously Armstrong had secretly withdrawn from the "new" 1917 agreement—almost immediately after signing it—and struck a fresh unilateral agreement with Mitsui covering only armament products. They were clearly limiting their risks. Vickers, realizing that they had been left overexposed by the Armstrong démarche, had no option but to seek a revision in similar terms. This was made active retrospectively from November 1919, and the Japanese side rather shrewdly limited its term to three years.

The optimistic pointers of 1918 and 1919 in the Japanese market, as in so many markets worldwide in these months, rapidly swung about. This was especially so for any business with interests in the defense sector. Almost all British operators in this field realized that, after the massive effort of servicing the domestic war economy, they would face a painful period of readjustment and forced diversification. However, they hoped for some relief from civilian engineering work and the more distant foreign markets. They were to be sorely disappointed.

In Japan, they faced almost as sharp a rebuff from the market as they encountered anywhere. The inevitable postwar contraction in the armament market was delivered to the naval sector—the one in which Japan was most interested and the main reason for Vickers's interest in Japan—in the formal shape of the Washington Naval Conference of 1922. The reductionist policy which emerged from the conference became public at about the time the Seikō Sho agreement came up for renewal. With the major powers cutting back on their warships, Japan saw no purpose in ordering more for herself. For Vickers, the consequence was that the Seikō Sho agreement was simply not renewed. Intelligibly, if brusquely, the Japanese interests behind the works at Muroran, that is, effectively Mitsui, terminated the agency arrangement and the system for passing on work to the British armorers. Vickers and Armstrong were left contemplating canceled contracts worth well over £1 million and reflecting once more on the delights of dealing with governments, their own or anybody else's.

Just as the armament multinationals were among the first international corporations to experience the attractions of the Japanese market, so they were unusually early in encountering its less attractive features.

By 1923 the two British multinationals had concluded that it was time to become less international. Certainly, they saw little prospect of profitable operation in the Japanese market, judging by its reaction to the new political influences, and they wished to get out. Rumors of a compensation scheme by which the Japanese government would reimburse Seikō Sho for its canceled contracts seemed to offer a way. Vickers suggested that they would forgo the compensation money if, in return, the Japanese government would purchase the British holding in the Muroran arsenal. This the government refused to do, and as J. D. Scott puts it, Vickers and Armstrong remained "compulsory shareholders" in Seikō Sho long after this first attempt to disengage.[31] The shares, now the only paying aspect of the connection, brought in an average of £34,000 per year from 1918 to 1925.

With similar withdrawals by governments occurring throughout the world defense market, the mightiest arms corporations of the prewar world fell upon hard times in the inter-war years. For Armstrong they were so hard that the firm disappeared as an independent organization. The new, fused company of Vickers-Armstrong was formed in 1928 in order to rationalize capacity and tailor it to shrunken markets. When Vickers-Armstrong took over the holding in Seikō Sho in 1928, the shares for which £766,612 had been paid were worth £150,000. Seikō Sho had also suffered its portion of shrunken markets in the preceding decade.

The final episode of the story is related to the Great Crash and the revival of militarism in Japan. In 1931, Seikō Sho was reconstituted as a limited company with a reduced capital, and the Wanishi Ironworks, which had been an additional source of difficulties in troubled markets ever since its acquisition, was split off. Wanishi was strongly affected by the reformist and "planning" tendencies of government during the radical phase of the middle and later 1930s. In 1934 it was incorporated into the industry-wide combine of iron and steel producers formed by government decree. The prospects for this great metal combine as the Japanese economy pulled out of the slump were good. Japan executed a rapid—to some western observers, startlingly fast—adjustment to the "new industries" of vehicles, aircraft, chemicals, and electrical engineering during the 1930s, and demand for plant from these sectors could only benefit the metal producers. However, the combine was formed too late, in a period of deteriorating international relations, to bring any benefit through Wanishi and Seikō Sho to Vickers-Armstrong.

Indeed, throughout the decade, the British firm pursued its efforts to get out of Japan. Scott believes that in 1928 "it was still not Board policy to treat all the foreign holdings as being fundamentally bad money,"[32] although this is scarcely a strong statement. In fact, the outlook for a British armament connection in Japan was not bright. This was so in the pre-Crash year, amid civilian governments and tendencies to disarmament. It remained just as true in the post-Crash phase, among expansionist governments and tendencies to rearmament. How could rearmament be bad for an armament multinational? For one thing, the political sympathy which had existed between Britain and Japan in the 1900s no longer obtained in the 1930s. For another, where rearmament had carried a deterrent connotation before 1914, it held quite different meanings by the 1930s.

But, more fundamentally, Japan simply did not need the technological assistance with this demanding industrial discipline that it had required in its apprenticeship phase. The manufacturing structure created in Manchukuo, under the framework of the Four-Year Plan—and, more immediately under the eye of the Kwantung Army—was heavily dependent on military demand and could make anything that the military required. Neither there nor on the main islands did Japanese shipbuilders, steel masters, engineers, or aircraft constructors need any further instruction from those who had led the field in the 1900s. Table 4 reveals just how rapidly the technological lag was drawn back, and technological absorption completed, in the case of naval shipbuilding.

The Vickers management was well aware of these considerations and from 1934 renewed serious efforts to dispose of their interest in Seikō Sho,

Table 4 Total Tonnage of Armored Ships Serving in the Imperial Japanese Navy by Source of Construction: 1908, 1931, 1940

Year	Total Tonnage	% Built in Japan	% by Japanese Private Yards	by % Foreign Private Yards	% by V & A
1908	307,071	57	0	43	28
1931	292,400	91	40	9	9
1940	432,640	90	38	10	6

Notes: (a) V & A=Vickers Ltd. & Armstrong, Whitworth & Co. Ltd.; from 1928 Vickers-Armstrong Ltd.

(b) In 1908 the IJN also contained a further 82,745 tons of heavy warships captured from the Russians at Tsushima. These vessels, built in Russia, the U.S.A., and France, are excluded because they do not represent original Japanese technological or design preferences.

(c) All Japanese home construction in 1908 was by the government dockyards at Kure and Yokosuka.

(d) Japanese private construction in 1931 and 1940 was by Asano, Kawasaki, and Mitsubishi.

(e) The number of fighting units represented by the tonnage figures were: 26 in 1908, 10 in 1931, and 22 in 1940.

Source: *Brassey's Naval Annual*, 1908, 1931, 1940.

this time trying to persuade Mitsui to purchase outright the British holding. Mitsui was not unamenable to the proposal to end what for them must have become a troublesome complication by this time. But it was scarcely an urgent consideration for the zaibatsu during the rearmament phase. Nor was the Japanese government of this era much minded to ensure recompense for a British connection that had outlived its usefulness. Viewed in the coldest light, there was little real interest for Japanese capital or Japanese officialdom in buying out the multinational interest; it might as well be allowed to die slowly until the holding was worth nothing.

VII. Parallel and Contrasting Cases: Chemicals and Explosives, 1905–30

Where suppliers of finished products, whether they be cotton cloth or cruisers, could only lose by the development of industrialization in new sectors of the world economy, the situation was more complicated for the manufacturers of semi-manufactured products, the inputs for other industries. The British chemical industry before 1914 was an important producer of such goods and, in the field of alkali exports, a highly competitive one. Another sector of the chemical industry produced an equally vital "software" input for the military machine, explosive propellants. In each department Britain possessed one of the most powerfully performing enterprises in the world: Brunner, Mond in alkalis and Nobel Explosives in propellants. Multinationals in their own right before 1914, these two organizations were merged in 1926 (along with United Alkali and British Dyestuffs) into one of the largest British multinationals of modern times, Imperial Chemical Industries. These two chemical producers, one military, the other civilian, offer a useful control on the experience of the great armament engineering companies, and on one another.

Japan by the 1900s presented a rich market for both military explosives and alkalis. The expanding Japanese army and navy needed propellants for the many guns and ships they were making and buying. An industrializing and urbanizing society needed alkalis for a variety of manufacturing processes, not least the production of glass. The differences in the methods used to market these products in Japan, and the differences in the commercial outcome, within this time period are instructive.

The Nobel Explosives Co. of Ardeer was a subsidiary of the enormous Anglo-German Nobel Dynamite Trust. It produced commercial explosives, primarily for the mining industry, and propellants, almost exclusively for governments. In Britain it controlled a specialist producer of military explosives called the Chilworth Gunpowder Co., and by 1914 had secretly absorbed almost all the half-dozen or so firms which supplied the British government with military explosives. It was linked through NDT with the bulk of the German explosives industry and with many companies in France, Italy, and Spain; in addition, the Nobel companies maintained enormously detailed market-sharing arrangements with the American explosives giant, Du Pont. The British Chilworth company was especially interesting, because from 1885 it was a wholly owned subsidiary of the Rheinisch-Westphalische Pulverfabriken, an important enterprise on the German side of the Anglo-German network. Chilworth was thus an outpost of the German military explosives industry, the Powder Group, within the British economy. Before 1914, few multinational organizations were as complex as this one.

In 1900, Nobel Explosives desired closer relations with the great British armament firms. It wished to improve its own capability for negotiating with governments by tapping the expertise of those more professionally committed to these skills than itself. And it wished to protect its own military trade from possible diversification by the gunmakers. It achieved these objectives by an agreement struck with Vickers in 1900. The capital structure of Chilworth was rearranged to give Vickers 40% of the equity, while the remaining 60% went to another representative of the Powder Trust, the Koln-Rottweiler company. In return, Vickers undertook to obtain all their propellant needs from Nobel companies, to tie weaponry orders to Nobel explosive orders wherever they could, and to keep out of the explosives trade.[33]

Nobel's introduction to Japan came about as one of the many results of the admiration of a fledgling for a senior naval power. Very few nations followed Britain into the adoption of cordite as their military propellant. But the Imperial Navy made Japan an exception. In 1899, it placed with Nobel's British factories a massive cordite order which took two years to manufacture. This was the first Japanese cordite contract, and the IJN was pleased with the product.

But it was concerned by the time taken to process large orders, and also by the delay in transporting them to Japan. As with Seikō Sho, the logical step was to set up manufacture in Japan. Again the technology was demanding, and there was no existing domestic base. So, "at the instance of the Japanese government,"[34] Nobel agreed to lead the development of the technology in Japan. True to form, they did not come alone. Correctly, they calculated that their friends in the armament trade would ease their path in dealings with an unfamiliar government. So when the Japan Explosives Company was incorporated in 1905, with a capital of £100,000, Armstrong put up £20,000 of it and the remaining £80,000 was contributed by the Vickers–Nobel–Chilworth connection. Thus, elements of British and German multinational capital, of heavy manufacturing and chemical processing, were all mobilized to create an explosives factory in Japan. Exceptionally, the whole of the capital was held by the foreign interests. This was not Vickers' style at all and it was far from the usual preference of the Japanese state. It is tempting to think that the enormous international leverage of the Nobel interest led that enterprise to insist on overall control, but there is no evidence on this score.

But not even Nobel money could prevent the Japan Explosives Co. from sharing the fortunes of Seikō Sho after 1918. Armament and explosives plants served the same masters and bent before the same winds.

Alkali makers faced less rigorous demands and experienced pleasanter breezes. They, too, found Japan an expanding market in the 1900s. Developing industrial economies indeed formed their favored stamping ground. The United Alkali Company exported 2,000 tons to Japan in 1901 and 10,000 tons in 1910, but it was far outstripped by Brunner, Mond, which sent out 27,000 tons in 1914. Denied access to the American market by the restrictions covering the working of the Solvay process, Brunner, Mond found in the manufacturers of Japan its biggest export market in the world by 1913. Yet, where the gun-making and explosives multinationals possessed operational factories in Japan by 1910, the highly entrepreneurial civilian producer, Brunner, Mond, did not even create a branch office there until 1918.

However, two years later, Brunners' upgraded its Japanese office into a local company on a footing with its similar offshoots in India and China. This operation was an enormous success during the 1920s. While the military producers wallowed in the wake of the Washington Conference, the civilian producer sewed up a market and won a famous competitive victory.

By 1924, Brunners' turnover in Japan was £2.5 million, but only one-third of this came from the sales of its own products. And it made nothing in Japan: all products were shipped out from Britain. This was a tactic in which ICI persevered against increasingly violent Japanese competition in the 1930s. Before the merger, the bulk of Brunner's Japanese turnover came not from its own chemical sales but from agency business on behalf of other, non-competing British companies in a variety of trades; that is, Brunners' provided a sales network for many other foreign manufacturers. Brunners' sold their local expertise for a commission to exporters less knowledgeable than themselves on the special features of Japanese markets.

However, this was far from irrelevant for the Japanese alkali trade. Indeed, the device allowed Brunners' to drive their own competitors to the wall. In the early 1920s the Magadi Soda Co. began off-loading alkali in Japan at knockdown prices. Despite the severity of the price competition, Brunners' were able to use their multifarious agency earnings to finance price reductions which Magadi proved unable to survive. By 1925, Brunners' were taking ¥1 million in profit from Japan, a return of 34% on the issued capital of the local company. This distinguished British enterprise fought the fiercest competitive battle of its career in its best market, in Japan during the 1920s. In order to do so, it relied upon selling industrial inputs, manufactured in Britain, to a still-expanding civilian economy. But in a Japanese market offering difficulties and high information costs to outsiders, Brunners' also made a considerable living by selling expertise. Crucially, however, it sold this expertise not to Japanese governments and manufacturers, who were quickly developing their own, but to other western capitalists who were somewhat slower to master the practices of Japanese commerce.

VIII. Conclusion

For this small array of high-technology British enterprises, the prime opportunity conditions within the Japanese business environment from

1900 to 1941 were technological and political. Before 1914, both types of conditions were strongly positive: Japan needed technical advice in the defense industries and chemical inputs in civilian manufacturing, and political relations were favorable. In the inter-war period, both types of conditions worsened. The political constraint fell upon the suppliers of finished military goods in the immediate aftermath of World War I; the technological constraint operated rather more slowly. But by the 1930s all constraints—adverse international relations, domestic political developments, technical self-sufficiency—were in place. Foreign suppliers of semi-finished civilian products prospered before 1914 and for longer after 1918. They were not affected by the changes in international relations in the 1920s, although, of course, they encountered problems from Japan's domestic political adjustments in the 1930s. Moreover, the nature of their product protected them from the technological backlash for longer.

But it is in the nature of all technological lags to be eroded. It is clear that British companies, "civilian" and "military," succeeded most readily when they had a technological lag to service. And it is axiomatic that this can offer only a temporary form of success.

Success for the defense supplier is, of course, uniquely dependent on international relations and upon relations with the host government. No other type of industrialist is so dependent upon the workings of these two political "markets." Unfortunately, of course, they are markets which have a tendency to alter drastically and suddenly. I have written in many places about the "special relationship" between governments and defense contractors.[35] The relationship can include such friendly devices as subsidies, research allowances, or non-competitive agreements, but it rarely includes considerate treatment when the cycle of international tension turns down or urgency subsides. This is true of many governments, but it will be particularly true of governments dealing with foreign defense suppliers, where not even the consideration of maintaining existing capacity against possible future crises is present. In the armaments industry the conventional commercial imperative is reversed: *caveat vendor*, let the seller beware.

It is this feature which explains why the Japanese market deteriorated earlier for the defense multinationals than for most other types of multinational, in the 1920s rather than the 1930s.

But, then again, the British defense firms did succeed when circumstances were in their favor, down to 1914. The cumulative worth for Vickers of the rewards which came through, or around, the Seikō Sho project was enormous. Within the global strategy of the British defense industry Japan before 1914 was a prime target. An industrializing economy generated wealth which could finance substantial purchases of weaponry. The country's strategic predicament required such purchases. The naval bias within strategy favored purchase from the world's premier maritime power. Proficient Japanese use of British warships was a good advertisement to other customers. Proficient Japanese manufacturing created—at least temporarily—a market in which arms technology could be sold when armament product was not required in the original quantities. Some other markets—Italy, Spain, Russia—offered some of these qualities. But Japan offered probably the best combination. However modest trade with, or investment in, Japan may have been at the macroeconomic level for the advanced western nations, these special features made the Japanese defense sector an outstandingly attractive marketplace for some of the largest international business ventures of the era.

For civilian semi-manufacturers, too, a rapidly growing economy of some competence, where restrictive license conditions did not apply, was an attractive spot on the globe. Japan was not only Vickers' most important market in the 1910s; it was also Brunner's most important market in the 1910s and 1920s. Special conditions of several types underwrote foreign success, while they lasted.

It is fairly clear, too, that defense technology was successfully transferred. There were many channels: the physical plant created at Muroran; ship designs; training of staff; advice to senior personnel, whether admirals or professors; the flotillas of naval inspectors who watched the big ships go together, rivet by rivet, at Barrow or Newcastle; and the careful imitation of these vessels by Japanese yards. Japan's metallurgy and her naval architecture, her ability to build for herself by the 1930s the biggest of big ships and vessels as direly complex as the submarine, compose a grim tribute to the effectiveness of this transfer. Western industrialists commented on the remarkable speed of technological absorption in Japan. In naval shipbuilding full confirmation of this is available: Table 4 provides entirely convincing proof of skills absorbed and technology domesticated. And difficult as they are to track or quantify, there will also have been gains to civilian shipbuilding, to general machine practice and to steel or turbine technology.

In the organizational sense, it is striking that the British defense producers replicated within pre-1914 Japan the relationships of the British military-industrial complex. The same dominant firms which built a special relationship with the British procurement departments, and with one another, are to be found repeating the process in Japan. Interestingly, of course, they associated the largest of Japanese industrial concerns with this development. The zaibatsu already had their own special relationships with government, but presumably found these new connections educative. They might have noted with surprise that the replication of the military-industrial relationships in Japan also included the replication of the strains and hostilities within the system.

The agreements and collusions employed by British firms at home and abroad never ruled out conflict. Compacts existed but they did not always bind. The competitive edge displayed in Japan between Armstrong and Vickers, *within* the framework of an agreement, is a good, but not isolated, example of this. The jockeying for position within the shareholding of Hokutan in the 1910s suggests matching tensions among the Japanese capital interests. And the friction which developed between Seikō Sho and Vickers over the *Kongō* contract shows that conflict need not be confined within the two national camps. Competition between the components of the armament multinationals was not uncommon before 1914. These organizations were rarely the coherent, coordinated, and monopolistic engines of exploitation which some sorts of radical criticism have long assumed.

If joint ventures were an effective method for technological transfer, they were not immune to internal stresses and strains. Learning processes and conflict processes are by no means mutually exclusive.

Notes

1. Vickers Archive (hereafter VA): Evidence prepared for submission to the Royal Commission on the Private Manufacture and Trading in Arms, 1936 (Bankes Commission), Cd. 5292.
2. C. Trebilcock, *The Vickers Brothers: Armaments and Enterprise, 1854–1914* (London, 1977), pp. 146–47.
3. By adding to its Sheffield steel works, the artillery works of the Maxim-Nordenfeld Company, and the shipyard of the Naval Construction Company.
4. VA: Evidence submission for Bankes Commission.
5. Almost certainly, also the order for the *Kongō* was influenced by a celebrated bribery scandal (the Fujii affair of 1913). Vickers were prepared to push very hard to achieve domination in Japan.
6. VA: Correspondence of Albert Vickers, 16 December 1903, citing a Japanese Admiralty source.
7. I am grateful to Professor T. Yoneyama for the provision of these Japan-side details.
8. VA: Evidence submission for the Bankes Commission.
9. VA: Letter Book 11; Douglas Vickers to Basil Winder, 15 February 1912.
10. *Ibid.*, 12, pp. 718–20; Report of Count Hirosawa to Albert Vickers, 2 June 1908.
11. *Ibid.*, A. Vickers to A. Noble, 24 March 1910.

12. *Ibid.*, 31; Albert Vickers to Isaac Rice, Electric Boat Company, 16 November 1909.
13. *Ibid.*, 33; Vickers Ltd. to B. Winder, 25 February 1911.
14. *Ibid.*, 8, p. 970; Sir J. McKechnie (Barrow) to B. Winder, 4 October 1911.
15. *Ibid.*, 8, p. 84; 12 August 1911.
16. *Ibid.*, 14, p. 251.
17. VA: Microfilm 307.
18. VA: Letter Book 8, p. 407; Sir Trevor Dawson, Vickers London, to Vickers Sheffield, 1 September 1911.
19. *Ibid.*, 7, p. 32; Dawson to Vickers, Barrow, 16 June 1911.
20. *Ibid.*, 11; quoted by Dawson to S. Watanabe of Mitsui Bussan, 15 January 1912. The chief controller was the IJN's senior material and technical supply officer.
21. *Ibid.*, 8: Sir J. McKechnie, Barrow, to B. Winder, 4 October 1911.
22. *Ibid.*, 8, p. 988; October 1911.
23. *Ibid.*, p. 116; Dawson to Harrison of Armstrong, 15 August 1911.
24. *Ibid.*, 11; Douglas Vickers to Winder, 15 February 1912; 12, p. 781, Vickers to Winder, 26 March 1912.
25. *Ibid.*
26. *Ibid.*, 12; D. Vickers to Winder, 1 April 1912.
27. *Ibid.*, 33; Vickers to Winder, 16 March 1911.
28. Vickers prepared a special file of evidence for the 1936 Bankes Commission on the Fujii scandal. It was also widely reported in *The Times* and the *Japan Chronicle* between February and July 1914. Fujii admitted to receiving ¥0.3 million from Vickers and was sentenced to four years' imprisonment. He had recommended that the *Kongo* order should go to Vickers, but so had other officers who had not received equivalent encouragement. The matter had never been before the Vickers board, and the firm concluded that McKechnie was personally responsible.
29. Again, I am indebted to Professor Yoneyama for these details on Hokutan shareholding.
30. J. D. Scott, *Vickers, A History* (London, 1962), p. 85.
31. *Op. cit.*, p. 147.
32. *Ibid.*, p. 191.
33. See W. J. Reader, *Imperial Chemical Industries: A History, Vol. I: The Forerunners, 1870–1926* (Oxford, 1970); also, Clive Trebilcock, "Legends of the British Armament Industry, 1890–1914: A Revision," in *Journal of Contemporary History*, 5 (1970), pp. 13–15.
34. Reader, *ibid.*, p. 148.
35. See, for example, Clive Trebilcock, "A 'Special Relationship'—Government, Rearmament and the Cordite Firms," in *Economic History Review*, 19 (1966), pp. 364–79.

Comment

Takau Yoneyama

Dr. Trebilcock has provided a concise and lucid account of the foreign business of British multinationals in the late 19th and early 20th centuries. He has replied quite appropriately to the questions Professor Udagawa put forward. Moreover, Trebilcock has proved some facts that had not been given by Japanese historians. It is useful for Japanese historians to be given other aspects on joint ventures.

On the first question, Trebilcock's replies are as follows: Both Vickers-Armstrong and Brunner, Mond regarded Japan as a promising market. Because Japan was becoming a modern nation promoting several industries, she was seen as an important customer alongside Russia, Turkey, and Italy. Moreover, there was an Anglo-Japanese political relationship and the friendship between Japanese naval officials and British armorers. So the arrangement of Nihon Seikō Sho had been unusually smooth. Seikō Sho was established in 1907, with half of its capital owned by Armstrong and Vickers and the other half owned by Hokkaido Tankō Kisen (Hokkaido Colliery Steamship Co.), often called Hokutan.

Secondly, there were questions on the activities of foreign businesses in Japan. As for the motives of the foreign companies, Trebilcock has presented two suggestions: the supply-side incentives and demand. For the defense industry, the influences mainly lay on the demand side. Because a new generation of world economies were arising from political nationalism, these countries possessed manufacturing competence, political will, and a sense of insecurity sufficient to create an appetite for advanced defense industries. Yet, they lacked crucial elements of expertise. On the other sub-question—namely, what difficulties they encountered in Japan—there are many answers. The expected large orders to Seikō Sho were postponed, so that the foundation period 1907–1911 was a hard time for profitability. From his managerial standpoint, Albert Vickers complained that the Japanese government had reneged on its undertakings. Moreover there were some difficulties in the managerial phases. There were sometimes different opinions within Seikō Sho. Relations between Vickers and Armstrong within the Japanese scheme, as within many of their joint prewar ventures, was often stormy. It is very interesting that there was a split between Vickers and Armstrong, a fact that is hardly pointed out by Japanese historians. Furthermore, it was aggravated by the antagonism between Inoue Kakugorō and Mitsui Bussan up to 1910. Although Trebilcock has not pointed it out, different intentions of Japanese-side management were whirling within Seikō Sho, which caused the company some difficulties.

Lastly, the third question presented by Udagawa was a little difficult to cope with. Because he questioned the impact of the foriegn businesses upon Japanese companies, we have to study other Japanese companies in the same industry. Although Seikō Sho was not, strictly speaking, Japanese, it became distinctly Japanese when it increased its capital in 1919. As a result, the share of Japanese capital rose from 50 to 75%, decreasing Vickers-Armstrong's share to 25%. So the process of technology transfer from Vickers-Armstrong to Seikō Sho is one reply to the third question. Vickers-Armstrong's impact was not only on technology transfer but also on cost-accounting and management methods. British foremen, smelters, and workmen came to Japan. Japanese officials and managers visited Britain to study how Vickers' shipyard and steel mills were managed. It seems that Vickers-Armstrong willingly gave the Japanese an opportunity to learn from their technology and know-how. In short, their impact on Japanese business was far from disturbing to Japanese industries. It was not "penetration."

There are some addenda that it may be worthwhile to add to Trebilcock's points. Firstly, it may be necessary to explain the circumstances of the formation of Seikō Sho. The Japanese parent company was Hokutan. Inoue, the chairman of Hokutan, was against nationalization of the iron and steel industry. Since being recruited to Hokutan, he had been interested in undertaking iron- and steelworking. He asked Vice-Admiral Yamanouchi to make a field investigation into iron sand around the Funka Bay. Yamanouchi persuaded Inoue to manufacture arms in an Anglo-Japanese joint venture. He was personally acquainted with Andrew Noble. Moreover the Imperial Japanese Navy felt a need for more arsenals. They had only the one arsenal of Kure. Meanwhile, the Japanese government promoted the nationalization of the railway companies, so Hokutan had to get a large sum in compensation for the buying out of their railroad department. Then Inoue decided to build an ironworks. At this point, it may be useful to point out three distinctive features of Hokutan. The first one was its semi-official nature. The largest shareholder was the Imperial Household Agency. The second was the strong leadership of its chairmen, such as Amemiya Keijirō and Inoue. The active method of raising money was the third feature. Hokutan depended more heavily on external money than other Japanese companies did. Accordingly, Mitsui's influence on Hokutan seemed to be very small until 1910. Inoue resigned in 1910, feeling responsible for the sluggishness of the business. The price of coal, the main product, was falling drastically and the initial costs of Seikō Sho increasing. Murota Yoshifumi took over after him, but he could not solve the problem and resigned in 1912. Afterward, Dan Takuma, from Mitsui interests, proposed a radical plan of reorganization. Accepting the plan, Hokutan came under Mitsui influence. Therefore, Hokutan, and in turn Seikō Sho, was under the authority of Mitsui since 1913. Looking into the formation and the early business activities, we can understand that both sets of interests behind Seikō Sho were not always brotherly.

What may not be clear are the agency contracts. Trebilcock says that Mitsui Bussan was the agent for Vickers in Japan until 1913, when it was replaced by Mitsubishi. But the company history states that Seikō Sho was the sole agent of Vickers and Armstrong since 1908. As the sole agent, how did Seikō Sho cope with Mitsui Bussan between 1908 and 1913? Moreover, why was it replaced as agent by Mitsubishi in 1913? Trebilcock pointed out the importance of the Fujii affair, but the Japanese did not know about the Fujii affair (a part of the Siemens problem) until 1914.

I will now point out two contrary pieces of evidence. The first one is about the payment of compensation. The problem of compensation was brought about by the disarmament. The government paid it in September 1926. As for Seikō Sho, the total sum was about ¥14 million. The other point may be less important. This paper stated that all constraints including technical self-sufficiency were in place by the 1930s. Although this was a rare case, the delegation of Cosmo Johns, an engineer of Vickers, in 1930 might have been very important for Seikō Sho. His contribution to their steel-making is admired in the company history.

This paper also explained the cases of Nobel Explosives and Brunner, Mond. Nobel Explosives made a subsidiary of which shares were fully owned by the Trust. On the other hand Brunner, Mond never formed factories, and concentrated on sales of their own and other British products. As an agency, Brunner, Mond made a large sum of profit in the 1920s. But Nobel Explosives did not seem to make so much profit in the 1920s, as Vickers-Armstrong did. The difference in these performances is partly explained by the nature of the industry. The defense industry was not *caveat emptor*, but *caveat vendor*. The case of foreign diversification of the above three or four companies presents very interesting and useful facts. Although we cannot immediately generalize about these cases to fit the pattern of multinationals, they constitute a great contribution to the study of foreign diversification before World War II.

Response

Clive Trebilcock

Professor Yoneyama has made two substantial points. The first concerns the Japan-side influences behind Hokutan. The second relates to the agency arrangements maintained by Vickers between 1908 and 1917. In a sense, both point arise out of differences between the British and Japanese sources.

For obvious reasons, there is little in the English-language archive on the inner politics of the Japanese parent to Seikō Sho. I am grateful to Yoneyama for making available the details from the Japanese-language archive; I have incorporated some of them in my text, where relevant. The effect is primarily to reveal that the uneasy balance between the British partners in the Seikō Sho project was matched by a contest for control of Hokutan between the major Japanese corporate interests. Certainly Mitsui emerges as a more powerful influence than could be guessed from the British sources. My argument that joint ventures, though often efficient places, may not be especially peaceful ones, gains added strength from this interesting material.

On the second point, the archives clash. Yoneyama cites the Japanese official history of Seikō Sho to support the contention that the Muroran venture became the sole Japanese agent for Vickers and Armstrong in 1908. By contrast, the documents submitted by Vickers to the great British investigation of the armaments industry, the Royal Commission on the Private Manufacture and Trading in Armaments in 1935–36, are clear that the Seikō Sho received no sole agency until 1917. By that time it scarcely mattered. Within one year the cessation of World War I produced the most severe contraction in the global arms market that the modern defense industries had experienced. Within two years Mitsui had 75% control of Seikō Sho.

What does matter is the form of the British armorers' agency arrangements in Japan between 1908 and 1917. There is no indication in the British company papers that Vickers contemplated appointing any sole agent for its thriving Japanese business before 1914. That is not surprising. Indeed, there are excellent reasons why Vickers and Armstrong should have avoided strenuously any limitation to a single agent.

To begin with, Vickers had expert local representation of its own in Tokyo, in the shape of their agent Basil Winder, a man whose diplomatic contacts and commercial influence had served the company well in the past. They would not be likely to jettison these assets. Secondly, Vickers and Armstrong were interested—and it was a shrewdly directed interest—in establishing a connection with zaibatsu power. This was an obviously sensible objective for a world-class company entering a strange market: a question of like calling to like, allowing for all necessary translations. Thirdly, the initial arrangements for business transferred to the United Kingdom via Seikō Sho were distinctly specialized. The notion was that work that could not be carried out at Muroran should be seconded to Barrow or Newcastle. The British partners were willing to pay a 2.5% commission on such transfers. But they were also free to refuse them, or to sublet them in any way they pleased. This type of "overspill" agency is not usual and its restrictive terms do not suggest that the British firms would be willing to commit themselves to a sole agency with an enterprise that they had already limited in this way. Moreover, the manifest irritation of the British firms when Muroran began to behave *as if it were* a sole agency, charging commissions on all work derived from Japan, is spontaneous evidence that the British did not believe that Seikō Sho was entitled to such powers.

Before 1914, Vickers wanted a multi-layered form of representation in Japan: Winder for local knowledge and western contacts; a zaibatsu link for general trade connections in the upper reaches of corporate industry and government; and a specialized arms producer with good military introductions. It would not have been good business sense to discount the first and second in favor of a monopoly for the third.

However, after three years of war and ten years of Japanese technological progress, and as part of a postwar strategy for the Asian market, it would have been logical in 1917 to take a different line.

Four possible conclusions emerge:

(a) Before 1914, it was not in Vickers' interest to appoint Seikō Sho as sole agent.

(b) Vickers did not believe that they had done so.

(c) It is possible that, by misunderstanding, Seikō Sho believed that they *had* been so appointed.

(d) It is possible, but unlikely, that Vickers had conceded a sole agency to Seikō Sho but then chose to disregard the fact.

A combination of these would explain the actual course of events. A genuine sole agency for Seikō Sho from as early as 1908 would not.

Ties Between Foreign Makers and Zaibatsu Enterprises in Prewar Japan: Case Studies of Mitsubishi Oil Co. and Mitsubishi Electric Manufacturing Co.

Nobuhisa Fujita

I. Introduction

In prewar Japan many companies, most of them zaibatsu enterprises, were engaged in tie-up relationships with foreign makers. These relationships encompassed a wide variety of manufacturing businesses, including heavy electrical equipment, rubber, oil, and machinery.

The purpose of this paper is to consider the nature of tie-up relationships between zaibatsu enterprises and foreign makers in prewar Japan, using the cases of Mitsubishi Denki and Mitsubishi Sekiyu (Electric and Oil respectively) as examples. More specifically, the expectations of the zaibatsu enterprises and the attitudes taken during the formation of the relationships will be examined. As a case in point, an inquiry will be made into the advantages gained by Mitsubishi-related enterprises through such tie-ups and the subsequent managerial manipulation of those advantages. For example, how did quality improve as a result of the introduction of technology? Given an improvement, how was this change reflected in managerial, manufacturing, and sales activities? In short, what managerial changes took place?

Additionally, much weight has come to be given to the view that zaibatsu enterprise capital was extremely closely held. Despite this, there is a certain logic to the idea that tie-ups with foreign makers would go so far as to violate this concept. The demonstration of this logic, as far as it is possible, is also a focus of this paper.

This paper provides an overview of zaibatsu enterprise/foreign maker tie-ups, followed by case studies of Mitsubishi Denki and Mitsubishi Sekiyu, which will demonstrate the following two hypotheses:

First, that entering into tie-ups with foreign makers that resulted in new joint ventures, while allowing diversification, was carried out only when indispensible resources (technology, technicians, production equipment, raw materials, etc.) were not held by the zaibatsu, and that industries thus entered were comparatively new, with promising futures.

Second, that when existing zaibatsu enterprises formed tie-ups with foreign makers, the enterprises in question had certain requirements (technical information, management know-how, etc.) that needed to be met, due to a late start (compared with international or domestic competitors). That is to say, without long-term managerial intervention, successful development of such enterprises could not be expected.

It should be noted that the term *zaibatsu enterprise* indicates zaibastu holding companies or their subsidiaries. Also, it should be kept in mind that foreign enterprises involved in tie-ups being considered here are limited to manufacturing enterprises.

II. Overview: Tie-up Classification

Appendix A lists 22 zaibatsu enterprises which had tie-up relationships with foreign makers during the prewar period.[1] The holding companies or subsidiaries of Mitsui, Mitsubishi, Sumitomo, Furukawa, Nissan, and Nitchitsu zaibatsu maintained foreign tie-ups in electrical equipment, machinery, and a variety of other fields. Although the timing, motivation, equity ratios, and other factors differ by case, through examination of factors such as method of establishment of joint ventures and type of advantage sought through tie-ups, it is possible to divide the enterprises on the list into three basic types.

Type 1 consists of joint ventures established by zaibatsu enterprises in conjunction with foreign makers, resulting in entrance into completely new lines of business. Type 2 is composed of existing zaibatsu enterprises that formed ties with foreign makers in order to expand existing businesses. Type 3 consists of foreign-controlled businesses in which zaibatsu enterprises invested. Let us consider the characteristics of the three types and look at a few examples.

Included in Type 1 are the Mitsui affiliates, Nihon Seikō Sho, Tōyō Carrier Kōgyō, Tōyō Otis Elevator, and Shibaura Kyōdō Kōgyō; the Furukawa affiliates, Yokohama Gomu Seizōsho, and Fuji Denki Seizō; the Sumitomo affiliate, Sumitomo Aluminum; the Nitchitsu affiliates, Nihon Bemberg Kenshi and Asahi Kenshoku; and ten enterprises held by Mitsubishi Sekiyu. Divided by industry, we find a wide variety including two enterprises each in electrical equipment, rayon, and machinery, and one each in rubber, aluminum, steel, and oil. Looking at time of establishment, we find a large number of joint ventures that were founded in the first years of the Shōwa period (beginning in 1926). Divided by the original equity ratio, we find that more than half were 50–50 ventures.

Specifically, stock in the joint venture was often given to the foreign firm in return for technology. The advantages gained by the zaibatsu enterprise from such an agreement varied by case, but generally the foreign partner built the factory and supplied production equipment or furnished necessary technical assistance or raw materials. In many cases the foreign partner agreed to dispatch technicians on an as needed basis. In other words, although the zaibatsu enterprises were diversifying, they were generally inferior to their foreign partners in terms of indespensible resources. Let us look, then, at two typical cases, those of Yokohama Gomu Seizōsho (Rubber Manufacturing Co.) and Tōyō Otis Elevator.

In 1917, Yokohama Rubber Manufacturing was established with initial capital of ¥2.5 million as a joint venture between the American company B.F. Goodrich, which had plans to build manufacturing facilities in Asian markets, and a Furukawa zaibatsu affiliate, Yokohama Electric Wire Manufacturing Co., which was planning expansion into rubber manufacturing as a step toward diversification. At the time of the new company's founding, the Japanese rubber industry was still in its infancy, and most domestic rubber products were inferior to imports. According to the new venture's articles of incorporation, each partner was to hold 50% of the stock. However, of the first capital installment of ¥1 million, YEWM paid ¥800,000 in exchange for its ¥500,000 share, thus giving Goodrich (which paid only ¥200,000) ¥300,000 worth of stock at no charge. The new company began construction of a factory in July of 1918, with Goodrich providing all plans for the factory layout in addition to purchasing all the production machinery. Goodrich also sent technicians to install the newly purchased equipment. The venture began test production in July of 1920 and gradually started actual production, but during the testing stage a total of seven Goodrich technicians provided technical guidance in the areas of compounding, molding, and the production of final products such as tires, belts, and hoses. The Goodrich technicians also gave technical advice on general manufacturing processes and quality control. Actual production was based on Goodrich's compounding process, and the necessary compound ingredients, cotton cloth, etc., were ordered from Goodrich. The new company's board of directors was composed of ten members, with Goodrich sending two directors in addition to the vice-president, who also served as chief financial officer. The heads of manufacturing and research were Japanese who had received technical training at Goodrich. The venture had not even begun full production, however, when the factory was destroyed by the Great Kantō Earthquake. In 1928 a new agreement was concluded and production began again. As full production was reached, performance began to improve, and by 1933 the company was able to pay a dividend.[2]

Next let us take a look at the case of Tōyō Otis Elevator. TOE was established with initial capital of ¥1 million (raised to ¥2 million after only a few months) in 1932 as a joint venture between Mitsui Bussan, which had been selling imported elevators, and the Tokyo branch of Otis Elevator Co. (of America), which had been established in 1927 to import and distribute elevators, and which had plans to establish a production base in the Far East. At that time, strong companies like Mitsubishi Denki (Electric) and Hitachi Works were already in place as makers of elevators, but Tōyō Otis was the first specialized manufacturer of lift equipment in Japan. The new venture began construction of a factory while completely taking over Otis's Tokyo branch. Ownership was set at 60% for Otis and 40% for Mitsui (with the same ratio after the increase). Whether or not Otis technical advisors were present for the construction of the factory is unclear, but all of the production equipment was brought in from America. Production materials such as steel, rope, and sheet metal were all of domestic origin. Not only did Otis provide free of charge the use of some 28 patents covering safety and control devices, specialized life motors, etc., but technicians were dispatched and information for technical improvement was sent whenever needed. As for managerial personnel, Otis supplied one director and an auditor, although only the director was posted to Japan. Detailed records of the venture's finances are not available, but 200 units were produced in 1938, generating sales of approximately ¥2.5 million and capturing 60% of the total Japanese market. Subsequently the company was compelled to curtail production because of wartime controls.[3]

Type 2 enterprises, the reader may recall, are those which were formed by existing zaibatsu enterprises that established ties with foreign makers in order to expand and develop existing businesses. They include the Mitsui affiliate, Shibaura Seisakusho (Shibaura Engineering Works), which formed ties with General Electric (GE); Mitsubishi Denki, which tied up with Westinghouse Electric; and Sumitomo Wire and Cable Manufacturing Co., which formed ties with International Standard Electric, for a total of three. Each of these enterprises was involved in the electrical machinery industry, and each accepted capital investment from foreign makers during the period from the 1900s to the 1920s. (Sumitomo Wire and Cable Co. also received technical guidance from Western Electric in 1920, with Nippon Denki serving as intermediary.) The foreign shares were relatively small. These enterprises had been attempting to develop under their own power, but accepted foreign investment as a means of improving management and, more importantly, in order to overcome technical handicaps by securing advanced technology.

Next, let us briefly examine the case of Shibaura Engineering Works.[4] The tie-up relationship between Shibaura Engineering Works and GE was begun in 1909. Shibaura Engineering Works's capital was ¥1 million, raised to ¥2 million in 1910, with 24.75% of the stock (9,900 of 40,000 shares) being transferred to GE. Discussion of a relationship had started around 1897, but concrete consideration did not occur until about 1907. At that time Shibaura was the sole domestic maker of heavy electrical machinery but was limited to generators of less than 100 kw, and was far below the level of western makers. Noting the company's position, a director expressed the need for a foreign alliance as follows:

> Through many hard struggles, our company, Shibaura Engineering Works, has managed to reach its current position. Having already built this base, future development will not present serious difficulty. When it becomes necessary to expand, it will not be a problem to secure the necessary capital in Japan and we need not rely on foreign capital. However, I have come to feel that it is technology, rather than capital, that we need. . . . Compared to western technology, Japanese technology cannot be thought of as being in the same dimension. The current [western technological] situation is far above Japan's and, what is more, the [western] level of progress is much faster. In short, foreign companies have greater economies of scale, better equipment, and more research and development. Japanese enterprises have much to learn.[5]

It can be seen from this that Shibaura Engineering Works saw technology as being more important than capital, and that it fully realized how far it was behind western manufacturers. As a result of the tie-up with GE, Shibaura not only acquired the ability to manufacture large generators, transformers, and induction motors but also saw productivity, profits, and dividends rise. In addition, entrance was facilitated into the areas of fans and household appliances and into radio communications, thereby establishing the foundations for development into a general electrical-equipment manufacturer. Of course, GE provided technical designs and dispatched personnel on both short- and long-term assignments to help with production. GE also supplied necessary raw materials and parts, but sent only one or two directors. GE received a royalty of 1% of sales.

Type 3 enterprises (foreign-controlled ventures in which zaibatsu enterprises invested) are the Mitsui affiliates, Tōyō Babcock and Nihon Kenchiku Zairyō (Nihon Structural Steel Co.); the Sumitomo affiliates, Nippon Denki (Nippon Electric Co.), Nichibei Ita Garasu (Nichibei Sheet Glass), and Teikoku Sanso (Teikoku Oxygen); the Nissan affiliates, Nihon Victor, Nihon Chikuonki Shōkai (Nipponophone Co.), and Daidō Match; and the Asano affiliate, Tōyō, Kamibukuro (Tōyō Paper Bag), for a total of nine companies. Characteristics of this group are: (1) with the exception of one or two cases, the period in which the zaibatsu investment was made was concentrated from the late 1920s through the 1930s; (2) that the nucleus of such participation was composed of the new zaibatsu firm, Nissan; and (3) that the fields of investment were not in heavy industry but rather in light electrical products and other areas of manufacturing. The reasons for participation in these ventures by zaibatsu enterprises vary widely by case, but the influence on business activity of restrictions and exclusion of foreign capital are considered to be a major factor. Also, the new zaibatsu and slightly weaker original zaibatsu like Sumitomo may have participated in order to strengthen their positions by absorbing enterprises with future promise. A look at the case of Nippon Electric Co. and Nihon Victor may be instructive.

Sumitomo's involvement in the management of Nippon Electric Company (NEC), which was founded in 1899 with a 54% investment by Western Electric (subsequently International Western Electric, and later International Standard Electric), started in 1932. As a prelude to this, NEC and Sumitomo Densen Seisakusho had concluded a contract concerning the use of patents for telephone "phantom" cable in 1920. The contract reflected the dovetailing of NEC's needs with those of Sumitomo Densen. NEC's copper-wire-materials supply problems, its emergence from the role of specialized manufacturer, and its consideration of entry into the public telephone business fit neatly with Sumitomo Densen's desire to expand its product range. The contract provided for NEC's aquisition of 25% of Sumitomo Densen's stock (50,000 shares) with the latter receiving 5% (10,000 shares) of NEC. An exchange of directors was also agreed upon. NEC signed over the use of Western Electric's "phantom" cable patents to Sumitomo Densen, and also provided the related manufacturing equipment. In addition, the two companies concluded a representative agency contract. Since these contracts were between NEC and Sumitomo Densen, there was no direct relationship between the latter and WE.[6] From 1926, however, conditions for NEC gradually began to worsen. A major factor was Depression induced government budget reduction, in particular a large reduction in allocations for telephone network expansion. As a result, NEC's sales fell from a peak of ¥18.54 million in 1925 to a low of ¥4.07 million in 1931. Also, with the Manchurian Incident of 1931, encouragement of domestic production was strengthened, leading to strong competition and gradually taking the form of pressure against foreign capital. Products of companies which were not at least 51% Japanese-owned were not viewed as domestically produced. Because of this, the leadership of NEC as well as International Standard Electric needed another (Japanese) enterprise to provide equity participation. Given the situation, and given the above-mentioned close relationship with NEC, Sumitomo was the prime candidate. While NEC was losing favor with the government because of its connection with ISE, Sumitomo's reputation with the government and the military was quite good due to its previous development. Also, the two companies' product lines were complementary, and attention was paid to the fact that both had the (prewar) Communications Ministry as a customer. For Sumitomo, the opportunity to enter the communications-equipment field, an area in which there was no participant from the Sumitomo zaibatsu, was a big plus. Thus, negotiations were begun between ISE and Sumitomo, but at the beginning no agreement could be reached concerning the problem of the ratio of stock to be exchanged. An agreement was reached in 1932, however, which resulted in ISE holding 50% of NEC's shares, with Sumitomo acquiring 29% (including the shares previously held by Sumitomo Densen). Sumitomo also took primary control over NEC's personnel decisions. Thus, Sumitomo's participation in the management of NEC was the product of NEC's response to foreign capital exclusion and Sumitomo's desire to enter the communications-equipment manufacturing field.[7]

It was in 1936 that Nissan took a stake in Victor Talking Machine Company of Japan, a company which had been formed in 1926 with its total capital of ¥2 million having been supplied by Victor Talking Machine Co. (which was in turn purchased by Radio Corporation of America in 1929). Although the Mitsubishi and Sumitomo zaibatsu had previously invested in VTMJ, they provided only one director each, and so the effective control was held by RCA. It is not clear why Mitsubishi and Sumitomo invested, but in 1930, VTMJ's capital was doubled, so it is thought that their role may have been to supply part of this additional capital. Having constructed a factory, VTMJ not only produced records but also gradually began to manufacture phonographs and radios. However, as stated in the NEC case, the gradual increase of government pressure against foreign makers, combined with the appearance of competitors, led to a worsening of the business environment. Given this situation, Nissan provided equity participation as part of its plans for diversification into the manufacture of musical devices and electric-wave apparatus. Hitachi Seisakusho was within the Nissan zaibatsu, but it did not make consumer electric products. Nissan acquired 42.5% (42,500 shares) of RCA's stake in VTMJ and took a role in management. At the same time, Mitsubishi and Sumitomo turned over their combined stake of 32,000 shares to Daiichi Seimei (Daiichi Life Insurance). This case can also be said to have been the product of a compromise between a foreign maker's response to foreign capital exclusion and a zaibatsu enterprise's diversification plans.[8]

III. Case Study: Mitsubishi Sekiyu[9]

1. *Mitsubishi Trading Co.'s Entry into the Petroleum Business*

The Mitsubishi zaibatsu first expressed its interest in oil by forming what was known as the Investigatory Committee on Liquid Fuel in 1923. There were a number of reasons for this interest. First, major changes were afoot in the structure of the market for fuel. With the advent of the internal combustion engine, a shift from coal to oil became evident from the late 1910s. For example, the navy began to increase its purchases of oil, and shipping companies began to change over from coal to oil. Along with this change in the structure of consumption came changes on the side of production as well. Both decreases in Japanese domestic petroleum production and, along with the post–World War I depression, a trend toward worldwide overproduction began to be seen. Given this environment, foreign oil companies were actively looking toward the Japanese market, and Mitsubishi's attention was drawn to the future of the oil trade. A second factor was a problem facing the management of Mitsubishi Trading Co. (MTC). Originally, MTC's primary function had been to manage sales of the coal produced by Mitsubishi's mining division. However, due to a number of factors, including a steep fall in the price of coal, MTC had turned its sole agency rights back over to Mitsubishi Mining Co. This resulted in having to find something to replace coal as its main line of business. Since it supplied fuel to Nihon Yūsen Kaisha (Japan Mail Steamship Co.) through an agency agreement, and since a sister company, Mitsubishi Zōsen Kaisha (Mitsubishi Shipbuilding Co.), had a close relationship with the navy by way of contracts for warships, MTC judged itself to be in an excellent position to enter the petroleum business.

One problem that loomed large, however, was that of securing stable supplies of oil, and so MTC began to look for an American oil company from which it could secure sole agency rights. Since companies like Rising Sun Petroleum Co. (Shell Group) and Standard Oil Co. were already active in the Japanese market, Associated Oil Company (AOC) of San Francisco was chosen as a candidate. Because AOC was beginning to face both overproduction problems in California and difficulties with its Japanese agency, it was considering a fresh start in Japan. Both companies were thinking along similar lines and negotiations began, leading to the conclusion of a sole agency contract in 1923. This was despite disagreement concerning which products were to be handled and the volume of procurement. However, the contract was gradually expanded to include more products, and by 1925, MTC was handling AOC's entire line. In addition, MTC acquired sole agency rights from Tidewater Oil Co., which had the same parent company as AOC. Along with the conclusion of these contracts, MTC began to prepare its sales network, and actual sales of petroleum products began in 1924. Distributionships were acquired in 1923 from Texaco when it left Japan, and the fuel section began other major dealings. With the commencement of shipments to the Tokuyama Naval Fuel Depot in 1924, MTC's petroleum trading developed favorably.

2. *The Tie-up Process*

Shortly after its entrance into petroleum, MTC clearly recognized that, in order to carry on stable long-term trade, it would have to move from sales to refining. First, there was the problem of tariffs. As the Japanese oil-refining industry was still in its infancy, plans for a policy to protect domestic refining had already led to a tariff increase in 1926, and the trend was toward further increases. Second, despite the rise in tariffs, Rising Sun and Standard had strong brands and were able to sell gasoline cheaply. Competing was no easy matter for MTC, but even so, a trend toward the displacement of foreign products by the domestic products of Ogura Oil Co. and Nippon Oil Co. was seen. Third was the high level of profits from petroleum refining. At the time, Nippon Oil and other domestic refiners were paying dividends of close to 10%, and it was the refining process that was thought to be yielding such profits. In addition, Nippon Oil and other domestic refiners were supplying about 20% of total domestic consumption, and so there was judged to be plenty of room for entrance. Thus, MTC began to seriously consider expansion into refining. To put it the other way around, if Mitsubishi did not go into refining, it would have been best to get out of petroleum altogether. On top of that, the head of the Mitsubishi zaibatsu, Iwasaki Koyata, was extremely supportive of petroleum, both because of its bright future and its national significance.[10]

But the key point in the expansion into refining was to ensure a stable supply of crude oil. Because it could not secure crude oil on its own, MTC began to negotiate tie-ups with a number of enterprises, including AOC. At first, seeing Standard's acquisition of General Oil (which had a sole-agency contract with Mitsui Trading) in 1925, and being concerned that AOC might be absorbed by Standard as well, MTC thought of approaching Standard. Standard, however, balked at the construction costs of a new refinery, and the intricate intertwining interests of AOC, Tidewater, Mitsui Trading, and others made for little progress in negotiations. In 1928, then, in accordance with the 1925 contract (which was made with the understanding that Mitsubishi Trading would buy or construct a refinery within three years), MTC decided to embark on a joint refining venture with AOC. At its March 1928 meeting, Mitsubishi Trading Co.'s board of directors decided to enter into negotiations with AOC by approving a draft calling for the new venture to have a capacity of 400,000 barrels per year, capital of ¥5 million, 50% participation by each partner with the possibility of 40% Mitsubishi and 60% AOC, for MTC to have sole agency rights, and for commissions to be fixed at 6%. The draft also specified that if AOC were to refuse equity participation, the venture would be called off, since reliable supplies of crude oil would be made impossible thereby. Negotiations proceeded smoothly, and in June of 1928, statements of understanding concerning basic principles were exchanged. The new company was to have capital of ¥5 million with 50% investment by each partner. It was to be headed by a president and a managing director from Mitsubishi and a vice-president from AOC, the three of whom would form a committee. The plant manager was to be sent by AOC. MTC was to have sole agency rights for all production, commissions were not to exceed 6%, as much crude as could be supplied was to be bought from AOC at a "reasonable price," and AOC was to send personnel for verification by the time of the signing of the contract. In 1929, though, AOC objected to MTC's sole agency rights, holding that the new company should sell its own products or that a separate sales company should be set up. This was so as not to incite its rivals in America and also to protect its rights with regard to the new company, but it was a point on which MTC could not compromise. At that point MTC offered a modified sales proposal and, should AOC refuse, decided to consider the independent entrance of the Mitsubishi zaibatsu into the oil-refining industry. When AOC was asked for its final answer in June of 1929, it replied that it would accept a 51/49 equity ratio and that the new company would be called Mitsubishi Sekiyu, but that sole agency rights would not be given to MTC, whereupon negotiations broke down. It was then decided to found a new company jointly capitalized by the Mitsubishi holding company, MTC, and Mitsubishi Mining. AOC had a sudden change in attitude and in November of 1929 it concluded a contract to establish the new venture with Mitsubishi.

3. The Establishment of Mitsubishi Sekiyu

Mitsubishi Sekiyu was founded in February of 1931. The content of the contract between Mitsubishi and AOC was essentially the same as Mitsubishi's proposal. Capital was ¥5 million (¥2.5 million paid in), with AOC providing 50% and Mitsubishi providing 50% (30% from the holding company, 10% from MTC, and 10% from Mitsubishi Mining). Mitsubishi installed Miyoshi Shigemichi of the holding company as president and Tsutsumi Kazushige of the fuels section of MTC as managing director. AOC sent D. D. MacGregor, chief of the mechanical division of its Avon refinery, to be the new vice-president.

Construction of the refinery began in November of 1930, prior to the formation of the new company. Capacity was 3,000 barrels per day of heavy crude and 1,000 per day of light crude. The advantages of the tie-up were realized even from the design stage. That is, although AOC did not provide equipment directly, all important apparatus was ordered under its guidance from the American company, Kellogg Co. As for the construction of the refinery, direct technical guidance was provided by Kellogg engineers; the acting plant manager, D. D. Stark; and an engineer from AOC's mechanical division. Stark, who had worked in the research and development division of AOC's Avon refinery, not only took charge of designing purification apparatus but also oversaw layout, the purchase of production equipment, assembly, and even the selection of technicians. This was of great significance for Mitsubishi, which had no technical experience in the oil-refining industry. The refinery's first phase was completed approximately one year after the start of construction, and operations began in December of 1931. While it goes without saying that crude was supplied by AOC, Mitsubishi Sekiyu was the first (domestic) oil company to purchase directly from abroad, as all the other companies were purchasing through trading companies. This meant that the new company had the considerable advantage of having reliable supplies of crude.

Although the new company made satisfactory progress under the guidance of foreign engineers, management faced a rather rocky start due to severe competition, tariff increases, restrictions on American oil production, and other factors. The industry gained temporary relief through pricing agreements, but it was not until 1935 that things really began to take a turn for the better. This was a result of an industry-wide agreement which stemmed from the Petroleum Industry Law of March 1934. Despite the problems facing management, Mitsubishi Sekiyu was able to take a definite share of the market immediately after its founding. Although its share was under 10%, it succeeded in establishing itself in the industry. There was no doubt about its technical ability to supply gasoline of competitive quality.

Thus, Mitsubishi, which had sales experience but no technical experience, entered the relatively new field of refining and received huge benefits from a tie-up with a foreign partner. In fact, it is difficult to imagine how it could have entered without the tie-up. That is to say, many elements indispensable to the new venture, in the form of a stable supply of raw materials, choice of production equipment, technology, and subsequent technical guidance, were secured via the tie-up.

IV. Case Study: Mitsubishi Denki

1. *The Business Environment*

Mitsubishi Denki was founded in February of 1921 and derived from Electric Works of Kobe, which was part of the Kobe shipyard of Mitsubishi Shipbuilding Co., which was in turn the starting point of the Mitsubishi holding company's efforts at expansion into heavy industry. From the start, the company made clear its intentions to aim for non-Mitsubishi zaibatsu demand. While this market included military demand, civilian demand was the primary target.[11] The company stated the following in the prospectus issued upon its founding:

> It is clear that in every field the process of electrification will continue in the future, and that demand will naturally increase. Our goal is to use the current lull to build factories and foster manufacturing capacity in order to respond to future large scale demand.[12]

The emphasis of the prospectus was the clear recognition that, in comparison with Shibaura Seisakusho, which had tied-up with GE and was growing to be a powerful maker of heavy electrical equipment, or with Hitachi Seisakusho, which had no foreign partner but had comparatively high technical capacity, Mitsubishi Denki had made quite a late start.

In response to an inquiry from the navy, the company held that it produced as many as 17 items including AC motors and generators, transformers, DC machines, alternators, traction motors, and switchboards. In fact, however, it had confidence only with DC equipment and was almost incapable of producing large capacity equipment. Technically related problems included a claim versus the company by the Ministry of Railways for deficiency due to constant breakdowns of the transformers and alternators. Also, of the 150-horsepower induction motors ordered by Nippon Flour Milling Co. in 1923, it was noted that the company "had never made this kind of motor before and lacked the appropriate plans." It was written of the devices that, "when started, the shafts weaken, the rotors slip, and they get hot." In 1924 the company took advantage of damage to Shibaura Seisakusho's factory to secure an order for 15,000 fans, but due to defects, many of them "did not rotate, got hot, and moved about by themselves." Over half were returned.[13] On the other hand, Shibaura, an early starter, was producing 10 of 16 heavy electric items at record levels throughout the 1920s. Even Mitsubishi Denki's management was heard to lament that ". . . most of our company's electrical equipment, experience, skill, and production methods are in . . . a miserable condition," or that "our company's position in the industry is indeed second rate, and perhaps less than second rate."[14] Management was in no doubt of its being behind.

For Mitsubishi Denki, which was starting from behind, problems stemming from its late development did not stop with technology. Management itself was definitely inferior compared with that of Shibaura or Hitachi. For the year of 1921, total sales were one-fifth of Shibaura's and one-third of Hitachi's, and there was a large gap in paid-in capital as well. Another large gap was noted in return on equity: Mitsubishi showed a loss of 4.1%, compared with returns of 37.3% for Shibaura and 11.6% for Hitachi. While technology was of course a problem, these gaps resulted from inattention to general management of development. That is, Mitsubishi Denki lacked management skills such as those for systematic securing of orders, cost accounting, and process control.

For example, the items that Mitsubishi Denki produced hardly changed from its founding until about 1925.[15] The managerial system remained unchanged from the shipyard days, and almost all production was to fill orders from MTC (a sole agency contract had been signed in 1922). In addition, systems for factory supervision, costing, and estimates were not well prepared. The following examples illustrate the situation:

> During production, theoretical problems are encountered, unsolved problems pile into mountains, amounts of half-finished products become wastefully large, and the factory is thrown into confusion. Deliveries are postponed. Worries over production are unceasing.

Or:

> Costing is extremely high in big factories and low in small ones and so on; the costing system is ill-prepared and results are irrational.

And:

> Estimates are nothing more than approximate guesses and, although profits are made occasionally, the sustaining of losses is not uncommon.[16]

Starting with technology, management in its entirety had serious problems. Thus, in order to catch up with Shibaura and Hitachi, which had started early, the late-starting Mitsubishi Denki decided that "conditions have definitely come to require a tie-up with a well-known Western electrical manufacturer, and even with comparative sacrifice, the establishment of a tie-up is desirable."[17]

2. *The Tie-up Process*

As a late entrant, Mitsubishi Denki had been on the lookout since its founding for a foreign tie-up partner in order to eliminate its disadvantages. Immediately following its founding in July of 1921, two of the company's managing directors departed on a trip to observe western enterprises and look for possible venture partners. The candidates which arose at that time were Westinghouse Electric (WH), Metropolitan Vickers of England (MV), and Siemens-Schuckert of Germany (SS).

Prior to this, WH had turned over sole agency rights to Takata Trading Co. and was planning local production. Although directors of WH were invited to Japan twice, in 1919 and 1921, negotiations with Mitsubishi Denki broke down due to disagreements over conditions. The condition which WH demanded was receipt of one-third of Mitsubishi Denki's stock at no cost.[18] Under these circumstances WH was eliminated as a candidate. Of the remaining two companies, Mitsubishi Denki leaned toward negotiations with MV. There was a reason for the placement of MV as the new number-one candidate.[19] The reason was a plan circulated by the Ministry of Railways for the start of domestic production of electric railway cars. That is, the ministry considered Shibaura, Hitachi, Kawasaki, and Mitsubishi as the four candidate enterprises, but all four had drawbacks. The Ministry of Railways evaluated each company and found that although Shibaura, due to its relations with GE, did not have problems with technology, it had difficulties with the manufacture of railway-car bodies. While Hitachi had no problem making car bodies, its lack of a foreign tie-up was a disadvantage. Kawasaki had gained the trust of the Ministry of Railways because of its experience in making steam locomotives, but could not be relied upon with respect to the electrical aspect. Mitsubishi, due to its close relations with Mitsubishi Shipbuilding, had no problem making railway-car bodies and was seen to be an independent electrical-equipment maker, but the snag was its ability to make use of foreign technology. If, through ties with a foreign maker, Mitsubishi could use foreign technology, there was the possibility of securing orders from the Ministry of Railways. This possibility was extremely attractive to the latecomer.

Mitsubishi Denki started negotiations right away with MV through the London branch of Mitsubishi Trading. The primary goal of the negotiations at that time was to gain the rights to manufacture MV's electric locomotives. It is not clear whether Mitsubishi Denki was thinking of a tie-up relationship, but in any case the negotiations foundered on hidden rocks: In September of 1922, two months after the start of negotiations, it became apparent that the manufacturing rights which were thought to belong to MV were actually held by WH. Because of past close relations with Mitsubishi, MV tried to bargain with WH in order to secure the rights, but WH refused. Thus, in December of the same year, Mitsubishi attempted direct negotiations with WH. WH, however, answered that it was unwilling to discuss the transfer of manufacturing rights to individual products, but that it would come to the bargaining table if a joint-venture arrangement would be discussed. At that point, talk of an equity agreement became more concrete. A tie-up with MV, however, was thought to be a more natural path due to a number of factors. These included changes in the agreement between MV and WH, a variety of prior contracts which had been made between MV and Mitsubishi zaibatsu companies, and the idea that MV desired a tie-up with Mitsubishi.

In March of 1923, MV replied that, according to its contract with WH, it could not tie up with Mitsubishi without WH's consent. Coupled with the fact that MV had entered into a representative agency agreement with Suzuki Trading Co. for its civilian products in Japan, negotiations ended unsuccessfully. At the same time SS presented a plan to Mitsubishi recommending that, together with Furukawa, the three companies form a new venture. Hence, Mitsubishi maneuvered delicately between WH and SS. Mitsubishi desperately needed a tie-up, but WH intended to secure the best conditions possible, and Mitsubishi did not feel itself able to submit to WH's demand for one-third of its stock. SS felt that its plan should go smoothly since Mitsubishi Mining had received stock in Furukawa Denko, but a three-company venture was not what

Mitsubishi Denki had in mind. Mitsubishi attempted to use SS's offer, though, as leverage in negotiations with WH.

In June of 1923, WH presented its basic conditions for a tie-up with Mitsubishi. These included exclusive use of certain WH patents, mutual factory inspection, transfer of part of Mitsubishi stock to WH without charge or purchase of additional stock, placement of WH directors on the board of Mitsubishi, and conditions related to Takata Trading Co.'s sales of WH products. The Mitsubishi side proceeded with caution since the amounts of stock to be received and/or purchased and the nature of the relationship between Mitsubishi and Takata Trading were still not clear. When WH loosened its conditions, however, the Mitsubishi board decided in October of 1923 to enter into a tie-up relationship with WH.

3. *The Merits of the Tie-up*

In this light, Mitsubishi Denki and Westinghouse Electric concluded a formal contract in November of 1923. Of Mitsubishi's total equity of ¥15 million, WH received ¥1 million worth of stock and purchased an additional ¥500,000 stake, giving WH a 10% share of Mitsubishi's stock. In the beginning, according to the agreement, Mitsubishi Denki received blueprints, technical information, production specifications, etc., and eventually came to have unrestricted use of almost all patents owned by WH. Also, Westinghouse allowed Mitsubishi technicians to visit and to be posted at its factories, while at the same time technical guidance was being received from WH engineers posted at Mitsubishi plants. In short, Mitsubishi received more than WH technology: It was also able to access managerial know-how like factory management and sales systems.[20]

Results did not appear immediately, though. After about a year, in September of 1924, the board of directors reported that

> our company's current condition is still one of preparation. The costs of training technicians, of sending them abroad, and of product improvement are mounting very high. . . . Effectiveness of the contract with Westinghouse is not born out by the current figures.[21]

It was not merely product design and technology but also production and factory management systems that were not yet solidly developed.

For Mitsubishi Denki, the merits of the tie-up did not manifest themselves until after 1926, when advantages appeared in the areas of technical improvement, product line expansion, scientific control methods, and standardization of materials/parts procurement. On the management side of things, improvements were seen in the areas of cost accounting and estimation systems, and in the sales structure.

Looking at the technical side, a technical section was established in the head office in February of 1924, and arrangements were made to host WH technicians. At the same time Mitsubishi technicians were sent for training at WH plants (by 1926 the number of trainees had mounted to 17), and in February of 1925 Mitsubishi's first full-time representative was posted to WH. Additionally, several WH technicians were invited to provide design assistance for transformers and AC equipment. Improvement in the technical level of products and expansion of the product line were seen as results of these efforts. Production of items such as hydraulic turbines, turbine generators, induction motors, transformers, and rotary converters reached record levels. Also, the ability to manufacture new items like synchronous motors and oil circuit breakers was acquired. All of this was the result of study under WH engineers or of the use of WH plans and designs. Mitsubishi Denki even produced versions of WH home appliances and motors for use in railways and agriculture. Especially during the depression period from 1927, railway related electrical products (transformers, railway motors, railway controllers, etc.) were ordered as total systems by rail companies. The capacity to fill these orders owed a lot to WH technology.[22]

Even in the area of managerial systems, great benefits were received from WH. Kobe Electric's experience of failure in the manufacture of fans was previously mentioned, and while this failure was partially a result of half-baked technology, irrationality in factory management was also a cause. Thus, in February of 1924, Mitsubishi sent engineers to WH to take a course in shop management. The course included instruction in time motion research, factory control, and cost accounting methods. The engineers brought back a variety of material which they tested out at the fan factory of the Kobe Works. A 24% savings in production time and benefits from a new wage system were the results. In 1924, Mitsubishi finished its Nagoya Works, built to produce standard products. WH reference material was used to accomplish standardization of parts.[23]

Establishment of the sales system, although a little late, was started in 1928 with the introduction of a sales department at company headquarters. Preparation for a sales section had been taking place gradually even prior to this through such measures as the training of sales engineers. In 1927, however, engineers were sent to study WH's sales organization and, by such means as shifting the estimate system from the technical section to the sales department, changes in structure were carried out.

Moreover, in the depression years from 1927, a budgeting system was introduced and a standard for financial control systems was developed. These, too, were learned from WH.[24] While it goes without saying that the introduction of WH technology was important, the introduction of various managerial systems was also of tremendous value in shedding the problems associated with a late start.

Thus, from about 1932, Mitsubishi, which had received not only technical know-how from WH but also general management know-how, gradually caught up to become a competitor equal to Shibaura and Hitachi.

V. Conclusion

In prewar Japan, many enterprises tied up with foreign makers in order to expand their business activities, and most of these were zaibatsu enterprises. It is possible to classify the motivations for these tie-ups into three broad categories.

First, zaibatsu enterprises formed joint ventures with foreign makers in order to secure resources necessary for development. While there were cases in which those resources were raw materials, other needs included products, production techniques, plant construction, and technical guidance. The case of Mitsubishi Sekiyu noted in this paper is a typical example of a case in which the securing of stable supplies of raw materials served as primary motivation, although this is characteristic of oil products.

Second, as seen in the case of Mitsubishi Denki, enterprises which started late (and found themselves behind the existing zaibatsu enterprises) sought to get rid of the accompanying disadvantages through tie-ups with foreign makers. The most important point was the merit of receiving technology, but general management was also strengthened through the absorption of managerial know-how from foreign makers.

Third, due to the intensifying ostracism of foreign capital following the Manchurian Incident, there were cases of equity participation in foreign makers by zaibatsu enterprises. These relationships were products of zaibatsu plans for expansion into new fields and of foreign makers' responses to exclusion of foreign investment.

The zaibatsu enterprises were not expecting to receive benefits from the financial aspect of foreign equity participation. In most cases it was not capital that was sought but rather managerial resources which the introduction of technology alone (through the use of patents or rights of manufacture) could not assure.

Notes

1. Nippon Kōgyō Ginkō Gaijibu (Foreign Affairs Div. of the Industrial Bank of Japan), ed., *Gaikoku Kaisha no Honpō Tōshi* (Foreign Capital Investment in Japan) (Nippon Kōgyō Ginkō, Tokyo), 1948; "Jitsugyōkai ni okeru Gaikokushihon no Katsudō (Activities of Foreign Capital in the Japanese Industry)," *Ekonomisuto* (Economist), 15 Dec. 1928, pp. 26–35; and history of each company. This list, however, has some limitations on the availability of research materials.

2. Yokohama Gomu Seizō Kabushiki Kaisha (Yokohama Rubber Mfg. Co.), ed., *40 Nen Shi* (40-Year History) (Yokohama Gomu, Tokyo), 1959, pp. 5–39, 51–62, 129–37, 217, and Nippon Kōgyō Ginkō, *op. cit.*, pp. 153–67.

3. Nippon Kōgyō Ginkō, *op. cit.*, pp. 255–66, and Mitsui Bussan Kabushiki Kaisha (Mitsui Trading Co.), ed., *Mitsui Bussan Kabushiki Kaisha 100 Nen Shi Kohon, I* (100-year History of Mitsui Trading Co., Manuscript I) (Nihon Keiei Shi Kenkyūsho, Tokyo), 1978, pp. 620–21.

4. On the case of Shibaura Works, Tokyo Shibaura Denki Kabushiki Kaisha (Tokyo Shibaura Electric Co.), ed., *Shibaura Seisakusho 65 Nen Shi* (65-Year History of Shibaura Works) (Tokyo Shibaura Denki, Tokyo), 1940, pp. 53–55; Takeuchi Hiroshi, *Denki Kikai Kōgyō* (Electric Machinery Industry); (Tōyō Keizai Shinpōsha, Tokyo), 1973, pp. 108–9, 117–19; and Nippon Kōgyō Ginkō, *op. cit.*, pp. 53–68.

5. Tokyo Shibaura Denki, *op. cit.*, p. 53.

6. Sumitomo Denki Kōgyō Kabushiki Kaisha (Sumitomo Electric Industries Ltd.), *Sha Shi Sumitomo Denki Kōgyō Kabushiki Kaisha* (History of Sumitomo Electric Industries) (Sumitomo Denki Kōgyō, Osaka), 1961, pp. 353–73, and Nippon Denki Kabushiki Kaisha (Nippon Electric Co.), *Nippon Denki Kabushiki Kaisha 70 Nen Shi* (70-Year History of Nippon Electric Co.) (Nippon Denki, Tokyo), 1972, pp. 100–108.

7. Sumitomo Denki Kōgyō, *op. cit.*, pp. 616–32, and Nippon Denki, *op. cit.*, pp. 138–60.

8. Nihon Victor Co., ed., *Nihon Victor 50 Nen Shi* (Victor Company of Japan's 50th Anniversary) (Nihon Victor Co., Tokyo), 1977, pp. 51–68, and Nippon Kōgyō Ginko, *op. cit.*, pp. 195–209.

9. The description of this chapter is based on: Mishima Yasuo, ed., *Mitsubishi Zaibatsu* (Nihon Keizai Shinbunsha, Tokyo), 1981, pp. 321–29; Kawabe Nobuo, *Sōgō Shōsha no Kenkyū* (Study of General Trading Companies) (Jikkyō Shuppan, Tokyo), 1982, chapter 2; Mitsubishi Sekiyu Kabushiki Kaisha (Mitsubishi Oil Co.), *Mitsubishi Sekiyu 50 Nen Shi* (50-Year History of Mitsubishi Oil Co.), 1981, pp. 1–33; and Mitsubishi Sha Shi Kankōkai (Publishing Committee of History of Mistsubishi Gōshi), ed., *Mitsubishi Sha Shi* (History of Mitsubishi Gōshi) (Univ. of Tokyo Press, Tokyo) 1981, reprint ed., vol. 36, pp. 493–507.

10. Iwasaki Ke Denki Kankō Kai (Biographical Committee of Iwasaki Koyata), ed., *Iwasaki Koyata Den* (Biography of Iwasaki Koyata), (Univ. of Tokyo Press, Tokyo) 1979, reprint ed., pp. 286–89.

11. On this point, refer to Fujita Nobuhisa, "Mitsubishi Denki no Keieishiteki Kenkyū, I (Business History of Mitsubishi Electric Manufacturing Co., I)," *Kōnan Ronshū* (Papers of Social Science), vol. 9, 1981.

12. Mitsubishi Denki Kabushiki Kaisha (Mitsubishi Electric Manufacturing

Co.), ed., *Kengyō Kaiko* (Retrospective of the Company's Foundation) (Mitsubishi Denki, Tokyo), 1951, p. 50.

13. *Ibid.*, pp. 59–62.

14. Yuasa Kōzō, *Takeda Hideo Den* (Biography of Takeda Hideo), Takeda Hideo Den Kankōkai (Biographical Committee of Hideo Takeda) (Mitsubishi Denki, Tokyo), 1944, pp. 383, 386.

15. On this point, refer to Mitsubishi Gōshi Kaisha, ed., *Mitsubishi Gōshi Kaisha Nenpō* (Annual Report of Mitsubishi Gōshi) (Mitsubishi Gōshi, Tokyo), each year, 1921–25.

16. Mitsubishi Denki, *op. cit.*, pp. 62–63.

17. Yuasa, *op. cit.*, p. 386.

18. Mitsubishi Denki, *op. cit.*, pp. 64–65.

19. On the tie-up process, *Mitsubishi Denki Kabushiki Kaisha Torishimariyakukai Gijiroku* (Minute Book of the Board of Directors), July–Dec. 1922, Jan.–Oct. 1923, and Mitsubishi Denki, *op. cit.*, pp. 65–68.

20. *Mitsubishi Denki Torishimariyakukai Gijiroku*, Nov. 1923.

21. *Ibid.*, 30 Sept. 1924.

22. Mitsubishi Denki, *op. cit.*, pp. 139, 143, 160–65, 192, 200–201.

23. Sasaki Satoshi, "Mitsubishi Denki ni Miru Kagakuteki Kanrihō no Dōnyu Katei" (The Introduction of Time Study Method into Mitsubishi Electric Co. at Kobe Works), *Keiei Shigaku* (Japan Business History Review), vol. 21, no. 4, 1987, pp. 37–38, 48–49; and Mitsubishi Denki, *op. cit.*, pp. 76–77.

24. Mitsubishi Denki, *op. cit.*, pp. 91–96, 307–8, 391–92.

Appendix A

Name of Venture		Year of Tie-up	Original Tie-up Capital
Nihon Seikō Sho	☆	1907	¥ 1,000,000
Tōyō Carrier Kōgyō	☆	1930	300,000
Tōyō Otis Elevator	☆	1932	1,000,000
Shibaura Kyōdō Kōgyō	☆	1939	16,000,000
Mitsubishi Sekiyu	★	1931	5,000,000
Sumitomo Aluminum	○	1931	3,500,000
Yokohama Gomu Seizōsho	●	1917	2,500,000
Fuji Denki Seizō	●	1923	10,000,000
Nihon Bemberg Kenshi	▼	1929	10,000,000
Asahi Kenshoku	▼	1922	2,000,000
Shibaura Seisakusho	☆	1909	2,000,000
Mitsubishi Denki	★	1923	15,000,000
Sumitomo Densen Seizōsho	○	1932	15,000,000
Tōyō Babcock Seizō	☆	1928	1,750,000
Nihon Kenchiku Zairyō	☆	1933	1,500,000
Nippon Denki	○	1932	12,500,000
Nichibei Ita Garasu	○	1922	3,000,000
Teikoku Sanso	○	1930	2,400,000
Nihon Victor	▽	1935	10,000,000
Nihon Chikuonki Shōkai	▽	1935	11,200,000
Daidō Match	□	1932	500,000
Tōyō Kamibukuro	□	1935	250,000

Note: Symbols represent zaibatsu affiliation as follows: ☆ =Mitsui, ★ = Mitsubishi, ○ =Sumitomo, ● =Furukawa, ▽ =Nissan, ▼ =Nitchitsu, □ =Asano.

Sources: Udagawa Masaru, "Senzen Nihon no Kigyō Keiei to Gaishikei Kigyō" (Business Management and Foreign-Affiliated Companies in Japan before World War II), *Keiei Shirin* (The Hōsei

Japanese Holdings	Foreign Partner	Remarks		
50	Armstrong, Vickers: E			
50	Carrier Corp.: A			
40	Otis Elevator: A			
51	United Engineering & Foundry : A			
50	Associated Oil: A			
50	Aluminum Ltd.: C			
50	B.F. Goodrich: A			
70	Siemens-Schuckertwerke+Siemens & Halske: G			
80	J.P. Bemberg: G			
80	Vereinigte Glanzstoff Fabriken: G			
76	General Electric: A			
90	Westinghouse Electric: A			
88	International Standard Electric: A			
		(Est.)	(Co.)	(Inv. %)
39	Babcock & Wilcox: E	1908	B&W	100
34	American Trading+Truscon Steel: A	1919	AS+TS	100
50	International Standard Electric: A	1899	WE	54
35	Libbey-Owens Sheet Glass: A	1918	LO	35
12	L'Air Liquide: F	1910	AL	100
67	Victor Talking Machine: A	1927	VTM	100
75	Columbia: A	1927	C	67
?	Sweden Match: S	1927	S	50
35	Bates International Bag: A	1927	BIB	99

Journal of Business), vol. 24, no. 1, 1987, table on pp. 18–20 (author's modification); Nihon Kōgyō Ginkō Gaijibu (Foreign Affairs Div., Industrial Bank of Japan), ed., *Gaikoku Kaisha no Honpō Tōshi* (Foreign Capital Investment in Japan) (Nihon Kōgyō Ginkō, Tokyo), 1948; official company histories of companies listed.

Comment

Hidemasa Morikawa

Professor Fujita's paper presents some interesting arguments. But I do not have enough time to deal with all of them, so I would like to choose only two problems in his paper for my comment. These two problems are closely related.

The first problem is the reason why zaibatsu enterprises cooperated with foreign enterprises in Japan more often and more actively than non-zaibatsu. We can answer this question in different ways. An example is that zaibatsu looked so credible to foreign enterprises that the latter gladly invested their managerial resources in the zaibatsu enterprise. In addition I want to point out the fact that the zaibatsu, a group of diversified enterprises owned exclusively by a single wealthy family, required the introduction of managerial resources from foreign enterprises in order to develop new businesses. Of course, not only zaibatsu but some non-zaibatsu enterprises adopted the diversification strategy. But the zaibatsu—which essentially meant diversified enterprises—were distinguished in this regard from the non-zaibatsu, which entailed single-product enterprises without a propensity to diversify.

If any company continues to insist on the single-product strategy within one industry for a long time, it can accumulate a lot of managerial skill and experience and needs no imports of technology, managerial know-how, or institutions from the outside. Zaibatsu, a group of diversified enterprises, always looked for new business opportunities and needed to introduce outside managerial resources to pursue such opportunities. In the case of newly developed or heavy industries, *outside* meant almost wholly *abroad*. Until recently those industries in Japan have lacked the accumulation of managerial resources even in the most advanced enterprises. On account of this, zaibatsu enterprises were willing to cooperate with foreign enterprises.

The second problem, the significance of tie-ups with foreign companies, has a very close relationship with the above-mentioned problem. The zaibatsu developed through their diversification strategy. However, there were two aspects. In one, the zaibatsu could grow large by adopting the diversification strategy. For example, Mitsubishi developed by entering into various industries in succession; coal mining, metal mining, banking, shipbuilding, real estate, and warehousing. In another aspect the big zaibatsu (which could grow large) diversified by investing their huge managerial resources. In pursuing eagerly the diversification strategy the zaibatsu worked hard, not only at growing bigger and bigger, but at lining up a more intensive network of diversified enterprises in order to win the highest status among the zaibatsu groups. This effort to line up diversified business left the disadvantages of late starting out of account. For instance, Mitsubishi, the number-two zaibatsu, wanted to enter into various new fields after World War I to rival Mitsui, the number-one zaibatsu. Mitsubishi's electric machinery manufacturing and petroleum refining, which Fujita mentioned in his paper, were good examples. Those were latecomers in each industry. Owing to their backwardness, they had to rely on cooperation with foreign companies. But they could not overcome this underdevelopment. In other words, their cooperation with foreign companies and the introduction of managerial resources from abroad were not so effective.

We have to sort out activities of foreign companies in modern Japan before World War II without drawing them uniformly. There were not a few examples of not indispensable and uneffective cooperation between zaibatsu and foreign companies. Mitsubishi Denki and Mitsubishi Sekiyu were such examples. Mitsubishi Denki could not catch up to Toshiba and Hitachi before and after World War II. Mitsubishi Sekiyu, as the annexed table indicates, had to accept the low quota among competitors during the war. Its status could not change in the postwar period.

TABLE 1 Quota of Petroleum Products Sales Among Large Companies, 1939 (unit, %)

	Gasoline	Heavy Oil	Machine Oil	Total
Nihon	27.0	17.3	25.3	23.0
Ogura	13.2	4.4	12.8	9.8
{Hayama	4.2	3.0	4.2	4.1
{Niitsu	2.7	0.5	2.5	1.5
{Asahi	—	7.1	3.6	3.7
{Mitsubishi Sekiyu	7.5	4.0	3.0	5.2
{Mitsubishi Trading	—	9.5	1.0	4.3
Mitsui Trading	—	16.1	—	8.8
Total	100.0	100.0	100.0	100.0

Source: Government statistics.

Response

Nobuhisa Fujita

I agree that because the zaibatsu enterprises were those controlled by a single family and their strategy was diversification, they felt it indispensable to find managerial resources outside. In the case of Japan, outside meant foreign countries. The formation of the close relationship between the zaibatsu enterprises and foreign firms was a natural outcome. But I am still inclined to assume that in access to foreign firms the requirement of technological know-how was a more important factor than the managerial one, especially in technologically intensive industries such as oil or electrical machinery, although this does not necessarily deny the importance of the latter requirement.

Also, regarding the second point—that in the case of latecoming enterprises "tie-up with foreign companies and introduction of managerial resources from abroad were not so effective," I would like to insist that it would still be indispensable for latecomers to rely on foreign companies. Because if they continued to rely on only domestic managerial as well as technical resources, they would never be able to catch up with the pioneers. Otherwise they would lose the game completely. In an attempt to stay, not ahead, in their respective industries, they chose to tie up with foreign firms.

Economic and Commercial Relations Between Switzerland and Japan Before World War I

François Jequier

I. Introduction

The economy of Switzerland has been sustained by its exports for hundreds of years. Foreign trade has always relied on a high level of exports, especially of manufactured goods (which represented 78.4% of Swiss exports in 1913),[1] and on a world rather than a local market. Textile goods, watches and machinery, and, since the end of the 19th century, food and chemical products are the main staples of Swiss exports.

It was not until 1885 that the federal administration created an office to establish foreign trade statistics, which published its first series in 1886. The period before 1886 is called pre-statistical by historians and, as we shall see, the only statistics available create a major problem for my subject. Right up until the end of the century the official foreign trade statistics did not even mention Japan as a separate country importing Swiss goods. Swiss exports to Japan were included in those to China, Korea, and other far eastern countries.[2] It is only from 1899 that figures are available.[3] Other possible sources are equally difficult to use, as Charles Favre-Brandt, Swiss vice-consul at Hyōgo-Osaka, explained in a letter dated 20 June 1878:

> Swiss imports and exports are impossible to ascertain, because nearly all goods pass through customs with certain printed formula which only require the name of the port of embarkation and not the country in question, which means that goods arrive here under the name of France, England, or Belgium, according to the port chosen [Switzerland having no international ports . . .].[4]

Therefore historians must be prudent when using any figures found in consular reports and other documents which quantify trade between Switzerland and Japan in the 19th century.

II. Swiss Residents in China and Japan Before 1859

Swiss merchants took advantage of the network created by the large shipping companies which dominated foreign trade in the Far East. Resident in Bombay, Calcutta, Singapore, and Batavia, they traded with the Chinese, who were particularly fond of their watches.[5] The Bovet family were the first Swiss traders to penetrate the complex Chinese market. Edouard Bovet, who since 1818 had repaired watches for the British company Charles Magniac in Canton, founded his own business in 1824 with his brother Charles, lately arrived in China. The rapid development of business, which the Treaty of Nanking in 1842 stimulated, had direct repercussions on the Val-de-Travers (Neuchâtel Jura), which specialized in this type of manufacture. Thus, watches for China were responsible for the prosperity of the Neuchâtel watchmakers for more than half a century.[6] Other Swiss watchmaking areas—Bienne, Saint-Imier, and Sonvilier—also started producing watches for the Chinese market. Textile manufacturers used the same maritime routes, and printed calicoes and raw silk followed the same distribution network.[7] From 1840 the Swiss calico printers and textile manufacturers sent their batiks and material woven with colored threads to the Dutch East Indies, Siam, and Burma.[8] Several decades before their first contacts with Japan, Swiss traders were already well acquainted with the main sea routes of the Far East, and several companies were established in the main ports open to European trade. Protected by the flags of other European nations already established in the Far East, the Swiss became good customers of the large Dutch, British, and French shipping firms.

Commercial relations preceded diplomatic contacts. During the long period of Japanese isolation (1639–1854), only the Dutch and the Chinese were authorized to trade with Japan, and then only in a very limited way.[9] Several Japanese princes bought Swiss watches through the Vereenigde Oist Indische Company, founded in 1602 and established in 1641 on the island of Deshima. Alfred Chapuis, who has studied the company archives, presents the development of watch sales to Japan—watches destined for the rich.[10] Japanese craftsmen were prompt not only to copy but also to adapt European watches and clocks to their national time of variable hours. The dial of the clock "had movable numerals, which were to take account of seasonal changes in the length of the temporal hours (each hour a twelfth part of day and night)."[11]

Professor Yamaguchi Ryūji has described in his numerous studies the ingenuity of these Japanese watchmakers, schooled in a long tradition of highly skilled metalwork. Handmade copies of European clocks and watches called *wadokei* were produced right up until the calendar reform of 1872.[12] During the last quarter of the 19th century, the Japanese government sent watchmakers to be trained in Europe so that they, in their turn, could start a watchmaking industry in Japan to compete with those in Switzerland and America.

The textile industry was, by necessity, extremely versatile, adapting its goods to changes in fashion and specific local requirements in each part of the world. Jules Kindt, visiting the calico-printing workshops of the Swiss company Greuter and Rieter in 1846, described this variety well: "I observed large calicoes, dyed Andrinople red [*en rouge d'Andrinople*], printed with a tiny black or blue clover pattern or a small two-colored flower pattern for the Japanese and Singapore markets. Pale oranges and small blue patterns . . . were for Java.[13]

Several years later, after mechanizing their textile and embroidery industries, the manufacturers of the Saint-Gall region succeeded in penetrating the far eastern markets. Orders rushed in from India, Indonesia, and even Japan.[14] As the Federal Council recalled in its message on 8 July 1861: "Until now, Swiss trade with Japan was in the hands of the Dutch East India Company, which benefited from a monopoly of Japanese trade, governing the trading colony of *Desima* from Batavia . . . Direct trade between Switzerland and Japan did not exist because no Swiss could live in the country and even less open a business. . . ."[15]

III. Americans Breach the Japanese Fortress

Since the opening of the Chinese market in 1842, expeditions from western powers, and especially those under the American flag, became more frequent in Japanese waters.[16] In 1845 the American Congress passed a resolution that the government should take measures to secure "commercial agreements" with Japan. Traders from New York and Baltimore persistently urged that this resolution should not remain a dead letter.[17] The annexation of California in 1848–49, the final stage of the migration westward to the Pacific, explains the sudden interest of Americans in the Far East. Two expeditions under the command of Commodore Perry in 1853 and 1854 opened Japan to American trade. The Treaty of Kanagawa, signed on 31 March 1854, initiated a series of commercial agreements which in their turn opened up new ports. All the other powers followed the American lead. Great Britain in October 1854 and in 1859; Russia in February 1855 and in 1859; Holland in January 1856; and France and Portugal in 1859 secured similar agreements. In the space of only four years and without armed resistance, the Japanese fortress was unlocked for the benefit of foreign trade.[18] These treaties, however, brought about a turning point in Japanese history. All nationalist opposition united against the shogun. Imperial power should be restored to banish foreigners. Xenophobic factions joined with the followers of the mikado to overthrow the shogun. Thus the commercial expansion of the western powers precipitated the terrible crisis of 1858–68, which overturned the political, social, and economic structures of Japan.[19]

IV. Private Enterprise Precedes Diplomatic Relations: The First Mission of the Watchmakers' Association in 1859 (Union Horlogère)

The textile manufacturers of eastern Switzerland and the watchmakers of the Neuchâtel mountain area followed closely the negotiations by western powers to open up the Japanese market. On February 25, 1858, the watchmakers of La Chaux-de-Fonds created the Watchmakers' Association, and its articles of constitution revealed that its members were working actively to find new markets for their products:

> Let us think carefully of the possible consequences of recent world events; for example, the outcome of the last eastern war, the insurrection of the East Indies, the present war with China, the opening of Japan to European trade. . . ."[20]

The Association was a discount, deposit, and export house, a sort of bank to assist watchmaking manufacturers in difficulty during the late 1850s.[21] Its members also decided to establish an Asian trading post to eliminate their dependence on the middle men of the maritime companies which controlled far eastern markets.[22] Jean-Marc Barrelet, associate archivist at Neuchâtel, has produced a detailed study of the political, commercial, and diplomatic activities of the president of this Watchmakers' Association, the Senator Aimé Humbert (1819–1900).[23]

> Through his political connection with the federal government, Humbert was well informed of the decline in Swiss exports, a decline which could well continue if nothing was done to improve the situation. With the help of his friend, Salomon Zellweger of Trogen, delegate of the silk industries, Humbert endeavored to find solutions to improve Swiss trade in the East. Under his guidance, the Watchmakers' Association became one of the first groups of watchmakers intent on both liberating themselves from bank control and marketing their own products with the help of the Confederation.[24]

Aimé Humbert, a member of the Swiss parliament, wrote several letters and reports to the federal authorities asking for the official support of the Swiss government.[25] The Zurich Chamber of Commerce and the industrialists of Saint-Gall followed a similar course.[26]

The first trade mission to the Far East was a joint venture by the Watchmakers' Association of La Chaux-de-Fonds and the "commercial directorate" of Saint-Gall (Kaufmannisches Direktorium von St. Gallen). They appointed the Prussian writer Rudolf Lindau (1829–1910) as head of the mission. Lindau, a gifted linguist, had numerous contacts in both commercial and diplomatic circles. He took his new job very seriously.[27] François Perregaux, from Le Locle, was chosen to establish the new far eastern trading post. The two men left Marseille on 28 April and arrived in Singapore on 31 May 1859. Lindau had been officially nominated delegate of the Department of Trade, Customs and Excise by the Swiss authorities.[28] Leaving Perregaux in Singapore, Lindau landed at Nagasaki on 3 September 1859, aboard a Dutch cargo ship. Two months later he managed to enter into negotiations with the Japanese government's representatives in Kanagawa.

Unfortunately the Japanese refused to discuss any commercial affairs after months of sterile negotiations.[29] In spite of his lack of success with the Japanese, Lindau gave a positive picture of Japan in his report dated 4 January 1860, written from Kanagawa:

> Japan is the least known of the important countries of the world. This nation, which should have lost everything from the artistic, scientific, and commercial point of view by its isolation and lack of contacts with the rest of the world, has, nevertheless, reached such a high level of prosperity and civilization that it is the most advanced country in the Far East. Japan's marvelous artistic treasures surpass in many ways those of Europe and America. . . .[30]

However, Lindau added how very difficult it was to establish a commercial relationship: "The Japanese are not traders. They have the mind of a small shopkeeper with whom it is practically impossible to do large-scale business."[31]

At the end of his second report, Lindau recommended that Swiss industrialists unite to confront the Japanese market. In spite of the failure of the diplomatic part of his mission, he approved of the establishment of a far eastern trading post by the Watchmakers' Association. The Association signed title deeds to land in Yokohama on March 18, 1860. This purchase created indescribable problems for its members in the following years, as we learn from the correspondence of Humbert. In April 1860, Humbert wrote to the Federal Council: "The Watchmakers' Association has established a trading post in Yokohama. It is run by Dutch and French employees, whose nationalities give the business the protection of those countries' treaties. It will probably take a long time before Swiss nationals can benefit from the same advantages as the dependents of the five maritime powers. . . ."[32]

Naturally the Swiss found themselves in an inferior position to those who traded under the protection of a commercial treaty. When Japan signed a commercial and friendship treaty with Portugal on 3 August 1860, Swiss business circles renewed their discussions to obtain a treaty. On 24 January 1861, Prussia secured similar privileges. On 29 January the General Council of the Netherlands announced that the Japanese authorities were ready to conclude a treaty with Switzerland.[33]

This time Humbert's plans appeared about to be realized. The Swiss Confederation's gazette (*La Feuille Fédérale de la Confédération Suisse*) published the first official reports of the Prussian delegation to Japan which mentioned briefly the commercial activities of Swiss firms: Ziegler and J.-B. Muller at Wyl, "whose Taffachellas are of excellent quality."[34] This long report described the Japanese ports and also gave a detailed analysis of imports to Japan and the particulars of the Japanese clientele. The report emphasized the tendency "of the Japanese to copy all objects which might be useful to them. They show great dexterity and determination in reproducing them."[35]

The announcement that the Japanese government was willing to conclude a treaty with Switzerland relieved the Swiss government of the difficult task of preliminary negotiations. The Swiss authorities contacted the business circles concerned with far eastern trade in order to send an official delegation to Japan.

V. The Vicissitudes of Diplomatic Negotiations (1861–64)

The Federal Council took an active interest in trade with the Far East at a time when Swiss foreign trade was going through a deep crisis, the worst of the period 1851–70. In 1861 the volume of exports was almost 28% below the level of 1859 and all economic circles complained of a decline in trade.[36] In July 1861 the Federal Assembly authorized the sending of a Swiss delegation to Japan and voted a credit of 100,000 francs to the enterprise, in spite of opposition from those who considered that Switzerland, without any sea power, could only survive under the protection of other foreign governments.[37] In August 1861, Aimé Humbert, president of the Watchmakers' Association of La Chaux-de-Fonds, was nominated head of the delegation, and the Federal Council invited the Chamber of Commerce and all the cantons to contribute gifts for the Japanese. The research of Paul Akio Nakai and of Jean-Marc Barrelet describe in detail the peripeties of these years of preparation. The confused situation in Japan, shaken by an outburst of xenophobia, did not simplify matters. On 20 November 1862, the Swiss delegation left Marseille with letters of recommendation from the Netherlands and under their protection.

The two official envoys—Aimé Humbert, plenipotentiary minister, and Caspar Brennwald (1838–99),[38] from Mannedorf, the commercial delegate—were accompanied by four other Swiss traveling at their own expense: James Favre-Brandt, watch manufacturer from Le Locle, who would establish his company in Yokohama; Major John Bringolf from Unterneuhaus;[39] Artillery Officer Ivan Kaiser from Zoug; and Edouard Bavier, silk merchant from Coire.[40]

The Swiss delegation arrived in Japan in April 1863. It experienced serious difficulties in a country on the brink of revolution. A guest of the Dutch legation, Humbert had to endure numerous delays and vexations before achieving his goal. In September 1863 the Federal Council, alarmed by the news coming from Japan, decided to recall the delegation. During this long period of waiting, Humbert never stopped writing to the Federal Council,[41] to the Watchmakers' Association, and to his wife, Marie.[42]

Humbert tried to reorganize the affairs of the association's far eastern trading post, founded in 1859, which had lost money in Yokohama.[43] These difficulties and financial losses did not affect his morale or prevent him from lauding the potential of the Japanese market:

> In spite of everything, I hope that you will maintain relations with the Far East. There is a huge future in these countries. Western civilization has difficulty penetrating this world, of course, but the wager is already won. Japan is going through a political crisis. The mikado issues warrants to expel all foreigners without distinction. Prince Nagato shoots at every foreign flag indiscriminately, but we are selling 30,000 bales of silk in one season at an average of 100 pounds sterling the bale and all the government officers I meet are proud to show me that they already have a watch. Who knows if we will not see all the imperial ports opening next year?[44]

On 2 January 1864, the Dutch general consul in Edo (Tokyo) warned the Japanese authorities that he would advise the Dutch government not to receive the Japanese mission leaving for Europe if Japan did not agree to enter into negotiations with the Swiss delegation. Under this Dutch pressure, the Japanese agreed to negotiate with the Swiss. In the Chōji temple in Edo, on 6 February 1864, Aimé Humbert signed the commercial and friendship treaty between Switzerland and Japan.[45] Mr. Daniel de Graeff de Poelsbrock, the Dutch government's agent in Japan, was appointed general consul of Switzerland, and the Dutch consul A.-J. Bauduin became Swiss consul in Nagasaki. The consulate in Yokohama was assigned to Dr. R. Lindau for a very short time.[46] As Switzerland had no intention of keeping an official Swiss diplomat in Japan, its diplomatic representation was entrusted to Holland and its consuls were dependent on that country's agent.[47]

One further point to add is that, on 26 April 1867, by special convention, the tariff agreement Japan had signed in 1866 with France, Great Britain, the Netherlands, and the United States, which lowered customs duties to 5% ad valorem, was extended to Switzerland, which thus benefited from the same clause as a most-favored nation. Henceforth, Swiss industrialists enjoyed the same status as their rivals from other countries. Slowly, they began to organize their affairs in the ports open to foreigners.

VI. The Development of Commercial Relations Between Switzerland and Japan: The Swiss in Japan

In 1863 there were eight Swiss citizens among the 242 foreigners resident in Japan.[48] Two years later, the following 12 Swiss signed a petition to the Federal Council asking them to nominate Rudolf Lindau as Swiss chargé d'affaires so that the Swiss consul would have the same status as the diplomatic representatives of other powers: Th. Luscher, Jean-Conrad Morf, August Mingard, Gaston Muller, Edouard Bavier, James Favre-Brandt, Charles Ziegler, Fritz Abegg, Charles Favre-Brandt, E. Alpiger, Henri-Frederic Schoene, and Alfred Mottu.[49]

One must add the names of Mr. Veuve, Swiss consul in Hakodate; Caspar Brennwald, who took over the consulate in Yokohama in February 1866, and his chancellor, Edouard Schnell; and, finally, François Perregaux, Ivan Kaiser, and Ledermann, who signed a new petition. Consulate registers enable the historian to count the approximate number of Swiss in Japan. The first 16 entries for the first decade 1863-73 were mostly traders. Nearly all of them stayed for more than 20 years in Japan. Arnold Dumelin, who arrived on 19 May 1866 did not return to Switzerland until 1899.[50]

James Favre-Brandt was the first Neuchâtel watchmaker to settle in Japan. In 1865 he sent for his brother Charles, who established a watchmaking business in Osaka. On 24 January 1876 he assumed the office of the Dutchman P. A. Fricke at the Swiss consular agency in Osaka. Favre-Brandt remained at this post until 1888. Henry Favre-Brandt, youngest son of James, succeeded his father as head of the company at the beginning of the 20th century.[51]

The Brandts established close contacts with young Japanese who would later rise to key positions in their country. These human bonds strengthened the relationship between Switzerland and Japan.[52] The Brandts began to organize the distribution of Swiss watches in Japan. The advantage of having a repair workshop permitted them to impose their goods and services on the market. They stopped the arrival of mediocre merchandise, which diminished the reputation for quality of Swiss watches. As Caspar Brennwald stressed in his general report, watch sales to Japan encountered serious difficulties:

> People are too poor to buy expensive watches, which, moreover, they are not in the habit of using. The Japanese have no notion of the value of time because in most cases they do not attach any importance to being on time.
>
> Important officials, princes, and some superior officers carry watches, but as objects of curiosity rather than instruments of precision. One can say without hesitation that it will take many years before imports of watches and jewelry gain the same importance as in China. . . . The British consulate's list in Kanagawa gives the value of imported watches, at 306 pounds sterling in 1861 and 406 pounds sterling in 1862.[53] These factors make it easy to understand why the Favre-Brandt company, founded in 1865 in Yokohama, also dealt in textiles, optical instruments, and armaments.[54]

Caspar Brennwald, one of the pioneers of the Swiss colony in Japan, also played an important role in the development of commercial relations between the two countries. During a visit to Switzerland in 1865 he met Hermann Siber, a young silk manufacturer from Zurich who lived in Bergamo, in northern Italy. He persuaded Siber to join him in establishing a commercial firm in Japan. In November 1865 a circular left London concerning the creation of the Siber and Brennwald Company in Yokohama. Shortly afterward the two young men left for Yokohama. Brennwald became Swiss consul of this port on 14 February 1866. In addition to importing Swiss manufactured goods to Japan, Siber and

Brennwald quickly realized the opportunities in exporting Japanese raw silk at a time when silk manufacturing was on the increase in Zurich. Thus the export of raw silk, formerly a British monopoly, became the principal activity of the Siber and Brennwald Company, which delivered its raw silk to Switzerland, the United States, France, Italy, and Germany. The two Swiss also improved the quality of the silk and organized the importation of the first silk spinning frames to Japan. This machinery helped the Japanese silk industry to become competitive and rival the Swiss silk industry. The Siber and Brennwald Company was the forerunner of the industrial empire of Siber, Hegner and Company.[55]

Edouard Bavier founded his own silk company in 1865. Ten years later the Swiss colony totaled 25 members, 8 of whom were real-estate owners. Six firms acknowledged their Swiss origins. The number of Swiss companies increased regularly: There were a dozen in 1880, when the Swiss colony acquired 36 members. Swiss firms seldom went bankrupt in Japan. In 1910 the consul noted that "for the first time for many years a Swiss factory went bankrupt!" At the beginning of the 20th century, 121 Swiss lived in Japan and 14 enterprises were in possession of land near Yokohama.

Living and working conditions were not easy for foreigners. The vice-consul in Osaka ended his 1877 report with several remarks on immigration: "For the last two or three years there have been no Swiss arrivals in these ports. Five or six have left for China and Java. Hence one can conclude that those countries offer more advantages to merchants."[56] The Swiss colony in Japan started to increase from 1880 onward (36 registrations). This figure doubled in the next ten years to reach 100 in 1893.

The dominant number of merchants needs no explanation. The war and the following economic crisis in the 1920s forced some Swiss to leave Japan. Jean de Rham estimated the number of Swiss in Japan at 169 in 1921: 16 in Tokyo, 94 in Yokohama, 51 in Kobe and Osaka, 7 in the Hokkaido region, and 1 in Kyushu.[57] During the 1930s the total number of Swiss ranged between 200 and 250, and in 1938 the head of the Swiss legation in Tokyo added the following commentary to the figure of 258 Swiss in Japan: "Total has been stationary for the last few years." At the outbreak of war in Asia in 1941, the Swiss colony was estimated at about 300 people.

The Swiss living in Yokohama managed to acquire a place in Japanese society. The Swiss Rifle Club, started in 1865, was immensely popular. Shooting competitions were attended by well-known Japanese personalities, such as Marshal Prince Oyama; the war minister, General Saigō;

the naval minister, Admiral Kawamura; General Murata; and members of the Imperial family.

The Swiss colony in Yokohama enjoyed such a good reputation among other foreign colonies in the town that Consul C. Brennwald was honored with the post of president of the Consular Council in 1874. In 1899 the news summary relates that two Swiss were among the reception committee to welcome His Majesty the Emperor of Japan during his first official visit to the "foreign settlement" in Yokohama. There was also an excellent relationship between the members of the Swiss Rifle Club and those of the British equivalent, the Yokohama Rifle Association. It is also worth mentioning that imports of arms from Switzerland played an important role in the insurrections which mark the end of the shogunate period.

Around 1880, several Swiss occupied prominent positions as exporters of raw silk or as experts in sericulture. Of these, Muller, Abegg, and Guiseani held the important position of public inspector of the silk factories in Yokohama.[58]

On 1 September 1923, Yokohama was destroyed by an earthquake and Tokyo badly damaged. Housing problems in the two devastated cities forced most Swiss to move to the Kobe region, which subsequently became the most important center of Swiss activity in Japan.

VII. The Slow Development of Commercial Relations from 1864 to 1899

The members of the Humbert mission who stayed behind in Japan played an essential part in the first direct commercial exchanges between Japan and Switzerland. During the first 20 years the Swiss firms in Yokohama principally exported raw silk and imported cotton goods, armaments, and watches. It was only after many years that the number of merchants increased and the range of merchandise expanded and diversified.

The absence of detailed statistics discourages any attempt to estimate the volume of each product in the flow of merchandise. We do know, however, that unbleached shirtings occupied an important position in the volume of cotton goods. Taffachellas also captured a dominant place in Swiss exports to Japan. In 1876 the consul noted in his report that Taffachellas were the leading Swiss export.[59] Then Andrinople red calicoes took the lead, followed by printed cotton in 1877. The consular reports reveal marked annual fluctuations in sales of each product. Sales could double if the product was seasonal. In 1878 the vice-consul Charles Favre-Brandt complained that the quantity of imported articles had largely exceeded the absorption capacities of the market, provoking a sharp fall in prices. He reminded merchants that the Japanese bought sheets and blankets only in winter and that they should make allowances for seasonal variations. These sudden fluctuations explain why certain products changed position in the list of exports.

Generally, cotton goods, silk, and later watches shared the principal place in Swiss exports to Japan, each series changing according to its own conjuncture. In 1880, *halbseidene schwarze* satins suddenly claimed the principal position in exports: 17,489 pieces were sold at a value of $347,326, whereas the previous year 8,268 pieces were sold for $167,421. In 1885, watches climbed to the top of the list of Swiss exports in spite of the "general slump in business": in 1883, about 21,556 pieces for about ¥132,206; in 1884, 29,439 for ¥160,478; and in 1885, 25,000 for ¥163,000.[60] Consul Paul Ritter also mentioned these strong fluctuations: "For many years Swiss industry has monopolized the Japanese market, providing 90% of total consumption. The commerce of watches went from a little more than ¥100,000 in 1890 to more than ¥3 million in 1898, only to fall to ¥400,000 in 1899. . . ."[61]

Colored dye (*Farbstoffe und Anilinfarben*) arrived on the market at the end of the 1870s, and condensed milk in 1888, according to information received from the Swiss company Nestlé. Sales of food products such as cheese and chocolate were insignificant.

Until the end of the century, consuls kept repeating that the statistics available were not sufficient to give a detailed and precise picture of Switzerland's share in Japan's foreign trade. In the table drawn up by Consul A. Wolff of Yokohama, Japanese imports increased from ¥15 million in 1868 to ¥37 million in 1890, whereas Japanese exports grew at a slower rate, from ¥20 to ¥27 million. The enthusiastic Swiss consul even estimated the value of the different imports and exports under separate headings, as well as the volume of shipping and the revenue of the customs office in Yokohama.[62]

In spite of the strong fluctuations mentioned above, commercial relations between Switzerland and Japan improved in the last quarter of the century. Switzerland profited from the extensive reforms which marked the economic and social evolution of Japan. The period from 1868 to 1890 is considered to be the starting point of the takeoff of Japanese economy.[63] The guilds were abolished in 1868 and the feudal system dissolved in 1871. The 1870s were difficult: a terrible crisis of inflation marked the years 1876–80, followed by a period of deflation from 1881 to 1885. More than 52,000 bankruptcies were recorded in the five years from 1875 to 1879.[64] It was not until the 1880s that Japan embarked on a period of steady growth. From 1880 to 1913, Japanese foreign trade multiplied eight times in volume. Between 1880 and 1900 many new industries developed whose products competed with those imported from Europe.

The Swiss played a significant role in the transfer of technology to Japan, as the Japanese historian Nakamura Takeshi remarks:

> The first to adopt machine filature in Japan was the feudal clan of Maehashi. In 1870 a Swiss resident at Kobe, Gustav Muller, was asked by the Maehashi clan to come and demonstrate the operation. Muller was then engaged by the Ono Company, the first civilian concern to practice machine manufacturing of silk. Afterward he worked for the government factory at Akasaka and taught the Italian method of silk manufacturing.[65]

Three other Swiss appear in the tables giving the origin of foreigners, which the above historian calculated at two or three thousand during "the entire Meiji period." The initiative of the Maehashi clan and the Ono Company in adopting machinery seems to have preceded that of the state, which introduced the first modern silk-winding factories and the first spinning machines. Charles Favre-Brandt, vice-consul in Osaka, had already observed a transfer of technology in another field of the textile industry:

> In 1875, in my yearly report, I pointed out that the item, knitted underwear, was now manufactured by the Japanese in Osaka with the help of a certain number of knitting machines, supplied by a Swiss company. The Japanese produce at least 400 to 500 dozen knitted articles a day. . . . I have already said that the Japanese always prefer imitations of the real article if the price is lower. . . . The textiles which they produced to rival certain European products are, as imitations, perfectly successful and the price defeats any competition. . . .[66]

Local competition was not the only problem for Swiss merchants in Japan. They fought among themselves for the best part of the market. This internal struggle among the Swiss merchants gave a considerable advantage to their Japanese counterparts, who quickly learned to profit from this weakness.

All the consular reports mention the 101 different ways which the Japanese used to lower prices. It is true the narrow-mindedness of the Europeans themselves played into their hands. The Swiss watchmakers gave a poor example when they accepted to sell on credit to capture the market from their colleagues. The bankruptcy of a Japanese watch salesman at the end of 1885 cost a fortune to the Swiss who did business against custom.[67] "Business was usually transacted in cash because of a wholly mutual lack of trust."[68] S. Sugiyama draws attention to the consequences of the absence of sale by credit which the Swiss watchmakers had tried to introduce. His point of view appears in Swiss commercial reports:

> Any Japanese merchant who wished to purchase imported goods therefore required a certain amount of capital, and the market was inevitably closed to those with small capital, who were unable to raise sufficient money for purchasing. The number of buyers was therefore limited and the business in imports had to be done inflexibly and on a limited scale. Money exchange dealers lent funds, presumably gained from foreign trade, to import merchants, who required cash.[69]

Under these circumstances it is easy to understand the necessity of being present in Japan and of having close contacts with the merchants of the ports like those Swiss companies in Yokohama: Favre-Brandt, Edouard Bavier, Ernest Borel, Courvoisier & Co., and above all Siber-Brennwald.[70]

Western experts were invited to work in Japan and were encouraged by the high salaries which Japan offered to entice foreigners: They could receive pay that was 12 times higher than that received by Japanese civil servants. During the period 1870 to 1891, salaries for foreigners never dropped below ¥50 per month, whereas 55% of Japanese civil servants earned ¥15 a month, and 25% of them only ¥10 a month. A quarter of the westerners employed by the government received a monthly salary of ¥50 to ¥200, and 7% of them received a salary of ¥500 to ¥1,000 a month.[71]

Numerous Japanese were sent to study abroad by their government. From 1868 until the end of the century, thousands of students and civil servants studied for one to three years in America and Europe.[72] Japanese historians mention Switzerland in their statistics of receiving countries, even if it is only a question of two, three, or four students studying engineering (mechanics, civil engineering, steel manufacturing, and electricity).[73] Ohno Moriyoshi, son of an important watchmaker, entered the school of watchmakers in Geneva in September 1877. After qualifying three years later, he spent a short time working at Patek Philippe & Co. in Geneva. In 1885 two young sons of watch merchants in Tokyo, Mizuno Taichi and Takenouchi Jizaburō, entered the school of watchmakers of

Le Locle on the recommendation of the Favre-Brandts of Yokohama. In spite of the failure of their projects to create watchmaking enterprises in Japan, "they nevertheless had a great influence on the evolution of the Japanese watchmaking industry. They opened up the path that others followed."[74]

The organization of the Polytechnical School in Zurich, founded in 1854 and opened in autumn 1855, seemed to have interested the Japanese:

> Dyner's College did provide, from 1873 to 1886, an elite of Japanese students, as well as their technical assistants, with an entrée into the modern world of 19th century technology.
>
> The organization of the college was based on that of the Polytechnic of Zurich. Both Hug Matison and Itō Hirobumi agreed that it was so. Yamao Yozo, later Minister of Works, also insisted that the inspiration came from Zurich.[75]

The situation changed abruptly in the last ten years of the 19th century. It is incredible to see how quickly Japan freed itself from western technical assistance. Edmond Rochette, Swiss general consul to Japan, complained of the sudden change in his report on the year 1891, dated 6 May 1892: "Up until last year, the ministries, the army, the administration, and Japanese enterprises employed a certain number of foreigners; now they are all being dismissed. . . . There is an evident reaction against foreigners. . . ."[76] For Japanese authorities, this desire to dispense with western scientific aid is part of a long maturing project of economic development.

VIII. The Rise of the Japanese Watchmaking Industry

Yamaguchi Ryūji divides the history of the Japanese clock and watchmaking industry into six main periods:[77] (1) 1549–78, importation of mechanical clocks from Europe; (2) 1579–1638, Japanese clockmakers copy European clocks; (3) 1639–1861, Japanese adaptation of European clocks to their own time scheme under the name *wadokei*; (4) 1862–91, the beginnings of the Japanese clock and watchmaking industry; (5) 1892–1945, development of the clock- and watchmaking industry; (6) 1945–69, introduction of Japanese watchmaking industry's production on the world market.

The rise of the watchmaking industry at the end of the 19th century was due to the initiative of several Japanese craftsmen who went to train in Holland and Switzerland. Unfortunately these enterprising individuals of the Ohno, Mizuno, and Takenouchi families failed in their attempts to found viable companies in Japan:

> The technology gap between Japan and the West was a gap between handicraft and mass production—so wide and so deep that the Japanese entrepreneurs who hoped to produce clocks and watches to compete with imports had no choice but to introduce the same machines and apply the same mass production methods as those used in the West. The first successful maker of modern clocks was Hayashi Ichibei, who founded a factory called Jiseisha in Nagoya in 1888. The largest clock merchant in that city, he had greatly prospered from his dealings with foreign tradesmen in Yokohama, and decided to invest his profits in an attempt to manufacture the same type of wall clocks as were being imported. . . .
>
> . . . Hayashi's clockshop began with 40 workers. The factory rapidly expanded, until in the single year of 1892, it produced more than ten thousand clocks turned out by 323 employees. Jiseisha had become a large corporation with a considerable volume of production by the time Japanese industry was taking off.[78]

All authors acknowledge the importance of the role played by Hattori Kintarō in the takeoff of the Japanese watchmaking industry:

> Hattori Kintarō began his career as an apprentice in a clock shop; in 1881 he opened his own business, purchasing watches from foreign tradesmen in Yokohama and selling them to retailers. He was very successful in the trade, by the 1890s importing watches directly from Switzerland and the United States. In 1892 he set up a clock factory called Seikōsha. . . .
>
> . . . Seikōsha also began producing alarm clocks and pocket watches, articles which had previously been considered impossible to produce in Japan. . . .
>
> In order to make alarm clocks it was necessary to develop techniques for plating the case and, especially important, to set a system for mass production of small-sized movements. The latter was finally made possible when Hattori purchased a complete set of machines for mass production of clock parts in Germany during his tour of Europe and the U.S. in 1899–1900. Improvements were made on the imported machines, and efforts continued to manufacture all parts within the Seikōsha factory.

> . . . During World War I, Britain and France ordered large numbers of alarm clocks from Japan in place of Germany, raising Seikōsha's annual production sharply to 500,000–600,000. After that, however, production declined to its pre-war level, while emphasis gradually shifted to the production of pocket watches and wristwatches.[79]

The production of pocket watches was particularly difficult because of Swiss and American competition. Paul Ritter, Swiss consul in Yokohama, described the terrible losses of Japanese companies which ventured into this field in his 1898 report:

> The Osaka Watch Company has almost completely abandoned the production of pocket watches. . . . The company suffered a complete failure and the money invested was lost. The Nihon Watch Company in Tokyo is also in a precarious position.[80]

It was Seikōsha that finally succeeded in establishing a viable watchmaking business in Japan. Hattori invested his profits from sale of imported watches into clockmaking, and when this, in turn, showed a profit, he diverted the surplus into making watch cases, which soon constituted a large part of the revenue from his business as a whole.

Hattori's tenacity was eventually rewarded. He endured many years of loss to develop his watchmaking division and profited from his voyages abroad to acquire advanced watchmaking machinery. His enterprise is a good example of the changeover from trade to production. Commercial profits fueled the takeoff and rapid development of manufacture at the beginning of the century. "Watch production at Seikōsha rose from 2,000 pieces per month in 1903 to 17,400 per month in 1918. With the failure of the Osaka Watch Company and the Nihon Watch Company, Seikōsha remained the only watch factory east of the Suez Canal as late as the end of World War I."[81]

In 1922 wristwatch production began; in 1930 watch production totaled 2.2 million pieces to reach 5.1 million in 1937, the highest point of these years of development. From 1938 production was reduced by a quarter before falling below 3 million pieces in 1941. During the war the watchmaking industry was entirely converted to armaments production.

IX. The Swiss Watchmaking Industry Dominates the Japanese Market

Swiss watchmakers have never been known for their modesty. Sure of their supremacy, they were convinced that they alone were capable of manufacturing good watches. Instead of combining, they competed ruthlessly with each other, damaging the reputation for quality of the label which was to become "Swiss Made." In the last quarter of the 19th century, Swiss watchmakers held about 80% of the Japanese market. This virtual monopoly blinded the Swiss to the changing mentality of the Japanese during this period, although the companies were obliged to adapt their merchandise to Japanese taste:

> The Japanese who buys a gold watch wants it to have a large diameter [caliber] (21–23 lines) and a heavy case (18–20 carats). He also wants it to be stamped with the federal hallmark, L'Helvétie, which is well-known and appreciated in Japan. When Swiss companies tried to introduce 14-carat watches on the market, they encountered no success at all. Japanese women do not yet wear watches.[82]

Having described the ruin of the Japanese watchmaking enterprises, Emile Bonjour, head of the Federal Chancellery, drawing his conclusion from talks with the principal Swiss exporters, feared no competition from the Japanese:

> The Japanese do not have the necessary aptitudes to become good watchmakers. If the factories engaged American or European workers, they would have to pay them higher salaries and, without even mentioning the question of quality, the subsequent goods produced by the local factories would, of course, be at a higher price than the European equivalent.[83]

According to this report to the federal authorities, the supremacy of Swiss watchmakers, whose exports made up 86% of the total market in 1896, was in no way threatened by local competition. This official point of view was not generally accepted; Paul Ritter, the Swiss consul in Yokohama, was more pessimistic than Bonjour. Ritter worried about the bad quality of the watches, a result of the cutthroat competition between Swiss companies. The shrewd connoisseur of the Japanese empire did not show the same contempt for the Japanese worker, whom he described as skillful, adroit, and, above all, cheap.

The situation changed suddenly at the end of the 19th century. Paul Ritter warned the appropriate business circles in his voluminous 1901 report in which he stressed the fall of Swiss exports from ¥2.4 million in 1898 to ¥228,161 in 1899.[84] Japan had suddenly stopped buying watches. He drew attention to the weaknesses of the watch trade, such as smuggling, to evade the new customs duties of the 1896 treaty, and also the development of a new direct commerce between Switzerland and Japan which competed with the intermediaries established in the archipelago. According to the consul "the Japanese tradesman is treacherous and quarrelsome, the judicial system long and expensive"; Swiss commercial interests did indeed seem in jeopardy. Several commercial houses, such as the Schneider Bros. and Herb & Co., went bankrupt. They were forced to liquidate large stocks of watches. Another major development was that American watchmakers had penetrated the Japanese market.[85]

The Americans were more responsive and compliant to the changing fashion in Japan than the conservative Swiss. The small American watches replaced the large Swiss ones. Whereas the Swiss dispatched finished goods, the Americans, past masters at evading customs duties, sent their watch movements and cases separately. The uniformity and simplicity of their calibers facilitated the assembling of the watches in Yokohama.

Switzerland's share in Japan's imports of watch products changed from 86% in 1896 to 76% in 1898 and 55% in 1900, reaching rock bottom in 1902 with only 47% of the market. In just a few years Swiss watchmakers had lost their preeminent position to American competition and also to the gradual domination by Japanese watchmakers of their own market.

X. Revision of Commercial Treaties in 1896 and 1911

In the period preceding World War I, the Swiss federal authorities and Swiss businessmen watched attentively the wave of international colonial expansion in the race for raw materials and new markets. Even if Switzerland did not participate in international politics, Swiss businessmen claimed state assistance to defend their commercial interests. In May 1896 the Vorort (the most important employers' association) financed an inquiry into economic relations between Switzerland and Japan.[86] The most detailed reports were the work of Paul Ritter, Swiss consul in Yokohama. Inasmuch as Japan had abolished the system of consulate jurisdiction and adopted a protectionist tariff legislation, the Swiss were obliged to negotiate a new commercial treaty in November 1896.[87] The import duty was raised to improve public finances and to promote the development of local industries. The tariff established a duty of 8–10% on current articles and 15–20% on luxury items. Watch products were taxed more heavily: 30% on gold watches, 25% on silver ones, and

15% on watch movements. On October 1, 1906, the taxes were increased to 50% on gold watches and 40% for the other two categories. These measures favored the introduction of unfinished articles to Japan. Watch movements and cases were imported separately and then assembled locally. The Japanese authorities remained indifferent to the Swiss watchmakers' complaints.[88]

In the same year, 1906, Switzerland finally decided to open a legation in Tokyo. Paul Ritter, consul in Yokohama since 1892, became the first official Swiss diplomatic representative in the Japanese empire, China, and Korea.[89] This step marked the importance of Japan in Swiss commercial relations in Asia, even if, in reality, commercial exchanges between the two countries only represented about 1% of their total imports and exports. In April 1910, Japan adopted a further series of tariffs affecting textile goods, condensed milk, tar colors, and watches, among other products. The list was joined to the Federal Council's message.[90] On 21 June 1911, the two countries signed a new treaty of commerce for 12 years. This treaty was renewed by both parties and was still enforced in 1964.

From the beginning of the 20th century to World War I, there was a deficit in the Swiss balance of trade with Japan except for the years 1905–8. During these four years it was the important volume of watch exports which gave Switzerland a surplus in the balance of trade. It was during the war that Switzerland's commercial deficit was most pronounced because its traders attempted to buy on the Japanese market at any price. The First World War offered Japan's industries a unique opportunity to expand. Even if all the conditions for the "takeoff" existed at the end of the 19th century, the war accelerated the growth of industry and the diversification of the Japanese economy, as confirmed by Ferdinand de Salis:

> If the export of metals rocketed, it was because of the constant demand from the nations at war. Machinery was the most important item to increase the volume of exports. Before the war, machinery and instruments were an important item of Japan's imports. A year ago [this report is dated June 28, 1917] the situation changed: Japan has become an exporter of machines. . . ."[91]

Two years later the same author remarked that the Japanese were capable of imitating or copying any foreign product.

The following report, written on 13 July 1917, mentioned the continuation of this period of prosperity and "all the exceptionally favorable conditions which stimulate economic activity to an unprecedented degree."

Japanese exports to Switzerland increased rapidly to 20.4 million Swiss francs in 1916, to 33.2 million in 1917, and to 73.7 million in 1918. In 1918 Swiss exports to Japan were worth only 21.3 million francs. This situation was dramatically reversed during the crisis of the 1920s and there was a surplus in the Swiss balance of trade between the two world wars. However, it would be prudent to mention that the commercial exchange figures of each country vary considerably, as the head of the Swiss legation in Tokyo acknowledged:

> The Japanese trade statistics give a completely false idea of commercial relations between Switzerland and Japan. A comparison of the Swiss and Japanese statistics shows that Japanese exports to Switzerland in 1906, 1907, and 1908 were about 218, 66, and 70 times higher according to Swiss figures than their Japanese equivalent. It is the same case for Swiss imports to Japan, which are also higher according to Swiss statistics, although the difference is not so marked as in the previous example.[92]

This is the reason why I have based my research work on figures mentioned in Swiss sources, thus avoiding erroneous conclusions.

XI. Nestlé in Japan

At the end of the 19th century, the Swiss company Nestlé began to expand, first in Europe, then in America. In 1907 the rise in customs duties in Australia forced Nestlé to buy the largest condensed milk company in that country, the Cressbrook Dairy Co. of Brisbane. Several years later Singapore became the center of distribution for Nestlé in the Far East. Warehouses were opened in Hong Kong, Calcutta, Madras, Bombay, and Colombo.[93]

In 1913, Nestlé established a company in Japan. It is useful to remember that it was only after 1899 that foreign companies were allowed to invest outside the "foreign settlements" in Japan. Nestlé's "Anglo-Swiss condensed milk company" imported and sold Nestlé milk products. Condensed and powdered milk were the main products sold in Japan until the end of the Second World War. The company started by buying offices in Yokohama. After the First World War, business developed slowly. By 1925 Nestlé realized a turnover of more than a million Swiss francs, two-thirds from condensed milk and the rest from the sale of lactogen (powdered baby food). One Swiss and ten Japanese worked in

Nestlé's office in Japan, which moved from Yokohama to Kobe after the 1923 earthquake. There was no local production because of the inadequate milk supply in Japan. Condensed milk was imported from Holland for both the Chinese and Japanese markets. In 1928, Edmond Mandelert joined seven Englishmen at the Shanghai branch in China. He was the first Swiss to work for Nestlé in China. Together they controlled 300 employees in five warehouses. Their turnover reached 2.5 million Swiss francs.[94]

In the early 1930s, Nestlé participated actively in the development of the Japanese milk industry. Nestlé also took an interest in the work of the local milk cooperatives created to teach local farmers. When an attempt to create a joint venture with the Japanese company Snow Brand failed, the Swiss directors decided to start their own local production. In 1933, Nestlé built their first factory on Awaji, a small island near Kobe. The factory supplied milk products such as Milkmaid, a concentrated, non-sweetened milk, and powdered milk. These high-quality products rapidly became popular. The Swiss engineer E. O. Schmidt, with the help of another engineer, Albrecht, built a canning factory. From 1933 onward Maurice Champoud managed the Nestlé factory with two other Swiss and about 100 Japanese employees. The factory produced 3,000–5,000 liters a day. In order to avoid certain local problems encountered by other foreign companies, Nestlé founded its own Japanese company, Awaji Rennyū, with a capital of ¥50,000. In 1935, Nestlé engaged a Swiss, Cyril Bovet, to build a second factory at Saidaji, near Okayama. Forty Japanese worked at the factory under the direction of Mr. Spettlau. The salary of the Japanese employees was between ¥25 and 40 a month; Swiss personnel received at least 20 to 30 times more. Only condensed milk was locally produced. Nestlé milk products competed with those of English and Dutch companies and of Japanese companies, such as Snow Brand of Hokkaido and Morinaga and Meiji, which were established in several towns throughout Japan. Nestlé's local factories only produced a limited range of products: condensed milk, both sweetened and non-sweetened, powdered baby food, and a little caramel from the surplus of sweetened condensed milk. Chocolate and coffee only came onto the market after World War II.

The scarcity of local milk was a constant problem during the 1920s and 1930s. Without pastureland, cows were fed with other food, which gave a strange taste to the milk. Nestlé imported bulls from Canada to improve the local stock, lent money to local farmers to buy more cows, and even engaged several veterinary surgeons to control breeding. These improvements were condemned by the Japan Milk Association, which tried to curtail all efforts to rationalize production. In 1934 the situation became critical when condensed milk imports were severely limited. Nestlé realized that it had to become self-sufficient. When the Japanese banned the European brand names Eagle and Milkmaid in 1936, Nestlé changed the labels on its products to its own Japanese brand name, Awaji Rennyū.

The 1920s and 1930s were extremely difficult years: The Swiss company realized a turnover of only 2 million francs and during the Second World War the company only just managed to survive with a skeleton staff. However, the presence of Nestlé in Japan from 1913 to 1941 and the experience gathered by its directors during this period were important factors in the success of the company after the war. An internal memo written by Nestlé in 1987 explains:

> Nestlé's Presence [in Japan] Before the Second World War:
> There is no doubt that Nestlé's presence in Japan before the war played an important role in its later success.
> —During the first 50 years Nestlé became familiar with Japan, the local market and the different economic and business circles.
> —Nestlé had also proved to Japanese consumers that it controlled the quality of its products. This good reputation was important when launching new products on the market.
> —Nestlé's experience of Japan was also important for recruiting locally. Most foreign companies have difficulty recruiting bright Japanese university graduates because:
> —They cannot offer the same social status to their staff as the Japanese companies.
> —The Japanese work philosophy is different from the Western one.
> —Foreign companies have little contact with local universities, which orientate their promising students toward industry. The lack of long-term strategy in foreign companies discourages young Japanese.
> Nestlé is recognized in Japan as a stable company capable of creating a satisfying work environment for ambitious young employees.

XII. Conclusion

Switzerland has always lived by its exports. In spite of its lack of raw materials and seaports, Switzerland sells its manufactured articles throughout the world. In the wake of American and European expansion, Swiss merchants and industrialists profited from the opening of the Japanese market. The pioneer merchants, following the example of their predecessors in China at the beginning of the 19th century, established themselves even under difficult conditions at Yokohama. The development of commercial relations between Switzerland and Japan is a direct result of the presence of this handful of traders followed by their companies in the Japanese ports.

The political authorities in Switzerland were persuaded by these businessmen and their companies to open consulates in Yokohama in 1864 and in Osaka in 1870 and a legation in Tokyo in 1906. The annual reports and the correspondence of first the consuls and then the legation constitute a documentary corpus of considerable value. These authors give a vision of Japan and the Japanese which is slightly stereotyped but which merits further study. The tremendous contrast between the different cultures and mentalities did not facilitate business relations. The Swiss found it difficult to accept the constant efforts of the Japanese to become independent of foreign know-how: "The Japanese is ambitious and wants to do everything himself. As long as he is unable to, he will continue to shun anything foreign; this state of affairs ceases when he feels confident and is able to produce articles to compete with any foreign products."[95]

This prophecy was to be realized after many years of copying foreign goods. This copying irritated the Swiss merchants:

> The European notion of "forgery" does not exist for the Japanese. To copy a model, reproduce a masterpiece, to imitate an idea, for a Japanese, is to honor the creator. . . . This is why it is worth paying continuous attention to the dangers of forgery and imitation that Swiss products undergo at the hands of the Japanese manufacturers.[96]

However, it should be remembered that the Japanese imitated Swiss manufactured goods with the machines which the Swiss eagerly sold them. In 1919 the Japanese manufactured western tool machines by copying the best models.

After highlighting the numerous fluctuations in commercial relations between Japan and Switzerland, it is important to add that this trade remained marginal. According to Swiss sources, trade with Japan accounted for only 1% of its total trade up to World War I.

Notes

1. Paul Bairoch, "Le volume des exportations de la Suisse de 1851 à 1975," *Revue Suisse d'histoire,* 1978, 1–2, p. 33; general books on Swiss economic history given in the bibliography.

2. *Développement du commerce extérieur de la Suisse dans les années 1886 à 1912*, Berne, Département fédéral des douanes s.d., pp. 376–79.

3. "Commerce de la Suisse avec le Japon 1899–1910, importation et exportation données en quantité et en valeur par rubrique," in *Feuille Fédérale de la Confédération suisse* (hereinafter F.F.) année 1911, vol. 111, pp. 1205–6.

4. Archives Fédérales Suisses (AFS) E 2400 Osaka: letter from the Vice-Consul Ch. Favre-Brandt to the Haut-Conseil Fédéral on 20 June 1878.

5. Georges Bonnant, "Quelques aspects du commerce d'horlogerie en Chine à la fin du XVIIIe et au cours du XIXe siècles," *La Suisse Horlogère*, no. 17, 23 April 1964, pp. 404–8, gives the names of the watchmakers and traders based in the Chinese ports open to foreign trade.

6. Alfred Chapuis, *Relations de l'horlogerie suisse avec la Chine. La montre chinoise.* Neuchâtel, Attinger (1919), 272 pp., still the best study on the subject. On Fleurier and watches for China, cf. François Jequier, *Une entreprise horlogère du Val-de-Travers: Fleurier Watch Co. S.A.*, Neuchâtel, La Baconnière, 1972, pp. 33–44 and bibliography, pp. 370–71.

7. Walter Bodmer, *Die Entwicklung der schweizerischen Textilwirtschaft im Rahmen der übrigen Industrien und Wirtschaftszweige.* Zurich, Verlag Berichthaus, 1960, 580 pp.

8. The different stages of this commercial expansion are described in Hermann Wartmann, *Atlas über die Entwicklung von Industrie und Handel der Schweiz in dem Zeitraum vom Jahre 1770 bis 1870.* Winterthur, 1873.

9. Ambassade du Japon, *Coup d'oeil sur les relations entre la Suisse et le Japon de 1586 à ce jour.* Berne, Ambassade du Japon, p. 1.

10. Alfred Chapuis, "Les Hollandais au Japon et l'horlogerie (1600–1857)," *Journal suisse d'horlogerie* (édition suisse), nos. 3–4, 1951, pp. 47–52.

11. David S. Landes, *L'heure qu'il est: Les horloges, la mesure du temps et la formation du monde moderne.* Paris, Gallimard, 1987, pp. 122–25.

12. Yamaguchi Ryūji, "Historique de l'industrie horlogère japonaise," *La Suisse Horlogère*, no. 40, 15 October 1970, pp. 1535–37.

13. Béatrice Veyrassat, *Négociants et fabricants dans l'industrie cotonnière suisse 1760–1840: Aux origines financières de l'industrialisation.* Lausanne, Payot, 1982, p. 39; Bodmer, *op. cit.*, pp. 345–46.

14. Veyrassat, *op. cit.*, p. 255.

15. Message from the Federal Council to the legislative councils concerning the delegation to Japan (8 July 1861), in F.F. 1861, vol. II, p. 323.

16. Paul Akamatsu, *Meiji: 1868 Révolution et contre-révolution au Japon.* Paris Calmann-Lévy, 1968, p. 107 ff. Vers l'ouverture.

17. Pierre Renouvin, *La question d'Extrême-Orient 1840/1940.* Paris, Hachette, 1946, p. 49.

18. *Ibid.*, p. 52–53; Akamatsu, *op. cit.* , pp. 107–43.

19. Akamatsu, *op. cit.*, p. 145ff.

20. Archives de l'Etat de Neuchâtel (AEN), carton brochures 113. Acte constitutif de l'Union horlogère, Cf. also Henri Grandjean, *Exposé des motifs de l'Association l'Union horlogère.* La Chaux-de-Fonds, 1858, 40 pp., which gives a good summary of the period.

21. Hans Rosenberg, *Die Weltwirtschaftskrise 1857–1859.* Goettingen, 1974, XXV+210 pp.; Frédéric Scheurer, *Les crises de l'industrie horlogère dans le canton de Neuchâtel*... Neuveville, Beerstecher, 1914, p. 56ff.

22. AEN, Brochure 113, Report from the Administrative Council of the

Watchmakers' Association to the general assembly of shareholders on 4 February 1860, p. 16.

23. Jean-Marc Barrelet, "Diplomatie, commerce et ethnographie: Le voyage d'Aimé Humbert au Japon 1862–1864," *Musée Neuchâtelois*, no. 4, 1986, pp. 145–66.

24. *Ibid.*, p. 150.

25. AEN, copies of the letters from Aimé Humbert.

26. AFS, E 6/39–40, Handelsverhältnisse mit Japan 1854–1867.

27. Paul Akio Nakai, *Das Verhältnis zwischen der Schweiz und Japan: Vom Beginn der diplomatischen Beziehungen 1958 bis 1968.* Bern und Stuttgart, Paul Haupt, 1967, p. 27; "Die Aufnahme der diplomatischen Beziehungen zwischen der Schweiz und Japan im Jahre 1864," in *Nippon-Helvetia 1864–1964.* Tokyo, Comité du Centenaire, 1964, pp. 11–68.

28. Nakai, *op. cit.*, p. 31; F.F. 1861, vol. II, p. 327.

29. Nakai, *op. cit.*, pp. 32–44, Rudolf Lindau in Japan. The Swiss point of view is given in the Federal Council's message concerning the delegation to Japan on 8 July, 1861, in F.F. 1861, vol. II, p. 327ff.

30. Among Lindau's numerous reports, two, addressed to the Swiss Department of Trade and Customs Duty, are particularly interesting:

(1) The English trading posts in the Straits of Malacca, Singapore, Penang, Malacca, dated the end of August 1859 in Shanghai 28 fol. ms, AFS E 60 40.

(2) On trade in Nagasaki and Yokohama and the future of trade with Japan, 30 fol. ms. AFS E 6 40.

31. AFS E 6 40, 7 fol. ms.

32. AFS E 6 40, letter from the President of the Watchmakers' Association, Aimé Humbert to Knüsel, Vice-President of the Federal Council. La Chaux-de-Fonds, 16 April 1860.

33. Ambassade du Japon, *op. cit.*, p. 2; F.F. 1861, vol. II, p. 329–30.

34. First official report written from Japan by Mr. Spiess, Saxon commissioner with the Prussian mission to Asia in F.F. 1861, t.I., pp. 439–65. On "Taffachellas," see note 59.

35. F.F. 1861, t.I. p. 443 *op. cit.*, p. 42.

36. Bairoch, *op. cit.*, p. 42.

37. Message from the Federal Council . . . concerning the delegation to Japan (8 July 1861) in F.F. 1861, vol. II, p. 319–32; John Ninet, *Pas de traité commercial avec le Japon!* Berne, Impr. Haller, 5 July 1861, 16 pp.

38. C. Brennwald published numerous reports between 1863 and 1865, e.g., *Mission suisse au Japon*, Berne, 1864, 23 pp. and his *Rapport général sur la partie commerciale de la mission suisse au Japon*, Berne, Weingart, 1865, 159 pp.

39. John Bringolf left Japan for San Francisco in the spring of 1863.

40. Barrelet, *op. cit.*, p. 152.

41. AFS E 13 (B) 198.

42. AEN, Fonds Aimé Humbert, copies of letters.

43. The decision to abandon the Asian trading post of the Watchmakers' Association was taken on 24 March 1864, by the Administrative Council. AEN Brochure 113, report to shareholders, 1 April 1865, p. 3.

44. On the events described by Aimé Humbert, cf. Akamatsu, *op. cit.*, p. 195ff.

45. Messages from the Federal Council to the Federal Assembly concerning

the ratification of the commercial treaty with Japan (27 June 1864), in F.F. 1984, vol. II, pp. 189–213, give the text of the treaty.

46. F.F. 1864, vol. II, p. 129.

47. Jean de Rham, "Les relations entre le Japon et la Suisse de 1864 à 1964," in *Nippon-Helvetia*, pp. 69–93. A consular agency in Hakodata, managed by Mr. Veuve, was closed in 1868, the one in Nagasaki in 1869. A Swiss consulate was in operation in Osaka for Hyōgo prefecture from 1870 to 1890. Cf. AFS E 2400 Osaka I. On 14 February 1866 Caspar Brennwald, commercial delegate of the Swiss mission to Japan (1862–64), succeeded the Dutch Consul in Yokohama and occupied the post until 1881.

48. Brennwald, *Rapport général, op. cit.*, p. 24.

49. AFS E 1508 Yokohama. The Federal Council refused to discuss the matter.

50. AFS 2200 Yokohama I Matrikel-Register 1863–1919.

51. Barrelet, *op. cit.*, pp. 162, and 166 n 13.

52. Eugène Jaquet and Alfred Chapuis, *Histoire et technique de la montre suisse des origines à nos jours*. Bâle, Urs Graf, 1945, pp. 141–42, "Trade with Japan."

53. Brennwald, *Rapport général, op. cit.*, pp. 46–48.

54. Nakai, *op. cit.*, in *Nippon-Helvetia*, p. 66.

55. *Siber-Hegner 1865–1965*, Jubiläumsschrift, Zürich, 1965; Lorenz Stucki, *L'empire occulte: Les secrets de la puissance helvétique*. Paris, Laffont, 1970, pp. 150–51.

56. AFS E 2400 Osaka: Report from the Swiss Vice-Consul at Osaka (M. Charles Favre-Brandt of Locle) for the year 1877.

57. de Rham, *op. cit.*, p. 78.

58. *Ibid.*, p. 77.

59. "Taffachellassen": cloth similar to cotton but stronger, which was made by the Dutch for the Japanese. It was used in the making of the national costume for both men and women. Switzerland destroyed the Dutch monopoly for the export of this article.

Brennwald, *Rapport général, op. cit.*, p. 29, H. Wartmann, *Industrie und Handel des Kantons St. Gallen am Ende 1866*, St. Gall, 1875, p. 517: " . . . during the last years of my report, Japan has opened her ports to goods from the textile industry of Toggenburg and has given this industry a lucrative trade in one particular article, the "Taffachelasse" (close-woven material with a double twisted thread with stripes, usually in rustic cloth of Toggenburg dark blue) . . . ." See also p. 589.

60. *Journal suisse d'horlogerie*, no. 4, Oct. 1886, p. 124. This preponderance increased at the end of the century, but with strong variations. The rate of the yen was fr. 4.50 in February 1885.

61. AFS E 6 40 Paul Ritter, "Watch and clock trade in Japan in 1901," p. 9.

62. AFS E 2300 Yokohama I. Bericht des schweiz. General-konsuls in Yokohama über das Jahr 1880, p. 461.

63. Pham-Van-Thuan. *Les fondements socio-économiques de la révolution industrielle du Japon*. Lausanne, 1966, p. 12.

64. Pierre Léon, *Histoire économique et sociale du monde*. Paris, Colin, 1978, t. 4, p. 247; W.W. Rostow, *Les étapes de la croissance économique*. Paris, Le Seuil, 1963, pp. 103–6.

65. Nakamura Takeshi, "The Contribution of Foreigners," in *Society, Science and Technology in Japan, Journal of World History*, vol. IX, 2, 1965, pp. 315–16; cf. also Pham-Van-Thuan, *op. cit.*, p. 159ff.

66. AFS E 2400 Osaka: Report for the year 1878, pp. 434–35.
67. *Journal Suisse d'Horlogerie*, no. 4, October 1886, pp. 124–25.
68. S. Sugiyama, *op. cit.*, p. 9.
69. *Ibid.*, p. 10.
70. *Siber-Hegner*, *op. cit.* This study relates in detail the evolution of the company in Japan and especially the role played by Arnold Wolff, who entered the company in 1869.
71. Pham-Van-Thuan, *op. cit.*, pp. 165–68. Later, in October 1900, Professor Louis Bridel (1852–1913), a Swiss living in Paris, was appointed to teach French law at the University of Tokyo (*Dictionnaire Historique et Bibliographique de la Suisse*, vol. II, p. 298).
72. *Ibid.*, p. 170ff. gives figures, charts, and diagrams based on source material.
73. Watanabe Minoru, "Japanese Students Abroad and the Acquisition of Scientific and Technical Knowledge," in *Society, Science and Technology in Japan*, *Journal of World History*, vol. IX, 2, 1965, pp. 277, 280, 282 ff.
74. Yamaguchi, *op. cit.*, p. 1536; Takagi Katsuji, "L'évolution du commerce horloger entre le Japon et la Suisse," *La Suisse Horlogère*, no. 40, 15 October 1970, p. 1568.
75. Olive Checkland, *The Scots Abroad: Labour, Capital and Enterprise 1750–1914*. London, Croom Helm, 1985, p. 262 (The Scots in Meiji Japan 1868–1912, pp. 251–71); cf. also Watanabe, *op. cit.*, p. 272. Nakayama Shigeru, "The Role Played by Universities in Scientific and Technological Development in Japan," in *Society, Science and Technology in Japan*, *Journal of World History*, vol. IX, 2, 1965, p. 345.
76. AFS E 2400 Yokohama.
77. Yamaguchi, *op. cit.*, pp. 1535–37; Erich Pauer, "Traditional Technology and Its Impact on Japan's Industry during the Early Period of the Industrial Revolution," in *Pre-Conditions to Industrialization in Japan*. Berne, 1986 (9th International Economic History Congress).
78. Uchida Hoshimi, "The Growth of Japan's Watchmaking Industry," in *Entrepreneurship: The Japanese Experience*, Kyoto, PHP Institute, 1983, pp. 14–15.
79. *Ibid.*, pp. 16–17.
80. AFS E 6/40. For more details, cf. Uchida, *op. cit.*, p. 17.
81. Uchida, *op. cit.*, pp. 17–18.
82. AFS E 6/40. Emile Bonjour, *Horlogerie au Japon*, 8 pp. ms.
83. *Ibid.*
84. AFS E 6/40. Paul Ritter, "The Watch Trade in Japan," 18 fol. ms. pp. Several excerpts are published in the *Feuille Officielle Suisse du Commerce*.
85. Ritter, *op. cit.*, Barrelet, *op. cit.*, p. 164.
86. AFS E 13 (B) 204.
87. On these negotiations, cf. the 1896 correspondence of Paul Ritter and AFS E 2007 (A) and the report of the Department of Trade and Industry (20 November 1896) on the future of commercial relations between Switzerland and Japan (AFS E 2001 (A)). Cf. also the Message of the Federal Council of the General Assembly concerning the treaty of friendship, settlement, and trade with Japan (10 November 1896), in F.F. 1896, no. 51, pp. 812–43.
88. *La Fédération Horlogère*, no. 47, 13 June 1897.
89. Yves Collart, Marco Durrer, and Verdiana Grossi, "Les relations extérieures de la Suisse à la fin du XIXe siècle . . .," in *Etudes et Sources*. Berne, 1983, no. 9, p. 117.

90. F.F. no. 32, 9 August 1911, pp. 1193–230.

91. AFS. "Tokyo Notices économiques sur le Japon," in *Rapports commerciaux de légations et consulats suisses de l'année 1917.* Berne, 1918, p. 85.

92. AFS E 2400 Tokyo 1–4. Report from the Swiss legation in Tokyo for the year 1909, pp. 31–32.

93. Jean Heer, *Reflets du Monde 1866–1966. Présence de Nestlé.* Lausanne, 1966, 230 pp.

94. Information from Mr. Edmond Mandelert during an interview at Nestlé's headquarters in Vevey on 6 March 1989. Mr. Mandelert worked for Nestlé in China from 1928 to 1945 before controlling Nestlé Japan from 1945 to 1955. I would also like to thank Mr. Franz Müller, who worked in Japan from 1966 to 1978. These interviews were arranged by Mr. Georges Speidel.

95. AFS E 2400 Tokyo 1–4: Report from the Swiss legation in Tokyo for the year 1909, p. 28.

96. AFS E 2400 Tokyo 5: Walther Thurnheer, Report from the Swiss legation in Japan, 1937, p. 32.

Comment

Terushi Hara

The paper by Professor Jequier describes the economic and commercial relations between Switzerland and Japan from the beginning to World War II, stressing mainly the watchmaking industry of the two nations. His paper is divided into two parts. In the first part, which is composed of sections I–VII, he shows us the following facts.

First, he writes about Swiss residents in China and Japan before 1859. At that time, Swiss trade with Japan was in the hands of the Dutch East India Company, which benefited from a monopoly on Japanese trade at Deshima. Then, after mentioning that the Americans breached the Japanese fortress, it is shown that private enterprise preceded diplomatic relations, and the activities of the first mission of a Watchmakers' Association in 1859 are shown. This mission did not succeed because of the attitude of the Japanese government. Then there was a time of vicissitudes of diplomatic negotiations from 1861 to 1864. In 1864, Aimé Humbert, who was the president of the Swiss delegation in Japan, signed the commercial and friendship treaty between the two countries. After this treaty there was a development of commercial relations between the two countries, but it was very slow from 1864 to 1899 and there were only a handful of Swiss who did business in Japan.

In the second part of his paper, Jequier describes the outline of the development of the Japanese watchmaking industry, citing especially the recent works of Japanese scholars.

First, he shows the rise of the Japanese watchmaking industry and the slow development of its independence. After that, it is shown that Swiss watchmakers held about 80% of the Japanese market. But after the revisions of commercial treaties in 1896 and 1911, Swiss watchmakers lost their dominant market share in Japan. These are the main points which Jequier's paper presented.

I have three questions about Jequier's paper. First, what was the relative importance of the Japanese watch market for the Swiss watchmaking industry in comparison to other foreign markets? What was the foreign investment and export policy of the Swiss watchmaking industry? And were there any differences between the policies for Japan and for other countries?

Second, the transfer of technology is important. Jequier says that traditional clockmasters were not directly transformed into modern clockmakers, but approached mechanical clockmaking after studying in western countries and being trained under European mechanics hired as advisers by Japanese government-owned factories.

Jequier's paper tells us that Japan sent some people to Switzerland to study the technology of watchmaking, but they did not succeed in establishing their business in Japan in the 1870s. In the case of Seikōsha, Hattori Kintarō imported watches from Switzerland in 1890 and succeeded in establishing his company in 1892. Can we conclude that it was useless to send people to Switzerland to study the technology? I would like to know the particular features of the transfer of technology of the watchmaking industry from Switzerland to Japan.

Third, according to Jequier's paper, Swiss watchmakers held about 80% of the Japanese watch market in the last quarter of the 19th century, but they lost their dominant market because of tariff protection by the Japanese government and the Japanese ability to copy foreign goods. His paper stresses the attitudes of the Japanese side. But were there any other factors which caused the departure of the Swiss watchmaking industry from the Japanese market on the Swiss side? Was it the Swiss watchmaking industry that lacked the innovation of technology, marketing activities, and entrepreneurship?

Response

François Jequier

From the 18th century onward, Swiss watchmakers sold their watches on the world market. After the Napoleonic wars, Swiss merchants explored the Far East, settling first in China and then, 50 years later, in Japan.

Japan's watch market was not important from a macroeconomic expert's point of view, but it was the main distribution channel for certain enterprises. A lot of watchmakers specialized in articles for specific places such as Japan, China, South America, Turkey, etc. It is not possible to distinguish any global export policy when studying the Swiss watchmaking industry. There were more than a 1,000 different companies and no central organization. Swiss watchmakers fought each other in every market in the world. The absence of any national commercial policy favored the foreign retailers who played the Swiss against each other to lower prices. There was no specific strategy for the Japanese market.

The study of technology transfer is fraught with difficulties. Numerous interpretations are possible. Japanese historians think that the transfer of technology was important. It is difficult for me to argue differently. Japan sent three to five young men to Switzerland through contacts with the Brandt family. Hattori's success was obviously due to his exceptional entrepreneurial capacities. He used profits from his clockmaking industry to finance his watchmaking industry. Hattori examined Swiss watches before producing his own, but I doubt that the contacts which he had with Swiss watch manufacturers were directly useful. He had access to American, English, and Swiss watches on the open market; he also had every opportunity to adapt these watches to the local market. Apart from the manufactured pieces, most watches were assembled and finished by craftsmen, and there is no doubt that the Japanese excelled in this type of work. Technology transfer is difficult to evaluate without tangible proof.

There are several factors which caused the decline of the Swiss watch industry. The first was the internal competition among Swiss watchmakers, who fought each other ruthlessly for command of the market. The second was the lack of organization in watch exportation. The third factor was the rise of American competition and the growth of American sales in Japan. The fourth factor was the lack of innovation of the Swiss watchmakers. The final factor which caused the decline of the Swiss watchmaking industry was the lack of entrepreneurship in this sector caused by its heterogeneous framework.

Watchmaking remained a craft industry. Each attempt to unite the watchmakers failed and each sector producing a particular part of a watch only saw its own short-term interests without ever having a global view of the whole industry. Hattori did not rely on outside contractors. His strength lay in his control of the entire watchmaking process.

With Reservations: Prewar Japan as Host to Western Electric and ITT

Mark Mason

I. Introduction

Why did so few foreign multinationals participate in the developing Japanese economy? This question frames the central debate in the literature on foreign direct investment in modern Japan. The most common explanation is that foreign multinationals did not seriously consider Japan as a site of operations—that these companies practiced what one observer has termed "benign neglect" of the Japanese market.[1] American and other foreign investors were "indifferent" toward or "ignorant" of opportunities in Japan, many critics contend, so they chose not to commit the the necessary resources.[2]

Other accounts point to government and other barriers to explain the relative lack of foreign multinational investment in Japan. "A century of experience makes it abundantly clear," according to one study, "that Japan resolved at an early date to avoid foreign business controls at any price, and the policy has been relentlessly pursued to date. . . ."[3] "As late as the 1960's," states another account, "the Japanese government by dint of a wide variety of protectionist devices did, in fact, make it very difficult for most foreign companies to do business in Japan. . . ."[4] Although these two viewpoints offer differing explanations, what they share is a common focus on the reasons foreign companies did *not* enter Japan.

Yet the prewar record alone offers many instances of foreign multination participation in the Japanese economy—even if the literature provides little explanation for why such firms operated in that economy. According to a 1932 study of the U.S. Department of Commerce, for example, at least 12 American corporations had directly invested in

The author would like to thank Dennis Encarnation, Laurence Goldfarb, Robert Mason, and Mira Wilkins for their helpful comments.

Japanese manufacturing operations by that year. Indeed, these corporations ranked among America's most prominent prewar multinationals —including Ford, General Electric, General Motors, International Telephone and Telegraph, and Otis Elevator.[5] These and other foreign companies acquired substantial interests in local operations in a whole range of important Japanese industries. The same 1932 Department of Commerce study shows, for instance, that almost all of these U.S. multinationals held 50% or more of the equity in their Japanese affiliates— including controlling interests in companies operating in such vital and growing sectors of the Japanese economy as automobiles, elevators, tires, and telephone equipment.

To ascertain why foreign multinationals undertook direct investments in the developing Japanese economy, the present article analyzes the history of Western Electric and ITT as direct investors in the prewar Japanese telephone industry. One conclusion is that the government played a critical role in promoting the entry and development of these foreign companies' investments in Japan, but that this official support later turned to opposition. The analysis then proceeds to ask whether prewar government policies toward these two companies fit into a larger strategy of national development.

II. Western Electric, ITT, and the Japanese Telephone Industry

The early history of the telephone in Japan is virtually inseparable from the policies and actions of the Japanese government.[6] Invented in Boston in March 1876 by Alexander Graham Bell, the telephone was first brought to Japan less than 20 months later by Japan's Ministry of Industry. The Osaka Police Department put the telephone to use in Japan shortly thereafter, and soon the principal government ministries in Tokyo operated phones for limited official purposes.[7]

The authorities, who recognized the importance of telephones almost immediately, encouraged their manufacture in Japan independent of foreign involvement. At the factory of the Ministry of Industry, for example, engineers tried to imitate imported sets with crude lathes and other limited equipment. By 1885, government workers had managed to produce 252 telephone sets based on the imported models. Still, the quality and technical sophistication of these devices continued to lag behind the latest examples from the West, and their manufacture could not keep pace with demand. Private Japanese firms such as Oki & Company also tried to match foreign phone makers, but proved little more successful in terms of quality or volume.[8]

Apparently dissatisfied with the results of these early efforts, the authorities chose to rely more on foreign producers to meet domestic needs. As a first step, Dr. Ōi Saitarō of the Ministry of Communications (MOC) was dispatched to the United States and Europe in 1888 to report on the state of foreign telephone companies and the systems they had established.[9] During his visit, Ōi met with top managers at Western Electric, among other firms, and upon his return to Japan the following year recommended that his government adopt some of the American company's telephone systems.[10]

The consequent shift in government policy, together with rising demand for the product's use, encouraged rapid diffusion of the telephone in Japan. With switchboards and other Western Electric equipment brought back from America by Ōi, the authorities inaugurated public telephone service as a government monopoly in 1890. Although there were just 200 subscribers in Tokyo and 40 in Yokohama during its first year of operation, the phone system served almost 3,000 customers just five years later, with many more applicants on long waiting lists. "In Tokyo they have 4,000 applications ahead for telephones and new applications are coming in at the rate of 130 per month," reported one observer in 1897, "yet the most they are trying to do is to connect 1,500 new subscribers next year."[11]

Western Electric began to manufacture telephones and invest in foreign markets shortly after Bell's invention, but during its first years of operation did no business with Japan. The American company, established in 1879, became the manufacturing arm of the Bell System two years later. Following its parent organization, Western Electric moved into foreign markets with dispatch. To supply telephones to Bell's newly created foreign division, International Bell Telephone (IBT), in 1882 Western Electric established a factory in Antwerp, Belgium, near the headquarters of IBT. Direct manufacturing investments into other European markets quickly followed, and by 1897 Western Electric owned and operated plants in London, Berlin, Paris, Milan, Vienna, and St. Petersburg in addition to Antwerp.[12]

Ōi's visit to the United States and Europe had established the first link between Japan and Western Electric, and relations expanded rapidly thereafter. Meeting with New York manager Harry Thayer, European manager F. R. Welles, and other Western Electric officials, Ōi had explained at length his government's interest in developing the telephone system in Japan. Apparently encouraged by his conversations with Ōi, Thayer began to make inquiries about developing an export business to Japan. Shortly after meeting Ōi, for example, Thayer approached Iwadare Kunihiko, a former telegraph engineer with the Japanese government who had left official duties to study at the Edison Machine Works in Schenectady, New York. Iwadare, however, proved unable to come up with the name of a suitable Japanese importer. Still, the Japanese government's continued interest in Western Electric products encouraged Thayer to persevere, and by 1891 the American company, in part through its Antwerp subsidiary, had begun to export telephone equipment to Japan via the commission merchant Takata & Company of Tokyo. Government demand rose steadily, and shipments continued to grow. To further expand business, the U.S. firm in 1895 transferred its exclusive agency agreement to the talented Iwadare, who had since returned to Japan to specialize in the importation of electrical goods from the United States.[13]

The Japanese government therefore played a critical role in stimulating Western Electric's interest in Japan. The MOC's Ōi Saitarō first alerted the American company to the possibilities of the Japanese market, and his government's decision to adopt Western Electric systems further encouraged the foreign firm to do business with Japan. New government moves soon would invite Western Electric to take additional steps to promote its interests in that market.

1. *Entry*

The government's desire to develop telephone service still further led the authorities to embark on a ¥13-million, seven-year telephone expansion program from April 1896. Plans called for an increase in telephone subscribers from 3,000 to 25,000, and the purchase and installation of 16,000 miles of long-distance circuits.[14] Once again, the government sent officials to the United States and Europe to survey the state of telephone systems in the West and meet with representatives of Western Electric and other telephone companies.[15] "All over our Empire now," Commissioner Mine of the MOC pronounced upon the official mission's landing in San Francisco in May 1896, "there is great interest in electrical power and in electrical lighting. Electricity has been introduced in several cities, but the Government wants it all over the country. It is the same way with telephones," he continued. "We have seen the value of them and desire to have them generally adopted."[16]

One of the mission's most important stops was in Chicago, where a member of the team met with E. M. Barton, the president of Western Electric. During a lengthy interview, Nakayama Riuji of the MOC described to Barton in great detail his government's plans to develop the Japanese phone system on a much grander scale. Projected demand would far outstrip domestic production capabilities, Nakayama explained, so the government would seek equipment from abroad. "So far as he can see," Barton later recounted of his conversation with Nakayama, the Japanese authorities "have no present intention of establishing the manufacture of telephone apparatus in their own country. The work is so urgent that there is no time for this. They must import their apparatus and cables and probably their copper wire for long lines."[17]

Once again, a direct representation from the Japanese government encouraged Western Electric to reassess its position in that country's market. Within months of his meeting with Nakayama, President Barton sent Thayer of the New York office to investigate business opportunities in Japan at first hand. As a result of his trip, Thayer recommended that the firm shift from simple exporting through a local agent to direct investment in concert with a Japanese firm. His reasons were several. For one thing, Thayer noted that a great many Western Electric products were damaged in shipping, and therefore advised the firm to set up an office and station in Japan a company expert who could have equipment repaired before delivery to the government: "With the amount of business secured and in sight," Thayer wrote from Japan, "it seems essential to me the that the stuff should be shipped early enough so that it can be tested and repaired if necessary before delivering it to the Government, and we should have some one here competent to do such a job right or to get it done."[18] For another, Thayer anticipated keener competition from local firms, and judged that partial production in Japan —of "such parts as come within the measure of skill possessed by the native"—could cut transportation and labor costs.[19] In addition, the policies of the Japanese government figured prominently in Thayer's decision. He noted, for example, that import duties significantly raised the local price of wholly imported goods, and that there was a "strong popular and governmental sentiment in favor of home manufactures."[20] By teaming up with a Japanese company, Thayer reasoned, Western Electric could further save on costs while at the same time satisfying the objectives of his local hosts. Current government regulations allowed foreign direct investment only in the open ports under existing treaties, but upon their revision in mid-1899 the authorities would permit such investment even in the interior of the country.

After obtaining management approval, Thayer sought to implement Western Electric's new Japan strategy. Thayer deputy W. T. Carleton traveled to Tokyo in late 1897 and negotiated a tentative agreement with Oki & Company, the local manufacturer with the most experience and the best facilities in the Japanese telephone industry.[21] According to the contract, Western Electric would establish an office in Yokohama to import and sell telephone equipment to the Japanese company. Oki, in turn, would manufacture those parts of Western Electric equipment which could be "made in Japan to better advantage," and sell the completed products to the government. The two firms would divide evenly the profits from the operation, and Western Electric would have the option to purchase a 50% interest in Oki upon treaty revision.[22] In the end, however, Oki backed out of the deal and all negotiations between the two companies were discontinued.[23]

Carleton then turned to Iwadare, Western Electric's importing agent. The American proposed that Iwadare set up a limited partnership to handle the same types of manufacturing and sales activities first under negotiation with Oki, and that the partnership be reorganized as a joint-stock company with Western Electric capital participation upon treaty revision. However, success would depend in part on Iwadare's ability to acquire for the new company a particular type of license, for selling telephone equipment to the government required a special permit before the necessary tenders could be submitted to the Ministry of Communications. Iwadare therefore approached an associate who held the requisite license, Maeda Takeshirō, and the two agreed that Maeda would enter into the partnership in exchange for transferral of his public permit to the new firm. The American company agreed to these arrangements, and on August 31, 1898, Iwadare and Maeda formally established Nippon Electric Limited Partnership. With technical assistance provided by Western Electric advisers, the new firm began partial production of telephone equipment at a factory it had acquired from the financially troubled Miyoshi Electrical Manufacturing Company. Finally, on July 17, 1899—the same day that the revised United States–Japanese treaty took effect—Nippon Electric Company, Limited (NEC) was established as a joint-stock company, with Western Electric holding a 54% direct stake, and the remainder of the equity owned by Iwadare, Maeda, and a number of their associates. For the first time in modern history, Japanese and foreign capital had joined to found a business enterprise in Japan.[24]

Once again, the Japanese government had played a crucial role in promoting Western Electric's involvement with the Japanese market. Just as the first official mission to the United States had encouraged the company to export to Japan, so the second mission promoted Western Electric's decision to directly invest in Japan. Government actions supported the investment decision in other ways as well. Official policies to increase telephone equipment purchases, levy tariffs on imported goods, and permit foreign direct investment throughout the nation after treaty revision also encouraged the American company in its decision.

2. Development

Official involvement remained strong as the Japanese telephone industry expanded still more rapidly from the turn of the century. Twice before 1930, the government enacted new national projects to expand the use and availability of the telephone. Modeled after the first such plan of 1896 but still more ambitious in its range, the government program of 1907 was initially funded by a Diet-approved budget of ¥20 million to be spent over a period of ten years.[25] The plan aimed to increase telephone subscribership by 95,000 customers, and to construct an additional 419 central telephone stations throughout the country. And in 1916, the Diet approved ¥22.5 million for yet a third telephone expansion program, which sought to enlarge the phone system by 75,000 new subscribers and to add more than 32,000 kilometers of new toll lines. Indeed, even these figures understate the size of government support, for rising labor and materials costs pushed annual expenditures during the third plan to more than ¥20 million *per year*.[26]

These government policies created explosive growth in the Japanese telephone industry during the early 1900s. Although by the close of the 19th century the authorities had managed to establish a limited phone system for use by public officials, important businesses, and some wealthy individuals, during the first quarter of the 20th century official support helped provide phone service to a far greater number of users. Thus, for example, in 1900 there were only 25 telephone exchanges serving about 19,000 customers, but just 11 years later more than 850 exchanges provided service to some 150,000 users throughout the nation. Even during Japan's financial difficulties in the early 1920s, the phone industry remained vigorous.[27]

Despite these gains, however, demand for telephones exceeded supply throughout the first decades of the new century. In 1918, for example, there were 90,000 unfilled applications for phone service on file in Tokyo alone. Annual government lotteries determined the assignment of new telephones, although an active secondary market controlled by phone brokers soon emerged as well.[28] "You folks don't know how lucky you are to have your own . . . telephone," wrote one American engineer resident in Japan in 1923. "The cost of installing a telephone in Tokyo is about 1,800 yen ($900) at present. This is because of a shortage of equipment."[29] Indeed, this observer could not have known it at the time, but the Great Kantō Earthquake, which would strike central Honshū just months after he had noted his observation, would make still greater the gap between the demand for and supply of telephones in Japan.

Western Electric–affiliated NEC benefited enormously from the government-sponsored phone boom. "The prospects in Japan are rather better than they are in any other section of the world in which we are doing business," wrote Thayer in 1908 to a colleague posted in Tokyo. "I hope the results will come up to the prospects."[30] Thayer was not to be disappointed. Government demand for telephones, cables, and switching equipment soared after the start of the second expansion plan, and again after the beginning of the third. Still more important from Western Electric's perspective, the Ministry of Communications regularly selected the products offered through the American company's local affiliate over those of even purely domestic phone makers such as Oki and Annaka.[31] Thus, NEC not only endured the depression of the early 1920s but, according to its official history, actually prospered—"due mainly to the large volume of business it had accrued through the Japanese government's third telephone expansion program."[32] Indeed, even during periods when the MOC cut back on telephone demand, such as the Russo-Japanese War years of 1904–1905, army and navy orders for communications equipment kept the U.S. affiliate "very busy."[33]

Official promotion of the American affiliate went beyond mere purchases of the company's equipment, however. Similar to its behavior toward many local companies entirely owned by Japanese interests, the government supported the placement of senior bureaucratic officials in the ranks of the Nippon company. In August 1919, for example, Dr. Ōi Saitarō—who, after his trip to the United States in 1888, had worked his way up the ranks to become the MOC's first Chief Engineer of Telephones and Telegraphs—left government service and became a member of NEC's board of directors. Similarly, MOC official Ohata Genichirō resigned from the ministry to join NEC in 1920 (and obtained the position of managing director six years later), as did engineers such as Niwa Yasujirō, who moved directly from the MOC to the Japanese company in 1924.[34] These early instances of former government officials going to work for NEC provided the U.S. affiliate with invaluable access to the very officials who crafted and implemented the government's telephone policies.

With official support such as this, it is hardly surprising that NEC developed rapidly during its first quarter century. From a single factory obtained through the Miyoshi acquisition in 1898, NEC had grown to own and operate as many as 11 plants by 1930, with employment totaling some 1,400 workers.[35] Moreover, the NEC operation provided Western Electric with unusually high returns from its Japanese investment. Western Electric's *President's Report* of 1909 stated, for example, that the American company earned some 43% on its investment in Japan during that banner year.[36] And internal firm data show that for the ten-year period 1915–1924, Western Electric realized an average annual return on its investment of almost 20%—even after adjusting for losses from the 1923 earthquake.[37] The performance of the Japanese investment is also impressive in international terms: For the period 1918–1922, for example, Western Electric's foreign investment world wide yielded an annual return of 11%, but for Japan alone the figure stood at almost 25%.[38]

Yet, Western Electric was not the only beneficiary of the NEC operation. The Japanese investors of the Nippon company, of course, enjoyed financial gains from their stake in the joint venture, and public- and private-sector subscribers benefited from the greater availability of advanced phone systems. At least as important a beneficiary, however, was Japanese industry, for the Nippon company acted as a critical link in the transfer of technology and know-how from America to Japan. After the establishment of NEC, for example, Western Electric licensed many of its most basic telephone technologies to the Japanese company, and sent to Japan leading American engineers to instruct Japanese employees in their use. In addition, Western Electric regularly brought NEC employees to its U.S. plants and laboratories, where they received instruction on the latest methods of telephone production. Indeed, NEC had absorbed so much American technology so quickly that the firm was producing virtually the entire Western Electric telephone apparatus in Japan just 12 years after its founding.[39] Finally, the U.S. firm trained NEC workers in western systems of labor management, accounting, administration, and other aspects of modern business management. Western Electric had therefore, in the words of the official NEC history, introduced innovations "which were quite significant in the history of Japanese industry, contributing greatly to the nation's modernization scheme."[40]

In sum, just as the government had encouraged the export of Western Electric products to Japan and the American company's later determination to directly invest in that market, so official actions had actively promoted the development of the American affiliate once the local operation had been established. Military agencies as well as the civilian communications bureaucracy fostered the firm's development through large purchases of NEC products throughout the first quarter of the century. In addition, placement of government officials in NEC promoted intimate relations and privileged (if informal) access to policymakers and others.

3. Withdrawal

Government participation in the telephone industry continued even after the telephone had become well established in the mid-1920s. Official demand for telephones and related equipment fell stagnant from the start of Japan's economic downturn in 1927, but picked up rapidly after the 1931 Manchurian Incident. From at least as early as 1933, the Diet approved greatly expanded budgets for the acquisition of telephones, radio equipment, and other communications gear. The outbreak of hostilities between Japan and China in 1937 created yet a new surge in government purchases of these goods.

Official procurement was not the only important aspect of government involvement with the telephone industry during the years preceding World War II, however. Equally important for foreign-affiliated NEC, from the late 1920s the authorities began to shift more of their purchases to Japanese-run manufacturers such as Oki Electric and Tōa Electric—which by now had become able producers of many types of communications equipment. The Ministry of Communications took this new aspect of public policy one step further when it decided in July 1930—more than one year *before* the Manchurian Incident and the growing influence of militarist elements in the government which soon followed—that only telephone manufacturers whose capital was primarily held by Japanese interests would qualify for privileged consideration as domestic producers.[41]

Thus, unlike earlier periods when the authorities had promoted the fortunes of Western Electric in Japan, the government now worked to reduce U.S. interests in the domestic communications industry. ITT, the American company which bought Western Electric's interest in NEC through a sweeping international transfer of U.S. overseas communications assets in 1925, began to sense the pressures from the Japanese government before the end of the 1920s.[42] Directly responding to these new official Japanese policies, ITT President Sosthenes Behn held talks with private Japanese circles from 1929, in an effort to reduce the American company's holdings in NEC and therefore enable the Nippon company to qualify as a domestic producer. Finally, in June 1932, ITT arranged to sell to the Sumitomo interests enough of its equity in NEC to lower the American company's total interest to just under 50%.[43] Government officials continued to force down the foreign equity position in NEC during the years preceding war with the United States, so that ITT's share of NEC capital stood at less than 25% in December 1940.[44] Private Japanese interests took over this last portion of American direct investment in NEC just days after the attack on Pearl Harbor.[45]

In sum, the Japanese government played a central role in the evolving relationship between American business and the Japanese telephone industry. Having first attracted Western Electric's interest in Japan as an export market, officials then encouraged the American company's decision to directly invest in Japan and the subsequent development of the company into which Western Electric had invested its capital and technology. After Japanese-run firms had developed an independent capacity to produce advanced telephones and other communications equipment, however, officials promoted the withdrawal of Western Electric successor ITT from the domestic market.[46]

III. Public Promotion of Foreign Business in Prewar Japan

Though unique in its particulars, the story of government interaction with Western Electric and ITT in prewar Japan is suggestive of official policies toward other foreign companies in the prewar period as well. Government action toward American direct investment in the Japanese automobile industry is a case in point. The authorities did not obstruct foreign direct investment in the domestic motor vehicle industry during the first three decades of this century, and in certain ways even encouraged it. Ford and General Motors dominated the Japanese market through exports after World War I, but began to explore direct investment strategies following the Great Kantō Earthquake. Attracted to Japan in part by a huge order for motor vehicles placed by the Tokyo municipal government in the wake of that calamity, Ford set up a plant in Yokohama in 1925 to assemble cars and trucks imported in "knocked-down" kits. Equally interested in the Japanese market and fearful that Ford might predominate there if unchallenged by other foreign automakers, GM followed suit by setting up an assembly plant in Osaka shortly thereafter. Neither Ford nor GM encountered government opposition to their entry, and the Osaka authorities even arranged for a package of tax abatements and other inducements to lure GM to their locale. Indeed, once operating in Japan, both companies benefited from substantial government purchases—which helped to raise Ford and GM's combined domestic market share to roughly 95% by the end of the decade. At the same time, the two U.S. companies brought to Japan new manufacturing, sales, management, and other skills, and earned very high returns on their Japanese investments.

During the 1930s, however, government policies changed. As domestic companies became increasingly expert at the manufacture of motor vehicles—thanks in large part to the transfer of techniques to Japan by the U.S. automakers themselves—the authorities placed increasingly severe restrictions on the development of the Ford and GM subsidiaries. Regulations issued under the Automobile Manufacturing Industry Law of 1936 assigned quotas and other limits to the operations of the local American operations, and provided subsidies and additional means of assistance to Japanese-controlled vehicle manufacturers. The government also began to restrict GM and Ford access to critically important foreign exchange and import licenses from 1937. Despite the wishes of both U.S. automakers to remain active in the local market, public policies forced their virtual withdrawal as hostilities approached.[47]

The U.S. record and phonograph manufacturer Victor Talking Machine had much the same experience. Founded in 1901, Victor began to export its products to Japan shortly thereafter. From the early 1920s, however, Victor found itself confronted with a stiff 100% tariff on phonographs and related products. To remain competitive in Japan, the American company directly invested in that market in 1927 by acquiring a controlling interest in the Nipponophone Company. Victor then transferred to its Japanese affiliate technologies and know-how critical for manufacturing, and instructed Japanese workers in their application. In return, the U.S. firm enjoyed returns on its investment for several years at annual rates ranging from 20% to 50%.

Yet here too, changed government policies promoted the eventual withdrawal of an American business from the Japanese market. By the early 1930s, after Japan Industries and other domestically controlled companies had acquired the requisite skills and could manufacture phonograph equipment independently of Victor, pressures on the American company to diminish its presence gradually increased. "Buy Japan" campaigns, discriminatory treatment by the Patent Bureau, and delays by the Ministry of Finance in granting foreign exchange permits to import critical parts forced Victor's parent, RCA, to reconsider its direct investment. These pressures, together with difficulties RCA encountered in the domestic U.S. market, prompted the American company to sell off its direct stake in the Japanese phonograph industry by 1939.[48]

Nor are these the sole examples. Singer Sewing Machine Company, which had directly invested in Japan six years after treaty revision to sell and repair its products there, was forced out of the market in the late 1930s after Japanese sewing machine firms had become competitive.[49]

Here, too, the government played a critical role in the withdrawal decision: "Our company," according to a ranking Singer manager in a memorandum of November 1945,

> ... has been doing business in Japan since January, 1905, having succeeded at that time to the business previously carried on for many years by branches of The Singer Manufacturing Company. The business developed steadily until 1937 during which year the Japanese Government imposed drastic restrictions on imports of sewing machines at the time of the outbreak of the "Chinese Incident." The Government's policy of refusing import licenses forced a gradual liquidation of the business.[50]

The American tire maker B.F. Goodrich had acquired a controlling interest in the Yokohama Rubber joint venture with Baron Furukawa in 1917, and transferred substantial expertise to that Japanese company to promote its development.[51] But in the 1930s, when Yokohama Rubber had developed the capability to produce tires without assistance from the American parent, the military authorities—who were major domestic consumers of tires—pressured Goodrich to withdraw from the joint venture.[52] General Electric's experiences followed the same general pattern. The U.S. firm, which had directly invested in Tokyo Electric Company in 1905 and had licensed this local firm to produce GE light bulbs in Japan, similarly found itself pressured to reduce its capital stake, now that the Japanese company presumably could make do without further support from General Electric.[53]

In each of these instances, the Japanese government appears to have followed a similar strategy. As the experiences of numerous foreign companies show, the authorities encouraged the entry of certain non-Japanese enterprises in the early decades of the century. Once established, these received crucial support from the government to aid their development. Western Electric's Japanese affiliate, for example, directly benefited from public procurement and the placement of former government officials in key positions in its organization. Yet even if the authorities initially supported foreign enterprise in the local market, that support turned to opposition once native enterprises had acquired the skills necessary to operate without foreign assistance. American companies such as B.F. Goodrich, Ford, General Electric, General Motors, ITT, RCA Victor, and Singer Sewing Machine had all invested in local affiliates before the end of the 1920s, but in each case the government later worked to remove the foreign company from Japan. In sum, the authorities promoted the entry and development—but also the withdrawal—of these foreign enterprises over the course of the prewar decades.

IV. Conclusion

The pattern of prewar official policy suggests that the government manipulated foreign direct investment in specific ways to further strictly national economic goals. Indeed, as one Japanese scholar has surmised, there is much evidence to suggest that only those foreign companies whose presence could contribute to the nation's industrialization process were permitted to operate in the local economy.[54] Like Western Electric and ITT, such foreign enterprises generally possessed advanced technologies or other special strengths not immediately available to Japanese entrepreneurs. However, once such strengths had been adequately absorbed by Japanese interests, the government moved to expel the outsider.

The story of Western Electric, ITT, and other foreign companies in prewar Japan invites comparisons with the experiences of the so-called foreign experts, or *oyatoi gaikokujin*, who came to Japan principally in the late 19th century. Hired by the Meiji government, several thousand engineers, teachers, and other professionals from the West were brought to Japan to teach skills judged critical to the nation's modernization program. The government compensated these foreigners handsomely for their work, but sent them home after their skills had been absorbed. In a certain respect, then, Japanese authorities treated foreign enterprise like the *oyatoi gaikokujin* of a later time.

Notes

1. Ozawa Terutomo, "Japanese Policy Toward Foreign Multinationals: Implications for Trade and Competitiveness," in Pugel, Thomas, ed. *Fragile Interdependence* (Lexington, Mass.: D.C. Heath, 1986), p. 147.
2. See, for example, Abegglen, James et al., *Kaisha: The Japanese Corporation* (New York: Basic Books, 1985), p. 217. Abegglen does suggest, however, that Japanese government controls partially explain the modest levels of foreign direct investment in postwar Japan.
3. Henderson, Dan Fenno, *Foreign Enterprise in Japan: Laws and Policies* (Tokyo: Charles Tuttle, 1973), p. 14.
4. Christopher, Robert, *Second to None: American Companies in Japan* (New York: Crown, 1986), p. 10.
5. See Mason, Mark, "Foreign Direct Investment and Japanese Economic

Development, 1899–1931," in *Business and Economic History*, second series, vol. 16, 1987, pp. 93–107.

6. This paper's focus on Japanese government policies toward foreign direct investment is not meant to imply that the initiative for these policies originated wholly—or even primarily—with the authorities themselves. Indeed, much evidence suggests that, at least from the 1930s, Japanese business played a critical role in the formulation and implementation of public measures toward foreign investment. Whatever their origin, however, such measures were ultimately applied through government channels.

7. NEC, *NEC Corporation: The First 80 Years* (Tokyo: NEC, 1984), p. 3; Rhodes, Frederick L., *John J. Carty: An Appreciation* (New York: privately printed, 1932), pp. 196–98; Elliot, D.F., "Twenty-five Years of Successful Cooperation in Japan," in *Electrical Communication*, October 1923, p. 95; and "Each in His Dearest Tongue," in *Bell Telephone Quarterly*, vol. XVI, 1937, pp. 184–85.

8. NEC, *op. cit.*, pp. 3–4.

9. The MOC was established in 1885.

10. Elliot, D. F., *op. cit.*, pp. 95–96; and Iwadare, K., "A History of the Nippon Denki Kabushiki Kaisha," in *Western Electric News*, March 1914, p. 1.

11. Letter, Thayer to Welles, January 28, 1897, ATT Archives, Box 1134.

12. Barton, E. M., "The Story of the Western Electric Company," parts I and II, April 1912, pp. 1–3, and May 1912, pp. 1–3; Leigh, W. E., "Some Features of Our Foreign Business As It Is To-Day," October 1913, pp. 1–3; and Pingree, G. E., "Our Foreign Business," November 1919; all in *Western Electric News*.

13. Autobiographical sketch of Iwadare Kunihiko, May 15, 1919, Edison Pioneers Records; interview with one of Iwadare's sons, Tokyo, 1965, from the files of Wilkins, Mira; Elliot, D. F., *op. cit.*, pp. 95–98. The silk house Bavier & Company in September 1877 had gained an exclusive license from Alexander Graham Bell to import telephones into Japan and China. ATT Archives, Box 1122.

14. Letter, Sabin to French, May 22, 1896, ATT Archives, Box 1134.

15. Various correspondence, ATT Archives, Box 1134.

16. *San Francisco Call*, May 17, 1896.

17. Letter, Barton to Welles, June 18, 1896, ATT Archives, Box 1134.

18. Letter, Thayer to Welles, January 14, 1897, ATT Archives, Box 1134.

19. Letter, Thayer to Hudson, April 18, 1898, ATT Archives, Box 1139.

20. *Ibid.*

21. At the time of the negotiations, Oki had already entered into arrangements with Western Electric to assemble and repair in Japan certain of the American company's exports to that market. See Hayashi Masayuki, "*Senzen ni okeru Amerika Takokuseki Kigyō no Nihon Shinshutsu* (The Prewar Entry of American Multinational Enterprise in Japan)," in *Kōnan Ronshū*, vol. 5, March 1977, p. 42.

22. Letter, Thayer to Hudson, April 18, 1898, ATT Archives, Box 1139.

23. NEC, *op. cit.*, p. 5. On the negotiations, see in particular Chokki Toshiaki, "*Nihon no Kigyō Keiei no Kindaika to Gaishi Setchi Kaisha—Meiji Jidai no Denki Kikai Kōgyō ni okeru Mitsui no Jirei* (The Modernization of Japanese Management and Foreign Joint Ventures—Three Cases from the Electrical Machinery Industry of the Meiji Period)," in *Keiei Shirin*, vol. 17, no. 4, January 1981, pp. 118–19.

24. NEC, *op. cit.*, pp. 2, 5–8.
25. According to one source, even this amount understates the actual total spent, for "further money was granted from time to time, and a considerably larger amount [than the ¥20 million] was spent." Elliot, D. F., *op. cit.*, p. 103.
26. NEC, *op. cit.*, pp. 12, 15.
27. *Ibid.*, pp. 15–16, and Iwadare Kunihiko, "A History of the Nippon Denki Kabushiki Kaisha," in *Western Electric News*, March 1914, p. 1.
28. "Only Lucky Have Telephones in Japan," in *The Northwestern Bell*, June 1924, pp. 1–3.
29. "Hawthorne Engineer Writes Interesting Letter from Japan," in *Western Electric News*, 1923, p. 21.
30. Letter, Thayer to Condict, April 8, 1908, Western Electric Archives, from the files of Wilkins, Mira.
31. NEC, *op. cit.*, pp. 8–9.
32. *Ibid.*, p. 16.
33. Elliot, D. F., *op. cit.*, p. 101.
34. NEC, *op. cit.*, pp. 22–24.
35. Elliot, D. F., *op. cit.*, p. 109; and United States National Archives, Record Group 151, Box 46, Special Report No. 17.
36. Western Electric Company, *President's Report for the Year Ending November 30, 1909*, p. 13, ATT Archives, Box 1380.
37. "Historical Statistics," ATT Archives, Box 265.
38. Du Bois, Charles, "The Foreign Business of the Western Electric Company," August 1923, ATT Archives, Box 46; and "Historical Statistics," ATT Archives, Box 265.
39. Elliot, D. F., *op. cit.*, p. 106.
40. NEC, *op. cit.*, p. 11.
41. *Ibid.*, pp. 24–25ff.
42. ITT, founded in 1920, first held a controlling interest in two telephone companies—the Puerto Rico Telephone Company and the Cuban Telephone Company. Through a transaction completed on September 30, 1925, ITT's overseas subsidiary, International Standard Electric, acquired the rights to Western Electric's foreign assets, held by its subsidiary International Western Electric. "Foreign Business and Non-Telephone Activities," ATT Archives, Box 2029; and ITT, *Facts About ITT* (New York: ITT, 1965), p. 4.
43. U.S. National Archives, Record Group 331, Box 3802, "Summary of Reports" p. 2. U.S. interests had held a controlling interest in NEC from the Japanese company's founding in 1899. This percentage varied from 54% to about 60% during the years 1899 to 1932. Industrial Bank of Japan, *Gaikoku Kaisha no Honpō Tōshi: Kako ni okeru Jirei no Kenkyū* (Foreign Capital Investment in Japan: A Study of Past Cases) (Tokyo: Industrial Bank of Japan, 1948), pp. 100–101; and various Western Electric financial records, ATT Archives. The Sumitomo group first took an equity position in NEC in 1920, when Sumitomo Electric Cable Manufacturing acquired 5% of NEC's stock. See NEC, *op. cit.*, p. 18. Still earlier, in 1917, Mitsui interests had gained a 5% stake in NEC. The Mitsui investment was undertaken at the behest of Western Electric's Gerard Swope, who hoped that closer ties between Mitsui and NEC would boost his firm's business in China. Western Electric, NEC, and the Chinese government

together established the China Electric Company in 1918 in furtherance of the American company's China strategy. Wilkins, Mira, *The Maturing of Multinational Enterprise: American Business Abroad from 1914 to 1970* (Cambridge, Mass.: Harvard University Press, 1974), p. 28; and Goldfarb, Laurence, "Pacific Overture: Western Electric in Japan, 1895–1925" (Senior Thesis, Harvard College, 1988), p. 86.

44. Industrial Bank of Japan, *op. cit.*, p. 101. "From time to time," reported an ITT representative about the period after 1932, "the principal Japanese stockholder (Sumitomo) . . . reported that it was being embarrassed by demands on the part of certain Japanese Government officials that the percentage of foreign ownership (in) Nippon Electric Co., Ltd. be further reduced, and . . . that expansion of the Company eventually would be hampered unless something could be done to meet the wishes of such Government officials." U.S. National Archives, Record Group 331, Box 3802, "Summary of Reports," pp. 2–3.

45. The government officially designated the ITT interests in NEC as "enemy property" on December 28, 1941, after which time the shares held by the American company were seized and transferred to Japanese interests. Industrial Bank of Japan, *op. cit.*, p. 98; and NEC, *op. cit.*, p. 29. After the war, ITT regained a roughly 32% interest in NEC, but gradually liquidated this position. In 1978, ITT sold its remaining interests in the Japanese company.

46. This latter aspect of government strategy toward the American investors was supported even by Iwadare. In a conversation with the head of Oki & Company, for example, Iwadare defended the inflow of direct investment from abroad—provided such investment brought with it technologies critical to Japan's development; "[We] must open the gates [of the nation] to induce the latest technology, absorb that technology, make it our own, and quickly catch up with the West." NEC, *Nippon Denki Kabushiki Kaisha 70 Nen Shi* (A 70-Year History of NEC) (Tokyo: NEC, 1973), p. 27.

47. See Mason, Mark, "United States Direct Investment in Japan: Studies in Government Policy and Corporate Strategy" (Ph.D. dissertation, Harvard University, 1988); Udagawa Masaru, "The Prewar Japanese Automobile Industry and American Manufacturers," in *Japanese Yearbook on Business History*, vol. 2, 1985, pp. 81–99; and Wilkins, Mira, *American Business Abroad: Ford on Six Continents* (Detroit, Mich.: Wayne State University Press, 1964). The Japanese subsidiaries of Ford and GM continued to operate even as Pearl Harbor came under attack, but by then the scope of their operations had been greatly reduced.

48. Mason, Mark, "United States Direct Investment," pp. 67–78, 157–64.

49. *Ibid.*, pp. 140, 153–54; and U.S. National Archives, Record Group 331, Box 3811.

50. United States National Archives, Record Group 331, Box 3811.

51. Wilkins, Mira, *American Business Abroad*, p. 29; and U.S. National Archives, Record Group 331, Box 3798.

52. Wilkins, Mira, "American-Japanese Direct Foreign Investment Relationships, 1930–1952," in *Business History Review*, 56: 4, Winter 1982, p. 502; and U.S. National Archives, Record Group 331, Box 3798.

53. Wilkins, "American-Japanese Direct Foreign Investment," p. 502; and U.S. National Archives, Record Group 331, Box 3801.

54. See the comments of Nakamura Takahide in *Dai 22 kai Taikai Tōitsu*

Rondai: 'Kindai Keiei no Tenkai to Kokusai Kankei' Tōgi Hōkoku (The Overall Theme of the 22nd General Meeting: A Report on the Discussion of 'The Development of Modern Management and International Relations'), in *Keiei Shigaku*, vol. 22, no. 1, April 1987, p. 79ff.

Comment

Hideki Yoshihara

Western Electric (its Japanese subsidiary was NEC), which is the subject of the author's analysis, and other foreign companies operating in Japan before World War II can be considered to have been *oyatoi gaikokujin*. In the beginning, foreign companies were welcomed for their excellent technology, and they were able to enjoy good performance. However, when the Japanese side (the Japanese partner in the joint ventures, Japanese competing firms, etc.) acquired the technology, the foreign companies were forced to leave Japan and return to their countries of origin. The main point of this paper may be summarized in this way.

The Japanese government played an important role in the whole process of Western Electric entering Japan, expanding its business in this country, and finally withdrawing from the Japanese market. When discussing the government involvement in matters related to foreign companies, the following variables have to be taken into account:

—The characteristics of the industry of the foreign company
—The stage of development of the recipient country (developed or underdeveloped)
—Nationalism in the recipient country
—Political and military situations of the recipient country.

A noticeable feature of Western Electric, vis-à-vis many other foreign companies operating in Japan, is related to the nature of the industry of the company. The telephone industry is, even today, a typical example of an industry where government regulation is strong. Wasn't the involvement of the Japanese government weaker in the case of foreign companies operating in industries such as automobiles, electricity, chemicals, tires, and machinery?

Around 1940 nearly all foreign companies were forced to withdraw from Japan, but it can be thought that this development was not due to the Japanese side acquiring the technology owned by the foreign companies but to the special circumstances of the war.

During the conference, the author elaborated on the recent attempts by the Japanese government and other institutions to attract foreign companies. If the *oyatoi gaikokujin* model is applied, those foreign companies that are attracted to Japan, just like the foreign companies operating in Japan before World War II, should have technological advantages relative to Japanese companies. Also, when in due time those foreign companies lose their technological superiority, they would have to leave Japan and return to their home countries.

However, when observing recent behavior of foreign companies expanding operations to Japan, some new features can be seen that are difficult to explain by means of the *oyatoi gaikokujin* model.

Foreign companies that expand their businesses to Japan do not necessarily have a technological advantage over Japanese firms. In some cases, the technological advantage belongs to Japanese firms, and one of the reasons for foreign companies to start operations in Japan is precisely the desire to acquire the superior technology of Japanese firms.

Recently, American and European companies, mainly in the electrical and chemical fields, are successively beginning to establish development centers and research laboratories in Japan. The purpose of expanding R&D activities into Japan is not to transfer to this country the technology of the parent company but to employ Japanese engineers and researchers, develop technology for its Japanese subsidiaries, and transfer that technology to the parent company in the country of origin.

The *oyatoi gaikokujin* model shares basic features with current theories of multinational enterprises. If the *oyatoi gaikokujin* model is insufficient to explain the behavior of foreign firms in Japan (especially its recent trends), then the theories of multinational enterprises are also insufficient. It is necessary to develop a theory of multinational companies that can explain recent trends of foreign companies in Japan, such as the fact that these companies start their Japanese operations in order to acquire superior Japanese technology and that, as a consequence, the transfer of technology takes place from the subsidiary in Japan to the parent company in the country of origin.

Response

Mark Mason

Professor Yoshihara offered three main points in his comments at the conference. I shall provide a brief summary and reply to each of these points.

First, Yoshihara contended that Japanese government policies toward Western Electric and ITT were unusually restrictive because these companies operated in a field of industry normally subject to strong government control. He then went on to ask, rhetorically, if public regulation of foreign companies was not weaker in other industries such as automobiles and machinery. Although Yoshihara is quite correct to state that public regulation of Western Electric and ITT was indeed severe, it is equally true that the Japanese government applied very stringent controls over a broad range of foreign companies operating in other fields as well. To take the case of the automobile industry, which Yoshihara would cite as a counterexample, there is abundant evidence to demonstrate that public intervention—most notably, implementation of the Automobile Manufacturing Industry Law of 1936—played a critical role in the eventual withdrawal of Ford and General Motors from the Japanese market. Indeed, prewar government regulation also exercised a fateful influence over the local operations of General Electric, Singer Sewing Machine, RCA Victor, B.F. Goodrich, and a host of other foreign companies in a great variety of industries in prewar Japan.

Second, Yoshihara argued that the withdrawal of foreign companies can be explained by the "special circumstances" of the Second World War, and that such companies could have remained in Japan had there been no war. Besides offering an unprovable hypothesis—it is difficult to analyze events which did not in fact take place—Yoshihara's argument fails to take account of a considerable body of evidence which suggests that perceived domestic economic gain—quite apart from any military rationale—motivated the government to force out foreign enterprise. To return once again to the automobile case, for example, it is clear that the government had been trying to promote a domestic motor vehicle industry years before the rise of the militarists in the 1930s.

Indeed, interviews with responsible officials indicate that, even during the mid-1930s, key bureaucrats charged with formulating and implementing the government's automobile policy identified Japanese economic development as a central reason for restricting the local Ford and GM operations. Although it might be reasonably argued that the occurrence of World War II affected the timing of government policies toward foreign automobile and other companies, I do not believe that the conflict altered the essential nature of those policies.

Third, Yoshihara stated that the operation of Japanese government policies as described in my paper fails to explain more recent trends in foreign direct investment in Japan. Specifically, he pointed out that many foreign companies now in Japan operate at a technological disadvantage vis-à-vis local competitors, and that these companies have chosen to enter the market in order to acquire advanced technologies from Japanese industry. Yoshihara has made a valid observation about the motives of certain foreign firms now operating in Japan, but his observation is not directly relevant to the thesis I present. My paper describes certain historical phenomena before World War II, rather than a general model of the behavior of foreign multinationals in Japan for every historical period. Indeed, it may well be that the current entry of foreign companies seeking advanced technologies offers testimony to the success of earlier Japanese government policies toward such companies.

"Japanese Business Management" in the Prewar Electrical Machinery Industry: The Emergence of Foreign Tie-up Companies and the Modernization of Indigenous Enterprises

Toshiaki Chokki

I. Introduction

This paper aims at describing the process of modernization of business management in prewar Japan, focusing mainly on the electrical machinery industry. The electrical machinery industry was one of the most highly developed industries in Japan before World War II. The period of my analysis is from around the 1870s to the 1920s, covering the Meiji, Taishō, and early Shōwa eras. The enterprises under discussion were producers of communication equipments, light bulbs, generators, transformers, motors, and so on.

The methodology is a kind of comparative study. I will compare the foreign tie-up companies with the indigenous enterprises, which had to produce electrical machinery under the challenge of the former companies during the period in question. The first foreign tie-up company was established in 1899. Some more appeared afterward. The indigenous enterprises were forerunners of the industry, but it was the foreign tie-up companies which took the initiative of modernizing the management and technology of the industry. Some indigenous enterprises were also active in modernizing their own management style. So the modernization of the Japanese electrical machinery industry was the result of competition between the two groups of enterprises.

I have terminated the analysis around the end of the 1920s, when several companies had almost completed the modernization of management. I will describe the process from the beginning.

II. Beginning of Domestic Production

1. Earlier Producers

In the early years of the Meiji era, Japanese industry, if any, was carried out by Japanese entrepreneurs. There were no foreign firms producing any industrial goods in those days. We can point out two major reasons for these situations: One was Japan's remoteness from the European world; the other was the innocence of western people about the future possibility of Japan's industrial development. The former reason was a physical one, so it did not change afterward. The latter was a social one, so it gradually changed. Around the 1880s there came some western people in search of a chance to conduct business in this far eastern country. Before that time, however, the industry in Japan was carried out by Japanese craftsmen, the government, and entrepreneurs. The units of industrial activity were usually small and the management method conventional. The electrical machinery industry was just such an industry.

The first electric machine produced in Japan was one for telegraphy.[1] Modernization of communications was an urgent priority for the Meiji government, which aimed at administrative and military modernization. As early as 1872 it had the well-known craftsman-turned-technician Tanaka Hisashige produce a Henry telegraph machine. Following this, in 1873, a factory was set up under the Kōbushō (Public Works Ministry), and here the production and repair of telegraph equipments and machines began. Foreign engineers directed production at the Kōbushō factory, and many Japanese telegraph engineers were trained under their leadership. Oki Kibatarō, who later founded Meikōsha, was one of these, and made a big contribution to domestic production of telephones and switchboards.

Indigenous production of electric generators also began in the 1880s. Miyoshi Shōichi constructed an Edison-type DC generator in 1885 and used it for incandescent electric lamps. Miyoshi was also a product of the factory of the Public Works Ministry; after becoming independent in 1883, he began the manufacturing of electrical machines and equipment.

The light bulb was another electrical product that was manufactured relatively early in Japan. The one who devoted himself to this enterprise was Fujioka Ichisuke, then a professor of the Engineering College (Kōbu Daigakkō). In 1884 he was sent by the Public Works Ministry to the Electrical Exhibition being held in Philadelphia, where he observed the most recent results related to electricity. At that time he also visited the New York Electric Light Company, carefully inspected incandescent light bulbs developed by Thomas A. Edison, and observed the production process. After returning to Japan, he gave up his faculty position at the Engineering College and became chief engineer of the Tokyo Electric Light Company, taking part in the initial domestic production of incandescent bulbs. Cooperating with Miyoshi Shōichi, the electric machinery maker from the same town (Iwakuni, Yamaguchi Prefecture), he founded in 1890 the first specialized electric light bulb manufacturing company, the Incandescent Co., Ltd. (Hakunetsu-sha), a subsidiary company of Tokyo Electric Light. By importing a set of production machinery from England, he began the domestic production of electric light bulbs. Japan's first incandescent light bulbs were produced in August of the same year.

Early production of electric bulbs by the Incandescent Company, however, was on a very small scale, and the cost was inevitably high. Also, technological know-how was inadequate and the proportion of good products quite low. In about June of 1895, the Incandescent Company was marketing 8- and 16-candle bulbs at 60 sen, 24-candle bulbs at 70 sen, and bulbs of over 50 candles at one yen apiece, but imported light bulbs were being bought by lighting companies at a little over half those prices. Therefore, as a result of appeals from the lighting companies, the Incandescent Company was obliged to lower its delivery prices, but this in turn damaged the earning power of the company. In 1896 the Incandescent Company was reorganized as a joint-stock company, but its business results were very poor, and its dividends, if there were any, were between 5 and 8%.

But to entrepreneurs of that time, the production of electrical equipment seemed to be a field of business with a future. The Mitsui Bank bought Tanaka Hisashige's factory in 1893 and turned it into the Shibaura Engineering Works. Its first general manager, Fujiyama Raita, actively sought orders for electrical equipment and pushed the factory forward as an electrical machinery maker.[2] This process was by no means smooth, and orders for electrical equipment were slow to increase. It was not until the latter part of 1900 that the factory got out of the red and gained profits with such main stream electrical goods as generators, electric motors, equipment for electric railways, and transformers. As its business situation was gradually improved, in 1904 the Works were reorganized as a joint-stock company with capital of ¥1 million. Its largest stockholders were eminent members of the Mitsui family, and it can be said to have been a direct affiliate of the Mitsui zaibatsu.

In this way, at the beginning of the 20th century, several competent enterprises appeared in the Japanese electrical machinery industry, and with them at the center, various kinds of electrical equipment were produced. But the turn of the century was also the turn of the industry. The domestic producers found themselves faced with severe competition from imported foreign products. Also, the users in Japan were demanding more and higher-quality electrical machinery.

2. Background of Modernization of the Industry

From the end of the 19th century through the beginning of the 20th, as a general phenomenon, electrical machinery was undergoing rapid technological progress. The telephone, invented by Alexander Graham Bell in 1876, at first performed poorly and was unsuitable for general use, but with subsequent modifications by Thomas Edison and others, its use spread rapidly. And with the improvement of switchboard equipment, telephone networks were constructed as a means of communication within cities and between them. In the field of electric light bulbs, in place of bamboo or cotton filaments, metal filaments were employed, and finally the age of the tungsten light bulb emerged. Even as the field of electrical generating equipment grew larger, high-voltage long-distance power transmission came into use, and large-capacity generators, powerful transformers, and various kinds of auxiliary equipment were gradually produced in Japan.

The 20th century spawned a veritable "Age of Electricity" and gave birth to many kinds of electrical machinery. Amid such diversification of electrical equipment and rapid technical advances, Japanese enterprises tried to confront the competitive force of foreign products in terms of quality and price solely by developing the ability to create new products by strengthening and perfecting the power of Japanese capital and technology. But soon after its formation, great difficulties were foreseen for this Japanese industry in consolidating such conditions by its own efforts over the short term. Given such a situation, some Japanese enterprises sought to create new opportunities by tying up with foreign enterprises. Others remained purely indigenous. So new lines of competition were drawn between foreign tie-up companies and indigenous enterprises. The former assumed the part of challenger and brought new methods of engineering and management to Japan.[3] The latter were followers or respondents in the dynamics of development. This challenger-response process resulted in the modernization process of the electrical machinery industry in prewar Japan.

III. The Challenge of Foreign Tie-up Companies

1. Emergence of Three American Tie-up Companies[4]

(1) Nippon Electric Company (NEC): The prominent U.S. telephone maker Western Electric Company sent its Foreign Department manager, H. B. Thayer, to Japan in 1896. Western Electric succeeded in selling telephones on the occasion of the Japanese government's first telephone expansion program. Thayer's purpose in coming to Japan, in addition to arranging delivery of his company's products, was to examine the possi-

bility of Japan becoming a future market for telephones and to sound out the potential for investment of capital. Thayer returned home the following year and reported to his head office that there were bright prospects.

Western Electric planned to establish itself in Japan by forming a joint venture, and as a tie-up partner first chose Oki Kibatarō. But these negotiations eventually failed, and as a result Western Electric made Iwadare Kunihiko, who had performed the role of intermediary in negotiations with Oki, their tie-up partner and thus achieved entry into Japan. This was the beginning of Nippon Electric Company, Ltd. (NEC) in 1899. The company was formed with investment of capital by Western Electric in Japan Electric, Ltd., established by Iwadare and others. At its inception, the company's capital was ¥200,000, and the initial Western Electric holding was 216 of the 400 shares, or 54%. Nippon Electric was the first joint venture with foreign capital in Japan.

(2) Tokyo Electric Company: Subsequently, in the field of electric light bulb production, too, a joint venture with foreign capital made its appearance. This was the joint venture formed with capital investment by the integrated American electrical equipment manufacturer General Electric Company in Tokyo Electric Co., Ltd. in 1905. The limited-partnership Incandescent Company (Hakunetsu-sha), founded by Fujioka Ichisuke and others, had been reorganized in 1896 into Tokyo Incandescent Electric Light Bulb Manufacturing Ltd., and changed its name again to the Tokyo Electric Co., Ltd. in 1899. At that time its capital was ¥150,000. The intense competition with imported light bulbs, however, continued, and business results showed no turn for the better. The company, therefore, at its board-of-directors' meeting in February of 1904, decided to "increase capital by raising ¥100,000, that is, 2,000 shares in the form of preferred shares, in order to redeem our obligations" and, appealing for the cooperation of shareholders, exert efforts to find new investors. But the attempt to raise capital in Japan was not successful, so the management eventually decided to form a joint-capital venture with General Electric Company.[5] In 1905, Tokyo Electric increased its capital by ¥250,000 to ¥400,000, and because ¥204,000 of this increase was allotted to General Electric, that company became the holder of the majority share in Tokyo Electric. The investment in Tokyo Electric was GE's first industrial investment in the Far East. This joint endeavor, moreover, was accompanied by a contract for technological assistance from General Electric to Tokyo Electric, and as the result of this assistance from GE, Tokyo Electric's light bulb production technology was rapidly modernized.

(3) Shibaura Engineering Works: After this, in May 1910, another venture joined a Japanese company with General Electric. This was the heavy electrical machinery maker Shibaura Engineering Works. As noted previously, the predecessor of the Shibaura Engineering Works was the Tanaka Hisashige plant, which after coming under the umbrella of the Mitsui Bank in 1883 had followed the path of a specialized electrical machinery maker. This plant was a pioneer among the electrical equipment makers of Japan, but even such a leader enterprise, in view of the ever-advancing development of electrical equipment technology, was faced with the necessity of forming a technological liaison with General Electric.

According to *The 65-Year History of the Shibaura Engineering Works* (1940), the groundwork for the tie-up between the Works and General Electric had already been laid in 1896, but concrete negotiations were not begun until 1907 and a contract was not actually signed until November 1909.[6] Thus in 1910 the capital was increased to ¥2 million and about one-quarter of the shares were allocated to General Electric and investors connected with it. At the same time it was arranged that the Shibaura Engineering Works would receive technological assistance from General Electric in the production of electrical machinery.

2. *Merits of Foreign Tie-up*

The greatest benefits in tie-ups with foreign enterprises were the introduction of machinery and plants by the tie-up partner and the rapid raising of technological levels through the acquisition of technological know-how in various fields, as well as the attainment of an advantageous position in competition between enterprises by modernizing their production systems. The process of acquiring new technology was made safe, new products were turned out reliably, and productivity could be raised smoothly.

For example, at Nippon Electric[7] the equipment used at its inauguration had been bought from the factory of Miyoshi Electric, which was too old-fashioned to produce delicate instruments like telephones. After the tie-up, however, the construction of a new factory was begun in 1900. Western Electric's secondhand machinery was installed in the factory, but at the time these machines were the most up-to-date in Japan. Then a master mechanic was dispatched from Western Electric to supervise the process and production methods, tools, etc., with all products manufactured to WE's specifications. In around 1907, electric power was introduced, and the machines could be located according to their function. Moreover, blueprints for new products were sent regularly from Western Electric and the production process was reorganized by using them.

At Tokyo Electric,[8] after the tie-up with General Electric, a system aimed at self-sufficiency in electric light bulbs was established. Encountering favorable circumstances after the Russo-Japanese War (1904–1905), the company drew up a plan to increase production to 4,000 units per day. All the necessary plant equipment was ordered from General Electric. In reality, the actual daily production in the first half of 1906 did not reach 4,000 (instead averaging only 2,500 bulbs), but even so, the output was twice what it had been and the benefits of cost reduction were large. Then, in October of 1906, capitalization was increased to ¥1.6 million at a single stroke and a plan devised to raise the level of self-sufficiency in raw materials and related parts. Previously there had been deficiencies in the capacity to produce carbon filaments and metal caps, and the shortages had been made up by imports from General Electric, but as a result of the rise in import duties due to promulgation of the Emergency Special Tariff Act in 1904, imported parts became expensive, raising the production cost of light bulbs. Consequently, production machinery with an output capacity of 10,000 carbon filaments per day and a set of metal-cap-fabricating machinery were imported from General Electric and installed, while self-sufficiency in raw materials was achieved. Thus, light bulbs produced by Tokyo Electric were marketed after October 1906 under the Edison trademark, and the brand impact was so strengthened that their acceptability was raised in the national market.

Concerning the results of the technological assistance agreement with General Electric at the Shibaura Engineering Works, the aforementioned *65-Year History of the Shibaura Engineering Works* has this to say:

> After this agreement had been made, as the first step in the immediate introduction of their technology to our factory, many key personnel dealing with design and production were sent to our counterpart in April 1910, to study their technology and visit their factories, so that we learned a great deal. Afterward we frequently sent trainees to them and occasionally dispatched employees to observe their work in order to maintain technological links.[9]

In that way, enterprises tied up with foreign enterprises while receiving the benefits of technological know-how and guidance in modernization as well as plant equipment from their foreign partners, and raised the technological level of electrical machinery production. At that time machinery that in the western countries was secondhand was brand new to Japan, and the integrated production system of large American companies (vertical integration) was a novel production method in Japan. Along with the adoption of such new production methods, the frequent dispatching of personnel to the tie-up partner encouraged those who led modern production of electrical machinery, and this was a very effective way to raise their competence.

3. *Japanese Managers in the Foreign Tie-up Companies: Their Positions and Expectations*

The top management of the above-mentioned three American tie-up companies consisted mainly of Japanese. The CEOs in each company at the beginning were Iwadare Kunihiko, managing director of NEC; Tamura Eiji, managing director (president) of Tokyo Electric; and Mitsui Morinosuke, chairman of the board of directors of the Shibaura Engineering Works. The highest-ranking foreign officers from the parent companies were E. W. Clement and W. T. Carlton, directors of NEC; J. R. Gearly, managing director (vice-president) of Tokyo Electric; and J. R. Gearly, director of the Shibaura Engineering Works. Iwadare of NEC kept his office until September 1929, when he resigned the chairman of the board of directors. He had been in the position of CEO for 30 years. At Tokyo Electric, E. W. Rice and J. R. Gearly each became president once: Rice's term of office was from June 1918 to June 1919, and Gearly's was from May 1921 to June 1927. Their terms were rather short compared with those of Japanese presidents. In the Shibaura Engineering Works, when Iwahara Kenzō was elected president, O. Pruessman became director alongside J. R. Gearly. But the directors from GE, the parent company, were ordinary directors and never given full-time executive positions.

As for the expectations of the Japanese side for the joint venture with the foreign company in the case of the Shibaura Engineering Works, Ōtaguro Jūgorō, managing director, revealed the "true nature" of the tie-up between his company and GE in a magazine article:

> In Japan as well, the technology for making machines has progressed enormously, people are being sent abroad, and talented men rise continually in this field, but if the situation is compared with that in Europe and America, there is no way we can compete with them yet. The present situation is such that no matter how much we progress, the rate of their progress is that much faster. That is to say, on their side, as well as having the advantages of scale and well-developed equipment, their research resources and opportunities are more numer-

ous. These are the most important factors which our entrepreneurs must consider.[10]

In the cases of NEC and Tokyo Electric Co., the expectation of Japanese managers was almost the same. Japanese managers found it necessary or favorable to tie up with foreign companies in order to raise the level of Japanese products to that of foreign-made products. They thought the gap of technology between Japan and western countries was too wide for Japanese enterprises to bridge themselves. Japanese business executives in any industry put the highest priority on catching up with western industry at that time. Iwadare said clearly that tying up with a foreign company was a nationalistic action when asked his opinion by Oki Kibatarō, who was facing the prospect of a joint venture with Western Electric Co.[11] Oki, as a craftsman-type entrepreneur, hesitated to tie up with a foreign company: He thought it might be an act of treachery against the nation, because tying up with a foreign company might injure the interest of the nation. But in Iwadare's opinion it was, rather, an act of national responsibility of businessmen to introduce advanced foreign technology through joint ventures: It could help make Japanese products strong in world industrial competition. It cannot be denyed that Japanese managers placed the highest priority on the national interest when they made this important managerial decision of the Meiji and Taishō periods.

IV. The Response of the Indigenous Enterprises

1. *"Self-Reliance in Technology" as Management Policy*

Within Japan during this period, however, there were enterprises which, in the rapid progress of electrical machinery technology from the end of the 19th century to the early part of the 20th, without relying on capital or technical tie-ups with specific foreign enterprises, gathered business resources from within and outside the country and developed their own products which could compete with foreign products, thus managing to continue and develop their businesses. And their numbers were certainly not small. What made the existence of such enterprises possible was the demand for a great variety of electrical equipment in the country and the high growth rate of the market for such equipment. Among such enterprises there were managers and companies which fostered a strong sense of rivalry in the competition with foreign enterprises and companies tied to foreign capital, and deliberately advocated "self-reliance in technology." As representative of this kind of entrepreneur in the Meiji and Taishō periods (1868–1926), we can cite Oki

Kibatarō of Oki Electric Co. and Odaira Namihei of Hitachi, Ltd.[12]

Oki Kibatarō was born in Hiroshima Prefecture in 1848. As a young man, he learned the craft of the silversmith, but at the age of 27 he moved to Tokyo and entered a factory of the Public Works Ministry as a low-level worker. Shortly after that he was promoted to the rank of junior engineer (*gishu*), and in 1878 joined the team making Bell telephones at the factory, enjoying the opportunity to become familiar with the mechanisms of the latest communication equipment. Believing in the future of equipment using electricity, he left government service and founded Meikōsha in 1881. At this plant, along with telegraph and telephone instruments, medical appliances which were just coming into use were produced and orders from customers filled.

In 1889 Oki Kibatarō renamed Meikōsha the Oki Electrical Machinery Plant. Building a modern factory at Kyōbashi in Tokyo in 1894, he began mass production of electrical equipments, giving priority to telegraph and telephone equipment. In 1896, Oki Electrical Machinery Plant was renamed Oki Shōkai.

Then, as mentioned above, Western Electric tried to form a tie-up with Oki Shōkai in 1898, but when that failed, the joint enterprise Nippon Electric was formed the next year. After that, Oki Shōkai and Nippon Electric engaged in intensive competition in producing and marketing telephones and exchange equipment. Oki Kibatarō nourished a sense of rivalry with Nippon Electric and, taking a stand in favor of indigenous products, worked to prevent the importation of foreign products. Nippon Electric responded to this, and on the occasion of tenders from the Ministry of Communications for telephones and switchboards, the two companies made ever-lower bids. For instance, a ¥55 solid-back magnetic telephone quickly dropped to the ¥20 level, and a bid of less than half the original price was said to have been proffered for a switchboard.[13] Oki Shōkai was the only purely Japanese telephone and switchboard maker at that time, and as a result of Oki Kibatarō's entrepreneurial skill, the company maintained a high level of capability in technological development and production.

2. *Management Improvement of Indigenous Enterprises (1): The Case of Oki Electric Co.*[14]

Oki Kibatarō, founder of Oki Electric Co., died in May 1906. The following year his company, Oki Shōkai, became a limited partnership. Its capital was ¥600,000. The share of the Oki family was 27%, that of the employees was 6%, and the rest (67%) was held by the influential financiers in those days, such as Asano Sōichirō, Shibusawa Eiichi,

Yasuda Zenjirō, and others. Oki Shōkai, which had started as "craftsman-type" business 30 years before, was reorganized into a modern capitalistic enterprise. Although the Oki family was the largest shareholder of the company, Oki Shōkai was under the control of the financiers mentioned above. Oki Take, widow of Kibatarō, held the highest position (representative), but Asano became the full-time consultant.[15] Actually he was the strongest man in the company. Asano also took the position of chairman of the board of directors when Oki Shōkai was merged into Oki Electric Co., Ltd. with a capital of ¥1,050,000 in 1917. Asano became CEO and controlled the company in fact as well as in name until November 1930.

The telephone business was still going well after Kibatarō's death. The government carried out the Second Telephone Expansion Program (1907–1912) and then the Third Program (1916–1920). Oki Shōkai and NEC received a large order for telephones and switchboards, and this made their business busy and profitable. But telephone technology progressed rapidly. Oki Shōkai found it necessary to strengthen the R&D function in order to catch up on progress. Oki was apparently behind NEC in R&D capability.

Early in the 20th century the government tried to adopt the "common electric" (*kyōden*)-type switchboard instead of the magnetic type, because the former had many advantages over the latter. This new model was a patent of Western Electric Co., so at first the government imported the machinery from the United States and installed it at each branch office. Next the government ordered the machinery from NEC, because the company could supply the product under the auspices of WE. Oki was able to complete the machinery in 1918 and supplied it to the government. It was nine years later that the first new-type switchboard was imported from the United States. This made the management of Oki recognize the importance of R&D activity. In June 1918 they established the R&D department. Kawazumi Kanshirō, manager of the research division of the Ministry of Communications, took the post of R&D manager of Oki Electric Co. and led the modern and organized activity of R&D for the company.

As for workers on the floor, Oki began to hire formally educated people. Hitherto the workers of Oki were trained under the *oyakata* system: They were hired as apprentices when very young (ordinarily in their early teens) and taught skills through face-to-face training by *oyakata*. These workers were the core work force in the Oki plants. But the ratio of workers of this kind began to decrease around this period and graduates from schools outside the company increased in number. However, the initiative of production on the work floor was still in the hands of the former group until around the end of the 1920s. At Oki's plants a kind of "subcontract system" was in practice for the first three decades of the twentieth century.

During World War I, Oki received a large number of orders from both inside and outside the country.[16] After the war the Ministry of Communications explained the "self-reliance" policy of telephone equipment more clearly. They thought "we should avoid excessive dependence on abroad for communication technology, which might be called the nervous system of the economy and human life of the nation." This policy created an all-the-more-favorable situation for domestic producers of telephone equipments such as Oki and NEC because they could expect more orders from the government. Also, the Great Kantō Earthquake in 1923, which damaged the telephone network near Tokyo, created a big demand for communication machinery from Oki Electric Co., for they suffered little from the earthquake and could supply equipment to hard-hit areas. Around 1923, Oki had three plants, and the number of employees was 1,201: White-collar workers numbered 468 and blue-collar, 733. The capital was ¥2,500,000 and in 1925 it doubled to ¥5,000,000. Oki was already a fairly large company in those days.

After World War I the Ministry of Communications announced two major policies: One was the commencement of radio broadcasting and the other was the adoption of an automatic telephone exchange system in a short time. Oki, as a major communication equipment maker, had to adapt to these new situations.

Even before World War I, Oki had already tried to make wireless communication devices and was successful to some extent. But in making a vacuum tube, they encountered a patent problem with Tokyo Electric Co. and were obliged to abandon vacuum-tube making. They planned to make radio sets but the plan was not carried out.

As for the second new business field, i.e., the production of automatic exchange switchboards, Oki had to face entirely new circumstances. Even in the western countries automatic exchangers were not widely used in the telephone business, because they were complex mechanisms and expensive to produce and maintain. But the officials at the Ministry of Communications were very eager to introduce this new machinery. They regretted the human losses resulting from the Great Kantō Earthquake, so they decided to adopt an automatic exchange switchboard in place of the older one. However, the production technology of the new model was so high that Japanese domestic makers could not produce it by their conventional method. The Ministry of Communications nominated the six western producers of the new model.[17] Japanese makers got the agency of importing the products of the nominated producers and made a bid for them when the tender was offered by the Ministry.

But at first, Oki could not find the foreign counterpart. They failed to get the agency of importing the authorized automatic exchangers. So for the time being, Oki was excluded from supplying the automatic exchange switchboard to the Ministry. This was a very serious situation for Oki. If they chose to develop the new machinery for themselves, it might take a long time to complete the model. Furthermore, they might encounter a patent problem on the way. Because the automatization of the switchboard was the established policy of the Ministry of Communications, Oki had no choice but to acquire from the outside the technology to make it. They finally decided to tie up with General Electric Co. of the U.K. to produce the automatic exchange switchboard. In 1927 they constructed Shibaura Plant to make new machinery. This tie-up was a technological one and entailed no capital relationship between the two companies. But the incident showed that the indigenous company could not idly remain in a vacuum while faced with the rapid technological progress of the industry.[18]

Besides Oki Kibatarō, we cannot fail to mention Odaira Namihei as an eminent indigenous entrepreneur during the Meiji, Taishō, and early Shōwa periods. He was the founder of Hitachi, Ltd.

3. *Management Improvement of Indigenous Enterprises (2): The Case of Hitachi, Ltd.*[19]

Odaira Namihei was born in Tochigi Prefecture in 1874. After graduating from the electrical engineering course at Tokyo Imperial University in 1900, he entered a partnership firm, Fujita-gumi, and worked at the Kosaka Mine as chief electrical engineer. His main work at the Kosaka Mine was the construction of a hydroelectric system. After this he changed employers, moving to the Hiroshima Hydroelectric Company and the Tokyo Electric Light Company, and with the latter participated in building the Komabashi Power Station on the Katsura River. The output of this power station was 15,000 kilowatts, and it was designed to deliver 55,000 volts of electricity to the Waseda Transformer Station in Tokyo, a distance of 80 kilometers. The construction of the generator plant for the generation and transmission of such a large output and high voltage required the importation of components from abroad and guidance from foreign, i.e., western, engineers.

Odaira keenly regretted this reliance on electrical equipment and technology from Europe and America. He had consistently favored the domestic production of electrical machinery, and on this occasion his desire for domestic capability was especially strong. In 1906, Odaira was approached by a newly rising entrepreneur of the day, Kuhara Fusanosuke, and joined his company as an engineer at the Hitachi Mines of Kuhara Mining Co. Kuhara set up the electrical machinery repair shop at the Hitachi Mines, which was intended for the repair of equipment used in the mines, but it also contributed to the realization of Odaira's vision of the domestication of electrical machinery production.

In reality, the repair of machinery was the first step toward the manufacture of machinery. At the time the electric motors at the Hitachi Mines were almost all made in the United States, but the way in which machines were used in the mines was extremely rough, and within less than a year many of them were scorched black. The nominal repairs that had to be made were so involved that the work was not much different from building them again from scratch. Consequently, while repairing electric motors, methods of manufacture and so on were studied and acquired with confidence. In 1910 "steel sheet presses were bought from England, and by doing all of the design and working drawings themselves, three 5-hp electric motors" were built.[20] These motors were used at the Hitachi Mines.

At that time large-capacity, high-voltage electrical machinery and equipment were generally imported, while small-capacity, low-voltage units were usually ordered from Japanese manufacturing plants. The products of the Hitachi Engineering Works were predominantly of small capacity and low voltage at first, but Odaira purposefully assembled young engineers graduating from universities and formed a technological coterie, so that the propensity to develop new products at the works grew stronger.

For example, upon receiving an order in 1911 from the Hitachi Mines for a 275-hp 3700-rpm motor for ventilation, they produced it, and this was one of the largest electric motors made in Japan at that time. Even at Hitachi, "because it turned at high speed, its manufacture was very difficult," but it was completed in August of the next year and delivered. This electric motor was baptized at the Hitachi Engineering Works as Product No. 1, and was worthy of commemoration.[21]

Enterprises promoting "the domestication of technology," of which the Hitachi Engineering Works was foremost, were most conspicuously active during the First World War (1914–18). Because the importation of various kinds of electrical equipment for which foreign countries had been relied on in the past was stopped during this period, orders poured into Japanese companies, and the domestic production of large-capacity, high-voltage electrical equipment proceeded rapidly. At the Hitachi Engineering Works, generators with capacities of up to 6,000 kva were produced, and in electric motors, as well as units of large capacity, high-speed units like the 3,600-rpm motor were turned out. Transformers of the 66,000 and 77,000-volt class with capacities of several thousand kva were delivered to a chemical fertilizer company and others. In 1916 the company was called upon by the electrical testing station of the Ministry of Communications to make a 350,000-volt experimental transformer, and at the end of the following year, after much effort, it was completed. Such new products "were all designed either by following materials in books or magazines or by sketching the external appearance of models imported from abroad."[22]

Taking the opportunity afforded by this cessation of imported foreign makes, Japanese enterprises manufacturing electrical machinery expanded the range of their products and raised their technological levels. Their technological standards, however, did not immediately reach those of Europe and the United States. Concerning the technological level at the Hitachi Engineering Works during this period, the company history says that, "looking at the quality of the products, it cannot be disputed that there were many deficiencies, such as inadequacy of design, lack of skill in production, mismatches of raw materials, and, as a result, delays in production deadlines."[23] For example, the above-mentioned 350,000-volt experimental transformer delivered to the electrical testing station of the Ministry of Communications underwent its formal test for acceptance in June of 1917, but it could not attain the required capacity, and only after many more attempts did it finally come up to standard in November of that year.

For the enterprises following the principle of domestic generation of technology, R&D was a vital function. The Hitachi Engineering Works set up a research section in 1918, which, in conjunction with research, undertook the responsibility of solving the urgent problem of ensuring the continuing improvement of products. Accordingly, the research section repeatedly negotiated with the design department and worked for the improvement of technology and products. For instance, tests concerning the rating of fuses, experiments with commutation in direct-current dynamos, testing of electric fans, and copper wire testing were entrusted to them and carried out. Without such trials and research, there could have been no improvement in the quality of domestically produced electrical equipment nor any reduction in costs.

In 1920, Hitachi Engineering Works was reorganized into Hitachi, Ltd., a subsidiary of Kuhara Mining Co. Odaira became managing director and conducted the company to the point of becoming a leading electrical machinery producer. He was a leader of both management and technology. The number of employees in the beginning was 2,701, comprising 281 *shain* (white-collar workers) and 2,420 *kōin* (blue-collar workers). After several years' stagnation the number increased to more than 3,000 in the latter half of 1920s,[24] with three factories.

V. Concluding Remarks: Modernization of Japanese Business Management: The Process of Mixing Japanese and Western Elements

1. *Five Common Features*

The producers of Japanese prewar electrical machinery industry consisted of two categories: one was the foreign tie-up company and the other was the indigenous enterprise. They were different in origin, but had several features in common. I will discuss five of them:

(1) Starting out as a domestic business: The electrical machine producers in Japan were basically inside-market-oriented. They started selling products to domestic users, be they private customers, business firms, or the government. So the executives of the companies were ordinarily Japanese who knew the domestic market well. Even in the foreign tie-up company the majority of directors and top managers were Japanese.

(2) Professionalism in management: In the cases of NEC and Oki Shōkai the top managers were big share holders, for example, K. Iwadare in NEC and K. Oki in Oki Shōkai. But in other companies the top managers were professionals. In the case of Shibaura Engineering Works the chairman of the board of directors was from Mitsui family, but the presidents were elected from among the competent employees who built careers as managers. The professional managers were ordinarily strong in technological innovation and active in enlarging business activities. Managerial and technological developments were effected by them both in the foreign tie-up company and the indigenous enterprise.

(3) The management ideology of "western talent with Japanese spirit" (*wakon yōsai*): "Western talent with Japanese spirit" was a motto among the modernization-minded people in the Meiji era. They insisted that the Japanese should learn western knowledge and acquire western skills but never abandon the Japanese spirit. Almost all Japanese business managers were advocates of this ideology. They thought highly of Japanese national interests, but the managerial style they adopted was very nearly western as far as structure was concerned.

(4) Growing industry and growing business: The electrical machinery

industry was the innovative industry of the time. The managers were professional and active in business affairs. The users were also open to accepting new products. Diffusion of electric lighting and power was very rapid during the Meiji and Taishō eras. It was quite natural that the managers of this industry should have been positive and active in adapting themselves to these situations.

(5) Accumulation of human resources inside the firm: In the prewar electrical machinery industry the turnover of managers and engineers was limited. This was not peculiar to this industry. The same phenomenon could be seen in the other manufacturing industries of the time. Executives were mainly from among the employees of the company. Engineers ordinarily stayed in the same company. But there was some turnover among the companies in the same interest group and between private companies and the governmental organization. Some earlier officers of Shibaura Engineering Works were moved in from the affiliates of the Mitsui zaibatsu. Some officials of the Ministry of Communications were offered high-ranking positions in Oki Electric Co. and others. There was also some turnover between private companies. But as the companies grew larger, the turnover of managers and engineers became less. Even the turnover of workers became less in the late 1920s. Each large company adopted "in-plant apprenticeship" (*yōseikō seido*) and tried to reduce the removal of workers from the companies. This closed system of business on the human side was called "Japanese-style management" later. "Japanese-style management" was a result of the endeavor to establish a unique human system by each Japanese large company facing severe competition both inside and outside the country. It was a product of the endeavor of Japanese companies (especially the indigenous enterprises in the case of the electrical machinery industry) to reach for a "strong" management system.[25]

2. *Major Differences*

But there were some differences in management system between the foreign tie-up company and the indigenous enterprise. I will point to one feature in each major managerial function, i.e., financing, production, and marketing.

(1) Stability of financing: In this regard the foreign tie-up company was much stabler than the indigenous one. The parent company of the former was transacting big business worldwide and could assist the subsidiary from the financial side. As for the indigenous enterprises, Hitachi was a subsidiary of Kuhara Mining Co., and Oki accepted financial support from influential capitalists of the day. Speaking of

minor indigenous enterprises, the financial problem was the most urgent matter for business management. They could not afford to enlarge production capacity for lack of money. This arrested the development of many minor indigenous enterprises in prewar Japan.

(2) Manual vs. "creative" methods: The foreign tie-up company received a production manual from the parent company. The indigenous enterprise had to create the method of production for itself. Thus, at first, the production method of the latter company might contain irrational procedures. Also the independently created method could result in failures or defects in production. But if the people were accustomed to production in this way, they might find more suitable methods for themselves: They could create new methods. Production according to the established manual could produce standardized and normal products from the beginning, but production by creation could open the way to new production systems.[26] Indigenous enterprises accumulated these methods, which formed a "Japanese way of production" afterward.

(3) Organized marketing vs. market-oriented management: The "world-famous" brand name is a powerful instrument in business competition. The foreign tie-up companies used this instrument and practiced organized marketing both inside and outside the country. On the other hand the indigenous enterprise had to create its own customers. In Hitachi, Ltd., Odaira, the founder, laid stress on marketing in carrying out his business. Marketing was the most important managerial function for him. Toward the middle of the 1920s the Japanese government began to encourage the people to use national products to keep the balance in international trade and to support domestic industries. This government policy developed into the national movement known as the *Kokusanhin aiyō undō* ("Buy Japanese goods" movement). The movement helped indigenous enterprises find more customers in the domestic market. The products of foreign tie-ups were not expelled: They were also national products. But many users, including the government, ordered more products from indigenous enterprises as a result of the movement. Thus the indigenous enterprises enlarged their markets and proceeded to modernize their production and sales systems during the 1920s.[27]

Notes

1. The several passages following are an abridgment of the first part of my previous work, "Modernization of Technology and Labor in Pre-war Japanese Electrical Machinery Enterprises," in *Japanese Yearbook on Business History*, 1987.

2. At this time the Shibaura Engineering Works was in an unstable position in the Mitsui zaibatsu. The parent company changed several times within the group. It could be called a "venture business" of the time.

3. The word "challenger" may be not clear as a technical term. I have used this word to mean the first mover to modernize management and technology.

4. This section is based upon my previous work, "Foreign Joint Ventures and Modernization of Business Management in Japan: Three Cases in Meiji Electric Machinery Industry" (English title), in *Keiei Shirin* (The Hōsei Journal of Business), January 1981, pp. 117ff.

5. The Tokyo Electric Company, like the Shibaura Engineering Works, was a "venture business" of the time. They failed in business on a national basis and asked the help of the foreign company. In deciding on the tie-up the success of NEC as a foreign joint venture was a strong and favorable factor for Fujioka and other Japanese people concerned.

6. Masuda Takashi visited the headquarters of General Electric Co. in 1907 and met President Coffin of GE. It is said that this was the actual starting point of the joint venture between the two companies. See *Shibaura Seisakusho 65 Nen Shi* (The 65-Year History of the Shibaura Engineering Works), 1940, pp. 53–55. Masuda was a very influential person in the Mitsui zaibatsu.

7. See *Nippon Denki Kabushiki Kaisha 70 Nen Shi* (The 70-Year History of NEC), 1972, pp. 53–56.

8. See *Tokyo Denki Kabushiki Kaisha 50 Nen Shi* (The 50-Year History of the Tokyo Electric Co.), 1940, pp. 102–10.

9. *Ibid.*, p. 55.

10. Ōtaguro, J., "*Shibaura Seisakusho to Beikoku Zeneraru-sha to Gōdō no Shinsō* (The True Nature of the Tie-up Between Shibaura Engineering Works and G.E. of America)," in *Jitsugyō no Nippon* (Business of Japan), vol. 13, no. 2 (Jan. 15, 1910), p. 13.

11. See Okamoto, S., *Iwadare Kunihiko* (biography), and also *Nippon Denki Kabushiki Kaisha 70 Nen Shi*, pp. 26–27.

12. For Oki, I have consulted Hisazumi, S., *Oki Kibatarō* (biography), 1932, and for Odaira, Fujita, T., *Nihon no Denki Sangyō o Kizuita Hito: Odaira Namihei-ō no Shōgai* (The Man Who Built the Japanese Electrical Machinery Industry: The Life of Odaira Namihei), Kokusei-sha, 1962. As entrepreneurs they had rather diametrically opposite backgrounds: Oki was a craftsman-type businessman without a formal education; Odaira was a modern engineer who had graduated from Tokyo Imperial University. But their management philosophies and ways of doing business were very much the same.

13. See Hisazumi, *op. cit.*, p. 105.

14. The main sources of this section are *Yutakana Jōhōshakai o Hiraku Oki Denkikōgyō* (Oki Electric Industry Opening the Affluent Information Society), 1972; *Oki Denki 100 Nen no Ayumi* (The 100-Year History of the Oki Electric Industry Co.), 1981; and *Nippon Denki Kabushiki Kaisha 70 Nen Shi.*

15. Asano was the leader of the Asano zaibatsu, a new zaibatsu after the 1910s. Oki Take was Mrs. Asano's aunt. Asano was a good adviser to Kibatarō while he was alive, especially in his later years.

16. The main overseas market was China.

17. The nominated six western producers were Automatic Telephone Manufacturing Co., Standard Telephone & Cables, Ltd., Automatic Electric, Inc.,

General Electric Co., Siemens Brothers & Co., Ltd., and Siemens & Halske Aktien Gesellschaft. Of these the first three companies were WE-related.

18. The technological tie-up with the English electrical machinery producers also accelerated the modernization of production on the work floor of the Oki Electric Co. See my previous work, "Modernization of Factory Management in Japan" (English title), in *Keiei Shirin*, April 1985, pp. 18–19.

19. The main sources of this section are Fujita, *op. cit.*; *Hitachi Seisakusho Shi* (The History of Hitachi, Ltd.), 1949; and *Japanese Yearbook on Business History*, 1987, pp. 34–39.

20. *Hitachi Seisakusho Shi*, pp. 16–17.

21. *Ibid.*, p. 25.

22. *Ibid.*, pp. 46–47.

23. *Ibid.*, p. 31.

24. Chokki, T., "Accumulation of Technology and the Work Force in Japanese Electric Machinery Manufacturing Companies Before World War II" (English title), in *Keiei Shirin*, October 1986, p. 19.

25. As for the general features of Japanese business management, see my recent work, "Principles of Japanese Business Management" (English title), *Keiei Shirin*, July 1988, pp. 1ff.

26. One characteristic method of production in Japanese industrial firms throughout history was "value analysis" or "value engineering," though they did not use such a word before World War II. See *ibid.*, pp. 13–14 and footnote 5 on p. 15.

27. After the so-called Manchurian Incident occurred in 1931, the three American tie-up companies changed ownership and management. In 1932, ISE (International Standard Electric Corporation, the parent company of NEC at the time) gave a 14.1% share of stock to the Sumitomo zaibatsu and accepted two directors (the chairman of the board of directors and the managing director) from Sumitomo. The American side supplied three ordinary directors out of six. In 1939, Tokyo Electric Co. and the Shibaura Engineering Works merged into the Tokyo Shibaura Electric Co. (now Toshiba). In the beginning IGE (the International General Electric Corporation) was the largest shareholder (32.8%). The second largest was the Mitsui zaibatsu, which held a 14.8% share. The president was from the Japanese side and one of the four vice-presidents was from GE. As for ordinary directors, GE supplied only one out of eight. As a whole, the dependence of the top management on the Japanese side seems to have become all the stronger.

Comment

Hisashi Watanabe

Professor Chokki limits his subject to the Japanese electrical machinery industry and mainly to its initial stage, the period from its very beginning until World War I. I believe that such limitation is effective in making clear the prototypes of some problems accompanying one of those industries which have developed most brilliantly in Japan.

Chokki points out the "challenge-response" process in the Japanese electrical machinery industry, which faced severe competition with foreign enterprises on the domestic market before World War I. On the one hand, there were such enterprises as NEC, Tokyo Electric, and Shibaura Engineering, which did not hesitate to affiliate with foreign enterprises (so-called foreign tie-up companies: I call them Type I). On the other hand, there were such enterprises as Oki and Hitachi, which were opposed to any affiliation (so-called indigenous enterprises: I call them Type II). According to Chokki, both types were equally national-interest-oriented. The difference between the both types is, therefore, not in the degree of orientation toward the national interest but in the method for catching up with advanced foreign enterprises. My first question is related to this difference: Where does this contrasting difference in catching-up strategy of enterprises come from? If I understand Chokki correctly, he is going to explain it by citing the difference in entrepreneurial personalities. It must be taken into consideration, however, that the Japanese government played a decisive role at that time, not only as general conductor of the industrialization process, but also as a factor in the consumption structure. The Japanese government was assumedly de facto the biggest organized and integrated consumer with the most effective demand for the products of this newly developing technology–intensive industry. In this first stage of the industrialization of Japan, a new consumption structure for newly introduced industries had to be created. For this purpose, government consumption undoubtedly played a key role. In order to build up the infrastructure of the government organization, a huge demand was created, affording the enterprises concerned a chance to do big business. So far, the government was in an almost monopolistic position as purchaser. That means the government could have influence on the catching-up strategy of each enterprise. Thus it might not be wrong to speculate that a strategy mix for catching up was in the interests of the government, because both "self-reliance" or "affiliation" had merits and demerits. In this sense the "challenge-response" process went on not only among the Japanese enterprises but also between the Japanese government and enterprises.

Secondly, insofar as foreign enterprises were aware of the decisively influential position of the Japanese government, they regarded it as most important in the selection of Japanese counterparts for joint ventures if their connection with the Japanese government was strong enough. Such was also the case in the joint-venture negotiations between Siemens and Furukawa immediately after World War I. Siemens attached great importance to the relationship between the Japanese government and Furukawa, and it was one of the major factors in Siemens's decision to cooperate with Furukawa that the current prime minister, Hara Kei, was regarded as a Furukawa-man. At the same time Siemens carried on direct negotiations with the Japanese navy, which was interested in Siemens's sophisticated technology for submarine equipments. Therefore the "challenge-response" process could be observed between the Japanese government and foreign enterprises too. In my opinion the "challenge-response" process figures into the triangular relationship as shown below.

My third question is related to the Japanese enterprises which are grouped into Type I. According to Chokki, it appears that the Japanese enterprises could sit at the negotiating table with foreign enterprises as equal partners. Was it really so? Then, I wonder how they had developed so rapidly and successfully that they could now carry out negotiations for joint ventures with gigantic foreign multinationals.

My fourth and last question refers to the last remark in Chokki's paper: He stresses that marketing was the most important managerial function of so-called indigenous enterprises. I agree with him insofar as indigenous enterprises, Type II, had to make the Japanese government their customer. However, the latter was interested in the highest possible performance of national products. As far as Type II enterprises had to follow the governmental postulate for a high technical level, should it not rather be called "technology-oriented management"?

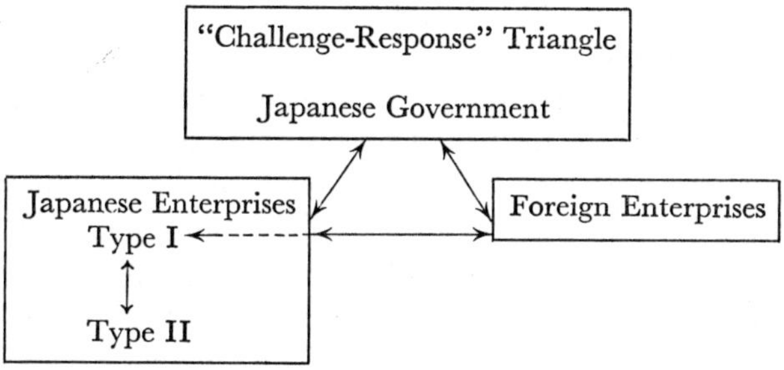

Response

Toshiaki Chokki

In answer to the first question: In my view the difference in catch-up strategy between types I and II (to use Professor Watanabe's terms) basically came from the entrepreneurial personality and his business ideology. Watanabe says there might have been an influence exerted by the government on the catch-up strategy of each enterprise. I admit that the government played a big, if not decisive, role as the last buyer of electrical machinery in those days, and it might have been the case that the government was gravely concerned about the tie-up of Japanese enterprises with foreign companies. But the industry was still in the infant stage of development in the Meiji era, and it was inconceivable that the government had established any definite industrial policy toward the electrical machinery industry. It is rather proper to think the three cases of American tie-ups I have mentioned in the paper were of an autonomous nature, not a political one.

To the second point: I admire Watanabe's presentation. The "challenge-response" process model should be considered in the triangular relationship between the Japanese government, Japanese enterprises, and foreign enterprises in the full-fledged stage. Furukawa and Siemens established Fuji Denki in 1923. This was a typical product of the triangular relationship. I have omitted the case of the Fuji Denki. If I had analyzed this case, I should have adopted an analytical framework very much like Watanabe's.

To the third question: I think the foreign enterprise recognized the Japanese counterpart as an "equal partner" for the three cases I mentioned in the paper. In my view they thought highly of Japanese managerial competence: Iwadare in NEC, Fujioka and Shinjo (the president from 1919 to 1921) in Tokyo Electric, and the Mitsui people in Shibaura Engineering. The Japanese enterprise was behind the foreign counterpart in money and technology, but I think there were no big differences insofar as human power was concerned.

To the fourth and the last question: I am afraid there is some misperception of the subject between us. Marketing is a very important managerial function for any enterprise. I have formulated "organized marketing vs. market-oriented management" as a different marketing feature of the two types of enterprises. And any user, including the government, was interested in a product's high performance. In that connection the indigenous enterprises should have been "technology-oriented," because they were behind their foreign rivals in that respect. But marketing came first for the indigenous producers in those days. I have mentioned the repetitive improvement of a delivered Hitachi-made 350,000-volt experimental transformer ordered by the Ministry of Communications in 1917. Both marketing and technology were (and are) indispensable to business activity. But I must say that Japanese enterprises were much more marketing-oriented than technology-oriented in the first stage of development. They were very anxious to find customers.

L'Air Liquide, Pioneer of French Industrial Presence in Japan Between 1910 and 1945

Jin-Mieung Li

I. Introduction

Although the French company L'Air Liquide was founded in 1902, it was not until 1905—the year in which Georges Claude first perfected the process for the industrial fabrication of oxygen—that it became truly active. Thereafter, it continued to expand rapidly both in France and the world at large throughout the period with which we are concerned here, i.e., up until 1945.

As early as 1906 the company decided to go multinational and created several subsidiaries and branches in other countries. The Japanese subsidiary was created in 1910 and developed rapidly after the installation of its first oxygen and acetylene works in Osaka in 1912, soon taking the lead in Japan's industrial-gas field and ranking second among all the Société L'Air Liquide affiliates by the start of the 1920s. In this study I shall try to trace its evolution and its role in the industrial history of interwar Japan, at the same time pointing out its place in the global strategy of the L'Air Liquide Group.

The period 1910–45 may be divided into three parts, corresponding to the three different forms of juridical status under which L'Air Liquide operated in Japan: the Société d'Oxygène et d'Acétylène du Japon, a company subject to French jurisdiction (1910–23); the Japanese division, under the direct control of L'Air Liquide (1924–30); and Teikoku Sanso KK, subject to Japanese law (from 1930 onward). The history of these three periods will be preceded by a section on the genesis and development of the parent company and its strategy of expansion.

I shall use the following abbreviations for certain words that appear frequently in the text: L'AL=L'Air Liquide; SOAJ=Société d'Oxygène et d'Acétylène du Japon (Japan Oxygen & Acetylene Company); Teikoku Sanso KK (Kabushiki Kaisha)=Société Impériale d'Oxygène (Imperial Oxygen Company).

II. The Birth, Development, and Expansion Strategy of the Société L'Air Liquide

The Société L'Air Liquide was officially formed on November 8, 1902, but its origins go back to 1899, the year in which two men, both highly talented in their own fields, first joined forces. They were scientist-inventor Georges Claude (1870–1960) and administrator-financier Paul Delorme (1866–1956).

Having perfected the process for the production of oxygen in 1905, L'AL developed rapidly. The first dividends were distributed in 1907 and have been distributed every year since, even during the two world wars. At current value its registered capital rose from F100,000 in 1902 to F500,000 in 1905 and had reached F386.5 million by 1946. Its credit rose from F1.7 million in 1907 to F1,405 million in 1945. The annual turnover was F50 million for 1920, F300 million for 1930, F600 million for 1940, and F1,100 million for 1945. Dividends rose unfailingly from 5% in 1907 to 35% in 1930, dropping only three times, in 1934–36, 1939, and 1944.[1]

In France, L'AL's first oxygen works was built in Paris (Boulogne) in 1906 and were 13 in number in 1920 and 17 by 1924. The works for acetylene solution were annexed to those for oxygen from 1917 on.

As of 1906, the company started establishing itself outside France: in Belgium (1906); Italy (1908); Indochina, Spain, Russia, and Greece (1909); Japan (1910); Canada and Sweden (1911); Algeria and Tunisia (1912); the United States (1916); etc.

L'AL was absent in certain countries. This was due to the fact that, from the time that this branch of industry first made its appearance around 1910, the world oxygen-acetylene market was shared by agreement, written or tacit, between L'Air Liquide, the British Oxygen Co. (which utilized the Linde process, and with which L'AL had several lawsuits between 1906 and 1910), and the Linde Company in Germany. Essentially the French company was effective in the European Latin countries and in the French colonies of Africa and Asia; the British company in Commonwealth countries; and the German company in the countries under German influence. Everywhere else it was a question of open competition conducted through their various subsidiaries and accredited concessionaries.

The multinational nature of these companies caused difficulties in the transport of their products, industrial gases. Before the First World War they were generally transported in 7-m³ or 10-m³ steel bottles weighing 70 kg or 80 kg; the cost of exporting a bottle of oxygen from France to

Japan, for example, was prohibitive. It was therefore logical to build a works there and quickly, more so since a single 20 m^3/h oxygen works was not a particularly expensive investment and the industrial production of this gas was awaited; it was henceforth necessary to get in ahead of any competition on the overseas market.

Another important reason for the transnationalization of this particular branch of activity was that its raw material, air, is in abundant supply and free all over the world.

Multiplication of subsidiaries and holdings represented an important proportion of the company's portfolio: at current value, F0.2 million in 1907, F2 million in 1910, F8.8 million in 1920, F136.4 million in 1930, F164.4 million in 1940 (F65.2 million in France, F99.2 million in foreign concerns), and F225.9 million in 1945 (F118.1 million in France, F107.8 million outside). This was in accordance with the financial policy of the group, which preferred to divide risks by forming separate companies, each of which was then called upon to show its own mettle. Only after several years of trial would they be judged worthy of being incorporated into the solidly established capital of the parent company.

Absorption or participation in other companies called for capital, for which L'AL began to depend more and more on investors (shareholders). To attract and keep them, profits had to be generated, which could then be distributed to them in more than comfortable dividends.

Thus, based on this strategy, in 1945 L'AL found itself head of a powerful organization comprising nearly 70 subsidiaries and foreign divisions: some 20 companies in France, 40-odd companies, and about 10 divisions in the world. In 1952, the L'AL Group owned 316 factories in 31 countries, 86 of which were in France and the remaining 230 abroad.

III. The Period of the Société d'Oxygène et d'Acétylène du Japon, 1910–23

The Société d'Oxygène et d'Acétylène du Japon (SOAJ, Nihon Okishijenu oyobi Asechirenu Kaisha, or Japan Oxygen & Acetylene Company) was a L'Air Liquide subsidiary, formed in Paris on July 9, 1910 with a capital of F400,000. A company under French jurisdiction, it operated in Japan through its central branch in Kobe until its absorption into the parent company in December 1923.

In 1909, before the foundation of the SOAJ, Charles Favre-Brandt, a Swiss watch representative established in Osaka, and Félix Ziégel, a naval engineer living in Paris, signed a series of agreements with three French companies: L'AL, which had a capital of F2.5 million at the time;

the Société Acétylène Dissous et Application d'Acétylène, founded by André Le Châtelier in 1909 with a capital of F1.4 million; and the Société Acétylène Dissous du Sud-Est, also founded by André Le Châtelier in Marseilles in 1903 with a capital of F100,000 (1 yen=F2.56 in 1909), to represent these companies and exploit their patents in Japan. But before Favre-Brandt had even started business, L'AL and the two companies had decided to take exploitation of their patents in Japan into their own hands. Engaging in negotiations with Favre-Brandt and Ziégel, they reached the agreements which gave birth to a company. The first constitutive assembly of the Société d'Oxygène et d'Acétylène du Japon (SOAJ) took place on June 18, 1910, in Paris, and the company was finally established during the second constitutive assembly on July 9.[2]

The SOAJ's first board of directors was made up of six members, elected for six years. As president, they chose 70-year-old Émile Bertin (1840–1924), retired director of shipbuilding in the French navy, who had served in Japan as counsel to the minister of the navy, and professor of maritime engineering at the Imperial University of Tokyo between 1886 and 1890. A member of the Académie des Sciences in 1903, he became president of the Société Franco-Japonaise de Paris (Nichifutsu Kyokai), founded in 1912, and a member of the Académie de la Marine (Academy of the Navy) in 1921.[3]

These same members, apart from Favre-Brandt, who was dismissed in 1916, were to remain the directorate of the company until 1923, still with Émile Bertin as president, although it was in fact Paul Delorme who held the reins of the Japanese subsidiary.

The SOAJ, created in Paris, was registered at the Kobe Tribunal on November 14, 1910. In the days following its establishment, it ordered oxygen- and acetylene-making equipment, as well as "tubes" (*bouteille* in French, *bombe* in German: i.e., steel bottles) and torches, from the parent company.[4]

In 1911 a group of excellent welders, under the orders of Georges Bouillon, ex-second production chief at L'AL's Boulogne works, were sent to Japan. Upon arrival, they set up an oxyacetylene repair workshop, which was the source of income until the opening of the works. They also organized lectures and demonstrations of welding and metal cutting for Japanese technicians from shipyards, railways, and metallurgical works. For this purpose, they utilized oxygen and acetylene produced in Saigon.[5] The first welding diplomas in the name of the company were delivered in August 1911.[6] Bouillon and his French welders gave a demonstration of liquid air and underwater metal cutting at the Tokyo

Ueno Exhibition. These techniques, unknown and revolutionary in Japan, created a sensation among spectators and were accepted with enthusiasm by industrialists.[7]

The construction of the first works met with administrative difficulties. The position of the president, Émile Bertin, should have eased the first steps, for he was still very fondly remembered in Japan. However, the civil servants in charge of granting construction permits and licenses to use the works turned out to be very wary of an industry using a process requiring such low temperatures and producing a substance such as oxygen, which was classified in Japan as dangerous. It thus took a relatively long time to get permission to construct the first works in the Sakurajima district of Osaka[8] on property belonging to the Osaka Iron Works Company, owned by Richard Hunter, an Englishman who had become a naturalized Japanese.[9]

The first works in Osaka began production of acetylene in January 1912. Production of oxygen was to begin on April 15 of the same year,[10] and this is the historic date of the first industrial production of oxygen in Japan. The Osaka works had one plant with a capacity of 20 m^3 of oxygen per hour, and with it they managed to produce 15,000 m^3 during 1912, the first year of exploitation.[11]

In the summer of the same year, Raymond Royer, ex-director of L'AL's Lille branch, was nominated director of the branch in Japan, and in July a sales office was opened in Tokyo.[12]

Business soon boomed for the SOAJ, largely through the shipyards, which were their main customers in a country with large mercantile and naval fleets. Its stock of oxygen bottles continually increased, becoming a sort of regular oddments.

Two years after its opening, the First World War broke out in Europe. The Japanese branch was cut off from its headquarters. Royer and Bouillon, its managers and sole French staff, were not mobilized and were thus able to carry on their work in Japan. Unable now to get new equipment and spare parts from France, they were obliged to open a small workshop at the Osaka works. Metal-cutting and -shaping torches were thus first fabricated in Japan in 1914, and it was there, too, that gas aluminum welding was first performed.[13]

In 1915 the company changed its name in Japanese from Nihon Okishijenu oyobi Asechirenu Kaisha to Teikoku Sanso-Asechirenu Kaisha (Imperial Oxygen-Acetylene Company),[14] although the legal position of the company as French remained unchanged. The addition of the adjective *teikoku* (*imperial*) made reference to the Teikoku Kaigun, or Imperial Navy, the company's largest client. In 1916 it received a gold medal at the Japanese Naval Show at Tokyo, a distinction crowning its efforts to introduce the very latest techniques in the domain of oxygen production, welding, and the cutting of metals.[15]

The site on which the Osaka works was built did not belong to the company, and when it was sold in December 1916, the company was obliged to move installations to Hyōgo-Kobe.[16] The opportunity was taken to augment production capacity so as to meet the increasing demand for oxygen, and the Hyōgo works had two plants, one of 20 m^3/h and the other of 10 m^3/h.[17] Two years later, in 1918, the works doubled in size. Although it is only 30 km from Osaka, the Kobe site was ideal. Not only was it one of the largest ports for foreign trade in Japan, with Yokohama in Kanagawa Prefecture, but the biggest shipyards, such as the Kawasaki and Mitsubishi dockyards, were also there.

Two other oxygen works were opened, one at Kanagawa in June 1917 with two 20 m^3/h plants, and the other at Osaka in 1918. An acetylene-solution installation was added to the Hyōgo works in 1919.[18] At the time, the SOAJ was the only French industrial establishment of any importance in Japan.[19]

Another of L'AL's fields of interest in Japan was the sale of Georges Claude's equipment and patents for the fabrication of nitrogen. The SOAJ had no more than an intermediary role in this particular line of business. By 1913, L'AL had sold a nitrogen production plant to the Nippon Chisso Hiryō Kaisha and work on its installation was completed by the beginning of 1914.[20] Between then and 1924, thirteen 500-m^3/h plants (nitrogen separators) were delivered to Japan, and two more in 1925.[21] Supplementary oxygen produced by these chemical fertilizer plants was sold to the SOAJ, which built residual oxygen compression installations near the fertilizer factories. In 1924 the SOAJ had five such installations (Minamata, Kagami, Nagaoka, Ome, and Takefu) providing oxygen to the neighboring districts.[22]

An explosion of acetylene and oxygen bottles occurred at Kobe Station on April 6, 1918, causing a dozen deaths and injuries and damage estimated at ¥1 million (F13 million). The Ministry of Railways brought charges against the SOAJ for damages. However handling within the station being under license, responsibility for the accident (resulting from the actions of one of the workers) devolved on the ministry, which lost the case.[23] The company did, nonetheless, pay the Japanese government an indemnity of F98,310 and drew up a reserve of F300,000 against future industrial risks.[24] The affair was thus settled, but the railway authorities refused to transport any more oxygen bottles. After negotiations, transport was reauthorized, but with drastic security requirements.[25]

Following this, the company was a victim of the Great Earthquake of

September 1, 1923, which caused considerable damage to its Kanagawa works. The works was quickly repaired and back in production by October.[26]

In 1921 the company reinforced its sales network by opening four branches (in Tokyo, Osaka, Kokura, and Nagasaki). The following year the network reorganized. Japan and its two colonies, Korea and Formosa, were divided into three zones.[27]

After Raymond Royer's return to France in 1919 and pending the arrival in Japan of Henri Melchior in October 1922, management of the business was entrusted to Eugène Jordan and to Pilet, a Belgian.

The SOAJ had grown spectacularly between 1910 and 1922. In terms of liabilities, capital went from F800,000 in 1914 to F2 million in 1918 and F4 million in 1921. Profits rose from F31,000 in 1912 to F946,000 in 1922. As for assets, they mounted from F663,000 in 1912 to F6.1 million in 1922: Their most important category, "equipment and tools," amounted to F290,000 in 1912 and F2.9 million in 1922.[28]

Relations between L'AL and its Japanese subsidiary, the SOAJ, were defined by the agreements drawn up on June 8, 1910, and June 7, 1921. The spirit of these agreements remained the same throughout the period studied here for both Japan and all other foreign subsidiaries and divisions of L'AL. These relations may be summarized as follows—for L'AL: (1) the transfer of patents, (2) the sharing of capital, and (3) the sale of machines, plants, and equipment to gain immediate profit; for subsidiaries: (1) the payment of royalties, (2) the distribution of dividends, and (3) the buying of machines, plants, and equipment.[29]

IV. The Period of the L'Air Liquide Japanese Division, 1924–30

From 1924 to 1930, business in Japan was under the direct management of L'Air Liquide, which expanded rapidly during this period but also met with hostility from its Japanese competitors, a fact which forced it to adapt itself to the socioeconomic climate of the country resulting from the Japanization of its affairs.

True to his conception of business conducted by rationalization of management through regrouping, Paul Delorme merged the SOAJ into the Société L'Air Liquide by acquisition toward the end of 1923. This operation took place two years after the preliminary measures of the 2,000 shares attributed to L'AL and the augmentation of the SOAJ's capital from F2 million to F4 million, taken in 1921. The proposition for the merger of the SOAJ with L'AL was adopted by the general assemblies of both companies, and the merger itself was back-dated to January 1, 1923.[30]

For procedure, L'AL put its 9,375 shares at the disposal of the liquidator of the SOAJ, at a nominal total value of F937,500 (their real value being F2,812,500). These L'AL shares were exchanged against 5,675 shares of the SOAJ, that is to say, at the rate of five F100-nominal-value L'AL shares for three F500 shares of the SOAJ. Moreover, L'AL dropped the 2,375 shares (representing 29.6% of the capital) it owned in the SOAJ.[31]

The SOAJ was dissolved on January 15, 1924. Business in Japan was taken over by the Japanese division. Émile Bertin, president of the SOAJ, died the same year at 84 years of age at La Glacerie (near Cherbourg, Manche).

The immediate effect of the direct control of business in Japan by L'AL was a change in the name used for the company in Japan to Ekitai Kūki Kaisha, the literal translation of Société L'Air Liquide. Around the same period, Henri Melchior, recently arrived in Japan as director of the Japanese branch, devised a program for expansion, and the production capacity of the works (Hyōgo, Osaka, Kanagawa) doubled between 1921 and 1924, from five oxygen plants with a total capacity of 190 m^3/h to eight plants with a total capacity of 405 m^3/h.[32]

Despite lively competition, in 1924, L'AL was supplying about 1.5 million m^3 of oxygen, representing two-thirds of the total consumption of Japan (2.5 million m^3), the remainder being shared among some 20 competitors.[33]

A detailed report on L'AL's position, drawn up by Melchior and annexed to the report dated November 24, 1924 of Hauchecorne, French consul in Kobe, also brought the following points into relief:[34]

—The French company owned five installations for the compression of residual oxygen from nitrogen plants which it had sold to the artificial fertilizer company, Nippon Chisso.

—The first oxygen works to be constructed outside the archipelago was started in Seoul, Korea, in 1923 and began production in December 1925, with a 20-m^3/h plant of a new type, producing oxygen at particularly low cost.

—There were two acetylene-solution works, one at Hyōgo, started in 1919, and the other in Kanagawa, started in 1924.

—The workshops of the Hyōgo works, over and above their work in oxyacetylene welding and repairs, had, since 1924, been making pressure gauges, torches, pressure reducers, and acetylene generators. In 1925 this works also began making welding flux, electric arcs, Picard underwater cutting torches, and, in 1929, electrodes for electric arc welding. Picard and Fouché torches were so well known in the country that nine-tenths of all torches used were either L'AL equipment or copies of it made by their competitors.

At the time, the company employed a total of 350 people in Japan, 200 white-collar employees (of whom a hundred worked in the Kobe area) and 150 workers.[35] There were 30 white-collar employees at the central office in Kobe, one third of whom were foreigners—Frenchmen, Germans, Syrians, and Filipinos. These held all key positions except in areas of general business entrusted to the Japanese.[36]

French personnel management showed marked differences from Japanese practice at the time. During the job interview the candidate was asked to state how much he expected to earn, even if it was not what he was finally accorded. If he had been solicited he might ask for more, but in general an employee earned ¥35 (F440) per month, more than the average Japanese salary. Those who learned the French language were favored in promotions.[37] Work went from 9:00 to 5:00, with a two-hour break for lunch during the week and, on Saturdays, morning work only.[38]

In 1927 the company raised production capacity once more by opening new oxygen works, branches, and sales offices. Thus, in 1927, L'AL had a total of seven oxygen works, five residual-oxygen-compression installations, three acetylene-solution works, and four branches (Tokyo, Seoul, Nagoya, and Kokura), not counting the head office in Kobe and two sales offices (Kyoto and Sasebo).

As far as equipment for the synthesis of ammonia was concerned, Georges Claude patented his technique in 1917, some time after the similar German Haber process. During negotiations for the assignment of these patents on ammonia production, started by L'AL in 1919, it was Suzuki Trading Company that prevailed over the Nippon Chisso Hiryō Kaisha in every area that the latter had had relations with L'AL in since 1913. An accord was drawn up between L'AL and the Suzuki Company. In 1924–25 two engineers and two foremen were sent from France to direct construction and oversee the starting up of the works at the expense of the Société de Fabrication d'Ammoniaque Synthétique Claude-Suzuki (Claude-Suzuki Synthetic Ammonia Fabrication Company). This plant, with a capacity of 50 tons per day, was built on the island of Hikoshima in the Straits of Shimonoseki.[39] The Claude-Suzuki Co. met with financial difficulties and losses had mounted to 214,000 by 1926.[40] Following the collapse of Suzuki Trading Company, the next year the synthetic ammonia business passed to the Mitsui group.[41]

In 1929 the Mitsui Mining Co., licensees for L'AL patents, undertook the construction of a large plant capable of producing 100 tons of ammonia per day using the hydrogen extracted from the gas from the coke ovens of the Miike coke works, which brought big orders for L'AL and its large subsidiary, the Société Chimique de la Grande-Paroisse. The works was started up in July 1931.[42] The following year the Mitsui Mining Co. bought back in advance the royalties it had undertaken to pay L'AL.[43]

As a producer of industrial gases, L'AL did not need to publicize itself with the general public. Its publicity and information were in the form of classes for welders and the publication of technical manuals. The Japanese subsidiary of L'AL began organizing demonstrations, talks, and classes for the training of welders since 1911. The classes were formalized as the School of Practical Welding & Cutting in 1928, the first and only one of its kind in Japan. The school also organized specific periodic courses and itinerant courses in the provinces. Students came from all branches of industry.

Parallel to its training of welders, L'AL also published and distributed free brochures and technical manuals. The first manual on welding in Japanese was published in December 1925 under the title *Practical Methods of Oxyacetylene Welding and Cutting*. This manual, rewritten and augmented, was published in October of 1928 as *Methods of Oxyacetylene and Electric Arc Welding*. A specialized review, *Welding & Cutting*, was also launched in February 1927. These publications were the sole sources of information for all Japanese interested in these techniques.[44]

Following the appearance in Japan of this branch of industrial activity at the start of the 1910s, the demand for oxygen grew rapidly. The Nihon Sanso Kaisha (1910) in Tokyo, using the Linde process, and the Dai Nihon Agagasu Seizōsho (1911) in Hiroshima, producing acetylene, were both founded almost at the same time as the SOAJ. Toward the end of the 1910s there were 30-odd companies, 20 of them large. Oxygen production in Japan doubled in a single year, going from 1.3 million m^3 in 1918 to 2.1 million m^3 in 1919, and thus provoked stiff competition between the producers. The price per cubic meter of oxygen dropped from ¥2.50 in 1918 to ¥1.50 in 1919.[45]

The almost anarchic situation finally led the Japanese government to implement rules concerning the fabrication, storage, transportation, and manipulation of compressed gases, putting the accent on safety. The first law on the regulation of compressed gases to be voted by the Diet, was enacted on April 11, 1922 and went into effect on June 1, 1923.[46] The legislation forced L'AL into exceptional expenditures for the modification of its equipment.[47] The law was revised and a new law implemented on August 1, 1936.

The 1920s were marked by economic crises and social upheaval. The shipyards, having cut down on activity subsequent to the treaty of Washington on arms reduction (1922), did not get back into the swing of things until the end of the decade, when they began construction of luxury liners.

This atmosphere aroused an economic nationalism among the Japanese, which had degenerated into a campaign against foreign products and capital by 1929–30. This campaign was orchestrated by the ministries of Commerce and Industry and of Railways.[48]

Profiting by this campaign, some 20 oxygen companies with local capital united against L'AL, the leader in the field with dominant position because of its advanced technology and commercial success. On January 18, 1930, these Japanese companies formed the Association of Japanese Oxygen Producers, whose stated goal was the promotion of friendly relations between itself and "national oxygen" users.[49] This was just a front. Their real intention was the destruction or, at the very least, reduction of L'AL.

L'AL found itself in a dilemma with this battle of one against 20. Henry Melchior suggested that the Paris headquarters form a Japanese company with joint capital. He charged ex-vice-admiral Arisaka Shōzō, adviser and director of the Tokyo branch and ex-pupil of Émile Bertin, with engaging in negotiations with Japanese groups. The partner could be neither a powerful zaibatsu, which would try to dominate, nor a small capitalist who risked being merged into a more ambitious group sooner or later. The Sumitomo Group seemed ideal but was not very tempted. Despite his shattering declaration, the Ministry of Railways secretly pushed the group to cooperate with L'AL.[50]

Negotiations culminated in the creation of a company under Japanese law. For L'AL this was the first step in the Japanization of its affairs.

V. The Period of the Teikoku Sanso (Imperial Oxygen) KK, 1930–45

The Société L'Air Liquide sent Pierre Philippon to Japan, charged with negotiations "for satisfying national [Japanese] preoccupations."[51] The Sumitomo Bank gave a favorable response to L'AL's propositions on May 8. On August 8, 1930, the Teikoku Sanso KK (*kabushiki kaisha*: limited-liability partnership with shared capital), or the Société Impériale d'Oxygène (Imperial Oxygen Company), was formed with capital of ¥2.4 million, or F30 million, divided into 48,000 ¥50 shares. L'AL owned 87.5% of the capital, the Sumitomo Bank 12.5%.[52]

The board of directors was composed of nine members, three Frenchmen and six Japanese. The retired vice-admiral, Arisaka, was nominated first president of the Japanese company, a position he held until his death in 1941. Both groups nominated their own executive director: Henri Melchior, who held the position until March 1943, for L'AL, and Odaka Chikashi, who held his post until March 1944, for the Sumitomo Bank. They signed jointly and were responsible for the direction of the company, but it was in fact Melchior who controlled the company almost single-handedly until March 1943.[53]

The company bought back most of L'AL's assets in Japan (business premises, sites, plants, and buildings) as well as the licenses under patent for a sum equal to its capital. It rented from L'AL bottles valued at ¥1.8 million and made F4 million cash available to the parent company. This operation allowed the French company a reduction of the order of F500,000 in its annual Japanese income-tax payments.[54]

This was a marked contrast to the attitude of English and American firms such as Dunlop, General Motors, and Standard Oil that had refused Japanese participation. The event was taken by the French diplomats in Japan as a sort of capitulation of the French firm before Japanese pressure and even as an important moral injury to France,[55] the more so since the company was the sole representative of French industry in that country.

Philippon took up the matter with De Martel, French ambassador to Japan, who sent a note of protest to the Japanese minister of foreign affairs, Baron Shidehara.[56]

There the affair rested, since the L'AL company seemed satisfied with the financial operation and the campaign against foreign products had slackened slightly. From then on the French directorate of the Teikoku Sanso KK held to a discreet attitude and avoided referring to the company as a foreign subsidiary (actually French) as such.

The Teikoku Sanso KK had a turnover of ¥3 million (F37.5 million) in 1930 and issued its first divided of 5% in 1932. These profits, converted into francs, were somewhat diminished because of currency fluctuation, one of the major concerns for a multinational company like L'AL. The dividend had risen to 8% in 1933. As of 1934 it remained steady at 15%. As finances became available to it, the Japanese company bought back oxygen and acetylene bottles rented by L'AL.[57]

The L'AL affair having been settled, the Association of Japanese Oxygen Producers no longer had a reason to exist. When the Teikoku Sanso KK joined, it became the National Association of Oxygen Producers and held its first assembly, in which a convention was adopted on November 7, 1930. The convention, which constituted a first step toward a terrible oxygen cartel on the lines of other industrial sectors, determined the price per cubic meter of oxygen and the respective sales zone. The oxygen cartel divided the archipelago into three zones and created a communal sales syndicate for each zone. Each company's share in the sale was determined according to their turnover during the preceding years. The sales offices took charge of collecting payment from clients prior to sharing among members. A stiff penalty was inflicted on contraveners, a measure which put an end to the merciless commercial war which had pushed the price of a cubic meter of oxygen to below 10 sen (1 yen=100 sen).[58]

Parallel with this association, the Federation of Pressurized Gas Producers was formed in October 1936. This was a scientific and technical organization which established norms, gave technical advice to administrative authorities, and organized talks and courses and in which the Teikoku Sanso KK played a principal role.[59]

The 1930s saw persistent economic crises and mounting militarism in Japan. As of 1930 the government reinforced its control over the main industries. Military authorities urged strategic industries such as oxygen production not only to set up on the continent but also to augment production capacity in Japan, particularly after the military coup d'etat of February 26, 1936. Responding to these demands and following the development of Japanese industry in general, the Teikoku Sanso KK multiplied its works and reinforced its sales network.[60]

On July 7, 1937, the Japanese and Chinese armies confronted each other on the outskirts of Beijing. Conflict had quickly spread from Shanghai to the center of China. In 1938, mobilization was proclaimed. All industries were placed under state control and priority was given to military requirements.

Imperial Oxygen (Teikoku Sanso) advanced onto the Asian continent along with the Imperial Army, sharing its fate with the Japanese Empire. Having set up its first works outside the archipelago at Seoul in 1925, it then successively established (1) three new works in Korea—Pyongyang (1931), Pusan (1935), and Sunchon (1941) on the Sino-Korean border; a branch in Seoul (1927); and two sales offices—in Pyongyang and Pusan (1936); (2) a sales office in Dairen, Manchuria (1930); (3) an oxygen works and a sales office in Taipei, Formosa (1931); and (4) an oxygen works and a sales office at Guanndong in China (1941).[61]

On the eve of the Second World War, the Teikoku Sanso KK was L'AL's chief foreign subsidiary and division with an annual oxygen production of as much as 80% of that produced by L'AL in France. It employed 600 people, including about 100 women.[62]

In 1938, the Japanese subsidiary had some difficulties transferring funds to L'AL because of exchange controls. The Compagnie des Messageries Maritimes found itself in the same straits.[63] A diplomat from the French embassy discussed the mounting French debt with the Japanese Ministry of Foreign Affairs (Gaimushō), who, after a series of negotiations, gave authorization in September for the transfer of ¥248,000 and another for ¥68,000 the next month. Faced with the impossibility of recovering its debts in Japan, L'AL decided to dedicate the sum frozen in Japan to increasing Teikoku Sanso's capital, raising it from ¥2.4 million to ¥3.3 million in April 1939. With the aid of the French authorities, L'AL continued to receive dividend transfers until 1942 and some repatriation of funds in 1943. Then, throughout the years 1944 and 1945, L'AL became completely cut off from its Japanese subsidiary.[64]

On September 3, 1939, Nazi Germany invaded Poland and started the Second World War. On December 8, 1941, Japan attacked Pearl Harbor. The leader of the oxygen industry, the Teikoku Sanso KK, was designated a "company under supervision" along with the Nihon Rika Kōgyo Kaisha. Forced to support the military effort and cut off from the parent company, it started to construct plants and machines on its own.[65]

The military authorities expressed hostility toward the French executives. The headquarters building of Teikoku Sanso KK was forcibly sold in February 1943 to the Kawasaki Heavy Industries Co. The headquarters moved to another building. The board of directors was forced to augment the capital to ¥7.5 million in April 1943. By order of the minister of the navy, the new shares, which should have been attributed to L'AL, were divided up and shared among various companies in the Sumitomo Group.[66]

At the same time, the company changed its name to the Imperial Compressed Gas Co. Murakami Shun'ichi, rear admiral–accountant, also an ex-pupil of Émile Bertin, was nominated to the post of president, vacant since the death of Arisaka in January 1941. The directorate was reorganized, with naval officers occupying all important posts including that of vice-president.[67]

The French executive director, Henri Melchior, and deputies, Marcel Requien and Pierre Saint-Loup, were arrested by the military police, accused of being "spies," and deported.[68]

Melchior, who had directed L'AL's affairs in Japan since 1922, was imprisoned by the Japanese military authorities in December 1943. He was then expelled from Japan in April 1944 and made to live under surveillance in Shanghai until the end of the hostilities. After returning to France at the end of 1944, he died there in May 1945.[69]

In October 1943, the Teikoku Sanso KK was named a "military enterprise" and placed under the direct control of the navy. On January 15, 1945, Yamamoto Hironori, rear admiral and naval construction engineer, was nominated president by the Sumitomo Group, following the death by illness of Murakami.[70]

The Kobe headquarters were destroyed on June 5, 1945 by an incendiary bomb dropped by an American plane. The directorate was temporarily housed in an office of the agency of the Sumitomo Bank, but the company's archives and oxygen works perished in the fire. The atom bomb which fell on August 9 wiped all personnel and installations at the Nagasaki works.[71]

Japan capitulated on August 15. As soon as the war ended, all naval officers and employees sent by the Sumitomo Group during the war disappeared. The group nominated a new director-general in the person of Iguchi Hiroshi. Headquarters moved provisionally to the second workshop at the Hyōgo works. The demobilized workers returned to work.

All the company's assets (works, branches, sales offices) in Korea, Formosa, Manchuria, and China were confiscated according to the terms of the armistice, committing ownership of the goods under Japanese jurisdiction to the respective governments concerned. L'AL sent Pierre Wary as delegate to return its subsidiary to the situation in which it had been before the war. On December 17, 1946, the company resumed its old name, the Teikoku Sanso KK. In the year following, Pierre Wary and Pierre Saint-Loup were nominated deputy directors. Wary became director-general in 1948. On November 30, 1949, the company reduced its capital from ¥7.5 million to ¥5.4 million, thus suppressing the forced augmentation effected during the war. It started up again with the Société L'Air Liquide once more the major shareholder. In 1950, it issued a dividend of 15% and in 1952 adopted a plan of re-equipment and modernization of all works for a fresh start.

VI. Conclusion

The only French firm which had invested in Japan before the Second World War, L'AL was the sole symbol of the French industrial establishment in Japan. It embodied a whole branch of specifically French industrial activity (the production of oxygen, acetylene, and nitrogen; the cutting and welding torches; and ammonia synthesis) based on the work of scholars and inventors such as Berthelot, Moisson, d'Arsonval, Cluade, Le Châtelier, Hesse, Picard, and Fouché.

The Japanese division or subsidiary was, like the L'AL group itself, a typical example of the principles on which a business depends fundamentally: survivability, profit, and growth.[72] Augmenting gains and profits, the Japanese subsidiary of L'AL quickly expanded to become the uncontested leader, controlling the Japanese oxygen market. The main reasons for this success were: (1) innovative and yet viable technology, (2) commercial success with active, even aggressive methods, (3) rationality due to the French way of directorship, and (4) the competence of the French managers, who, thanks to their long residence of, in general, more than 10 years, knew well the country and the milieu in which they worked.

The Teikoku Sanso KK integrated itself perfectly with Japanese economic life and contributed, in its own way, to the industrial development of the country. L'Air Liquide in Japan, through its subsidiary, was the very image of the success of a pioneer in an environment that was culturally different and sometimes even hostile throughout that period, in a country where French industry was practically nonexistent.

Notes

For this study, besides those works cited in the notes, we have consulted the annual reports (minutes of ordinary and extraordinary general assemblies) of the Société L'Air Liquide for the years 1902–52, those of the Société d'Oxygène et d'Acétylène du Japon for the years 1910–23, and also the diplomatic documents, *Série E, Asie-Océanie, Japon*, for the period 1910–45 from the archives of the French Ministry of Foreign Affairs.

Abbreviations—EGA: extraordinary general assembly; FMFA: French Ministry (or Minister) of Foreign Affairs; L'AL: L'Air Liquide; OGA: ordinary general assembly; SOAJ: Société d'Oxygène et d'Acétylène du Japon; Teisan: Teikoku Sanso KK.

1. *Cf.*: (1) Rosset, Alfred: "*Les petits débuts d'une grande société: L'Air Liquide,*" *Histoire, information et documents* (review), May 1970, 15 pp.; (2) Jehn, J.: "*La liquéfaction des gaz, un des facteurs de l'expansion française à l'étranger,*" *La revue des ingénieurs,* Feb. 1959, no. 103, 5 pp.; (3) Lebrun, Maurice: *La soudure, le brassage et l'oxycoupage des métaux,* "*Communications et mémoires,*" Académie de la Marine, Paris, 1958, 134 pp.; (4) *Cinquantenaire de la Société L'Air Liquide, octobre 1902–octobre 1952,* published by L'AL, 1952, 42 pp.; (5) "*L'Air Liquide, 1902–1952,*" brochure, 1952, 28 pp.; (6) "*Discours prononcés au banquet offert à son personnel par la Société L'Air Liquide à l'occasion de son vingt-cinquième anniversaire, le 13 octobre 1927,*" brochure, 29 pp.; (7) "*Centenaire de la naissance de Georges Claude* (*1870–1960*)," brochure, 18 pp.; (8) Deschars, Christian: "*Histoire de L'Air Liquide,*" brochure, 1978, 4 pp.; Minutes, OGA and EGA of L'AL, 1902–52.

2. EGA of the SOAJ, June 18 and 27, 1910; Sept. 5, 1916.

3. Li, Jin-Mieung: *Les relations économiques et financières entre la France et le Japon, de 1859 à 1914,* 3rd cycle doctoral thesis, University of Paris IV (Sorbonne), May 1977, 500 pp., and an appendix of 92 pp.—statistics, typed, p. 335; Togari

(Commander): "*Louis-Emile Bertin, son rôle dans la création de la Marine japonaise,*" publication of the Société Franco-Japonaise de Paris, 1935, 38 pp.

4. Minutes, EGA of the SOAJ, June 26, 1912.
5. *Ibid.*
6. *Teikoku Sanso no Ayumi* (quoted as "*Teisan*" hereafter) (History of Teikoku Sanso), published by the company, 1981, 251 pp., p. 19.
7. Minutes, EGA of the SOAJ, June 26, 1912.
8. "*TSKK* (*Teikoku Sanso Kabushiki Kaisha*)—*cinquante ans de présence de L'Air Liquide au Japon,*" brochure, 1960, 33 pp.
9. *Teisan, op. cit.*, pp. 16–17.
10. Report of Charles Wall, auditor of contributions, dated Oct. 27, 1921, in the minutes of the SOAJ, Oct. 26, 1921; FMFA, *Série E, Japon,* vol. 80, Hauchecorne, the French consul in Kobe, to Herriot, president of the cabinet and FMFA, Kobe, Nov. 23, 1924, appendix: report of Henri Melchior, director of L'AL's Kobe head branch.
11. *Ibid.*
12. TSKK, *op. cit.*; *Teisan, op. cit.*, pp. 18–19 and 227.
13. TSKK, *op. cit.*
14. *Teisan, op. cit.*, pp. 19–20.
15. Minutes, OGA of the SOAJ, Sept. 5, 1916.
16. *Ibid.*, Sept. 3, 1917.
17. *Ibid.*, June 27, 1918, June 20, 1919, and June 26, 1920; *Teisan, op. cit.*, pp. 20 and 227.
18. *Ibid.*
19. FMFA, *Série E, Japon,* vol. 8, report of Ernest Outrey, Senator, Aug. 16, 1919.
20. Minutes, OGA of the SOAJ, June 29, 1914.
21. FMFA, *Série E, Japon,* vol. 80, Hauchecorne to Herriot, Kobe, Nov. 23, 1924; report of Melchior, *op. cit.*
22. *Ibid.*
23. Uda, Tadashi: "*Nihon Kindaishi ni okeru Shakai-Keizaiteki Furansu Zō, Teikoku Sanso Kabushiki Kaisha no Enkaku o Megutte* (France's Image of the Socioeconomic Viewpoint, Through the History of the Teikoku Sanso Kabushiki Kaisha)," *Otemon Keizai Ronshū* (The Otemon Economic Review), vol. V, nos. 1 and 2, Dec. 1970, pp. 160–61; *Teisan, op. cit.*, pp. 21–22.
24. Minutes, OGA of the SOAJ, June 26, 1920.
25. *Teisan, op. cit.*, pp. 22–23.
26. Minutes, OGA of L'AL, June 18, 1924.
27. *Teisan, op. cit.*, pp. 30–31.
28. Minutes, EGA and OGA of the SOAJ, 1910–23.
29. Report of Charles Wall, Dec. 17, 1923, *op. cit.*
30. *Ibid.*; Minutes, OGA of L'AL.
31. *Petites-Affiches, journal officiel d'annonces légales,* Jan. 15, 1924.
32. FMFA, *Série E, Japon,* vol. 80, Hauchecorne to Herriot, Kobe, Nov. 23, 1924; report of Melchior, *op. cit.*
33. *Ibid.*
34. *Ibid.*
35. *Ibid.*
36. *Teisan, op. cit.*, p. 30.

37. Miwa Kazuichi: "*Teisan 50 Nen* (50 Years of Teisan)," quoted in Uda, *op. cit.*, pp. 172–73; Ōoka, Shōhei, *Sanso* (Oxygen), 1955, Shinchō Japanese literature series, no. 43, p. 364.
38. *Ibid.*
39. Minutes, OGA of L'AL, June 28, 1920; Uda, *op. cit.*, p. 163.
40. FMFA, *Série E, Japon*, vol. 83, report of the Commercial Attaché, no. 507, Tokyo, June 3, 1927, article in the *Teikoku Kōshinjo Nippō* (journal).
41. Uda, *op. cit.*, p. 163.
42. FMFA, *Série E, Japon*, vol. 172, carton E-566, De Martel, ambassador of France, to Aristide Briand, FMFA, Tokyo, June 23, 1931; minutes, OGA of L'AL, 1929–34.
43. Minutes, OGA of L'AL, June 2, 1933.
44. *Teisan, op. cit.*, pp. 28–29.
45. *Ibid.*, p. 23.
46. *Ibid.*, p. 24.
47. Minutes, OGA of L'AL, June 1, 1926.
48. *Teisan, op. cit.*, p. 35.
49. *Ibid.*, pp. 33–34; Uda, *op. cit.*, p. 166.
50. TSKK, *op.cit.*; *Teisan, op. cit.*, pp. 35–36; Uda, *op. cit.*, p. 166.
51. Minutes, OGA of L'AL, June 18, 1931.
52. FMFA, *Série E, Japon*, vol. 172, carton E-566, De Martel to Briand, Aug. 22, 1930; vol. 65, De Martel to Briand, Tokyo, April 17, 1931.
53. *Teisan, op. cit.*, list of directors, p. 207.
54. Minutes, OGA of L'AL, June 18, 1931; FMFA, *Série E. Japon*, vol. 172, carton E-566, De Martel to Briand, Aug. 22, 1930.
55. FMFA, *Série E, Japon*, vol. 172, carton E-566, *op. cit.*
56. *Ibid.*, De Martel to Baron Shidehara, Japanese Minister of Foreign Affairs, Tokyo, Aug. 22, 1930.
57. Minutes, OGA of L'AL, 1932–45.
58. *Teisan, op. cit.*, p. 39.
59. *Ibid.*, pp. 43–44.
60. *Ibid.*, pp. 227–34.
61. *Ibid.*, pp. 42–43 and 230–34.
62. TSKK, *op. cit.*
63. FMFA, *Série E, Japon*, vol. 173, telegrams, French ambassador to Japan to FMFA, FMFA to Ambassador, July–Oct. 1938.
64. Minutes, OGA of L'AL, June 21, 1945, and June 21, 1946.
65. *Teisan, op. cit.*, pp. 46 and 231–33.
66. *Ibid.*, p. 49.
67. *Ibid.*
68. Minutes, OGA of L'AL, June 21, 1946.
69. *Ibid.*
70. *Teisan, op. cit.*, pp. 54–55.
71. *Ibid.*
72. Ghertman, Michel, *Les multinationales*, "*Que sais-je?*" no. 2068, PUF, 1985, 127 pp., pp. 36–37.

Comment

Akira Kudō

Professor Li provides us with a most comprehensive and intensive description of Teikoku Sanso and its predecessors, practically the only French-owned company of any importance in Japan before 1945, taking L'AL's Japan strategy into consideration. Let me address a few questions or remarks mainly concerning the same points on which Li concentrates. Those are L'AL's early direct investment in Japan, its response to its declining dominance in the Japanese market, its strategy for adaptation and ownership policy; and the influences of L'AL's activities on Japanese firms and economy.

Li refers to the agreement of the big three oxygen companies and writes, "Essentially the French company was effective in the European Latin countries and in the French colonies of Africa and Asia; the British company in Commonwealth countries; and the German company in the countries under German influence. Everywhere else it was a question of open competition. . . ." I think we can safely assume from this statement that Japan was subjected to "open competition" from the big three. L'AL and Linde were in fact active in Japan. The former made direct investment as early as in 1910, while the latter did not establish any subsidiary or local company, but only sold machines and equipment through its agencies in Japan.

My first question is why this contrast was brought about: Why did L'AL prefer direct investment to licensing, and why did Linde prefer licensing to direct investment? Did the agreement between the big three include any articles relating to the "form" of their activities in the world market? Did the Japanese patents of L'AL play any role in restricting Linde's investment? Or should we instead explain this contrast through some difference of strategic decision-making of the two companies? I suppose that L'AL had a firm uniform principle (French rationalism?) to make direct investment all over the world and also applied this principle to the Japanese market. I would be interested to have more details in this regard from Li if possible, especially since I am ignorant of the internal strategic decision-making of the Linde Company (the company in West Germany recently informed me that it had no relevant documents on its activities in prewar Japan).

My second remark refers to the declining dominance of L'AL in the Japanese market. The Japanese market is often characterized by stiff competition, and the oxygen market was apparently no exception to this. Before the First World War the market was almost completely monopolized by L'AL's subsidiary and Nihon Sanso, which imported the oxygen separator of the Hilbrandt process, not of the Linde process (Nihon Sanso, *Fifty-Year History of Nihon Sanso*, 1966, p. 6). The stoppage on importing from Germany and the increasing demand from the shipbuilding industry and other industries during the First World War caused a lot of new entries. Many firms began their operations only after the war, which placed them in more difficult conditions during the postwar depression. The reconstruction demand after the earthquake of 1923 and other demands, however, promoted further new entries and more investment from existing firms. Some of them replaced Hilbrandt machines with Heiland machines. From 1927, when the financial crisis occurred in Japan, the operation of new machines and the threat of increasing supplementary oxygen caused cutthroat competition up to 1930, when the abolition of the embargo of gold was enforced (Tōyō Sanso, *Forty-Year History*, 1959, pp. 9–10). The nationalistic or even chauvinistic campaign against L'AL in 1929–30 can be interpreted as an expression of the troubled Japanese firms. It is noteworthy that this campaign resulted in the construction of a nationwide network of regional cartels in the oxygen industry including the most dominant foreign company. I suppose that the campaign played a decisive role in forcing L'AL, a possible outsider, to participate in the cartel.

The competitive pressure may even have placed L'AL's subsidiary in a difficult position around 1930. In the 1930s it, together with other producers, enjoyed an increasing volume of sales thanks to the stable price. Its market share may have fallen in that decade from about 60% to about 30% (Tōyō Sanso, *op. cit.*, p. 10). It grew rapidly in the 1930s, while some rivals grew more rapidly. In 1940 it employed 667 employees, while Nihon Sanso, for example, employed almost 1,000 people (Teikoku Sanso, *Teikoku Sanso no Ayumi*, Appendix; Nihon Sanso, *op. cit.*, Appendix). It could, however, share in an ever increasing profit in the 1930s.

My third point concerns L'AL's strategy for adaptation and ownership policy. I interpret the reorganization in 1923, from subsidiary to direct control, as the result of an application of L'AL's uniform ownership policy. That is, it adopted the policy of applying its global uniform principle rather than the policy of adapting itself to local conditions.

The neutral name of Ekitai Kūki Kaisha (Liquid Air Co.) is perhaps symbolic. I am, however, inclined to ask Li for more concrete details on the decision-making processes—for example, how they observed the present and future market situation in Japan. The growing importance of private heavy-industry companies may have influenced the decision to change its name.

I agree that "meeting with hostility" from Japanese competitors of L'AL "forced it to adapt itself to the socioeconomic climate of the country resulting from the Japanization of its affairs," that is, by the establishment of Teikoku Sanso as a Japanese company in 1930. But I am not quite sure, whether even "a powerful zaibatsu" could dominate the company through its minor participation of only 12.5%, and why it chose as its partner the Sumitomo zaibatsu, which was in fact powerful enough to dominate it in the 1940s!

Moreover, I would like to stress the stiff competition around 1930 as the most important "socioeconomic climate of the country" and characterize the reorganization of 1930 as a tactical device to L'AL to participate in the network of cartels and a skillful compromise between adaptation and application (ownership policy).

My last comment relates to the influence of L'AL's activities on Japanese firms and economy. It is really a pity that the presence of French companies was so weak in prewar Japan, since otherwise Japanese would have been able to enjoy a two-hour lunch break during the week! In technological education the influence of L'AL may have been stronger. It also at least partially succeeded in its marketing policy in applying its own direct sales organization. I would like to ask Li to suggest to what degree it succeeded in applying its personnel, technological, and marketing policies in Japan compared to other countries.

Response

Jin-Mieung Li

To Professor Kudō's important question of why L'AL preferred direct investment to licensing, and why the Linde Company preferred licensing to direct investment, I would like to say that the difference was due to the strategy and style of management of the two firms. Who managed the Linde company? If it was Linde himself, he probably had much less skill to handle industrial and financial affairs, because he was both a professor and inventor. Then, the German company preferred the way of facility, exporting its machines rather than direct investment, which involved different kinds of risks.

In the case of the French company, research and the technical domain were assumed by the inventor Georges Claude; the management was taken on by Paul Delorme, a skillful and able administrator, having received engineering training. Delorme established a financial and technical combination for creating affiliates, in contrast with other small companies in the gas and welding fields. The other, more important reason for L'AL's direct investment policy was protection of its patents at all costs. Even in regard to its subsidiaries, L'AL imposed very tight conditions for protecting these patents.

The "big three's" agreement or entente concerned the geographical sharing of the world oxygen market. I think that each company tried to avoid any activity in the countries under the control of its competitors. In other countries it was a question of open competition. I therefore think that the patents of L'AL did not play any role in restricting Linde's activities in Japan.

In the second part of his comment, Kudō gives L'AL's market share in the 1930s, which I could not find. The figure shows only partial results, but it clarifies Teikoku Sanso's situation at the time.

The third point, the absorption of the SOAJ in the L'AL group, is the result of application of L'AL's uniform ownership, as Kudō points out.

"Japanization" means creation of a subsidiary (in this case, Teikoku Sanso) under Japanese law with participation of Japanese capital and managers in the directorate. The French company kept the agreement with Sumitomo Bank a secret from the general public. It appeared as if the French company had entirely sold out its Japanese affairs to the Sumitomo Group, and it worked well, but in fact it was only a ruse. L'AL maintained the dominant position in its Japanese subsidiary. On the other hand, it adopted a very discreet attitude, avoiding referring to the latter as a foreign company.

Why did L'AL choose the Sumitomo Group? According to *Teikoku Sanso no Ayumi*, the Japanese group in 1930 was the least internationalized of the zaibatsu. It maintained the Japanese traditional style of business and was not very interested in L'AL's proposition to embark on a joint venture. The group had also good relations with the Japanese government. This appealed to L'AL, whose most important clients in Japan were the navy, the Ministry of Railways, and the shipyards, both public and private.

Apart from L'AL, no French industrial enterprise made a direct investment. France was interested in the Japanese market for the purchase of raw silk in the second half of the 19th century. At the same time, its exports to Japan constituted a very small proportion of Japanese imports. Importation of Japanese raw silk into France diminished, following the decline of the silk industry in Lyons at the beginning of the 20th century. French banks and capitalists actively took part in Japanese public foreign loans launched in the European financial markets between 1905 and 1914. But the French general public, as well as the merchants and industrialists, ignored the Asian market, including the Japanese. This disinterest explains the quasi-absence of the French commercial, banking, and industrial presence in Japan during the interwar period.

German Companies in Japan in the Interwar Period: Attitudes and Performance

Erich Pauer

I. Introduction

During the interwar period, the economy and policy of East Asia was hardly a point of interest in Germany and other European countries. The public usually had no concrete idea of what this region actually was. Merchants with overseas connections regarded the region as nothing more than a supplier of raw materials. It was not before the conflict between China and Japan in 1937 that East Asia became an item in European discussions, and the Tripartite Pact in 1940 made East Asia and especially Japan a major point of attention in Germany.[1] This was true not only for the general public in Germany but for most companies and industrialists also. For the latter, Japan had in fact been quite "far" in the east, and it was this view that influenced their attitudes against the Japanese, as well as German performance on the Japanese market.

Concerning the general economic and technical relations between Germany and Japan in the interwar period, several articles have already been published.[2] Therefore, instead of repeating already-known facts, one should now lay more weight on problems on the microeconomic level, such as attitudes of certain companies with regard to the Japanese market or their actual performance there. This paper consists of two main parts. Firstly the general condition and the political background of the relations of Germany and Japan are described, followed by examples of small and medium-size enterprises doing business in Japan. Most German companies in Japan in the interwar period belonged to this group, but to contrast this, in the second part, the rather exceptional case of I.G. Farben as a large company is dealt with. Even though it has to be acknowledged that any research in this field can be based on only a very small part of the original sources, some of them preserved by accident, it seems to be worthwhile to undertake such a task, because it reveals insights into the driving forces of as well as the obstacles to the development of the bilateral relations between Germany and Japan in general which cannot be gained otherwise.

II. The Framework: Attitudes and Government Policy in the Interwar Period

There was a significant difference in the policies of the governments and companies of both countries in the 1920s and 1930s.

During World War I the Japanese had become acquainted with the high technical standards and high quality of German industrial goods. To improve on Japanese techniques, an increasing number of Japanese companies approached German manufacturers shortly after the end of the war. In some cases, Japanese industrialists even went to Germany personally. For example, Matsukata Kōjirō, president of the Kawasaki Shipyard, managed to get hold of certain German submarine blueprints and employed several German engineers.[3] German aircraft manufacturers like Rohrbach, Dornier, Heinkel, and Junkers were also eager to give advice to the Japanese army and navy and to sell licenses to Japan. They sent engineers to train Japanese technicians and even established joint ventures there.[4] Another case was the Furukawa group, which succeeded in reestablishing its good contacts with Siemens, which had been built up before World War I, by offering to participate in a joint venture project in Japan.[5] In the case of joint ventures, usually Japanese companies offered capital which German companies lacked in exchange for German know-how, patents, and licenses. In some areas the Japanese search for new technology became the starting point for long-term German-Japanese relations.

It is noteworthy, though, that while some companies, such as Krupp, Bosch, Daimler-Benz, responded positively, there were also a great number of German companies which had had bad experiences in Japan during the wartime period and therefore had had enough of the Far East (i.e., Japan) . . . companies such as Thyssen and Mannesmann.[6] The reason for the negative attitude of these companies was that Japan in 1917 had lifted protection of patents granted to these companies, and the German counterparts concerned were therefore extremely reluctant to reestablish ties with Japan.

Besides such contacts on a personal basis between the companies, official Japan was not very keen on expanding trade in the early 1920s, because the Germans were regarded as a competing threat to some branches of fledgling Japanese industry. However, negotiations regarding a new commercial treaty between Japan and Germany started in Berlin in late 1924 and were continued in Tokyo. After three years of negotiations a new treaty was signed on July 20, 1927. This treaty put German residents on an equal footing with Japanese nationals in several respects, especially in the case of establishing and operating commercial and industrial enterprises. However, overall protection against import or export barriers was not granted by the treaty, because the Japanese government insisted on its right to monitor foreign trade.[7]

In contrast to the 1920s, when German and Japanese companies viewed each other as complementary partners and the Japanese government at last agreed to the right of Germans to establish enterprises and subsidiaries in Japan, the world economic crisis on the one hand and industrial and technological development especially in Japan on the other changed the situation rapidly. In the early 1930s, German economic and foreign trade policies in general were not conducive to trading with the Far East. In the interwar period, the German trade balance with Belgium, France, and Great Britain became unfavorable due to increased imports of raw materials, especially from the respective colonies of these countries. Therefore German trade policy concentrated on shifting the flow of goods from these countries to countries in southeastern Europe. Under the influence of Hjalmar Schacht, who become president of the German Central Bank in 1933, political ideology changed to favoring the Balkans and Latin America.[8] The Far East once more made its exit from the German stage. Furthermore, reciprocity became a point of contention. The German catchphrase of the time was "*Kaufe bei deinem Kunden*" (Buy at your customer's).[9] The policy was meant to untie Germany from world trade and instead establish close ties with certain countries based on preferential treaties and bilateral clearing agreements.[10] This corresponded with Japanese economic and foreign trade policy since the early 1930s, which favored the "yen bloc" and tried to exclude other countries from these markets. This resulted in two major problems: For one thing, companies involved in trading outside these "trading blocs" (and this concerned German trading companies doing business between the two countries and between two blocs) faced severe difficulties in clearing their transactions, while foreign-exchange control policy created a second obstacle and sometimes discouraged even the most enthusiastic entrepreneur from continuing to do business in Asia.

On top of all this, a fundamental reason limiting German-Japanese trade was the German attitude that East Asia first of all meant China, not Japan. China had been the favorite trading partner since the 19th century, even if not all the dreams could come true. In 1931, German exports to Japan and China had roughly the same value. However, exports to Japan were expected to decrease, because the growing Japanese economy had become a competitor not only in their domestic market but also in the world market. Thus, while Japan and Germany had been complementary partners in the 1920s, they became rivals in the 1930s.

III. The Approach: German Companies in Japan

The number of joint ventures was—despite the famous and often described case of Siemens and Furukawa—negligible. Germany's economic relations to Japan basically depended on (mostly German) trading companies and representative offices of German companies in Japan, the main tasks of which were buying raw materials, commodities, and other consumer goods from Japan (and later also Manchuria) and selling mostly capital goods, blueprints, patents, and licenses. For transferring technical know-how to Japan, human capital was also used.

1. Trading Companies and Subsidiaries

The general attitude of German industry toward the Japanese market had always been that it was not a major playing field. The situation did not change very much in the 1920s, as German industry continued to concentrate on the domestic market. Few advances to Far Eastern markets could be observed; rather, they were hampered by obstacles caused by the companies themselves or by the protectionist policies of Japan. Even after the world economic crisis, when in the early 1930s Japanese companies became interested in buying more German products, the bad performance of German manufacturers and trading companies restricted the growth of the German market share. Neither did the increased demand for German equipment or machinery lead to a corresponding increase in the number of subsidiaries in Japan.

German companies seem to have been arrogant enough to expect the Japanese to clamor for products labeled Made in Germany, and it took them a long time to understand that the Japanese were quite happy without German or western goods.[11] This misconception was due to an underestimation of the structural changes in Japanese industry during and shortly after World War I and their neglecting the variety and quality of Japanese products. The direct results of this misjudgment, however, was that German companies tried to market the wrong goods in Japan.

The major reason for such misconceptions about the Japanese industry was a lack of knowledge of the Japanese language, not only at most of the German trading companies, but even more so at the representative offices of German companies in Japan. In their research on the Japanese market, these companies had to rely on second hand information from Japanese newspapers in English or on research conducted by other companies, possibly their competitors. Knowledge of the Japanese language would have enabled the companies to read Japanese newspapers, journals, and technical newsletters, which in turn would have made it possible to quickly react to the rapid developments in Japanese industry in the 1920s.

On the other hand, German companies complained about what they called "dishonest practices" of the Japanese merchants, who were viewed as odd people, not to be taken seriously by gentlemen like the Germans. However, old German "Japan hands" would point out that it was the German companies which had to adapt to Japanese business practices if they wanted to be successful in the Japanese market.[12] The most common mistake in approaching the Japanese market was to contact Japanese customers directly in search of offers. Only later, when some of these German companies had gained access to the Japanese market in other ways, was it understood that a trading company had to be used for such offers. But trading companies were necessary for various other reason too. The overhead for running a representative office or subsidiary in Japan was the most decisive concern for German companies, and given their limited market share and limited interest in the Japanese market (and the far eastern market in general), the option was mostly put down. Therefore, it was only the big companies like I.G. Farben, Krupp, Demag, Vereinigte Stahlwerke, Schoeller-Bleckmann, Carl Zeiß, and those which had been in Japan before World War I, such as Siemens-Schuckert, Mannesmann, Gebr. Böhler, and some others that ran offices in Japan.[13] Other companies interested in the Japanese market and exporting to the Far East mostly were represented by one of the trading companies in Japan, who acted as agents for them.[14]

As in the period prior to World War I and also in the interwar period, most of the German companies relied on German trading companies for distribution of their goods in Japan. Most common were German trading companies acting as agents who were granted exclusive rights but had the obligation to be the exclusive agents for the products concerned. But there were also agents who were sent to Japan by companies for the sole purpose of distributing products.

These two types of agents were the most common ones, but as the following example shows, even the use of such agents was not always a guarantee for success. The agent of the big German cable manufacturer Felten & Guilleaume in Japan, the trading company C. Illies & Co., could sell only a small number of submarine cables due to a limited number of Japanese orders. In addition to limited market exposure, the trading company also lacked contacts with bureaucrats and government officials, which was especially detrimental to trading in Manchuria in the 1930s, where Illies & Co. had exclusive selling rights. Communication was bad in that Illies & Co. sometimes did not inform the home office of F & G in Germany about oncoming tenders so that F & G was unable to participate in business decisions. A private representative office would have performed much better, but the small market share in Japan did not justify the establishment of such an office.[15]

On the other hand, there were numerous complaints by the trading companies that most of the German manufacturers, not aware of market chances, would not, for example, put in tenders or send catalogs and other information on the company to the trading companies in Japan who acted as their agents.

In the 1930s, there were cases when Japanese companies sent representatives to Germany to persuade German companies to sell to Japanese trading companies or even the ultimate purchasers directly, thereby circumventing German trading companies in Japan. Such attempts to gradually oust German trading companies were recorded even for those products a German trading company had exclusive selling rights to in Japan.[16]

In answer to such approaches, a number of German manufacturers stressed that under no circumstances should the agent be one of the three big Japanese trading companies (Mitsui, Mitsubishi, and Ōkura).[17] These trading companies were regarded as unreliable because they had manufacturing companies within their own groups and soon would release news about German activities to their group members, which happened to be competitors of German manufacturers.

2. *Changing Business Conditions in Japan*

Owing to rapidly changing market conditions in Japan in the late 1920s and early 1930s, the tendency of specializing in certain branches or commodities within the group of German trading companies accelerated. Due to this specialization, competition between the German merchants decreased and most companies fared much better than before.

Difficulties in selling German goods in Japan in the 1930s arose mainly due to two factors: the aforementioned changing market conditions and technical problems. Because of the importation of sophisticated technology in the early 1930s, Japanese manufacturers had reached quite a high technical standard of production, and therefore products manufactured in Japan became competitive with imported German products.

This reduced the necessity of imports, but only a few German manufacturers realized the change in trading conditions,[18] mostly because they lacked sufficient information. "Strong domestic competition" and "a decreasing interest in imports" made it difficult to maintain market shares, even in the case of goods which had long been important export commodities of German industry.[19]

Together with the changing needs of Japanese customers, technical problems arose. A point of continuous contention, even before World War I,[20] had been that sales did not normally include the transfer of technical knowledge. The problem was that sales clerks were usually deficient in such knowledge. To alleviate the situation, some German companies sent engineers to East Asia, and especially Japan, who would in some cases become the heads of the respective representative offices.[21] However, World War I put an end to this agreement, and in the 1920s nearly the same problems arose once more. The solution of technical problems was restricted to an occasional visit by an engineer, but the growing need for technical advice in the late 1920s and 1930s made the presence of engineers an absolute necessity. Smaller German manufacturers which could not afford independent representative offices in Japan had to look for a more suitable solution.

How smaller companies reacted to changing conditions on the Japanese market can be described using the example of the Dr. C. Otto & Co., a medium-sized but technically high-competitive coke-oven manufacturer located in Bochum, in the Ruhr area, the main industrial zone of Germany. Efforts to open business with the Japanese had failed until the 1930s because the company usually approached Japanese customers directly. Later on, the company sold its product to the trading company L. Leybold in Tokyo, which then sold it to Japanese customers, usually to Mitsubishi Shōji or, less frequently, to one of the other big Japanese trading companies. The Japanese trading company then became the agent for the product and signed a contract with the ultimate purchaser. In early cases paperwork and blueprints were prepared in Germany, while hardware was usually bought in Japan. The geographical distance between the original bidder, the planning head office in Germany, and the ultimate buyer complicated the process. Engineers and technicians had to be sent from Germany to Japan, but as the company could not afford a representative office, the engineering staff literally found shelter under the roof of a German trading company, L. Leybold KK, in Tokyo. There the blueprints from Germany were redesigned for the Japanese customer and to this end draughtswomen were employed and paid by the Leybold company but placed at the disposal of the "Otto-

Bureau." In the long run, the good performance of these designers made the initial German blueprints superfluous, and sometimes original blueprints came to be designed in Japan. This hastened the execution of contracts and led to an increased inflow of orders.[22]

As the larger German trading companies like C. Illies & Co. or L. Leybold & Co. were in possession of spacious buildings, they offered office space to numerous other smaller German companies (like Dr. C. Otto & Co.) where Japanese customers could call at. Such agreements enabled German manufacturers to cut overhead because the administrative work was taken over by the personnel of the trading company, while staff from Germany was reduced to mainly engineers and technicians. Obviously, despite numerous failures to gain access to the Japanese market, some companies showed sufficient adaptability not only to reach the market but also to stay in business even during difficult years. But it has to be admitted that these companies were not in the majority.

IV. Obstacles I: Japanese Protectionist Policy

Business conditions were strongly affected by Japanese government's policy, and most complaints by German companies in Japan during the interwar period were in regard to obstacles and barriers put up by the government.

As early as the years preceding World War I, a strong tendency could be observed among Japanese firms to concentrate on channels controlled by Japanese trading companies for their imports. The habit became more pronounced after World War I, accompanied by the view that government agencies and organizations, public bodies, and government-guided institutions should rely on domestic products. It was proposed to exclude foreign companies from participation in public tenders. Until the 1930s, quite a number of German companies were driven out of the Japanese market.[23]

In the 1930s, usually regarded as a period in which Japan and Germany developed very special political relations, economic relations did not develop along similar lines. This is shown very clearly in the many practical problems occurring after the mid-1930s.

As already shown, most German manufacturers needed trading companies to be present on the Japanese market. Therefore, an obstacle which materialized in the late 1930s meant a severe blow to their exports. German trading companies were generally not admitted to the various Japanese control associations (*tōsei kumiai*) formed in the years after the outbreak of the Sino-Japanese War in 1937. A German company could join only if it it was indispensable to the importation of a certain commodity. Before admitting this company, the Japanese would first try to directly contact the supplier in Germany. The severity of the situation is testified to by the fact that the German chamber of commerce in Tokyo repeatedly urged the German Ministry of Economic Affairs and representatives of German industry to stick to their representative offices or trading companies in Japan and to conduct business in Japan via this route only. Also, German manufacturers were requested to refer to their German trading companies in Japan when approached by Japanese firms.[24]

German manufacturers had a hard time understanding that even if contracts were sanctioned by the Japanese government, contracts could not be fulfilled because the same government (or one of its agencies) would not issue importation or transfer permits. In early 1937 a contract for shipping 10,000 tons of tubes annually to Japan was signed and approved by the Japanese government. Only ten months later, the German tube manufacturers' association complained that the agreement was not really being observed by the Japanese side. The importing Japanese companies obviously still had to apply for importation permits, and by refraining from issuing such permits the government—which at one time had sanctioned the agreement—shortly afterward nullified it on the quiet. The Germans suspected that the contract had been signed in order to find a way to exclude German competitors from the Japanese market.[25] Generally speaking, import conditions had been deteriorating because "import permits are required, however rarely granted."[26]

Even if a trading company had been granted an import permit, the Bank of Japan (or, in Manchuria, the Manchurian Central Bank) would keep the company waiting and delay importation by not issuing the necessary amount of foreign exchange. Similar obstacles also affected business in Manchuria. The possibility of replacing imported German products with Japanese products, in accordance with the "Buy Japanese" slogan, and simultaneously saving foreign currency led to the introduction of a black list in Manchuria shortly after 1937. The list contained all commodities not to be imported,[27] which were especially those which could also be bought in Japan without an importation permit. This black list not only affected various items which had been major constituents of German exports to Manchuria but also put German firms and trading companies in an awkward position: Existing treaties on a specified volume of exports from Manchuria to Germany could no longer be balanced by imports, because import permits were no issued by the Manchurian government—which, at the same time, urged German trading companies to adhere to the contracts the two governments had agreed upon.

The German trading companies' and trading agents' performance in Manchuria was also heavily influenced by the "controlled economy" of the late 1930s. There were numerous complaints about protectionist trade policies by governmental institutions, ministries, and banks, but to no avail. Trade restrictions could even be oppressive; for instance, ships could be prohibited from anchoring at the mole and had to wait outside the harbor to let the Japanese ships clear first. German trading agents were kept waiting in front of the various overdue for several weeks.[28] These non-tariff barriers were the main reason why German exports to Manchuria did not increase as the German government had hoped they would.

A major reason why the Japanese in Manchuria adopted such measures was the shortage of foreign exchange. Secondly, in the late 1930s, German trading companies had their eyes mainly on China, on the assumption that a non-industrialized country like China would still need several years to catch up and therefore remain dependent on western products for quite a while. This promised good profit opportunities for the trade between Germany and China in the years ahead without having to fear that a rival would arise at the same time. Japan estimated quite differently: The Japanese were only interested in a limited number of special items, and they had become a strong competitor in many fields in the meantime. Moreover, it was an open secret, to the Japanese as well as to the Germans, that the representatives of German trading companies in China and Manchuria were "China-friends" and "Japan-haters." Officials of German companies on their return from a business trip to East Asia strongly urged replacing all these representatives because one had the strong suspicion that they would destroy any opportunity to trade with Manchuria[29]—which they actually did before long.

There might as well have been a psychological barrier which barred the trading agents from considering the Japanese to be entitled to success and business as the Europeans were.[30] This developed into a passive resistance against the Japanese and the Japanese bureaucracy in Manchuria. It comes as no surprise that the Japanese strongly reacted to this kind of arrogance.

The lack of foreign currency proved to be the hardest obstacle to overcome. Usually a German customer would transfer the amount invoiced by a Japanese or Manchurian exporter to an account held at a German bank. Due to severe foreign-exchange controls, money was not sent to Japan or Manchuria but was kept in Germany. The Otto-

Wolff group, a big trading company heavily involved in imports from Manchuria, came to think of a way to make use of the foreign currency held in such accounts. In 1937 a credit agreement was signed between the Central Bank of Manchuria and the Otto-Wolff group. The limit on the first loan (which was later to be followed by a second and third loan) was placed at £2 million sterling (35 million yuan); maturity was six years (ending in 1944), with a fixed interest of 5.5%. Ninety percent of the loan had to be paid off from a Manchurian reichsmark account, while the rest was due in pounds sterling. Items to be purchased by Manchuria under this agreement were limited to heavy industrial goods.[31] The advantage for Manchuria was that it could spare most of its foreign currency holdings. The actual performance of the deal, however, could not be observed because of the deterioration of trade relations and problems with shipments to Japan during its term.

The agreement was an exception, because hardly any of the other trading companies would have been able to provide for such a credit frame. The lack of foreign currency and the controls imposed on it made several Japanese companies try to pay German companies in yen. Most of the German companies, however, were not interested in yen holdings, because it was only the big companies which had the chance or the need to pay for products in yen. For smaller firms the same held true as for Dr. C. Otto & Co.: They sold technical drawings or licenses to Japan without importing anything in exchange for it.

V. Obstacles II: Problems with Patents and Licenses in Japan

A further impediment to good performace in Japan was the constant quarrel about patents and licenses. Feelings of apprehension made German companies limit their activities on the Japanese market. It had long been customary for German manufacturers to sell licenses and drawings rather than to ship whole plants to Japan. When famous German companies lost their patent rights in Japan during World War I, they became reluctant, and in the 1920s they came to explicitly mistrust any Japanese approach concerning licenses.

Japanese zeal to obtain German licenses, however, was unabated in the 1930s. As before, Japanese came to Germany as tourists and tried to visit certain companies in order to take new technical know-how home. In other cases Japanese engineers were sent to Germany with the vague prospect of future negotiations; one sent letters in order to gain information on new production processes, operations, and inventions.[32] More often than not, negotiations would fail without reason shortly after they had started, or even after they had reached a very concrete stage. Only from hindsight was it understood that the Japanese had elicited enough information about the new production processes during negotiations to manufacture the very product without buying the license.[33]

Fears of being exploited and cheated hampered business activities in Japan, and negotiations between German companies and Japanese manufacturers about patents and licenses at times reached a dead end. In addition, Japanese companies would sometimes purchase licenses without actually using them for production. German companies argued that these licenses were bought only to prevent potential Japanese competitors on the domestic market from buying them.[34] It is obvious why German companies would be reluctant to further cooperate with their Japanese counterparts under these circumstances.

On the other hand, Japanese patents granted to German companies very often did not live up to their purposes. For one thing, German knowledge of the Japanese patent system and its application procedures was restricted.[35] Secondly, once a Japanese patent had been granted, often it became clear that the wording was much too general, thus facilitating an evasion (*Patentumgehung*) by the Japanese company. Thirdly, German companies were amazed to see the ease with which the Japanese evaded certain patent details, as engineers, chemists, and technicians were well educated and had completely mastered processes and operations.

German companies that applied for patents in Japan also faced a lot of difficulties with patent claims or patent protection. For example, patents that were only slightly different from the German originals were taken out in Japan and used for the production of exactly the same items.[36] Also, it seems as if only the more experienced firms knew how to handle Japanese patent procedures. The files of Dr. C. Otto & Co. reveal that patent application was regarded as an efficient way of product protection and, more importantly, that the company used patents for marketing purposes. Employing patents for public relations may well have been a major contributing factor to the company's success in Japan. Dr. C. Otto & Co. even considered litigating patent infringements by relying on experienced lawyers,[37] an action other companies were reluctant to take.

With the exception of a few companies like Dr. C. Otto & Co., however, patent problems exemplify the general German attitude against Japanese companies and Japan as a whole. This attitude was based on the perception of Japanese "misbehavior" according to German standards and on a general lack of knowledge on Japan. In the opinion of German firms, everyone living in an industrialized country should behave "industrialized," i.e., like an American, an Englishmen, or a German. Even as a latecomer, Japan was expected to behave like any other western country, but not the way it did.

Problems with patents and licenses in Japan were not restricted to the company level. Slowly the German government, too, went into the ring. In the 1920s, German officials were still occupied with their own problems to a degree that left little room for worrying about Japan as an economic partner. In the 1930s the situation changed, with the result that the government became aware of what was called "industrial espionage of Japanese citizens." It was concluded that it was because of this industrial espionage that German manufacturers lost their market share against their Japanese competitors. Therefore, fighting industrial espionage became a major point of governmental industrial policy, and the new term *Industrieverschleppung* ("industrial abduction") was created in the mid-1930s. The government advised companies not to give certain licenses to Japanese firms, and it also limited the issuing of permissions for starting production with German technology in Japan, even if there were no competitors for the product concerned.[38]

It was not before 1938 that the fact that foreign production subsidiaries meant the exportation of German goods (hence the increase in foreign exchange holdings) was seen to be strong enough to allow the free flow of licenses to Japan. This was too late to have much effect on German-Japanese commercial relations. Moreover, only three years later, in 1941, the Ministry of Economic Affairs (*Reichswirtschaftskammer*) decided that business in Japan had to be conducted under the ministry's supervision.[39] But this new policy of restraint did not have any effect as trade between the two countries had practically come to an end due to the worsening world situation.

VI. A Case Study: I.G. Farben and Japan

In late 1925 eight former members of a cartel-like interest group called Interessengemeinschaft merged into the single corporation that was then called Interessengemeinschaft Farben AG (abbreviated I.G. Farben), thus becoming one of the largest corporations and at the same time one of the largest chemical companies in the world. During those years, exports preferably went to European countries, especially to the direct neighbors of Germany, but exports to East Asia, and especially to Japan, had also become substantial. The member companies had already been important exporters of dyestuffs, nitrogenous fertilizer, and other chemical products.

World War I, however, had reduced dyestuff imports to Japan (80% of which had come from Germany) to almost zero because Japan, with the help of government subsidies, had begun to establish its own dyestuff industry during the war. However, the quality of the products seems to have been very poor.[40]

In order to protect Japanese manufacturers during the years of the postwar recession, a tariff barrier was established which first put pressure on American competitors and, to a lesser extent, also on German companies, which had just begun to re-enter the Japanese market. Nevertheless, the Germans once more saw their chance on the Japanese market. But only after a special agreement between I.G. Farben and the Japanese government had been signed—in which I.G. Farben committed itself to exporting certain dyestuffs only in coordination with the Japanese party concerned—the way was open for the commercial treaty signed in 1927.

1. Basic Strategy of I.G. Farben: The Market and Agreements

When I.G. Farben was established in 1926, the board of directors "set its sights on the export trade and embarked on an ambitious rationalization program."[41] A special strategy was designed because it seemed to be quite difficult to regain the chemical industries' former position after World War I through an ordinary market-oriented strategy. According to this, "I.G. Farben's management . . . promoted advantageous national and international trade agreements and supported the establishment of foreign subsidiaries."[42] How, then, was Japan included in such a strategy? The various agreements signed between the big chemical companies of Europe and America in connection with exports to the Far East reveal that, first of all, most companies focused on the China market. This was true until the early 1930s, even though in most agreements China, Japan, India, and the Dutch Indies were all listed as export destinations. Exports to East Asia made up around one quarter of the total I.G. Farben exports in the mid-1930s,[43] but Japan never became the major export target.[44] A number of European and American companies signed a Three-Party Cartel Agreement and also several Six-Party Quota Agreements, but not before 1935 was a Japanese company included in an agreement called the Mitsui Indigo Agreement. This agreement tied down that, "in return for an agreement by Mitsui to limit its exports of Indigo [to China], the parties of the China Six-Party Agreements [I.G. Farben, Swiss I.G., C.M.C., Dupont, Nacco] accepted a small sales quota for Japan."[45] In other words, Mitsui (Bussan) thereby agreed to export indigo to China only (an amount of 40,000 piculs was agreed on), while the foreign companies were granted a 15% sales quota for Japan. This agreement, however, implied the total regulation of competition on the China market.

Only two dyestuff agreements were made between I.G. Farben and its Japanese competitor, NSK (Nippon Senryō Seizō KK, Osaka). Dyestuff contract no. 16 (signed on February 1, 1934) was designed to "regulate competition in Astraphloxine between the parties in Japan, and eliminate it outside Japan."[46] NSK agreed not to sell outside Japan. Sales quotas were set up for sales in Japan (including Korea and Formosa) at a ratio of 50:50. The second contract (no. 17, signed on March 24, 1935 [Japan Variamine Blue Agreement]) was signed to "settle a dispute as to the validity of Japanese patents of I.G. and the manufacture and application of Variamine Blue and Naphthol AS dyestuffs, and to regulate competition in those products by a price and quota agreement for the Japanese market and a prohibition of exports by N.S.K."[47] Again, NSK agreed not to sell outside Japan (including Korea and Formosa), and for sales in Japan the quota for the I.G. Farben was increased to 68%.

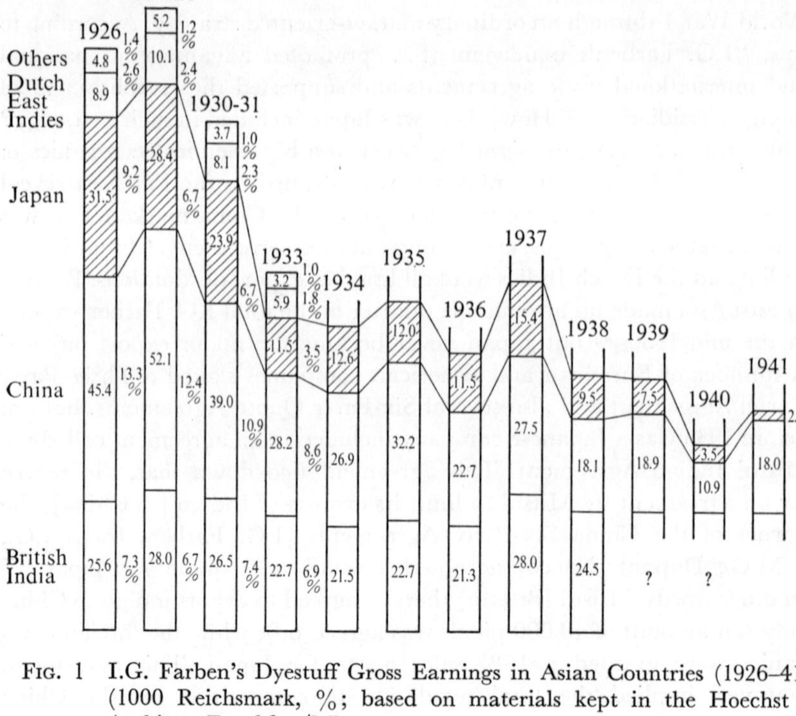

FIG. 1 I.G. Farben's Dyestuff Gross Earnings in Asian Countries (1926–41) (1000 Reichsmark, %; based on materials kept in the Hoechst Archives, Frankfurt/M)

However, the agreements focused only on the Chinese market: Asian markets, at least for dyestuffs, meant China, not Japan. (For I.G. Farben, the Japanese market for dyestuffs was of minor importance.) Around 50% of Japanese imports of dyestuff came from Germany until 1928, when the figures began to decline sharply.[48] (See export figures in Fig. 1.) Therefore, market strategy for dyestuff exports was to prevent Japanese manufacturers from exporting to China or India and to reach certain agreements, but not to open the Japanese market to European products.[49]

Exports of nitrogenous fertilizer to East Asia behaved in a similar way. As early as the 1920s, European manufacturers started negotiations about market shares, market access, and export quotas. Agreements were signed in 1927 and 1929, but a new round of negotiations became necessary after the world depression. Like the imperial powers of the world, the British firm ICI and the German firm I.G. Farben divided the world into several "reserved regions" where they had exclusive rights, and in some areas, like China and Japan, export quotas (Japan: 40% for ICI and 60% for I.G. Farben) were fixed.[50] Nitrogenous fertilizer was important in that nearly 20% of total production by the German chemical industry went to Japan, while nearly one-third of all Japanese fertilizer imports came from Germany.[51]

2. *Subsidiaries of I.G. Farben in Japan*

Most of the companies that merged into I.G. Farben in 1925 had already set up agents or sales bureaus in Japan. Shortly after the merger, special companies in every major business field were established according to Japanese law. For example, Doitsu Senryō Gōmei Kaisha was founded for the dyestuff business, pharmaceuticals were coordinated by Bayer Yakuhin Gōmei Kaisha, and AGFA Gōmei Kaisha became responsible for photographics. The only sales agent which did not change its name was the trading company H. Ahrens & Co., Nachf., located in Kobe, which had after World War I been in charge of BASF and the German nitrogenous syndicate in Japan.[52] However, the establishment of these companies was a change in the legal standing of already existing bureaus rather than a real foreign capital investment. Also, the tasks of these companies did not change much from those of the former bureaus.

In general, I.G. Farben, as most of the German chemical industry, pursued a rather restrictive policy of foreign investment.[53] The establishment of production subsidiaries was restricted to countries where they were indispensable for maintaining a given market share; hence foreign investment had a strong "defensive character."[54] Direct or indirect I.G. Farben capital investment in manufacturing companies subject to Japanese law numbered only 11 (as revealed after World War II),[55] and five of these were production sites only and not involved in trading.

A handwritten comment in the I.G. Farben files reveals that, for example, the foundation of Titan Kōgyō KK, Tokyo, was in some way a concerted action of European and American companies directed against the Japanese.[56] The major reason for fear of market loss instead of an increase in sales also becomes evident in the discussion around the establishment of Carbon Black manufacturing company in 1932: in reaction to the increase of the Japanese market share in China, the setup of a production site in China was being considered.[57]

3. Changing Markets and Changing Marketing Strategies for Japan

The companies I.G. Farben had established in Japan, with the exception of the Doitsu Senryō Gōmei Kaisha, mainly engaged in sales promotion. Doitsu Senryō Gōmei Kaisha became very important to I.G. Farben as its "antenna" in Japan: It collected data on the Japanese economy in general, the Japanese market, and competing Japanese companies. This data, together with clippings from technical and chemical journals and newspapers and even translations of articles, were then sent to the Economic Research Department (Volkswirtschaftliche Abteilung, established in 1929) of I.G. Farben in Berlin, where it was analyzed. This department built up a widespread network all over the world using sales offices, production subsidiaries, and other affiliates to gather information. Within a couple of years the department not only collected economic and statistical data for I.G. Farben export strategies but also furnished the German government with data.[58] Although at a lower level of the I.G. Farben hierarchy the importance of continuous and systematic collection of data for long-term economic analyses was realized quite early, at the upper level its usefulness was not seen immediately. Decision-making bodies within I.G. Farben were not greatly interested in East Asia, and it was only after Max Ilgner, one of the organizers of the worldwide information network, delivered an *Ostasienbericht* (report on East Asia) upon returning from a trip to East Asia, that Manchuria was "discovered" as the new and most important export target.[59] Shortly afterward, in late 1935, a Far Eastern Committee (*Ostasien-Ausschuß*) was created within I.G. Farben, which in a sense was a reaction to the mounting export difficulties in the far eastern markets.

However, despite these activities and all the information available, I.G. Farben hesitated to decide on its strategy for the Japanese market. The Far Eastern Committee, as all other departments, favored China and India as future export markets. Japan's rapid industrialization was analyzed[60] only in the context of how it affected I.G. Farben exports to Asian markets, not to Japan itself.

Max Ilgner himself called for increased exports to East Asia in 1937. He must have been well aware of the upper floors' reluctance to engage in East Asia. He stressed the importance of leading businessmen being sent to the new markets themselves in order for them to get the right feeling for the Asian environment by being exposed to people and circumstances there. Ilgner also realized that the most impressive report written by the most intelligent representative in Asia was useless unless those responsible at home were able to understand, reflect, and evaluate the report from the background of personal experience. Due to a lack of reflection and personal experience, he wrote,[61] changing economic conditions and structural changes in the export markets were simply declared to be cyclical downswings. These misconceptions ruled out a correct evaluation of export markets and denied the possibility of making the right decisions. Ilgner's opinions were supported by the later director of the Economics Research Department, Anton Reithinger, who returned from East Asia with the insight that I.G. Farben was in danger of being trapped between North China and Manchuria, thus becoming the political enemy of the Chinese and the economic foe of the Japanese.[62] It is noteworthy, though, that any report by I.G. Farben representatives in the late 1930s depicted Japan as a rival, not as an ally.

On the whole, there was no clear-cut marketing strategy concerning East Asia, China, or Japan in the 1930s. However, in spite of the preference for China as the future export market, the Far Eastern Committee decided to take an active stance toward Japan and Manchuria in 1939. Difficulties in Japan were clearly seen: reduced importation of products that the Japanese had started to manufacture themselves, tariff barriers, blacklists, and many others. Four proposals were made:

(1) increasing sales of raw materials and semi-finished goods,
(2) exporting capital goods,
(3) selling licenses and technical innovations, and
(4) starting production through a subsidiary or joint venture.[63]

This new strategy was clearly adjusted to real market conditions and it bears the handwriting of experts on Manchuria and Japan within the Economic Research Department. However, the decision came too late to live up to its theory because of the rapidly worsening international environment.

4. *Licenses for the Japanese Industry*

Selling licenses to Japan was nothing new for I.G. Farben, but the reluctance to give away licenses led to a new strategy in the 1930s which could be called a "delaying strategy." It was applied especially in countries where exports were expected to be reduced in the near future because those countries were starting their own production. For example, when the Japanese applied for I.G. Farben licenses for methyl alcohol and nitrogenous fertilizer, they had to wait for a reply. I.G. Farben sources disclose why methyl alcohol was an item on the "delaying list": First, it was a question of losing exports to Japan; second, demand in Japan seemed to be small, and because license fees were partly paid according to the volume, selling the license would not have been profitable;[64] third, Japanese companies planned to use methyl alcohol as a substitute for fuel, and this ran counter to an agreement between I.G. Farben and Standard Oil which stipulated that licenses were not to be sold to countries where methyl alcohol was to be used for fuel purposes.

Even though I.G. Farben delayed the giving of the license to Japan, the market was lost anyway because Japanese companies had at last succeeded in producing methyl alcohol without the help of I.G. Farben. Still, I.G. Farben was sure to hold a certain market share because of the better quality of their product. However, even this soon proved to be wrong as well: Japanese customers bought the Japanese product because, even if inferior, it was after all Japanese!

I.G. Farben decided that under these conditions it might as well grant the license to a Japanese company, but the decision came too late. Therefore, the German market share was lost because of a lack of understanding of the Japanese industrial reality as well as the Japanese consumer mentality.

The experience with nitrogenous fertilizer was hardly different. Knowing that the market for this product would be lost in the near future, I.G. Farben delayed license negotiations and, in the meantime, tried to sell as much nitrogenous fertilizer to Japan as possible before Japan could start its own production.[65]

When, in the early 1930s, I.G. Farben managers became aware that market share in other products would also be lost, because the Japanese were increasingly developing their own production processes (thereby also affecting payments on license rights), they decided to shift to a new strategy in negotiations on future license transfers. In early 1936 the Far Eastern Committee recommended not to agree on continuous payment in percentage profits, because production and therefore profits in Japan had turned out to be extremely low. A lump-sum payment should be agreed upon, supplemented, if possible, by a certain ratio according to production.[66]

In contrast, licenses on products not directly connected with I.G. Farben export strategies were granted without long-winded negotiations, especially if new technologies were involved (i.e., the production of magnesium alloy and others).[67] However, as it happened with hydrogenation patents (a similar example is Buna, the synthetic rubber), I.G. Farben became immediately suspicious as there was the "impression that the Japanese negotiations were not prompted by a genuine desire to adopt the I.G. process, [but that] their intention [was] to get the Germans to help them out of their difficulties." Within the company the "view was expressed that the Japanese were using the German [hydrogenation] plant as a subterfuge to get German technicians to Japan to help to remedy the defects in their existing plants."[68] I.G. Farben managers felt they were being exploited and became non-cooperative.

The Japanese view on license transfer was quite different. I.G. Farben was said to be blocking the further development of the Japanese chemical industry, especially the dyestuff industry. While certain products could not be manufactured in Japan because of German patents, buying these patents was considered to be much too expensive.[69]

Therefore in the case of I.G. Farben an arrangement concerning the transfer of advanced technology agreeable to both sides was found only in minor licenses. The impact on Japan's chemical industry must not be overrated.

5. I.G. Farben's Attitudes and Performance Revisited

The case of I.G. Farben in Japan is an exceptional one and hardly to be generalized. Based on a global market–oriented strategy on trade (or quota) agreements and the establishment of foreign subsidiaries, the company tried to regain competitiveness in the late 1920s. The special treaty signed with the Japanese government was one part of such a strategy for penetrating the Japanese market despite bad circumstances, but the world economic crisis was a severe blow to all efforts and I.G. Farben never managed to regain its position. In general, in the interwar period Japan was not viewed as a prospective market by I.G. Farben. Japan and Japanese companies were regarded as severe competitors, especially in the Chinese market.

But why did I.G. Farben lose even its small market share in Japan? By establishing sales subsidiaries in Japan, I.G. Farben thought that they had done enough to secure their market shares. Even though most interesting information on Japan was forwarded from a subsidiary in Japan to the economic research office of I.G. Farben, the management mostly ignored the reports prepared for them. Most members of the management looked upon the Japanese as mere copiers, unable to develop something by themselves without foreign help. They often refused to give patents, licenses, or even simple technical assistance to Japanese companies, because the Germans hoped to maintain the market share in the future by keeping the Japanese ignorant. This hope was soon destroyed as the Japanese companies without foreign help developed several chemical processes from which the import of foreign products received a strong blow. In cases when Japanese firms approached I.G. Farben to deliver selected advanced technologies, this was soon regarded as industrial espionage. Altogether, there was hardly a common view shared by the Germans and the Japanese. While I.G. Farben was neither in the know nor understanding of the Japanese attitude, the Japanese did everything to let misunderstanding arise.

VII. Conclusion

In contrast to the widely accepted view that the relationship between Germany and Japan in the interwar period was based on a certain "friendship," a closer look reveals that neither in political nor in economic terms could the two countries be called friends.

Economically, outspoken dissension began with the Germans being annoyed because Japan had entered World War I on the side of Germany's enemies and had taken restrictive measures against German companies operating in Japan, which lead to the dissolution of some of these firms during or shortly after the war. On the other hand, in the 1920s the Japanese were afraid that uncontrolled importation of German goods, especially dyestuff, chemicals, and machinery, would destroy the respective Japanese industries which had just started production. With the exception of a small number of German success stories in the Japanese market during the 1920s, the overall role played by German companies in Japan remained only a minor one.

During the interwar period, numerous Japanese companies, often represented by managers with engineering backgrounds, repeatedly tried to persuade German manufacturers to export advanced technology to Japan. However, in contrast to the 1920s, when a broad spectrum of German technology was of interest to Japanese companies, in the 1930s the Japanese asked for selected and highly specialized technology only. At the same time German companies were just vaguely interested in establishing branches in Japan; there were only a few joint ventures launched in the interwar period. Capital inflow from Germany to Japan was insignificant and, especially in the 1920s, due to Germany's limited capital resources. Therefore, technical assistance and licensing was much more important than joint ventures or capital investment in the interwar period.

The most important factor for technical assistance was human capital. In some instances technology was transferred to Japan quite freely, but more often than not the Germans were rather reluctant to provide for German technology. One reason for this disfavor was that the Japanese had already proved able to catch up very quickly and soon become a competitor on the market. The disfavor developed into a "spy-mania" due to several cases of Japanese industrial espionage; this made a transfer of technical know-how even more difficult, because not only companies but also the German government turned suspicious.

The situation was even worse for commodities and goods than it was for merchandizing German technology, licenses, and patents. An analysis of the actual situation, however, suggests that it was the Germans who have to be blamed for most of the failures. First of all, German companies did not regard Japan as a major market; even to those companies which focused on "East Asia," the term meant China first, not Japan. Generally, German companies had only limited knowledge about Japan and its economic potential; they were unaware of marketing strategies in Japan, and they sometimes did not even receive information through their trading agents in Japan on business opportunities. At the same time Japan built up several barriers against foreign competitors, which effectively restricted market penetration by German companies. Most importantly, Japanese trading companies tried to take over imports to Japan themselves. This strategy could be observed as early as the beginning of the 20th century, but it was pushed forward with increased pertinacity in the interwar period. Next to that, import tariff barriers as well as quite a number of non-tariff barriers hampered a more positive approach by German companies to Japan.

Most obstacles to the performance of German companies in Japan in the interwar period could have been overcome by a more positive attitude of the Germans toward the Japanese. However, the Germans instead tended to regard themselves as the industrialized power trading with a minor partner; despite increased contacts between German companies and Japanese importers, and numerous cases of important technology transfers in the interwar period (and even more so in the 1930s), the German performance compares badly with that of other countries on the Japanese market.

Given the adverse circumstances, establishing a subsidiary in Japan was not an attractive idea to most German companies. While only a handful of big German companies ventured to make an investment, most other "medium-size" companies relied on already well-established German trading companies in Japan. The practice of a bigger trading company housing several "bureaus" of German companies while acting as the agent and financial manager developed into a peculiar German approach to the Japanese market. However, due to a lack of data, the number of "shelter companies" and their clientele during this period is not available.

Politically, the German performance was severely impeded in the late 1930s, when—despite the "friendship" officially announced by politicians of both countries—distrust came to the fore in real life. A kind of "spy-mania" that arose in Germany as well as in Japan dried up the already diminished interest in exporting to Japan. Also, in pushing forward their "controlled economy," the Japanese took numerous measures to further reduce German activities. The limited number of German success stories in the interwar Japanese market cannot disguise the fact that both countries thoroughly lacked mutual understanding. The resulting recriminations denied the possibility of a smooth and efficient exchange of ideas as well as progress in real economy.

Notes

1. According to a press release from the German news agency Deutscher Montan Dienst, March 1942: 1; see Bundesarchiv Koblenz, R7/970.
2. Erich Pauer, "Die wirtschaftlichen Beziehungen zwischen Japan und Deutschland 1900–1945," in J. Kreiner (ed.), *Deutschland-Japan. Historische Kontakte*, Bonn: Bouvier, 1984, pp. 161–210; Erich Pauer, "Lots of Friendship, but Few Orders," in Ian Nish (ed.), *German-Japanese Relations in the 1930s* (International Studies 86/140, STICERD/LSE), London, 1986, pp. 10–37; Erich Pauer, "Deutsche Ingenieure in Japan, japanische Ingenieure in Deutschland in der Zwischenkriegszeit," in J. Kreiner (ed.), *Deutschland-Japan in der Zwischenkriegszeit*, Bonn: Bouvier, 1990 (in print).
3. For more details, see my article "Deutsche Ingenieure in Japan . . ." (*ibid.*), based on Fujimoto Mitsushiro, *Matsukata Kaneko monogatari*, Kobe, 1960, pp. 233, 242.
4. For details, see Pauer, "Die wirtschaftlichen Beziehungen . . ." (*op. cit.*), p. 171, and also the article by John W. M. Chapman, "Japan in German Aviation Policies of the Weimar Period," in J. Kreiner (ed.), *Japan und die Mittelmächte*, Bonn: Bouvier, 1986, pp. 155–73.
5. Fuji Denki KK (ed.), *Fuji Denki Sha Shi* (History of Fuji Denki Ltd.), Tokyo, 1957, pp. 6–7.
6. Karl Vogt, *Aus der Lebenschronik eines Japandeutschen, 1897–1941*, Tokyo, OAG, 1962, pp. 174–75.
7. Ostasiatischer Verein (ed.), *Achtundzwanzigster Jahresbericht für das Jahr 1927*, Hamburg, 1928, pp. 43–44.

8. Paul Hövel, *Grundfragen deutscher Wirtschaftspolitik*, Berlin: Springer, 1935, pp. 136–37; George W. F. Hallgarten & Joachim Radkau, *Deutsche Industrie & Politik von Bismarck bis heute*, Frankfurt: EVA, 1974, p. 329.

9. Hövel, *ibid.*, p. 138.

10. Hallgarten/Radkau, *op. cit.*, p. 327.

11. Leopold Katscher, "Gesichtspunkte für den Handelsverkehr mit Japan," in *Weltwirtschaft*, vol. 13, pp. 183–84.

12. *Ibid.*, p. 183.

13. Kurt Meissner, *Deutsche in Japan 1639–1939*, Stuttgart: DVA, 1940, p. 106.

14. E.g., the following companies were represented by the trading company C. Illies & Co. in the interwar period: MAN, Augsburg; Deutsche Schiffs und Maschinenbau AG, Bremen; Rheinmetall-Borsig, Berlin; Henschel & Sohn AG, Kassel; BMW AG, Munich; Robert Bosch GmbH, Stuttgart; Bleichert Transportanlagen GmbH; Vereinigte Kugellagerfabriken AG, Schweinfurt; Dornier-Werke, Friedrichshafen; Sächsische Textilmaschinenfabrik, Chemnitz; Anschütz & Co., Kiel, Dräger-Werke, Lübeck; Hapag, Hamburg; see Käthe Molsen, *C. Illies & Co. 1859–1959*, Hamburg: Hanseatischer Merkur, p. 93.

15. Wilfried Feldenkirchen, "Big Business in Interwar Germany: Organizational Innovation at Vereinigte Stahlwerke, I.G. Farben, and Siemens," in *Business History Review*, vol. 6, no. 3, pp. 417–51 and esp. pp. 180–81.

16. *Jahresbericht der deutschen Handelskammer Tokyo*, p. 18; see Bundesarchiv Koblenz, R 11/1282a.

17. According to a report of H. Reuter, representative of the Mannesmann tube works who went to Japan in 1928; manuscript in the Mannesmann Archives D 1.980/1.

18. A rare example is to be found in a letter from Norddeutscher Lloyd to Mannesmann tube works in 1939, in which it is said that "Japan today buys foreign goods only if it is absolutely necessary. In such cases usually special goods are imported in a field where Germany is extremely strong, or which, because of other reasons, could only be imported from Germany"; Mannesmann Archives M 19.420.

19. Mentioned in a paper on Bayer pharmaceutical products titled "A General View of Market Conditions," written in 1938; see Economics Division, Decartelization Branch, Control Office/I.G.-Farbenindustrie A.G., U.S. Zone (comp.), *Activities of former "Bayer" I.G. Farbenindustrie A.G. in the Pharmaceuticals Industry* (Sept. 30, 1946); Hoechst Archives, Frankfurt.

20. For more details, see the unpublished Ph.D. thesis by Michael Rauck, *Die Beziehungen zwischen Japan und Deutschland 1859–1914*, 1988, p. 604.

21. For a list of representative offices of German companies before World War I in Japan, see *ibid.*, pp. 612–14.

22. Gerhard Lorenzen, *Das Fernostgeschäft der Firma Dr. C. Otto & Co. GmbH* (manuscript written in 1947 in the archives of the Dr. C. Otto & Co. in Bochum), especially pp. 7–8; see also various materials still kept in the archives of the Dr. C. Otto & Co., Bochum.

During World War II, the autonomous "Otto Bureau" remained in business even though all communications with the German head office were cut off. Employees of other German manufacturers' branch offices who had gone a different way and were not able to pursue independently of their respective head offices were employed by the Otto Bureau. Until the end of World War II, "roof companies" like L. Leybold and C. Illies thrived and gave shelter to an increasing number of smaller manufacturing companies. (Details according to a personal interview with Herbert Doberer, employee of the "Otto Bureau" in Tokyo during the wartime period. Interview made on Nov. 5, 1985.)

23. For example, the German cable manufacturing company Felten & Guilleaume, which had exported submarine cables to Japan in the 1920s, lost the market share because of such a "Buy Japanese" campaign. Another reason was that Japanese manufacturers in the 1930s became able to supply Japanese customers with goods of a quality equivalent to foreign ones. F & G completely wrote off the Japanese market in 1933. See Feldenkirchen, *op. cit.*, pp. 167, 176–77.

24. *Jahresbericht* . . . , pp. 3, 18.

25. Letter from Röhrenverband to Mannesmann tube works, 29.12.1937; Mannesmann Archives M 80.030.

26. See note 19: *Activities* . . . , p. 90.

27. Bundesarchiv Koblenz, Files of the Reichswirtschaftskammer R11/1282d, pp. 30–35.

28. Such measures are described in several reports of the meetings of the German Chamber of Commerce in Harbin; Bundesarchiv Koblenz, Folders of the Reichswirtschaftskammer R 11/1282d (for example, p. 92); such obstacles are also described in a report written by Anton Reithinger of I.G. Farben in 1938, Imperial War Museum, London, Speer Collection, 4854/45 R.

29. Such a concern was brought up by A. Reithinger after his visit to East Asia in 1937/38; Karl Drechsler, *Deutschland-China-Japan 1933–1939*, Berlin: Akademie Verlag, 1959, p. 59.

30. Anton Reithinger of I.G. Farben used such a description in his report of 1928, Imperial War Museum, London, Speer Collection, 4854/45 R.

31. Public Records Office, London, FO 371/22144–F 543/543/10 German Manchukuo commercial relations, Jan. 14, 1938; for details, see also Tōyō Keizai Shinpō-sha, *Nihon Keizai Nenpō* (Shōwa 12-nen, Dai 4-shū), Tokyo, 1937, pp. 216–20.

32. A good example for such a case can be found in the I.G. Farben material in the Hoechst Archives, Frankfurt, folder 193, p. 27.

33. See also Hoechst Archives, Frankfurt, folder 191, in which some cases are to be found which illustrate such actions.

34. This happened to Mannesmann and an American tube manufacturer which sold the Friets-Moon license for tube manufacturing to Nippon Kōkan. See the letter from Ofenbau Union to Deutsche Röhrenwerke, 14.4.1936; Mannesmann Archives R4 5357.

35. Even I.G. Farben had its problems, and therefore in 1936 a proposal was made to the East Asia Committee to create the post of patent engineer in Japan as well as in Germany, both of whom would concentrate on Japanese patent problems; see Hoechst Archives, Frankfurt, folder 191/2. Report from a meeting of the Ostasienausschuss, 16.1.1936.

36. A good example of such a case is described in Hoechst Archives, Frankfurt, folder 191, concerning a washing agent.

37. Examples show that Dr. C. Otto & Co. company won several lawsuits against patent infringements by Japanese companies; see Lorenzen, *op. cit.*, p. 6.

38. Hoechst Archives, I.G. Farben files, room 24, group 18, folder 193: "Industrieverschleppung."

39. This statement by the Reichswirtschaftskammer can be found in *ibid.*

40. For details, see Rolf Harzheim, *Die Entwicklungsgeschichte der Teerfarbenindustrie in Deutschland* (Ph.D. thesis, Köln), 1952, pp. 128–29.

41. Feldenkirchen, *op. cit.*, p. 438.

42. Helmut Tammen, *Die I.G. Farbenindustrie Aktiengesellschaft* (*1925–1933*), Berlin, 1978, p. 215; see also *ibid.*, p. 439.

43. Verena Schröter, *Die deutsche Industrie auf dem Weltmarkt, 1929 bis 1933*, Peter Lang, Frankfurt, 1984, p. 227, note 330.

44. Unfortunately an overall view of activities and sales of the I.G. Farben in Japan is still lacking.

45. Department of Commerce/Office of the Publication Board (ed.), *Activities of I.G. Farbenindustrie A.G. in the Dyestuffs Industry*, Washington, 1946 (PB A 57.373), p. 86; for general remarks, see pp. 35–39.

46. *Ibid.*, pp. 88–89.

47. *Ibid.*, pp. 90–91.

48. Harzheim, *op. cit.*, p. 130.

49. For this, see Schröter, *op. cit.*, p. 311.

50. *Ibid.*, pp. 316–17 and 367.

51. *Ibid.*, pp. 110–11.

52. Karl Vogt, *Aus der Lebenschronik eines Japandeutschen 1897–1941*, OAG, Tokyo, 1962, pp. 231–32.

53. The number of production subsidiaries of the German chemical industry in 1913 amounted to 150; the figure decreased to 77 cases in 1930. The number of cases for overseas direct investment (outside Europe) was 17 (U.S.A., 11; South America, 4; Japan, 1; others 1). Figures presented by Harm Schröter, Berlin, at the Historikertag, Bamberg, 1988.

54. This term is used by Schröter, *op. cit.*, p. 385.

55. B. Bernstein, *Report on the Investigation of I.G. Farbenindustrie* (U.S. Dept. of Commerce, Office of Technical Series) (PB 25.681), Washington, 1945, p. 175; see also OMGUS (ed.), *Ermittlungen gegen die I.G. Farben*, Greno, Nördlingen, 1986, p. 273. The following companies are listed:

Asahi Bemberg Kenshi KK	Titan Tokyo KK
Nippon Tokushu Seizō KK	Cassella GK
Bayer Yakuhin GK	Delacamp, Piper & Co.
Doitsu Senryō GK	Titan Kōgyō KK
H. Ahrens & Co. Nachf.	Edogawa Kōgyō KK
AGFA GK	

56. "Einheitliches Zusammengehen der europ. am. Gruppe gegenüber den Japanern," Hoechst Archives, Frankfurt, folder 259: "Auslandslizenzen."

57. Hoechst Archives, folder 350: "Produktion im Ausland."

58. Schröter, *op. cit.*, p. 182.

59. Drechsler, *op. cit.*, p. 15.

60. Schröter, *op. cit.*, p. 183.

61. A report entitled "Die Exportförderung im Rahmen des Vierteljahresplanes" written by Max Ilgner, circa 1937; Bundesarchiv Koblenz, All.Proz., 2 NI/Nos. 1517–75, doc. no. NI 1570, p. 27.

62. Hallgarten/Radkau, *op. cit.*, pp. 352–53; Drechsler, *op. cit.*, p. 59.
63. Hoechst Archives, Frankfurt, folder 191, Ostasienausschuss, 9.Sitzung, June 15, 1939, p. 2.
64. See also Pauer, "Die wirtschaftlichen Beziehungen . . . ," pp. 171–72.
65. Schröter, *op. cit.*, p. 249.
66. Ostasienausschuß, 2.Sitzung, Jan. 16, 1936; Hoechst Archives, Frankfurt, folder 191.
67. Schröter, *op. cit.*, p. 241.
68. National Archives, Washington, RG 243, USSBS, 110d 229: "German Interrogation on Japanese Oil Industry," June 21, 1945.
69. This view was expressed in a report in *Kagaku to Kōgyō*, no. 1937, concerning the development of the Japanese dyestuff industry, translated for I.G. Farben and presented to the Ostasienausschuß; Hoechst Archives, Frankfurt, folder 191.

Comment

Tetsuo Abo

Professor Pauer's paper deals with the attitudes and performance of German companies in the interwar period, in particular the problems they faced in Japan. Although the author stresses that there is a lack of sources for such a study, much useful information is incorporated into the paper. The following are some comments on a few interesting issues raised in the paper and some questions that have arisen from this.

First of all, I think this paper is successful in illuminating the extent to which, the areas in which, and the reasons why the interests of German and Japanese companies (and goverments) differed during the period, sometimes leading to confrontation. The two decades are especially noteworthy in that, as a result of the world economic disorder following World War I, German industries on the one hand were struggling to recover from the massive damage wrought by the war and striving to compete against American and British industries while, on the other hand, Japanese industries, which benefited from the war, were rapidly catching up to their Western counterparts. The conflict of interest between German and Japanese companies also stemmed from a lack of understanding of Japanese conditions by the Germans. However, this is not a question of simple misunderstanding and is related to the next point.

Second, it is very interesting to learn that German companies, as well as the German government, were very reluctant to enter the Japanese market to any considerable extent, because they misunderstood the Japanese economy and companies and underestimated their possibilities of expanding in the Japanese market. In contrast to this, they overestimated the Chinese (and Indian) market. With respect to the Chinese market, it is also well known that the United States overestimated the potentials of that market since the end of 19th century. The question that I want to pose here is: Why was it so difficult for the Germans to understand the Japanese business practices (they called them "dishonest practices"), the consumer mentality, and the like. What circumstances were peculiar to Japan and how could German or Western companies have adapted to them? Also, German trading companies assisted somehow the German manufacturing firms when they faced problems overseas. How can we compare the function and nature of these German trading companies with those of Japan or other western countries?

Third, the paper focuses on the economic rivalry between German and Japanese industries in regard to technological transfers, in particular the strategem for licensing by I.G. Farben to Japanese companies. The governments of both countries were closely involved in the negotiating processes. The structure of the opposition between the two countries is clearly revealed in this: There was a conflict of interest in that Germany was pushing exports while Japan sought to impose import restrictions. The problem of licensing thus came to be the central issue in the negotiations. The hard and complicated negotiations, however, continued, with Germany suspecting the Japanese of "industrial espionage" and with Japan believing that the Germans were blocking the transfer of technological know-how. This eventually resulted in the too-late decision of the late 1930s by which I.G. gave licenses to Japanese companies.

My main question here is why I.G. did not pay more consideration to local production via foreign direct investment. The author points out that foreign direct investment policy was in general "restrictive" in I.G.'s strategy. Was there a shortage of resources for this, such as foreign exchange, or in terms of managerial personnel? Did they harbor pessimistic market prospects for Japan, or were there restrictive policies imposed by both governments? Regarding the licensing negotiations, the author indicates the importance of the German government's policy of fighting industrial espionage, but Professor Kudō in a recent paper emphasized the difference of opinions between the two top leaders of German chemical industries, Carl Bosch (former leader of BASF) and Fritz Haber (chemical scientist), as being of more importance (Akira Kudō, "The Strategy of I.G. Farben Toward Japan in the Case of Dyestuffs," *The Proceeding of the Department of Social Sciences*, University of Tokyo, Vol. 36, March 1987 ([in Japanese]). How do we reconcile these two conclusions?

The last question concerns the "obstacles" which German industries faced in entering the Japanese market in the 1920s. The author points to three major "obstacles": belated delivery, disregard for the particular needs of Japanese customers, and poor quality. What significance does this have in terms of the competitiveness of German industries? What similarities or differences do we encounter when we compare the German case with the performance of British or American companies?

Response

Erich Pauer

Professor Abo's comment brought the situation to this point: From our point of view Germany underestimated its opportunities on the Japanese market and heavily overestimated its chances on the China market. This is valid not only for the 19th century, or the interwar period, but for today as well. The answer to the question of why it was so difficult to understand Japanese business practices is quite simple. There had not been any contact between Germany and Japan since 1914, and the Germans, due to World War I, were not interested in Japan afterward. Therefore, what was known about Japan was usually outdated, and the success of industrialization in Japan between 1916 and 1920 remained largely unknown. Those few Germans who came to Japan in the 1920s behaved like their fathers had in 1900, their attitudes being that they were superior to the Japanese. Compared with European culture, Japanese manners and Japanese behavior was mostly regarded as inferior.

However, even if you question the term "dishonest practices," the fact that you can draw a long list of such practices has to be admitted even by the most fervent admirers of Japan. There is a huge number of instances such as "registration" of trademarks of a German company when negotiations had hardly begun, the selling of German licenses by Japanese companies without permission, patent violations, and so forth. However, the underlying reason why such a situation developed in the first place is the different approach toward trading. In German opinion, partners had to fulfill a contract once they signed it, whereas the Japanese feeling was that a contract became invalid if circumstances changed. A lot of misunderstandings arose, and neither could accept the other's view.

Concerning the nature and function of German trading companies in Japan as compared with Japanese trading companies, the Japanese firms were different in that they provided information on foreign markets to companies of their respective zaibatsu groups. In this way they acted like "antennas" in Germany also: The staff would read newspapers and scientific journals and subsequently send the information to Tokyo, where it was distributed. On the other hand, the role of German companies was restricted to mere "intermediaties." There was only I.G. Farben's Doitsu Senryō, which acted as the Japanese trading companies did for Japanese firms.

Next, regarding industrial espionage, call it "gaining information" and the term will lack the negative connotation of "spying." However, "gaining information" describes what the Japanese did and what the Germans conceived to be espionage. This is not to say that espionage was the basic strategy of Japanese companies but it was added by a different element in Japanese industrial organization, which made the Germans highly suspicious. When the Germans designed a plant, they started at the end: "What we need is an output of so-many tons." Then the prerequisites were pondered and planned, and next came the raising of funds. The Japanese way, at least in the 1920s and 1930s, was in exactly the opposite manner: First, all available data concerning a certain process was collected by various means, then how many of the prerequisites were available was discussed, the amount of money that could be afforded, and so on. The conclusion was how big the plant could be. Therefore, the Japanese wanted every bit of available information in step one, and Japanese visitors to German companies asked for all the details. This made the Germans distrust the Japanese and led to what I call the German "spy-mania." More often than not, the story was based on a misunderstanding, but it has to be stressed that real espionage also occurred; the extent, however, was smaller than the Germans supposed.

The last question is concerned with the reason why I.G. Farben had no interest in establishing a production subsidiary in Japan. There were certainly several factors involved: (1) pessimistic market prospects; (2) specific measurements raised by the government in order to fight industrial espionage and to prevent the establishment of subsidiaries equipped with German technology, because this would have meant nothing less than helping the Japanese to get hold of new techniques; and (3) different opinions held by Bosch and Haber. For instance, Haber's view was to keep technical know-how clear and better not to convey it to the Japanese, given that this special knowledge was the basis of I.G. Farben's strong position in Japan. At the same time, Haber saw that for those goods of equal quality produced by Americans, it would be better to pass on the know-how to the Japanese *before* other manufacturers made it available; being stubborn in this respect would only mean giving up a profit chance in Japan. However, such farsightedness was rather the exception at I.G. Farben. Letters from Japanese companies to the dyestuff department often carried handwritten comments by its head, Fritz ter Meer, which usually read: "Don't reveal details!" or "Not worth answering"—all of them revealing a strong anti-Japanese attitude. Therefore we could say that, to some extent, it was the personal views of some people within I.G. Farben's management which prevented the establishment of German production subsidiaries in Japan.

Summary of the Concluding Discussion

Masaru Udagawa

Three topics were selected for the concluding discussion, based on the ten papers given at the conference: (1) the ways in which foreign businesses advanced into the Japanese market, (2) factors within Japan which enabled foreign businesses to advance, and (3) the impact of foreign businesses on the development of Japanese industries and management.

I. Descriptions of Topics

Masaru Udagawa described each topic as follows. The first topic—the means of advance into Japan taken by foreign businesses—was found to be twofold, namely, licensing and direct investment, where investment is classified into 100% ownership, majority ownership, 50% ownership, and minority ownership. Udagawa then presented his hypothesis that a combination of four factors common to both host country and home country—namely, national influence, entrepreneurship, industrial characteristics, and technology—determined what form of advance a foreign company took as it entered the Japanese market.

For example, Ford and General Motors (GM) made direct investments in Japan in the 1920s. Both companies had advantages over Japanese automobile manufacturers in all of the four areas mentioned above, and therefore arranged their management in the form of 100% ownership.

In the electric-machinery sector of industry, foreign businesses elected to embark on joint ventures with Japanese businesses as they tried to gain a foothold in Japan. General Electric (GE) extended capital participation to Tokyo Electric Company, and Western Electric participated in the management of the Nippon Electric Company. Both foreign companies obtained majority ownership because they had more advantages over their Japanese counterparts than vice versa. On the other hand, Japanese businesses earned majority ownership in capital participation with GE at the Shibaura Works and with Westinghouse at Mitsubishi Electric Manufacturing, and in a joint venture by Siemens of Germany and Furukawa Electric Industry which established Fuji Electric Manufacturing, since in these three cases the Japanese companies possessed more advantages than the foreign businesses.

Udagawa also pointed out that the above four factors possessed by both foreign and Japanese businesses changed in relative weight to one another or in combination over time as the business environment changed. He described how Japanese businesses gained more advantages over foreign companies as time passed.

In order to illustrate the second topic, Udagawa pointed out three factors intrinsic to Japan which enabled foreign businesses to enter Japan. First, as a basic factor, it is a historical fact that Japan was behind the advanced European and North American nations in industrialization. The second factor is more subjective—namely, the attitude taken by the Japanese government and private companies toward foreign businesses entering Japan. Since the Meiji Restoration of 1868, the Japanese government had been aiming at modernizing and industrializing Japan. Therefore the Meiji government adopted favorable policies toward foreign businesses in Japan, since these businesses functioned as gateways by which advanced technology and modern management systems could be introduced, except during times of a national security crisis. The Japanese businesses enthusiastically sought licenses from foreign companies or joint ventures with them because they had to learn managerial activities and methods practiced by the foreign businesses in order to compete and grow. The third factor is objective, i.e., the magnetism of the Japanese market. The Japanese market expanded rapidly since the late 19th century, and its location was ideal as a stepping-stone to the East Asian markets. Moreover, compared with other developing nations, Japan's political and social environment was quite stable, making it one of a small number of countries which posed little risk for foreign companies conducting overseas business. An example of this can be found in postwar Japanese business history. The outbreak of World War II inevitably forced the foreign businesses that were involved in joint ventures with Japanese zaibatsu group companies to leave Japan. After this, the Japanese companies held royalties and dividends which were to have been paid to their foreign partners, and paid them after the war.

The third topic focused on two of the major impacts that the foreign businesses, especially through their direct investment, had on various aspects of Japan's industry and management. The first impact to be considered, Udagawa pointed out, was the impact on the Japanese market structure. The majority of the foreign companies that entered Japan were, at the time, prestigious and powerful multinationals, which gained large market shares regardless of whether they made individual advances or embarked on joint ventures. However, no single foreign company was successful in dominating a certain market for a long time because of competition since most markets were attractive. Competition came from other foreign companies, or from Japanese companies inspired by the advance of foreign businesses in the domestic market. In the latter case, once a Japanese company entered a market, it organized a management structure comparable to those of foreign businesses in the early stages in order to enhance its competitiveness. So there was always tough competition, either among foreign companies or between foreign companies and strong Japanese companies. Paradoxically, oligopolies were created in attractive markets while the powerful companies vigorously competed with one another.

The second impact was the transfer of technology from foreign to Japanese businesses, which occurred in two forms. One was the direct transfer of technology in the case of joint ventures between foreign and Japanese companies: The foreign companies actively transferred their production techniques and systems, as well as their managerial systems, to the joint-venture companies established in Japan as their subsidiaries or affiliated companies in order to develop them and improve their competitiveness. The other was indirect transfer: As mentioned above, the Japanese businesses tried to learn the production and managerial systems and methods of the foreign companies; therefore, they actively incorporated them into their own production and management. An effective means to accomplish this was to employ Japanese operatives who had previously worked for foreign companies and learned their managerial systems and methods.

In other words, the foreign businesses were vehicles by which to transfer advanced production technology and management systems and methods and other "know-how" to Japanese businesses.

II. Forms of Foreign Business Advancement in Japan

A concluding discussion of the first topic began with examinations of the validity of Udagawa's hypothesis that the form of advancement taken by a foreign business was determined by a combination of the four factors possessed by both its home and host countries. Following this discussion, we came to an agreement that this hypothesis was valid as a framework in which to consider forms of overseas expansion taken by multinationals.

This consensus was followed by examinations of the four factors, and there were intense arguments on the relative importance of nationality with regard to the several aspects of national influence. In this discussion Udagawa pointed out that European companies were more active in extending licenses than American companies as they tried to expand their business into the Japanese market, and that they were likely to seek either complete or majority ownership in the case of direct investment. Therefore, he maintained, the nationalities of the foreign businesses largely determined the forms of their advance into Japan.

However, against this assertion, the majority of the participants argued that the nationality of the foreign companies was not a major factor at the time of their advancement, although tensions and troubles between the foreign companies and the Japanese government created by wars and other events were largely responsible for the form of their expansion. They contended that there was no significant difference in the nature of foreign business advances on the basis of the nationality of the companies. Many of them further argued that any difference in the forms of business expansion among the various nationalities were reflections of cultural factors behind business activities characteristic of each nation or of a difference in business climate rather than a consequence of the nationalities themselves.

At this point Mira Wilkins presented this question: Which of the above four factors had the strongest impact on the forms of foreign business advance? The answer to this question, we concluded, was that it is impossible to point out any definite factor as the most important because the situations were very different from one industry to another and because the relative importance of each factor changed as time progressed. However, in relation to this matter, Akira Kudō pointed out that the foreign businesses tended to choose licensing rather than direct investment in the chemical industry, while the joint venture was the most favored form of advancement among electric-machinery manufacturers. Wilkins added that all the American automotive manufacturers took the form of 100% ownership as they expanded their businesses abroad. Kudō and Wilkins emphasized that there were certain patterns specific to some industry sectors as the foreign businesses entered the Japanese market, and that such patterns were highly dependent on the characteristics of the industries and types of technologies employed in those sectors. Their views were supported by the majority of the participants.

In summary, the forms of foreign business advancement into Japan were largely influenced by the stages of development of the industrial sectors they entered, and by the presence and competitiveness of the

Japanese companies which existed in these sectors. In other words, advantages in the four factors possessed by Japan as the host country over the foreign businesses primarily determined the forms of their business expansion into Japan and the nature of their development after their entry.

III. Factors Within Japan Which Enabled Foreign Businesses to Advance

Terushi Hara opened the discussion of the second topic by asking if the Japanese market before World War II was attractive to foreign businesses. Hiroaki Yamazaki and Kudō took the stance that the Japanese market, which had expanded rapidly since the late 19th century, was an excellent arena for the foreign companies to conduct their business activities in. Yamazaki emphasized that many foreign businesses entered the Japanese heavy and chemical industries, which had entered a developmental stage after World War I.

Hidemasa Morikawa, on the other hand, claimed that the foreign companies did not enter Japan because they were attracted by the Japanese market itself but because they needed a base to extend their business to the East Asian market. On the role of Japan as a bridge to the Eastern Asian market, Jun Sakudō, Clive Trebilcock, and Jin-Mieung Li pointed out that the relative importance of the Japanese market for American companies was different from that for companies from Britain, France, and Germany, which possessed colonies in Eastern Asia before entering Japan. However, many of the participants from abroad agreed that the Japanese market possessed more advantages than other East Asian countries as a base for the foreign businesses attempting to enter the East Asian market.

Erich Pauer, on this issue, presented the fact that the Chinese market was more attractive than the Japanese market for German companies, and pointed out that the attractiveness of the Japanese market differed largely by products and over a period of time. Pauer maintained that the Japanese market had once been very important for companies manufacturing heavy and chemical goods such as nitrogenous fertilizer and industrial dyestuffs, but the attractiveness of the Japanese market for this particular sector decreased rapidly in the 1930s when Japanese businesses gained control and the Japanese government started to suppress foreign businesses. Hisashi Watanabe responded to Pauer by pointing out the fact that the governments of many nations adopted a policy of protecting and subsidizing domestic industries in the 1930s to cope with a block economy, and Japan was not an exception. He suggested that the foreign businesses had regarded Japan as a part of the East Asian market and had not made a clear distinction between the two.

Pauer's opinion—that the attractiveness of the Japanese market changed over time—led us to examine subjective factors within Japan for receiving foreign businesses, i.e., foreign-capital policies undertaken by the government and the attitude of private businesses toward foreign companies.

Mark Mason stated that the foreign-capital policies adopted by the Japanese government changed drastically over time. He stated that the Japanese policies toward foreign capital before the complete abolishment of the principle of extraterritoriality and the full enforcement of the Commercial Law in 1899 were basically to exclude them from the Japanese market. Although the policies were changed after 1899 to positively accept foreign capital, the outbreak of the Manchurian Incident in 1931 brought back the exclusionist policies. Mason explained the cause for such changes after 1931, saying that Japanese businesses were highly independent by that time and no longer needed help from foreign businesses. He added that the favorable attitude of the Japanese companies toward foreign businesses declined in the 1930s. Mason's opinion was accepted by Wilkins, Trebilcock, Stephen Nicholas, and Tetsuo Abo, each of whom gave explanations for the Japanese government's suppressive policies toward foreign businesses after 1931, and the resulting difficulties that the foreign businesses had to face in conducting their business activities.

Against such opinions, Keiichirō Nakagawa emphasized that the underlying tone beneath the Japanese foreign-capital policies was favorable to the foreign businesses. He pointed out that the foreign companies were performing free business activities in their domiciles of choice even before 1899. He also asserted that the cause of the difficulties that the foreign companies encountered in the 1930s was multifaceted—namely, the changing international environment, the establishment of the block economy, the development of a controlled economic system, the aggravation of the international balance of payments, and the rise of military power. Morikawa, too, indicated that the Japanese government in the 1930s was not a monolithic entity, i.e., there were two groups of bureaucracies antagonistic to each other in the process of formulating industrial policies. One group consisted of bureaucracies in the ministries of Finance and Foreign Affairs and took the liberal interpretation of international cooperation. The other group included the army, which sought exclusionism and nationalism, and other "reformist" bureaucracies that were oriented toward a controlled economy. Morikawa also stressed that the managements of Japanese companies which had established joint ventures with foreign businesses, especially those of zaibatsu group companies, were consistently taking favorable attitudes toward their foreign partners. Then Udagawa related that the progress of the controlled economic system in the 1930s largely restricted the autonomous business activities of the Japanese companies as well.

Through the course of discussion of this topic, it became clear that foreign businesses more or less faced difficulties in their activities in any country during the 1930s, and that therefore such a situation was not unique to the foreign companies in Japan. However, we failed to reach a definite conclusion as to whether the policies of the Japanese government toward foreign businesses were consistently favorable to them or whether its stance changed largely over time. Also, we could not agree on the issue of whether the Japanese government's foreign-capital policies of the 1930s were more exclusionist than those of other host countries.

IV. The Impact of Foreign Businesses on the Development of Japanese Industries and Management

A discussion of the third topic began with an examination of the impact that foreign business expansion had on the Japanese market. As a result of the discussion, we came to support the opinion that Udagawa presented earlier that the advancement of foreign businesses into Japan intensified competition among both the foreign companies and the Japanese companies, resulting in the very competitive nature of the market structure itself. On this subject, some participants suggested that the foreign businesses in Japan sometimes created anew or expanded previously existing markets. François Jequier and Li introduced the example of the industrial gas market created by L'Air Liquide, and Wilkins presented another example, that of the automobile market developed by Ford and GM.

The reaching of the above consensus was followed by a discussion of the issue of technological transfer from foreign businesses to the Japanese companies. Many non-Japanese participants described the process of technological transfer and unanimously asserted that the foreign businesses played the role of a gateway for such an introduction. Toshiaki Chokki and Nobuhisa Fujita stated that the largest factor behind the Japanese businesses' decisions to form joint ventures with the foreign companies was the introduction of technology from their foreign partners. Chokki further suggested that, in the electric-machinery industry, managerial success recorded by the first Japan-foreign joint venture formed by Nippon Electric Company and its partner encouraged subsequent joint ventures in this industry. Nicholas suggested that the favorable business performances recorded by Anglo-Japanese joint ventures before 1931 encouraged the smooth transfer of technology thereafter. He also pointed out that the British companies were more active in technological transfer when they possessed majority ownership of their joint ventures.

Hideki Yoshihara pointed out that the Japanese companies learned the technology introduced from their foreign partners quite quickly, and suggested that we should discuss the ability of Japanese companies to absorb and digest new technology. Many participants agreed with Yoshihara. Wilkins, in particular, evaluated the high quality and ability of the Japanese engineers and workers as a factor behind the smooth absorption of foreign technology. Her example of technological transfer was that extended by Ford and GM to Mexican and Brazilian companies where the absorption of production techniques and managerial methods was much slower than in Japan. At this point Udagawa explained that the major Japanese companies actively employed engineers with an upper-level-education diploma, and such qualified engineers worked in tandem with workers in workshops, thereby contributing significantly to the excellent ability to absorb the foreign technology. Udagawa also indicated that, in the 20th century, increasing numbers of salaried managers were promoted to top management, and were more enthusiastic about introducing foreign technology than owner-managers because they assumed that the highest priority was the growth of their companies. Watanabe suggested that many of the joint ventures with the foreign businesses were formed by zaibatsu group companies, which had strong management structures to introduce and absorb the foreign technology. It was also suggested that, in Japan, there was a network of technological information between scholars, industries, and the government from an early stage, which improved the Japanese companies' ability to absorb foreign technology and accelerated its spread among Japanese companies. Some Japanese participants suggested that the Japanese businesses spared no effort in their own technological development when introducing foreign technology. This was given as one of the reasons why the foreign businesses could not dominate a market for a long period of time. Some participants from abroad suggested that such an effort by the Japanese companies to introduce and absorb foreign technology before World War II is an important aspect when considering the present industrialization of developing nations.

As a concluding comment on this course of discussion, Nakagawa stated that it is vital to consider the issue of technological transfer from both aspects of the foreign businesses, the transferor and the Japanese businesses, the transferee, and also that it is important to take into account the motives and business activities of both sides as well as the conflicts between the two. The participants agreed with Nakagawa and confirmed that we would continue research and the exchange of information on this issue.

Organizing Committee for the Fourth Series of the International Conference on Business History

Chairman:	Yuzawa Takeshi	(Gakushuin University)
Vice Chairman:	Udagawa Masaru	(Hosei University)
	Abe Etsuo	(Meiji University)
	Hiroyama Kensuke	(Nagasaki University)
	Kawabe Nobuo	(Hiroshima University)
	Kikkawa Takeo	(Aoyama Gakuin University)
	Kudō Akira	(University of Tokyo)
	Sakudō Jun	(Kobe Gakuin University)
	Yonekura Seiichirō	(Hitotsubashi University)
Advisers:	Wakimura Yoshitarō	(University of Tokyo)
	Nakagawa Keiichirō	(Aoyama Gakuin University)
	Yasuoka Shigeaki	(Doshisha University)

Project Leader and Editor for the First Meeting:

Udagawa Masaru
(Hosei University)

Yuzawa Takeshi
(Gakushuin University)

Participants:

Abo Tetsuo
(University of Tokyo)

Chokki Toshiaki
(Hosei University)

Fujita Nobuhisa
(Ryukoku University)

Hara Terushi
(Waseda University)

Jequier, François
(Université de Lausanne)

Kawabe Nobuo
(Hiroshima University)

Kudō Akira
(University of Tokyo)

Li Jin-Mieung
(Université Lyon III)

Mason, Mark
(Harvard University)

Morikawa Hidemasa
(Yokohama National University)

Nakagawa Keiichirō
(Aoyama Gakuin University)

Nicholas, Stephen
(University of New South Wales)

Pauer, Erich
(Universität Marburg)

Trebilcock, Clive
(University of Cambridge)

Watanabe Hisashi
(Kyoto University)
Wilkins, Mira
(Florida International University)
Yamazaki Hiroaki
(University of Tokyo)
Yoneyama Takau
(Kyoto Sangyo University)
Yoshihara Hideki
(Kobe University)

Secretariat:	Hiroyama Kensuke	(Nagasaki University)
	Sakudō Jun	(Kobe Gakuin University)
	Gross, David	(Hitotsubashi University)
	Pak, Sejin	(University of Tokyo)
	Shinomiya Masachika	(Tokuyama University)
	Yagi Yoshio	(Hosei University)

Index